MALE–MALE MURDER

In *Male–Male Murder*, Dobash and Dobash – experienced researchers, award winning authors, and long-time collaborators use evidence from their Murder Study to examine 424 men who murdered another man. Using both quantitative and qualitative data drawn from a wider study of 866 homicide casefiles and 200 in-depth interviews with murderers in prison, they focus on Five Types of male–male murder: confrontational/fighters; murder for money/financial gain; murder between men in the family; sexual murder between men; and murder of older men. Each type is examined in depth and detail in a separate chapter that begins with a brief overview of relevant research and is followed by a comprehensive examination of the murder event including subtypes that illustrate the diversity within each type of murder. Following the examination of the Five Types of male–male murder, the focus turns to the lifecourse of the perpetrators including childhood, adulthood, and their time in prison. Lastly, they reflect on the body of findings from the murder study, and stress the importance of gender in understanding these lethal events. The Dobashes bring their research skills and insights to the complex task of covering the entire scope of homicide cases in which men murder men. This is an essential text for students, professionals, policy makers, and researchers studying violence, gender, and homicide.

Russell P. Dobash is a Professor Emeritus, Criminology, University of Manchester, Manchester, UK, Distinguished Visiting Professor, Arizona State University, USA.

Rebecca Emerson Dobash is a Professor Emeritus, Criminology, University of Manchester, Manchester, UK, Distinguished Visiting Professor, Arizona State University, USA.

MALE–MALE MURDER

*Russell P. Dobash and
Rebecca Emerson Dobash*

LONDON AND NEW YORK

First published 2020
by Routledge
2 Park Square, Milton Park, Abingdon, Oxon OX14 4RN

and by Routledge
52 Vanderbilt Avenue, New York, NY 10017

Routledge is an imprint of the Taylor & Francis Group, an informa business

© 2020 Russell P. Dobash and Rebecca Emerson Dobash

The right of Russell P. Dobash and Rebecca Emerson Dobash to be identified as authors of this work has been asserted by them in accordance

with sections 77 and 78 of the Copyright, Designs and Patents Act 1988.

All rights reserved. No part of this book may be reprinted or reproduced or utilized in any form or by any electronic, mechanical, or other means, now known or hereafter invented, including photocopying and recording, or in any information storage or retrieval system, without permission in writing from the publishers.

Trademark notice: Product or corporate names may be trademarks or registered trademarks, and are used only for identification and explanation without intent to infringe.

British Library Cataloguing-in-Publication Data
A catalogue record for this book is available from the British Library

Library of Congress Cataloging-in-Publication Data
A catalog record has been requested for this book

ISBN: 978-0-367-43852-4 (hbk)
ISBN: 978-0-367-43596-7 (pbk)
ISBN: 978-1-003-00453-0 (ebk)

Typeset in Bembo
by Wearset Ltd, Boldon, Tyne and Wear

R²D²
on
Valentine's Day

CONTENTS

	List of tables	*viii*
	Acknowledgments	*ix*
1	Male–male murder – the evidence so far	1
2	Confrontational murder (fighters)	39
3	Murder for money/financial gain	74
4	Murder between men in the family	107
5	Sexual murder between men	141
6	Murder of older men	178
7	Lifecourse of male–male murderers – childhood	212
8	Lifecourse of male–male murderers – adulthood and in prison	249
9	Male–male murder – evidence from the Murder Study	291
	Name index	*300*
	Subject index	*304*

TABLES

Murder Event – Each Type of Male–Male Murder and Others
(each Type of Male–Male Murder Compared to Other.Murders not
of that type

2.1	Murder Event. Confrontational.Murders and Other.Murders	71
3.1	Murder Event. Money.Murders and Other.Murders	104
4.1	Murder Event. Family.Murders and Other.Murders	136
5.1	Murder Event. Sexual.Murders and Other.Murders	172
6.1	Murder Event. Murders of Older.Men and Other.Murders	208

Lifecourse – Each Type of Male–Male Murderer and Others
(each Type of Male–Male Murderers Compared to Others not of that type)

7.1	Lifecourse-Childhood. Each Type of Male–Male Murderer and Others	243
8.1	Lifecourse-Adulthood. Each Type of Male–Male Murderer and Others	286
8.2	Lifecourse-In.Prison. Each Type of Male–Male Murderer and Others	288

ACKNOWLEDGMENTS

We owe thanks to many unnamed individuals who facilitated our research in the prisons in which we examined casefiles and conducted interviews, to the men and women in prison who agreed to be interviewed, to the prison services in England/Wales and Scotland, and to the staff within each of the separate prisons who allowed access to their records and facilitated our research within the context of the many and varied demands of their daily routines.

To the ESRC, Economic and Social Research Council, for funding the research.

To Kate Cavanagh and Ruth Lewis, co-researchers, who spent countless hours working with us as we developed the data collection instruments, collected data from the casefiles, conducted interviews, and prepared the quantitative and qualitative data for analysis. Their dedication and professional approach was invaluable in the process of conducting a very difficult and demanding piece of research, and their friendship, sense of humor and optimism were equally as valuable.

To Routledge for publishing the book, Charlotte Endersby for commissioning the book, Arunima Aditya, Editorial Assistant, for attention to queries as the manuscript developed, Ravinder Dhindsa for copy editing, Pip Clubbs, Project Manager, and Tom who worked on the design of the cover, and many unnamed others who worked on typesetting, printing and distribution, and Lydia de Cruz who will see it on the other side. A special thanks to everyone as all of the final work was completed during the worldwide response to Covid-19, the coronavirus pandemic that affected us all.

Thank you, and stay safe.

1

MALE–MALE MURDER

The evidence so far

It is nearly impossible to escape the public and media obsession with 'true crime' murder. There appears to be a fascination with serial killers, women killers, psychopaths, and mass murderers, but few homicides actually match this profile. So, what is the reality of homicide? Most murders are committed one-at-a-time. Most are committed by men who kill other men, followed by men who kill women. Women rarely commit murder, and most murderers are not psychopaths. We focus on 'real life murders,' and use 424 cases of male–male murder from a larger study of murder conducted in England/Wales and Scotland that included 866 cases of all types of murder against men, women and children. In examining the 424 cases of male–male murder, we focus on the situations and circumstances at the time of the murders, the murder events, and the life course of the men who committed these murders including childhood, adulthood, and their time in prison.

We begin with a brief discussion of the worldwide prevalence of homicide and some historical patterns. This is followed by a consideration of some contemporary approaches to explaining crime, violence, and homicide which constitute the foundations of the approach taken here. This includes a focus on poverty and inequality, cultures and sub-cultures, the murder event and what men were thinking at the time they committed murder. The Murder Study, from which the 424 cases are drawn, uses a socio-cultural approach with a particular focus on the murder event. We used a mix-method and multi-disciplinary approach, including both quantitative and qualitative evidence from the casefiles of convicted murderers and from 180 interviews with men in prison for murder. Main findings from the Murder Study are presented in five chapters each devoted to a different type of male–male murder: Confrontational Fighters, Money/Financial Gain, Family, Sexual Murders, and Murders of Older.Men. The last chapters focus on the life course of the men who commit murder including their childhood, adulthood,

2 Male–male murder – the evidence so far

and life in prison. The final chapter provides a summary of the evidence and consider the problem's men will face when and if they leave prison.

A brief history of murder

Violence is a persistent and recurring feature of societies, and homicide has often been the main marker of the levels of interpersonal violence across the centuries. As early as the thirteenth century, fairly reliable evidence from several European countries reveals substantial levels of homicide with estimates as high as 30–50 per 100,000 members of the population (Eisner, 2003a). Historians report that medieval Europe was characterized by feuding families and clans where street fights and brawls were everyday events involving men prepared to use 'unrestrained' violence to settle disputes and maintain their 'honor.' This was not confined to the 'lower orders' of society but was a part of the lives of the ruling classes some of whom were reported to be leaders of 'armed bands.' In the sixteenth and seventeenth centuries, the rates of homicide in Europe began to decline and continued to do so for several centuries with important reductions in the late twentieth century. Over the last two decades, the rates of homicide in some European countries have declined even further (especially in Scandinavia), and are now as low as 1 or 2 per 100,000 in various countries including England/Wales and Scotland although there has been an increase in England/Wales in the last few years (for historical accounts see, Elias, 1978; Elwert, 2003; Eisner, 2003a, 2003b; Spierenburg, 1998a, 2008, pp. 12–42; Beeghley, 2003; D'Cruze, Walklate, and Pegg, 2011). (For current patterns and rates see Soothill and Francis, 2013; Home Office, 2019; Scottish Government, 2019).

Rates of homicide fluctuate over time and in different locations, and while rates have declined in many European countries, they are now extremely high in some Central American, African and Caribbean countries, and in some cities in the United States. In 2016, the rate of homicides among males in El Salvador was 159/100,000 members of the population, and 103/100,000 in Honduras. Homicide rates are usually highest in urban areas such as Caracas, Venezuela with a rate of 111/100,000 population, and some American cities such St Louis with 66/100,000, as well as Detroit and New Orleans with rates of 40/100,000. A number of factors drive these high rates including waring drug gangs, inequality, and firearms (Beeghley, 2003). Although not considered here, extremely high levels of death and destruction have also been associated with numerous wars, armed conflicts, and genocides in the twentieth century that have destroyed the lives of millions of individuals in the military and civilian populations in numerous countries.

Gender and murder – it is men who kill

All existing data from whatever source provide overwhelming and irrefutable evidence about the gendered nature of homicide. In the past, in the present, and in every nation, city or locality, those who kill are overwhelmingly men. It is only in popular films and novels that women killers seem to abound, but not in real life. In his anthology, *Male Violence*, John Archer (1994), a British psychologist noted that apart from sensationalist reporting, the female murderer is rare, and that it is men who kill. In the same volume, Gilbert, a clinical psychologist and academic, noted that, 'Male violence may even outrank disease and famine as the major source of human suffering' (Gilbert, 1994, p. 354). In some countries, men constitute as high as 90% of the perpetrators of all homicides, and a UN report on 53 countries estimated that 95% of all those convicted of homicide were men (UNODC, 2013, p. 13). The evidence so far is both clear and unequivocal. Overwhelmingly, it is *men who kill other men, men who kill women, and men who kill children.* The evidence about women and murder is clear and unequivocal: while many women are murdered, very few women commit murder.

Explaining historical trends – reductions in violence and homicide

The dramatic reduction in violence and homicide in some European countries requires consideration. In Norbert Elias's 'Theory of Civilization' (1978), he suggests that the changing nature of violence and its reduction were associated with the rise of the modern state, changes in socio-cultural patterns, and changes in personality types that gradually resulted in the transformation of European patterns of behavior. His explanation relies heavily on assumptions about the rise of social control and self-control. While violence among the upper classes never matched the levels of violence among the laboring poor, duels and 'hot' tempers among the ruling elites were not uncommon and were associated with a considerable amount of violence, but this began to wane with the criminalization of dueling and the use of firearms which were more likely to be lethal than swords.

What is often missing from most historical accounts is an explicit consideration of the significance of gender despite the overwhelming evidence of the asymmetrical nature of violence and homicide. In contrast, Spierenburg (1998a, 1998b) locates his historical analysis of the reductions in violence in the context of the 'crucial role of gender.' Violence was associated with a strong culture of masculinity that was linked to bodily violence and honor which 'depended on physical courage, bravery and a propensity for violence' (Spierenburg, 2008, p. 8). This culture began to recede in the early modern period, especially among the elites but also among the 'lower orders.'

A culture of 'male honor' gradually came 'to be associated with inner virtues,' a process he calls 'the spiritualization of honor' which is exemplified in the demise of dueling among elites and the reduction in incidents of knife fighting in the Netherlands (Spierenburg, 1998a, pp. 8–9). What began to develop, especially among the elites and the expanding middle classes, was an emphasis on manners, including table manners, and the regulation of emotions such as anger (Elias,

4 Male–male murder – the evidence so far

1978). At the same time, we see the rise of the modern state with a legal monopoly on violence. Although the vendetta and personal vengeance did not completely disappear, they began to recede as a way of dealing with disputes. Legal responses to family problems and economic disputes began to replace kin-based means of settling disputes, and the regulation of society and the economy was increasingly governed by the rule of law and agencies of the state. Contemporary evidence of the importance of the state in controlling and reducing violence and homicide is demonstrated by the especially high rates of violence in the weak, nearly power-less states in Central America and on the African continent, and certain areas of the United States where agencies of the state are unable and/or unwilling to engage with the cultural patterns associated with violence (for excellent over-views, see Levoy, 2015; Beeghley, 2003, Figure 3.3, pp. 67–69).

Long before Elias (1978) suggested that the reduction in violence was associ-ated with the 'rise of the modern state with its legal monopoly on violence,' Emile Durkheim argued that a reduction in violence and homicide was associated with the 'liberation of individuals from collective responsibility' as embodied in kinship relationships (1951 original 1897; Eisner, 2003a, p. 131). Which meant that at least some men could now use the law and criminal justice to settle disputes between individuals and groups. Nonetheless, some men continued to behave in a collective fashion albeit in slightly different ways within modern society (Eisner, 2003b). Group allegiance continued to be associated with an intense sense of group membership similar to the bonds that once connected family, kin and clans, 'demanded' loyalty, and required responses to slights, insults, and the like (Spiers, 2018). This continues to make sense for certain types of violence, particularly the violence of young men. Membership of a group (gang or club) may be demon-strated in dress, bodily comportment and other symbols they view as vital to their personal identity which helps explain their individual actions and some forms of violence. Loyalty to a group such as 'their' football team may be intense (and may sometimes erupt into violent encounters with the 'opposition'). Similarly, intense identification with different religions can involve antagonisms, violence and even murder such as in Northern Ireland during the time known as 'The Troubles.' Other examples include strong identification with 'their' street, 'their' city, 'their' nation, and other loyalties that shape 'their' identity and locate them (and their friends) and define their relationship to others who differ from them.

Max Weber's early exposition of the Protestant Ethic and the Spirit of Cap-italism (1905), provides another way of thinking about the historical reduction in levels of violence. Although not often cited in the literature about violence, it is grounded in the emergence of an emphasis on 'rationality' and a moral lan-guage emphasizing individual 'self-discipline' and 'collective, popular discipline.' This suggests that is it was not just the shedding of group membership and the emergence of a stable state and rule of law that contributed to a reduction in the levels of violence, but also an institutional structure (Protestantism) that promulgated new norms of self-regulation and a reliance on one's own normative values

(Weber, 1905, trans. 1930, reprinted 2001; Gorski, 1993). Social institutions and cultural practices emphasized 'duty, sobriety, frugality' and 'a methodic conduct of life' (Eisner, 2003a, p. 130).

These explanations of historical reductions in the levels of violence over very different periods of time and in different places, share one thing in common. In their different ways, they all suggest the importance of understanding the wider social context in which violence and homicide actually occur. This focus on the wider social contexts in which violence and murder occurred in earlier time periods is of central importance in the effort to make sense of what was happening then, but what about now? How have scholars tried to explain violence and homicide in more contemporary times and places?

Modern societies and cultures, crime, violence and murder

Poverty and inequality have long been linked to elevated levels of interpersonal violence and homicide (Pridemore, 2011). Some researchers argue that it is 'abject poverty' that determines elevated rates of homicide; others argue that 'relative poverty,' or inequality, is the link to elevated rates of homicide (Daly and Wilson, 1988; Daly, 2016 discusses this debate with a strong emphasis on relative deprivation and inequality). Using an evolutionary perspective, Daly (2016) has proposed that competition and conflict are distinct characteristics of human society, and that these characteristics are fundamental to levels of violence with inequality playing a major role in the variation of rates. For Daly, inequality is an especially potent factor that leads men to seek social status and economic success through a variety of means including the use of violence. These factors are particularly salient in the context of scarce resources, disadvantage, and limited opportunity. While those who propose the thesis of 'relative deprivation' sometimes fail to connect the structural pattern of inequality to actual violence, it is possible to argue that inequality 'generates alienation, despair, and pent-up aggression' (Beeghley, 2003, p. 150). In addition, inequality can have a detrimental impact on social relationships including 'trust and social capital' (Wilkinson, Kawachi, and Kennedy, 1998).

Sociologist have long argued for the importance of 'relative deprivation' and 'inequality' in criminal behavior and violence. In the mid-twentieth century, sociologists focusing on the sources of delinquent behavior in disadvantaged areas in the United States identified relative deprivation, scarce resources, status frustration and blocked opportunity as sources of discontent leading to delinquency (Cohen, 1955; Cloward and Ohlin, 1960). This helped explain the elevated levels of crime and gang formation, particularly among working-class boys. In the US, delinquent solutions to these conditions were linked to the American dream that anyone can improve their social and economic status because opportunity and success are open to anyone who works for it. But this egalitarian ideology ignored

6 Male–male murder – the evidence so far

the problems of 'differential opportunity' based on social class, ethnicity and limited educational opportunities. Instead, Cohen proposed that 'position discontent' and 'status frustration' arising from reactions to inequality led to delinquent solutions. Cloward and Ohlin proposed three collective solutions to thwarted or blocked opportunities in the neighborhoods and cultures they studied. The three pathways included: 'crime, conflict, and/or retreatism.' Solutions based on 'conflict' were the most likely to lead to violence and crime. Gang formation and property crime were much more likely within a criminal subculture. The criminal subculture attracted those who failed in the legitimate culture but had the skills associated with 'career criminals,' and adult career criminals socialized youngsters into criminal norms and techniques. Here, Cloward and Ohlin focused on organized crime. Their thesis helped tie together wider structural factors, inequality, cultural patterns, and crime. Although they did not deal with the crime of murder/homicide, their thesis is nonetheless relevant in efforts to explain the use of violence. For example, worldwide there are very few upper-class or middle-class violent gangs, and those with economic and social opportunities rarely become violent criminals even though such individuals may commit other types of crime.

Structural factors such as inequality and geographic concentrations of the poor and various racial or ethnic groups, contribute to social and cultural patterns that are linked to crime, violence and homicide. Locations, particularly in cities, that contain high levels of disadvantage are often associated with violence linked to illegal economic activities such as the sale and distribution of illegal drugs. About the US, Beeghley notes, 'the greater the residential segregation, the greater the African-American homicide rate,' and this is a 'very reliable finding' (2003, p. 137). The exceptional rise in murder rates in the US in the 1980s and 1990s was clearly related to the crack cocaine epidemic. It was not so much the use of drugs that contributed to the violence but rather the dealing in illegal drugs that generated conflicts and disputes leading to violent means of resolution, including murder. Similar patterns are apparent in Central American and Caribbean countries where extremely high levels of violence and homicide are linked to poverty, lack of legitimate economic opportunities, and the formation of gangs dealing in the illegal drug business. In 'A Brief History of Seven Killings,' James (2014) offers a narrative account of several attempts on the life of Bob Marley, a famous reggae singer-song writer, that was set in the overall context of drug dealing in Jamaica which was linked to demand for drugs in the US.

Cultures and subcultures of violence and crime

The importance of culture (beliefs, norms, values, and patterns of behavior) was first linked to crime and violence in the research and thinking of the Chicago School of Sociology in the early twentieth century. The School focused on the study of social problems and drew heavily on an 'ecological,' spatial approach to the explanation of human behavior. Demographic factors, population distributions, neighborhoods and culture in American cities were linked to crime and violence that, they argued, was rooted in 'social disorganization' and lack of 'social control.' Edwin Sutherland (*Principles of Criminology*, 1924) and Fredrick Thrasher, (*The Gang*, 1927) carried out ground-breaking research that established the foundations of American criminology (see Wikipedia, Chicago School of Sociology for a summary), and this early focus on 'location' and 'culture' was significant in thinking about delinquency and crime.

In the 1960s, Wolfgang and Ferracuti developed a subcultural theory of violence (1967). They defined 'subculture' as a relatively distinct system of values, norms and behavior, and offered a clearly defined and delimited exposition of these attributes. While not all members of the 'subculture' endorse violence, it is consistently 'demanded' in certain circumstances, and norms supporting its use are widely endorsed and rarely condemned. While the use of violence is not dictated for all circumstances, it is deemed to be 'necessary' in certain contexts. Anticipatory actions such as carrying knives or firearms may be condoned, and this obviously increases the possibility of serious violence and murder. Identification of violence 'provoking' circumstances is especially salient among males from 'particular ethnic groups' from 'late adolescence to middle age,' and is learned through imitation and socialization within subcultures of violence that specify the situations that 'require' the use of aggression and violence. Adhering to these norms of violence is usually status conferring, and failing to conform may result in shaming and even 'expulsion' from the subcultural group. In short 'Violence becomes a part of a life style' a means of 'solving difficult problems or problem situations' (Wolfgang and Ferracuti, 1967, pp. 159, 161).

In proposing a subcultural explanation of violence, Wolfgang and Ferracuti drew on patterns in American society that appeared to be more prevalent within certain ethnic groups, and subsequent research in the US, particularly ethnographic observational research pioneered in the Chicago School, provided strong evidence of this pattern. Some scholars encapsulate these subcultures in the phrase, 'code of the streets.' Sociologists such as Anderson (1994) suggest that this 'code' emerges from circumstances in the 'ghetto' in American cities which dictates that, 'one's bearing must send the unmistakable [message]… that one is capable of violence and mayhem.' Although not all exchanges and challenges require violence, the message must be clear: 'I am someone that should not be messed with' (Anderson, 1990, p. 2, 1994). Short and Strodtbeck (1965, p. 81) described these processes as 'signifying' one's identity which is related to signs, badges, tattoos, and other insignia. For Anderson, 'signs' of strength and threat exist alongside other 'decent' values rooted in a resistance to the 'Code' and based on notions of a 'strong, loving decent family committed to middle-class values' (1994, p. 85).

'In Search of Respect: Selling Crack in El Barrio,' Bourgois (1995) used an ethnographic method to provide a fulsome account of a street culture in a New York Barrio that was geared to the use of violence and illegal activities. He gathered evidence about a group of men involved in the drug business, an 'alternative

8 Male–male murder – the evidence so far

income strategy,' in which violence was widely used as a means of enforcing, controlling and maintaining their business. Using qualitative evidence, he illustrated 'the street's overarching culture of terror by intimidating everyone.' In the following example, he recounts an episode of violence committed by Caesar, an 'enforcer' in a drug dealing den.

> [He] was talking shit for a long time [boasting]. We were trying to take it calm until he starts talkin about how he gonna drop a dime on us [report to the police]. That's when I grabbed the bat. I want something that's going to be short and compact. I only got to swing a short distance to clock the shit out of this guy [result – a fractured skull]. The bottom line … is the survival of the fittest.
>
> (Bourgois, 1995, p. 88)

Southern states have some of the highest rates of violence and homicide in the US. In an effort to explain the high levels of violence and homicide in the southeastern states of America, an experiment was conducted at the University of Michigan. In the experiment, 83 undergraduate white males were exposed to a series of verbal insults directed at 41 males from the South and 42 males from the North. There was a marked difference in the responses of these two groups of young men, with Southerners more likely than Northerners to react with anger, and even aggression, when confronted with the same 'annoying' situation. All of the young men were white and the researchers concluded that the different responses were linked to variations in the cultural contexts in which they had grown up (Southern vs. Northern states in the USA). Nisbett and Cohen, (1996), both psychologists, offered a cultural explanation of why the Southerners rose to anger and Northerners were less likely to do so. They invoked the importance of a historical background of a pastoral ethic associated with an economy based on herding that was more common in the legacy of those who first settled in the Southern states, elements of which have been retained in much of their contemporary culture, including the necessity of self-reliance, sensitivity to 'their' territory, and the like. While this is only one small experimental study conducted with university students in a laboratory setting, and must be viewed as such, similar findings and conclusions have also been reported by historians and anthropologists who have noted the residual effects of a 'culture of honor,' particularly in states in the American southeast whose early settlers were from Scottish and Irish backgrounds rooted in herding societies with strong clan-based cultures that depended on the use of violence to settle disputes (Fischer,1989; Wyatt-Brown, 1982). This pattern has also been found in anthropological studies of other economies based on herding in Spain, Greece and other societies (Pitt-Rivers, 1954, 1965; Peristiany, 1965; Herzfeld, 1985).

Historians have also explored the nature of a culture of 'honor' and violence in the Southern states of the US, not only in relation to cultural contexts associated with agrarian societies, but also those associated with poverty and the violence of slavery (Wyatt-Brown, 1982). Historians documented the differences between Southern and Northern men in the US Congress in the mid-1800s that reflected different cultural codes of behavior originating in the geographical origins of these early statesmen. While Southern congressmen seemed to consider violence an appropriate test of manhood, men from the Northern states were less likely to hold these views. In some accounts, when Southern congressmen were 'inflamed' by anti-slavery speeches, they started physical fights, drew their knives, and challenged their anti-slavery opponents to a duel (Freeman, 2018; Oakes, 2019). Today, researchers continue to note the high levels of poverty and inequality in the rural south of the US, a strong culture of firearm ownership and usage. Southern states have some of the highest levels of gun ownership in the US. Other scholars have noted the importance of obtaining personal justice in a context of limited state presence and/or intervention as an explanation of the higher rates of violence in the Southern states (Powdermaker, 1939; Vandal, 2000). While this North–South divide in the US may reflect cultural differences in approaches to resolving conflicts and differential levels of violence, other contexts also contain elements of importance in relation to the use of violence, and particularly lethal violence. Cities, particularly very large urban areas with high levels of poverty, have high levels of homicide. Other cultural contexts associated with high levels of violence and orientations to encounters between men that 'support' violence can be seen in the three examples from Jamaica, Australia and the southern US.

Subcultures of violence – three examples illustrating the importance of context

Three examples illustrate the importance of cultural contexts in relation to high levels of violence: political group violence in Jamaica; booze, blokes and brawling in Australia; and bar fighters in the southern US. Jamaica has one of the highest murder rates in the world, and in their penetrating analysis, Morris and Graycar (2011) illustrate the link between political parties, violence and the historical roots of the societies in which they emerge and develop. Beginning in the post WWII era and extending into the 1980s, Jamaica was democratically governed by two opposing parties that exchanged electoral dominance throughout this period. When in power, each political party used their position to reward their constituents and to 'buy' their allegiance and votes. Focusing on the metropolitan area of Kingston, Morris and Graycar argue that the main reward was housing which was in short supply, and thousands of homes were built usually in seriously disadvantaged locations. These policies resulted in geographic areas that were politically segregated with clearly defined boundaries. This led to the establishment of 'garrison' districts of the city with military style social structures and specific leaders, 'dons,' and hit men dubbed 'gunmen,' or 'shottas,' who dealt with 'all aspects of life.' Violence between rival political factions became endemic, and spiked during elections. In 1980, homicide was rampant and involved groups of

10 Male–male murder – the evidence so far

men in open gun battles using heavy weapons. In the 1990s, the control of political areas and violence shifted to drug dealing between various factions which quickly 'migrated' to cities in the US and Britain. Morris and Graycar conclude that in Jamaica, institutions of the state actually contributed to high levels of violence rather than trying to reduce them. Instead, institutions of the state penetrated into areas of deprivation and through various policies 'bought' political allegiance that resulted in the establishment of neighborhood structures that were linked to serious violence.

Historical and contemporary evidence confirms that it is men who are most likely to engage in serious violence, and the following examples illustrate how this can be amplified when men are on their own without the influence of women. Cartwright (1996, p. 87) notes that disorder, violence and homicide in the early American West of the nineteenth century was much more prevalent in locations primarily inhabited by single men where belligerent masculinity fueled by solons and drunkenness contributed to high levels of violence. By contrast, locations that were predominately populated by married 'settlers' of men and women primarily engaged in agriculture had much lower levels of violence. 'The price of wide-spread bachelorhood for society was more violence and disorder' (1996, p. 65). Similarly, Carrington, McIntosh, and Scott (2010) report on violence in a nearly all-male context in the Australian 'outback' in the early part of the twenty-first century. A small town experiencing a mining boom was nearly overrun with young men who migrated from the cities to take advantage of the employment opportunities. Rapid economic growth, community expansion and highly skewed gender asymmetry were associated with exceptionally high levels of crime and violence linked to 'hyper-masculinity.' Men worked and lived in sparse, densely populated camps, yet they were not suffering from economic deprivation. Quite the contrary, their average earnings were significantly higher than the average wage in the local area. What these men 'suffered' from was not poverty but bore-dom and a lack of excitement which they alleviated by engaging in serious brawls in public locations, mostly in and around pubs. Fighting was entertainment, a form of 'manufactured excitement.' A local magistrate described these brawls as 'a form of sport.' One notorious pub was unofficially named the 'Brawlers,' and one of the miners aptly noted that 'no one drinks socially … everyone drinks to get drunk.' Drinking and brawling were status conferring among these young men. While the authors do not report on homicides, their evidence suggests that these brawls often resulted in serious injuries.

The third example involves bar fighters in a southern US city who saw themselves as 'peaceful warriors' (Copes, Hochstetler, and Forsythe, 2013). This ethnographic research revealed a subcultural 'code' associated with the use and regulation of what the fighters described as 'functional violence.' Bar fighters were not necessarily young: the average age was 33 and ranged from 22–48 years. They saw their use of violence as appropriate, legitimate male behavior associated with problem solving, and viewed violence as 'useful for settling disputes.' As one of the fighters put it, 'aggression and violence were useful in controlling annoying, aggressive and violent patrons.' Another fighter said, 'these aggro dudes get drunk … have something to prove and are just looking for trouble.' The fighters argued that their violence was principled, measured, controlled, and limited, saying such things as: 'I'm not trying to *seriously* kill nobody, bones heal. You can get teeth fixed. Bloody nose ain't going to kill nobody' (Copes, Hochstetler, and Forsythe, 2013, p. 777).

The fighters presented themselves as in control and moderated by temperament, skills, and an 'idealized' code. The 'code' specified that fighters must be dependable, step-in when needed, and be 'willing to defend principles.' Yet, they also told the researchers that the 'code of control' was sometimes overridden by their own anger and drunkenness. The violence was serious, as one fighter suggested, fights are finished when 'someone can't get up' or 'when they [customers] can't defend themselves anymore' (Copes, Hochstetler, and Forsythe, 2013, p. 778). The impression projected by these bar fighters in their attempts to valorize their own masculine identities, was 'we're not chumps.' While offering examples of self-regarding commendable ideals, much of the 'code' involved justifications, rationalizations, and excuses for the use of what was often described in their own words as rather dangerous violence. The researchers provided little evidence about the victims or about the types and levels of violence used, although other research on violence confirms how fighting, and especially the use of certain forms of violence such as stamping or jumping on the victim, can lead to very serious injury and even death. Even a single punch can kill.

Summary of violent cultures and contexts

The evidence reviewed establishes some basic patterns. The first is so obvious that it is almost possible to overlook it, i.e. it is men who usually kill other men, and it is also important to note that it is also men who usually murder women and children. Historical and contemporary evidence as well as various explanatory accounts lead to several conclusions. First, male violence and homicide is a persistent and deeply rooted aspect of most if not all societies. Second, the level of violence and the contexts in which it occurs have changed over time and in different societies. Third, historically some European and 'western societies' experienced significant reductions in interpersonal violence and homicide from levels that had previously been much higher. Fourth, explanations of this decline vary but include such developments as the rise of the modern state, the advance of rationality, and the 'rule of law' that resulted in different methods of settling disputes. Still today, as in the past, murders between men often occur in a context of male encounters involving 'character contests' leading to disputes and violence. While historical evidence suggests that violence was not exclusively committed by members of the 'lower orders' as demonstrated by the existence of dueling among elites, evidence about contemporary societies suggests that homicides are

12 Male–male murder – the evidence so far

primarily committed by disadvantaged men living in urban areas in economically and socially deprived communities and, in some countries, communities that are ethnically segregated.

Scholars debate the specific aspects of deprivation that may be of importance. Some argue that abject poverty is the important context of violence, while others suggest it is inequality and relative deprivation that elevated the levels of violence. Relative deprivation is very important although in some societies widespread poverty (which is highly correlated with inequality) contributes to high rates of homicide that are generally linked to illegal activities such as drug dealing and human trafficking. Locations of deprivation are often characterized by cultures/ subcultures that endorse the use violence to settle disputes, and usually have, or create, adversaries such as other gang members, opposing football (soccer) teams, school rivalries, and particularly members of other racial, ethnic and religious groups. Identifying adversaries usually legitimatizes violence as violent men 'search for insults,' often contrived, in order to rationalize their violent behavior. These patterns shed light on the nature of the wider cultural and sub-cultural contexts in which violence and homicide occur. Now, we shift our focus away from these wider sweeps across historical periods in time, and away from the various cultural and sub-cultural contexts in which violence and homicide occur, to a much narrower focus on the violent event itself.

Focusing on violent events

Although we turn away from the wider sweeps of historical time and the various cultural and sub-cultural contexts in which violence and homicides occur in order to focus on the violent event itself, this does not mean that these wider landscapes are forgotten or have become irrelevant. On the contrary, they remain the background in which violent events occur and are an essential part of the understanding of these events, but we need to know still more about the violent event itself if we are to gain a fuller understanding of what is happening and why.

In *Violent Men: An Inquiry into the Psychology of Violence* (1969), Hans Toch and his colleagues focused on violent events and men's use of violence. Using a novel approach to the study of violent events, in-depth interviews were conducted with three groups: men imprisoned for violence; men on probation primarily for assaults; and police officers who had either committed an assault and/or were the victims of violence from a suspect. Toch used the peers of each of these groups in all stages of the research including: the formulation of the study, construction of interview schedules, and conducting the interviews. Ex-convicts interviewed 44 prison inmates, 33 parolees, and 19 men who had been assaulted by a police officer, and police officers interviewed 32 serving police officers who had been assaulted. He noted that if we want to understand why men use violence, 'we must examine these acts, and we must understand the contexts in which they occurred… [and]…. We must know how these acts are conceived and perceived, and how they fit into the lives of their perpetrators' (Toch, 1969, p. 5, reprinted in 2017). Toch argued that these interviewers were better able to judge the veracity and validity of what they were being told, and were better placed to see through the obfuscations and self-deceptions of the interviewees and to assess the validity of their claims. The evidence from these interviews provides many insights into the nature of violent events and the men who perpetrate them.

Using qualitative evidence, Toch developed a typology of Violent Events and reflected on the personalities of the male perpetrators with terms such as 'reputation defending,' 'norm enforcing,' 'self-image compensation,' 'self-defending,' 'self-promoting,' and 'pressure removing.' Despite differences between them, most of the men seemed to be engaged, in a 'contest of character' intended to convey an image of someone who is 'formidable and fearless,' and willing to use violence to 'impress the victim and the audience.' Despite this image of bravura, he also identified an element of uncertainty among some of the men who were actually 'unsure' of themselves, 'irritated others,' and 'manufactured' situations in which their status was questioned' which, in turn, allowed them to demonstrate their 'toughness and potency' (Toch, 1969, pp. 135–136). The findings stress the importance of 'the maintenance of character' in a verbal contest when perpetrators 'feel' they have been disrespected and see this as demanding a violent response particularly if the encounter takes place in front of a 'chorus,' e.g. his friends or colleagues. With his ground-breaking research, Toch demonstrated the importance of studying the dynamics of violent events as well as the orientations of perpetrators within different contexts. For Toch, violence is often a group activity even when the group is not present but exists only as a point of reference. Finally, he described the men he studied as having the characteristics of 'violent prone' individuals.

In the 1970s, Luckenbill examined the circumstances in which homicides occur in a major US city (1977). Building on Wolfgang's conceptions of 'victim precipitation,' he used a dramaturgical approach linked to the 'symbolic interactionism' and characterized murder events as 'interactive' disputes between two people where the putative victim was equally as likely to become the perpetrator. The outcome was uncertain as to who would become the victim, who would be the perpetrator. Using evidence from police records of 70 murder convictions, Luckenbill described the murder event as a 'situated transaction' between the murderer and the victim that involved six sequential stages.

> Stage 1) an '*opening move*' of the victim is defined as 'damaging to the offender's sense of self.'

> Stage 2) the *victim refuses* the perpetrators 'request' to comply with his/her wishes, and the *perpetrator interprets* this 'action as a denial of the [offender's] ability/right to command obedience'.

> Stage 3) 'offender response' perpetrator delivers an 'ultimatum': 'either apologize, flee the situation, discontinue your inappropriate conduct, or

14 Male–male murder – the evidence so far

face physical harm or death'. In demanding these responses, offenders seemed to be suggesting to the victim a 'definition of the situation' as one in which 'violence is suitable in settling these questions of face and reputation'. At this stage, 86% of offenders used a verbal or physical challenge, and 14% killed the victim.

Stage 4) victims who were not 'eliminated' by this stage, are placed in a problematic and consequential position: either 'stand up' to the challenge (demonstrate strength of character), *or* 'back down' (apologize; discontinue his/her 'inappropriate' behavior; withdraw verbal statements the offender views as an insult).
– Most of those who were still standing, then come to a 'working agreement' or 'definition of the situation' as one suited to violence'. Then the 'battle' begins and the perpetrator 'drops' (kills) the victim'.

Stage 5) in 'many cases victims appeared to be committed to the battle'.

Stage 6) after the murder, 'moves that marked the end of the *transaction*': 58% or perpetrators flee; one-third remain; and a few are held by others who are by-standers.

(Luckenbill, 1977, pp. 181–186)

Some of Lukenbill's evidence regarding homicide events corroborates Toch's findings about non-lethal violent events, particularly when conflicts and disputes seem to be associated with men's sense of their own status and reputation, and when confrontations occur in the presence of observers. In some cases, the victim was seemingly the first person to use violence, which suggests the possible relevance of the notion of 'victim precipitation,' but only in these particular circumstances and perhaps not even in these cases which might have involved acts of 'self-defense' rather than pre-emptive acts of violence or aggression by the person who becomes the victim.

We have serious reservations about whether this 'six stage 'drama' of the homicide event' actually applies to all types of homicide, or may apply only to a small sub-set. Having spent several decades researching violence and murder in many different settings involving different perpetrators (men and women) and different types of victims (men, women and children), we find that many of these claims do not apply to many homicides that simply do not follow this script and do not fit into this 'six stage drama.' The claim that victims 'agree' to engage in 'violent combat' is suspect, particularly concerning 'battles' in which men murder women, when men kill children, and even in most encounters in which men murder other men.

Particularly puzzling is Luckenbill's claim that his conclusions apply to all types of homicides regardless of, 'age, sex, race, time and place, use of alcohol, and proffered motive' (Luckenbill, 1977, p. 186). In our other studies about the physical violence and murder of women by men, we did not find 'working agreements' (on the part of women victims) to men's use of violence against them. Instead, women usually tried to persuade the man not to use violence against them and beseeched him to stop. Verbal responses, defensive moves and arguments from the woman were usually met with an escalation of violence from the man. The evidence from our studies of men's use of non-lethal violence against women and the violent events in which men kill women do not follow this 'six stage drama' in which the women/victims 'agree' to a physical fight with their male attacker (Dobash and Dobash, 1979, 1984, 2004, 2015). In addition, other evidence from the Murder Study about murder events in which men kill children reveals 'zero agreement' on the part of the children to violent 'battle.' Our analysis of events in which men killed children provided no support for the notion that there was a 'working agreement' between child victims and their adult murderers that the 'situation was suited to the use of violence' against them, nor did our evidence support Luckenbill's notion that in 'many cases victims appeared to be committed to the battle' (Luckenbill's Stage 5). For evidence about child murders, see Cavanaugh, Dobash, and Dobash (2005, 2007) and Dobash and Dobash (2018). For similar criticisms of Luckenbill's claims, see Polk (1994) and Brookman (2005).

Polk's (1994) study of 380 cases of homicide in Australia, revealed that 'relationship types' (such as strangers vs friends) that are commonly used as descriptors of homicides, did not provide meaningful explanations of homicide. For Polk, contexts, such as the desire for revenge, ongoing disputes, immediate circumstances, and intentions shaped the use of lethal violence. Where Luckenbill focuses on interpretations, Polk reports on the more concrete aspects of murder, such as locations, actions, weapons, and the like. Many of the murders occurred in the context of assaults and heavy drinking in 'social settings' such as pubs, clubs, parties and BBQs. Most of these homicides were witnessed by groups of men, although in contrast to research from some other countries, he found little or no evidence of gangs. Firearms were used in about one-quarter of the homicides, and the most commonly used weapons were knives brought to the scene of the murder. Unlike Luckenbill, Polk found scant evidence of a sequence or stages in most of the murders. The violence was often 'vicious and unprovoked,' and the victim sometimes played no role in the build-up to the events in which he/she was killed. For Polk and many other researchers and commentators, the context and immediate circumstances of these events exhibited a 'masculine willingness to resolve disputes with violence' (Polk, 1994, p. 134).

In their ethnographic study of Latino 'clubs' in Chicago, Horowitz and Schwartz (1974), focused on the context and circumstances of violence and found a complex social nexus of both conventional and problematic behaviors among young men from deprived neighborhoods where norms and values emphasized the display of violent 'collective responses' in bars and on the street. Challenges were associated with their perceptions that they had been insulted, belittled and humiliated. These were provocative encounters, especially if they occurred in the presence of on-lookers, in which these young men felt they could not back-off.

16 Male–male murder – the evidence so far

'You got your pride, don't you? You can't let anyone step on you. You have to protect yourself ... and there's things we have to do.' Alongside such attitudes, they also found that these young men lived and acted in a context of 'ambiguity' where other cultural norms and ways of acting would sometimes 'override' violent solutions and shape non-violent and more conventional solutions. (Horowitz & Schwartz, (1974, p. 242).

Using participant observation, Benson and Archer (2002) investigated men's perceptions of what constituted a good 'night out' in a Northern English city. A good night out involved 'having a laff,' 'getting off with a woman' and 'fighting' in the city center. Drinking copious amounts of alcohol and 'getting pissed' was fundamental to a 'having a 'laff,' and for some, 'having a laff' also included violence. Conflicts and arguments appeared to be related to trivial issues such a spilled drink or a stare, and such acts, whether intentional or otherwise, were often interpreted as a 'challenge' to their 'manhood' that required a response in order to gain and/or maintain a reputation as a 'hard man.' While not all men reacted in this manner, for those who seemed to be 'prone to violence' this was an excuse to retaliate. Men who 'picked a fight' were careful to choose men who they considered to be a 'soft target' and thus unlikely to retaliate. These 'fighters' started fights, often accompanied by their friends, with a man they judged to be 'an unsuccessful fighter' (Benson and Archer, 2002, p. 12). In short, these encounters did not resemble a 'fair fight' with all parties 'agreeing' to a fight. Instead, they were one-sided affairs in which 'the fighters' attempted to pick a fight that they knew they could win as a means of illustrating their own status and prowess as a 'fighter.' In many ways these men looked more like cowards and bullies who knew they would always win against someone who was weaker, smaller, older or drunker than themselves, and nothing like an opponent in a 'fair fight' against whom he might actually lose.

Alcohol, weapons and murder

In the forgoing section we considered evidence and explanations associated with violent events, including homicide. They suggest the importance of certain contexts and specific characteristics of encounters that are linked to murder. Two of considerable importance are the consumption of alcohol, and the carrying and use of weapons. Without a doubt, overwhelming evidence suggests that the consumption of alcohol is related to the use of violence. Unfortunately, the findings regarding homicides often do not provide enough information to consider when and how drinking might make a difference. Large national population-based studies do not always report on alcohol consumption and violence, and when they do it is usually to report only if the offender and/or victim 'had been drinking.' Although interesting, such reports are not particularly informative since on any weekend night a considerable proportion of the adult populations of cities in North America and Europe could be classified as 'had been drinking.' People drink for all sorts of reasons, believing that: alcohol warms us up, makes us feel better, eases pain, is self-medication, helps overcome inhibitions, increases sociability, makes us livelier, and funnier, and so on. But alcohol can also contribute to aggression and violence. In the main, the problems associated with alcohol consumption are about 'excessive' consumption and especially inebriation.

Europeans, especially Northern and Eastern European countries have some of the highest levels of consumption of alcohol in the world followed by the USA, Canada and Australia (Forest, 2019). National evidence for England/Wales suggests that levels of alcohol consumption among those aged 18–24 is decreasing. However, in 2017, 30% of this age group reported binge drinking the week before they were interviewed (ONS, 2018; see also Alcohol Change UK, 2010). Worldwide health research carried out in 189 countries assessed annual levels of alcohol consumption from 1990–2017 (Manthey et al., 2019). UK evidence about 5,400 British adults found that, 26% reported 51 episodes of binge drinking in a year, which is almost 'once a week' (Manthey et al., 2019). Clearly, drinking to intoxication is not unusual among UK citizens. Providing further evidence of drinking in the UK, the organization, Alcohol Focus Scotland (2019), reported that Scotland is near the top of the world league tables for underage drinking with one-third of children having tried alcohol before their thirteenth birthday, and two-thirds before age 15. National population based evidence such as this should alert us to the necessity of conducting careful investigations of the possible relationships between alcohol consumption, violence and murder.

Bye (2013, p. 232) produced a comprehensive review of the evidence and explanations about the relationship between alcohol and violence. She noted that there are various ways of thinking about this connection. First, there may be a direct disinhibiting effect, i.e. drink alcohol, become violent. Second, alcohol may have an intervening facilitating effect on other factors such as an individual history of violence. Third, it may moderate violence. Fourth, in the strongest position it could be that alcohol has no direct effect whatsoever. All of these positions have been proposed and continue to enter into the discussions. What is clear is that wider social and cultural factors are positively related to drinking and violence. As expressed in Rehm's and colleagues 'hazard' measurement, several social and cultural factors are related to problematic and dangerous levels of consumption (Bye, 2013, p. 235). Drinking-related problems are associated with cultures involving lifestyles of heavy drinking, drinking in public places, festive drinking, acceptance of drinking to intoxication and public drunkenness, drinking without consuming food and a low rate of daily drinking (Bye, 2013, p. 235). These practices and patterns are more common in Northern and Eastern European countries which have some of the highest levels 'alcohol related homicide' in the world, and are especially linked to male–male homicide. For example, Russia has a very high level of alcohol related homicide, and binge drinking appears to be a common activity with one-third of Russian men reporting binge drinking once a month (Pridemore, 2004). Reliable evidence for Finland, Norway, and Sweden, indicates that 70% to 80% of all homicides involve an 'Offender under the influence

18 Male–male murder – the evidence so far

of alcohol' (Bye, 2013, Table 14.3, p. 236). It should not be assumed that these patterns result in exceptionally high rates of homicide in these countries. Quite the contrary, Nordic countries have some of the lowest rates in the world. By contrast, southern European countries such as France and Italy with cultures of daily drinking of moderate levels of alcohol with meals, and much lower social tolerance of drunkenness, also have relatively low levels of violence and homicide associated with alcohol consumption. This rather condensed version of the importance of alcohol consumption to violence, should alert us to the need for a careful consideration of the issue and the importance of context as well as 'mere' drinking (see Miles, 2012).

Weapons, violence and murder

While the word 'weapon' conjures up images of a gun or knife, a weapon can be any object or instrument used to injure, defeat or destroy. It can be a gun or knife, but it may be a baseball bat, a lamp, a car, a bomb, or any object that can be used to inflict injury or death. During the last few years, there appears to be a rising incidence in the use of knives as weapons on the streets of large cities in the UK. The following example of such an attack and murder was part of the opening statement of the prosecution of a defendant and four others as reported in *The Guardian* (Dodd, 2019, p. 28).

> The boy, 14, was knocked off his moped and stabbed by a rival gang. He suffered catastrophic injuries from nine stab wounds inflicted in seven seconds as he lay in the road. This defendant was part of an armed [with knives] group that went looking for a rival and, once they found him, the group chased their target, produced their weapons and butchered him. They first rammed him with their stolen Mercedes and then three of the males got out of the car ran up to the victim, who was lying defenceless and seriously injured on the ground. Rather than help him, the three embarked upon a violent frenzied attack, repeatedly stabbing him with knives that they must have armed themselves with for the purpose of attacking him. When the defendant caught up, he too stabbed him several times with a large knife. More people then joined the attack.

While punching, kicking and stamping is a common form of lethal attack, the main method of murder in Britain involves the use of a knife or sharp instrument such as a screwdriver or broken bottle. In 2019, there were 285 murders with a sharp instrument/knife, 39% of all homicides. This was the highest number of murders with a sharp instrument since the National Homicide Index began reporting in 1946 (Brookman, 2019). Clearly this represents a potentially worrying development which may reflect a significant trend since the proportions in the 1990s and the first decade of the twenty-first century were around 30%.

Male–male murder – the evidence so far **19**

A recent survey of young people age 11–18 'declared knife crime their biggest concern' (Brookman, 2019). Until recently, the proportion of stabbings in Scotland was quite a bit higher than in England/Wales, almost half of all homicides, but this has now fallen to around 44%, but of course this is still high (Eades et al., 2007, pp. 18–19). By contrast, the main method of killing in the US is with a firearm, about 65%–70% each year (Beeghley, 2003; U.S. Department of Justice, 2017; CDC, 2018). In the US, there is endless and acrimonious debate about the significance of firearms in the extraordinary levels of firearm deaths in the US. One side argues that it is not guns but people who are the issue. The other side argues that the evidence indicates it is the availability and widespread use of guns that contributes to the high rates of homicide in the US. As Beeghley (2003, p. 108) points out, 'All the extant data suggest that fatality rates are higher in [all violent encounters] when a gun is used, compared to a knife, club, or bare hands.' The Swiss social scientists, Killias (1993) conducted an analysis of homicide rates and firearms in 14 countries, including the US, and found a strong positive correlation between household gun ownership and the homicide rate, the more guns the higher the rate. Killias notes that guns are not the only contributor to high levels of homicide, but he concluded that 'guns matter.' In the England/Wales in 2018, 5% of homicide deaths resulted from the use of a firearm.

While the US continues to engage in unending debates about the use of firearms, particularly in mass murders committed in schools and other public places, discussions in Britain concern generally focus on incidents involving the use of knives, particularly among the young, and evidence about this issue is growing (Lemos, 2004; Eades et al., 2007; McVie, 2010). Carrying and using a weapon in early life may be a precursor to the use of serious violence. The first question to address is who carries knives, and why? Research in Scotland and England/ Wales revels that carrying a 'weapon' is not unusual among young people (Eades, et al. 2007; McVie, 2010). Detailed evidence comes from Scotland. The Edinburgh Study of Youth Transitions and Crime included a sample of 4,300 of young people between the ages of 13–17, and found that 30% reported ever carrying a knife, and 10% carried another type of weapon (McVie, 2010). Surveys do not usually ask questions about the nature of the weapon that a young person may be carrying such as: pen-knife (pocket-knife in the US)? Or, pepper spray? Or, a sharp-bladed knife? While the Scottish-based research identified two categories, knives and other, the evidence is mostly not clear on this issue. What is clear is that 'carrying' is infrequent and sporadic. Most young people are not 'hard core' carriers' intent on using a weapon. In the Edinburgh research a 'hard core' of frequent carriers were about 6% of the young people who were responsible for 25% of all knife-related incidents (McVie, 2010, p. iii). A rather counter-intuitive finding is that most carriers were the least likely to have used a weapon or to have inflicted an injury. It may be that 'carrying' is intended as a mode of protection, or to enhance individual status, or to threaten and/or intimidate others but not to engage in a knife fight or a violent encounter.

20 Male–male murder – the evidence so far

Who are these weapons carriers? In contrast to the young people who did not carry a weapon, weapon carriers were more likely to drink alcohol once a week, to do drugs, to hang out in public locations such as streets and parks, usually with other young males engaged in risky and anti-social behavior and offending, including violence. They were more likely to truant and to be excluded from school. On a personal level, they were more likely than non-carriers to have low self-esteem and elevated levels of alienation. Additionally, their backgrounds included a 'lack of parental guidance, feelings of social isolation, poor self-esteem, and a tendency to inflict injuries on themselves [self-harming] … and were at "risk of becoming a persistent offender"' (McVie, 2017, p. iv). Given this litany of problematic experiences it is not surprising that these young people reported 'adversarial contact with the police' and to be 'formerly warned or charged' with a crime, yet official action was rather rare.

What were they thinking – 'cognitive scripts' and violence

In the Murder Study, we investigated the 'ways of thinking' or 'cognitive scripts' used 'before' and 'after' murder events in order to 'facilitate' violence and justify its use. Social and behavioral scientists have long been interested in the techniques used to justify and rationalize crime and violence. In an early attempt to describe responses to 'deviant' and criminal behavior committed by juvenile delinquents, Sykes and Matza (1957) identified various 'techniques of neutralization' used to justify and rationalize deviant actions. These include: denying responsibility for the act, denying injury, and/or denying that the individual was actually a victim. In addition, they condemn the condemners (i.e. police and courts), and claim that others (group/gang) required them to behave in this way. These norms and values not only rationalize 'deviant' behavior but also prepare the groundwork for other such acts (Sykes and Matza, 1957, p. 669; see also Lamnek, 2003).

Drawing on English moral philosophers and a symbolic interactionist perspective, Scott and Lyman (1968) view the nature of 'accounts' offered for 'unanticipated and untoward behavior' as exculpatory and of two types: excuses and justifications. 'Excuses' vary and involve an admission that the act was 'bad, wrong or inappropriate' but also include a 'denial of responsibility.' 'Justifications' involve attempts to 'neutralize' an 'act' and at the same time include a claim that the act was 'permissible' or 'inevitable' under certain circumstances. In these accounts, 'sad tales' are offered, with the wrongdoer reconstructing their biography in order to create the impression of a 'dismal past' that 'explains' and thus 'justifies' their deviant behavior (Scott and Lyman, 1968, p. 52, note 29). In the process of giving an account, the offender is engaged in 'alter casting,' attempting to construct a specific situational identity. For example, a murderer may present himself as a 'reasonable man,' who like any other reasonable man, would respond with violence under similar circumstances.

Working on moral development, psychologists such as Bandura (1991) have focused on the interpretations and perceptions of individuals engaged in problematic behavior including violence. Bandura's research, explanations and interpretations are extremely important in an understanding of the thinking of violent offenders. He juxtaposes two types of individuals in terms of their thinking and actions. The 'ideal' adult is 'self-approving' and 'self-critical,' 'empathetic,' able to consider the reactions and evaluations of others and adverse effects upon others, is empathetic, and develops within a social context. By contrast, those who engage in 'reprehensible, anti-social, and harmful behaviors' base this on 'moral reasoning' that is 'weak on empathy,' 'lacks self-sanction,' and includes a range of ideologies, beliefs and cultural prescriptions that allow a 'reasonable' person to act violently. According to Bandura, violence and other forms of oppressive behavior can be made 'righteous through cognitive restructuring,' and delineates the mechanisms associated with attempts to justify and or excuse collective or individual violent behavior (Bandura, 1991, p. 73).

How is this done? A brief summation includes:

- *Advantageous comparisons* – 'others do worse than me';
- *Displacement and/or diffusion of responsibility* – 'someone else did it; I didn't mean it to end like that;
- *Advantageous comparisons* – 'it was trifling or even a benevolent' compared to the acts of others – I prevented you from 'reckless' or bad behavior;
- *Displacement and/or diffusion of responsibility* – obscures the relationship between acts and their impact with consequences defined as unintended or 'dictates of the situation' and, as such, personal acts are disowned and agency denied;
- *Disregard or distortion of consequences* – selective inattention and cognitive distortions that distance themselves from the consequences of their acts;
- *Dehumanization and impersonalization* – divesting victims of human qualities, thus blunting self-sanctions when individuals are no longer worthy of respect or fail to obey;
- *Attribution of blame* – assign responsibility for the violence to the victim, e.g. justifying sexual violence by saying 'it was consensual,' or 'the victim wanted it,' or 'anticipatory self-censure' is eliminated when the traumatic effects of sexual assault are 'twisted into pleasurable ones for the victim';
- *Disengagement of self-sanctions and self-deception* – offenders distance themselves from the act and the victim while attempting to enhance their own sense of self. They remain intentionally 'uninformed' about their violent acts, and are incredulous, or challenge other accounts and/or twist them to fit their own views.

(Bandura, 1991, p. 93; see also Tavuchis, 1991)

An integral aspect of our own research on men's use of violence against women and other men has always included attempts to capture the perpetrator's perceptions of what we refer to as, 'what were they thinking?' (Dobash and Dobash, 2011).

22 Male–male murder – the evidence so far

The objective is to try to capture the perpetrators own notions about what they did (violent event) and why (rationalizations, justifications, minimization, etc.). In a previous study of *Changing Violent Men* (Dobash et al., 2000), and in the current examination of 'Murder,' it is interesting that perpetrator's accounts of non-lethal violent events and of murder events almost always begin with what the other person said or did that 'started' the event and/or 'caused' the violence. Men's narrative accounts of violent events almost never began with something 'they did' or something 'they said.'[1]

We will see similar patterns in the following chapters as we focus on the different types of male–male murder, and hear perpetrators accounts, many of which offered exculpatory and excusatory explanations, and are devoid of a sense of responsibility, empathy and/or remorse. Victims are blamed, responsibility is deflected, and excuses are given. As will be shown, men's accounts of the murder events frequently began by implicating the victim, or excusing and/or rationalizing their own violence. What was often apparent in our interviews with violent men was the objectification of the victim. Events were often externalized as a whole group of circumstances were rolled into one, and in the end 'somebody died.' This sort of externalizing is not unusual. From their point of view, some of the men even saw themselves as norm enforcers upholding 'high moral values,' and their use of violence as acceptable when someone was 'out of line.' Many of the men viewed themselves as 'justified' in using violence to impose their will, and their beliefs and orientations provided a cognitive script that justified violence/murder and allowed them to have little or no remorse. There is a wealth of historical, anthropological and contemporary evidence regarding the manner in which individuals offer 'moral' justifications for their use of violence, and use 'techniques of neutralization.'

Many such accounts were given by the men in the Murder Study, and will be presented throughout this book, but first we turn to a discussion of the research methods used in the Murder Study, issues about typologies, and the development of our own Five Types of Male–Male Murder. As shown above, violence and homicide are embedded in the culture and time periods in which they occur and need to be considered in a 'context specific' manner that relates to the societies, locations, historical periods, cultures and circumstances in which they take place. Our own attempts to understand homicide/murder are not undertaken on a wide world stage focused on whole societies or grand sweeps of time such as those discussed above, but on a narrower stage focused on the social and personal contexts in which particular murder events take place and a close examination of the murder event itself. Unlike those who propose a universal theory of violence (Karstedt and Eisner, 2009), we have long argued for the importance of adopting a 'context specific approach' to the study of violence in its many forms (Dobash and Dobash, 1983; for a different approach to contextual explanations see Miethe and Regoeczi, 2004). We also emphasize the importance of empirical research as central in the twin tasks of revealing the nature of violent events and seeking explanations about when and why violence occurs

The murder study – research methods and data

A close examination of 'murder events' and the 'situations and circumstances' in which they take place are central to our efforts to provide a fuller understanding of when men murder other men. The evidence used here is taken from our wider study of murder which includes data gathered from a sample of 866 men (786) and women (80) convicted of murder drawn from casefiles held in prison headquarters in England/Wales, prison headquarters in Scotland, and seven prisons in the two distinct jurisdictions. Additional, qualitative evidence was collected in 200 in-depth semi-structured interviews conducted in seven prisons with 180 men and 20 women serving a sentence for murder. In the Murder Study, all types of murder (not manslaughter) were examined including different types of perpetrators (men, women and children aged 16 and under) and different types of victims (men, women and children age 16 and under) (Dobash and Dobash, 2015, pp. 265–280). The casefiles contain extensive details of the murder itself including the circumstances at the time, (locations, disputes, drinking, method of killing, actions after the murder, etc.). Details about the lives of the perpetrators included numerous reports about childhood, family, school, employment, and offending. Information about adult life included employment, marital status, use of medical and social services, and contacts with the criminal justice system including police, convictions, probation, and prison. Information about their time in prison included reports from prison staff and various professionals engaged in work, education and rehabilitation.

The information contained in the casefiles is extremely 'content rich' because those convicted of murder (but not those convicted of manslaughter) are sentenced to 'life' imprisonment and are given a 'tariff' (now called 'minimum term') specifying the number of years they must serve in prison before they can be considered for parole and possible release back into the community, but they will always remain on a 'life license' meaning that they can be returned to prison under certain circumstances. In order to be considered for parole, those convicted of murder must participate in specialized offender programs in which they are required to confront their culpability, accept responsibility for the murder, express genuine remorse, and seek to reform. Details of their daily behavior in prison as well as their progress on these offender programs is contained in their casefile.

Each casefile could be over 100 pages in length. From them, we were able to gather quantitative data for over 400 variables about the murder and the lives of these men as well as an extensive amount of qualitative text about the crime and their lives before imprisonment (for further details about the Murder Study, see Dobash and Dobash, 2015, pp. 11–17, pp. 265–278). Overall, the Murder Study included 786 male murderers which represents 22% of all men serving a life sentence for murder at the time of the study. Of these 786 male perpetrators, 424 (54%) murdered an adult male, 271 (34%) murdered and adult female (see Dobash et al., 2007; Dobash and Dobash, 2011, 2015) and 91 (12%) murdered a

24 Male–male murder – the evidence so far

child under age 16 (see Cavanagh, Dobash, and Dobash, 2005, 2007; Dobash and Dobash, 2018). Here, we focus only on the 424 cases of adult men (age 16 and older) who murdered another adult man.

Interviews were conducted in seven prisons selected as 'strategic sites' because they held different categories of prisoners and were located in different areas across the country. We used a mixed-method approach collecting quantitative and qualitative evidence. Most interviews lasted between 1.5–2 hours, were tape-recorded (with the prisoner's permission), and transcribed. This produced several-thousand pages of text that were coded for analysis of qualitative data using Nud*ist/QSR. Face-to-face interviews provided direct accounts about the actions and thinking of these men as well as their own interpretations of their use of lethal violence and the murder event, all of which is relatively rare in a sample of this size. In the interviews, we began by focusing on the life histories of the men, beginning with their parents and family, their lives as children and adults, the murder event including situations and circumstances at the time, and ending with their life in prison and reflections on the murder they committed, and some thoughts about the future. All of the data were collected by ourselves and two long-time colleagues Dr. Kate Cavanagh and Dr. Ruth Lewis. The collection of over 400 variables from each of the 424 casefiles of male–male murders, along with text from the interviews with these men, provide both a treasure trove of data and a massive challenge of how to systematically examine and classify all of this material in an effort to delve more deeply into these murder events and the lives of the men who committed murder. Clearly, a typology (or typologies) of murder was essential, but this task was far from straightforward.

The importance of typologies

Philosophers of science and natural and social scientists have long considered the utility of using typologies in research (Hempel, 1961; Kuhn, 1962; Lazarsfeld and Barton, 1964; Kaplan, 1964; Millon, 1991; Collier, LaPorte and Seawright, 2012). Identifying 'types' and their 'attributes' requires great care since they are important for concept formation, explanations, and as guides to empirical research. A meaningful typology is one that has an explicit structure and begins with a main system of classification, such as 'different types of murder,' and proceeds to identify central and crucial dimensions of each type. Both what is included as well as what is not included define a type. Identifying and specifying the crucial dimension of any type is best done using an interpretative/reflexive process since the parameters of types are rarely air-tight. There is always overlap, and it is best to think in terms of 'characterizations' rather than precise and immutable classifications. For example, the use of 'relationship type' such as homicides involving 'strangers' could mean a victim who had 'never seen' the perpetrator, but might also include those who had briefly 'exchanged words,' or a perpetrator who had secretly 'observed' the victim over a long period of time but was unknown to the victim. Should they all be considered 'strangers'? This illustrates even the most basic of questions about what might constitute an adequate typology of a murder between 'strangers,' and provides a glimpse at the sort of problems associated with developing any typology of murder.

So, what might constitute an adequate typology of homicide? In the social sciences, major figures in sociology such as Max Weber (1949) and Emile Durkheim (1951), asked questions about the wider social world and included problems related to crime as well as violence and homicide and produced important typologies. Durkheim, noted that, 'homicide, like suicide, is not a single, indivisible criminological entity, but must include a variety of [types] very different from one another' (cited in Flewelling and Williams, 1999, p. 98). In the twentieth century, the American sociologist Robert K. Merton, considered to be the founder of modern sociology, adapted Durkheim's concept of 'anomie' (normlessness), and translated it into what is commonly termed 'strain theory' which was intended to explain the relatively high rate of crime in the US by identifying a disjuncture between cultural goals and structural means of success. The 'strain' created by this disjuncture led to five adaptions (types): conformity, innovation, ritualism, retreatism and rebellion (Merton, 1938). Two of these are related to crime and violence: innovation demonstrated by organized gang crime and rebellion associated with rejecting both the means and the cultural goals of society which today might be linked to terrorism.

Typologies of violence and homicide

Most typologies of violence and homicide reflect Marvin Wolfgang's early systems of classification developed in the US in the 1950s that included 11 types of 'relationships between the victim and offender' such as 'stranger and acquaintance' (Wolfgang, 1958). This conceptualization was later modified to include the concept of 'relational distance' ranging from 'intimates to strangers' (Silverman and Kennedy, 1987). Wolfgang focused on '13 types of murder including 'altercation of a trivial origin' and 'victim precipitated' that emphasized motives' and the importance of 'contextual and situational factors' (Polk, 1994, p. 20). These were later translated by Luckenbill (1977) into a series of exchanges typifying 'disputes and conflicts' between victims and offenders. Although Wolfgang mentioned the need to consider the 'situations and circumstances' in which violence occurred, this was not taken up until Luckenbill translated them into his scheme of exchanges typifying disputes and conflicts between victims and offenders as considered above.

In 1994, Ken Polk presented a comprehensive and penetrating critique of the ever expanding approaches to classification in homicide research. He noted that the US FBI Supplementary Homicide Report contained 30 categories associated with homicide, that 'various classification schemes were more "diverse" than consistent,' and that 'each employed its own description of victim/offender relationship so that it is highly likely that no two lists will be the same' which made

26 Male–male murder – the evidence so far

it difficult to build consistent and valid typologies of homicide (Polk, 1994, p. 20, see also, Wilson, 1993a, 1993b; D'Cruze, Walklate, and Pegg, 2011; Hough and McCorkle, 2017). In addition to all of this diversity, other typologies focused on 'motives' making a distinction between 'expressive' and 'instrumental' homicides, with the former driven by emotions such as anger and the latter related to material gain such as theft and larceny (Block and Zimring, 1973; Block, 1988). Polk concluded that, 'The fundamental problem with exiting codes is that ... they do not provide enough information to inform theoretical analysis of why people kill' (Polk, 1994, p. 21).

The preeminent homicide researchers, Daly and Wilson also noted that, 'criminological conceptions of motives in homicide is a woolly amalgam ... and [represents] only a relatively small dose of the substantive issues that [people] mean when they speak of motives,' and pointed out that what is needed is research results and typologies that provide more information about the context and circumstances of murder along with the thinking, intentions and actions of the murderers (Daly and Wilson, 1988, pp. 173–174). The American homicide researcher, Zahn, listed four pressing needs in homicide research including more attention to the identification of different 'types of homicides including the recognition that homicide was a multidimensional rather than a unidimensional phenomenon' (Zahn, 1991, p. 17). Similarly, the British criminologists, Brookman and colleagues. noted that, 'Homicide comes in numerous guises [and] understanding ... requires disaggregation of homicide into conceptually meaningful subtypes' (Brookman, Jones, and Pike, 2017, p. 340). In our own examination of, 'When Men Murder Women,' we identified three types of male–female murder (Dobash and Dobash, 2015). Much existing research on homicide fails to classify murders, and at best employs rudimentary categories such as age, sex and ethnicity of victims and offenders as well as geographic locations where homicides occurred. While such information is essential for comparing rates of homicide, it is basically a list of attributes rather than a typology of homicides that constitutes an attempt to examine more closely what happens in murder events and why they might have occurred.

While Polk offered a number of criticisms of existing typologies, he used an inductive method involving the collection of qualitive evidence to construct a typology of various types of homicide in his Australian sample. Excluding the cases that were 'bizarre' and unclassifiable, he identified six main types: Homicide in the context of sexual intimacy, homicides originating in family intimacy (mostly children), other family victims, confrontational homicide, conflict resolution and victims of mass killers (Polk, 1994, p. 23). Of the 380 cases, the largest proportion (27%) involved the 'context of sexual intimacy' – most of these cases were men killing women, usually intimate partners. This main type was followed by 'confrontational homicides' (22%) and homicides originating in another crime (16%). Those involving 'confrontations' or 'sexual intimacy' were classified as 'masculine violence.' As the majority of mounting evidence demonstrates, when men kill in

Male–male murder – the evidence so far **27**

the context of sexual intimacy, they usually kill women intimate partners as acts of possessiveness and jealousy (Polk and Ranson, 1991; Polk, 1994, Chapter 3). By contrast, 'confrontational homicides' usually involve men killing other men.

Polk's evidence suggests that 'confrontational homicides' are usually spontaneous, emerge in a context of verbal and/or physical fights, and usually occurred in and around pubs. Alcohol consumption and men in groups are important in characterizing this type of murder: 'Without question, the collective of males is a central feature of the conflict' supplying 'participants and [a] social audience' (Polk, 1993, p. 49). These groups of men are not 'gangs' as identified in the US literature. Perpetrators often used lethal violence because the victim had 'shamed' or 'humiliated' them often in front of an audience. Although these slights might seem trivial to most people, Polk and other observers suggest that these encounters are extremely important to men without status. For Polk (1994, p. 169), the fundamental aspects of 'confrontational' homicides involves character contests, challenges, and a 'masculine readiness to engage in physical violence in response to such challenges.' These are the two types of homicide that Polk explicitly labeled as 'masculine.' However, a close reading of the evidence and conclusions suggests there are two additional types of homicide that might also be labeled 'masculine': 'conflict resolution' and 'homicide originating in another crime,' both of which mostly involved men killing other men. 'Conflict resolution' homicides involved men in conflict over such things as personal disputes, debts, and the sharing of legal and illegal resources. Much of the violence occurred in the context of illegal activities such as drug dealing among men who had 'close ties to a criminal way of life.' These homicides were much more likely to occur between men who knew each other. The violence was rarely spontaneous, but was usually planned and deliberate. The 'homicide and other crime' type mostly involved robbery and burglary among male perpetrators and victims. Of the 61 cases, only 5 involved a woman perpetrator (Polk, 1994, p. 111). Most of the victims in this category were not strangers. According to Polk what was important to the murder was not the relationship between the victim and perpetrator but the 'nature of the crime,' i.e. theft.

Reporting on 178 homicides in the Netherlands, researchers noted that homicide is 'governed by men' (Nieuwbeerta and Leistra, 2007; Ganpat and Liem, 2013). Employing data gathered through the Dutch Homicide Monitor system and focusing on the offender victim relationships and the context of murders nine 'categories' were identified. Four types involved killing in a family and between intimate partners which constituted one-quarter of all homicides. About 5% involved 'other' family, including for example, honor and blood feuds. Two types were criminally related, and most included drug dealing and drug users (11%). Another crime-related type involved murders in the context of robbery or burglary (7%). Conflicts, quarrels in various types of relationships excluding families, accounted for 20% of murders. Sexual murders constituted 4% of all the murders. A very heterogenous group of murders were labeled 'other' and made up 10% of

28 Male–male murder – the evidence so far

the murders. An important aspect of these types and the evidence upon which they were built was the veracity and reliability of the evidence.

Much of Brookman's research on homicide appeared in 'Understanding Homicide' (2005), where she identified and analyzed various types of homicide, such as 'men killing women,' 'the killing of children and infants' and 'multiple homicide.' Of particular significance for male–male murders is her identification of two types she labels, following Polk 'masculine homicide.' In her research into police files in three jurisdictions in England and Wales she identified 97 cases of homicide. In 54 cases, men killed other adult males and these were about equally divided into two main types: *confrontational* (19 cases) and *revenge* (18 cases) (Brookman, 2003, p. 40). 'Confrontational murders' usually involved 'face-to-face' spontaneous violent reactions associated with trivial issues where men 'agreed' 'to allow the confrontation to develop and escalate.' The violence usually occurred in a public location such as a pub or club, and included an audience and support- ers. Importantly, it seems in most cases there was no intention to kill. Evidence regarding 'revenge killings' suggests a history of 'strife' between the victim and offender who were usually known to each other. Revenge killings were rarely spontaneous, rather they often involved planning and were purposeful and delib- erate. For Brookman, revenge homicides involved lethal intent. Using a wealth of contextual- and individual-based evidence, this makes additional distinctions between these two 'masculine' based homicides.

The murder study – developing a typology of male–male murder

Like others before us, we began by attempting to develop a typology by focus- ing on the 'relational distance' between perpetrators and their victims, from strangers to acquittances, friends and family members. As well as the apparently straightforward nature of the relationship, we also included the length of the relationship, from no relationship, to an acquaintance of a few hours, to many years. At the most basic level, it would seem that relationships mattered. We went through numerous iterations in our efforts to develop a typology of the male–male murders based on relationships, but most of these efforts did not reflect what seemed to 'count' or make sense in terms of what was happening. After much deliberation, we concluded that while a focus on relationships did contain elements that were useful in the development of a typology, this was not enough and much more thinking and refinement of other factors was needed in order to develop a typology that best reflected what was happening when men murdered other men.

We went back to square one and continued 'constructing' a typology by shift- ing our focus onto the murder event itself. Originally, all of the casefiles and interviews were given what we called a 'thumbnail' sketch, a brief description of some of the distinguishing characteristics of the murder. Re-reading all of the

424 thumbnails, along with many of the casefiles and the full text of some of the interviews, helped us re-think how the cases might best be categorized in ways that captured the most salient elements of the murders. In the end, we developed a typology of Five Types of Male–Male Murder. We included the type of *relationship* between the perpetrator and his victim, but the primary focus shifted to the *murder event* itself and the *context and circumstances* in which it occurred as these elements provided more meaningful categorization of the murders. Throughout this process, we used the quantitative evidence to assess the robustness of the various provisional typologies, and the qualitative evidence to assess the meaningfulness of the typology for understanding what happened, when, and why (for the use of qualitative research see D'Cruze, Walklate, and Pegg (2011)).

The murder study – five types of male–male murder

Based on evidence from the Murder Study, the five main types of male–male murder are: Confrontational Fighters, Money/Finance, Family, Sexual, and Older. Men. A single chapter is devoted to each type of murder in which we present findings about the murder event, the wider context in which it occurs, as well as the perpetrator–victim relationship. These dimensions include a number of clusters: the nature of the relationship between perpetrators and victims; circumstances such as ongoing disputes and the nature of disputes; confrontations at the time of the murder; previous violence between the victim and perpetrator; the use/ abuse of alcohol and drugs; the location of the murder; the nature of the violence used in the violent event that ended in murder; as well as some notions about the apparent motives and thinking of the murderers (see Dobash and Dobash (2015, pp. 267–275) for details of the development of a typology of male–female murders in the Murder Study). Quantitative evidence is employed in a systematic analysis of all the critical dimensions, and qualitative evidence is presented in subtypes we constructed that demonstrate the diversity within each main type as well as the dynamic elements of these murders. Some of the cases might have belonged in more than one type, and decisions about the 'best fit' were made following discussions about the details of that particular case. Finally, murder is both multi-faceted and messy, and the more you know the more difficult it is to classify events and individuals into a typology that matches the definition of what constitutes the attributes of a specific type and does not stray from that definition. Because murder events contain many facets that are of importance, and these sometimes overlap across the different 'types' of murder, we adopted a case-by-case approach when dimensions involved some form of overlap. For example, a man who was both *sexually assaulted* and *robbed* during the murder, could have been placed in two of our Five Types of Male–Male Murder ('money' and 'sexual murder'). In such cases, the classification of murder was based on the most dominant characteristic in relation to the murder event. We were *not* able to classify

30 Male–male murder – the evidence so far

41 of the 424 cases (10%) because of missing data relative to the type of murder.[2] Although each of the Five Types will be examined separately and in detail, here we provide a brief overview of the five types of male–male murder. (note – in the tables, calculations for 'All' murders include the 41 unclassified cases).

Confrontational fighters and murder

Of the 424 cases of male–male murder, Confrontational/Fighters constitute the largest category of the Five Types of Male–Male Murder, ($n = 158$, 37%). The distinguishing characteristic of these murder events involved direct confrontations. Most involved only one perpetrator and his victim, although some included several men on one or both sides of a confrontation. While confrontations sometimes occurred in other types of murder, fighting and attacking constituted the most important dynamic aspect of these murders. Some involved a previous encounter between the men in which the perpetrator believed he had been humiliated and/or bested by the victim, and he retaliated in a murderous attack. In other cases, the killer created a confrontation in which he could place the victim in a position that, in his eyes, legitimized the use of lethal force such as claiming that the victim had 'bumped into him' or had 'disrespected him' with a 'look' or a 'comment.' For some Confrontational/Fighters, group activity or allegiance was important in the murders, although gang membership as such was not prevalent in these events. Defense of the group, or 'suffering' an insult in front of friends and or in front of enemies appeared to be felt acutely. Revenge and retaliation were sometimes immediate but insults and grudges often festered over a longer period of time. These murders were frequently fueled by the consumption of a considerable amount of alcohol by offenders, victims, or both. Many 'Fighters' appeared to be 'searching for respect,' 'defending their pride,' boosting a reputation that had been damaged or needed to be enhanced, and used serious violence as a means of establishing or maintaining their personal sense of self-worth and identity.

Murder for money/financial gain

As with most of the labels used in this typology, there was considerable deliberation about the name of this type of murder, ultimately, we decided 'why not be explicit.' These murders were committed in the context of an attempt to obtain money and/or resources. Most of the 81 murders (19% of 424) were committed in the context of a burglary or robbery. Others involved disputes about the 'share-out' of resources/money acquired through a theft or fraud, legal and illegal loans, and profits from drug dealing, prostitution, or people trafficking. Other murders involved conflict between individuals or government officials about legal or illegal activities that had financial consequences, and a few murders involved a 'contract' to kill. It may be assumed that such killings do not involve emotions and are defined simply as instrumental, but some are in fact highly emotional and reputational. For example, a drug dealer might be enraged when a supplier fails to deliver, and kills him out of anger and/or because his personal reputation (and business activities) would be seriously damaged if this act went unpunished. Many of these killings involved some form of burglary in which the perpetrator responded with anger when 'challenged' by a victim who tried to stop the burglary, the theft of his property, or the intrusion into his home.

Family murders

There were 72 murders (17% of 424) committed by men against other men within the context of the family. Family murders were disaggregated into several sub-types including 'blood' relatives within the immediate family (grandfathers, fathers, brothers, sons, uncles and cousins) as well as in-laws; same sex intimate partners; collateral murders; and murders committed by 'brothers' acting together to kill an outsider, as well as feuds between families. Some men killed another man because they believed he had 'stolen' their wife – we term this subtype a 'collateral' murder because they occurred in the context of ongoing violence/ aggression against a woman intimate partner but ended in the murder of another man. While other issues such as theft or a bad loan, were sometimes involved in these murders, data from the casefiles and interviews indicated that the murder was primarily about relations located within the context of the 'family.'

Sexual murders

With the exception of hate violence perpetrated against gay men, very little attention has been devoted to the murder of men within various male–male sexual contexts. Using the 32 cases of sexual murder (8% of 424), we begin with a consideration of hate crimes against gay men and describe the context and circumstance of these murders which, in many cases, were also related to muggings. In the family chapter, we consider same-sex intimate partner murder. Here, we consider other additional contexts involving sex: murders related to sex in exchange for material goods such as money or accommodation; murder in the context of 'baiting and luring' a gay man into a sexual encounter and then killing him both as a part of a hate crime but also as part of a theft where the victim was unlikely to report the violence. In murders involving heterosexual prostitution, it is usually women sex workers who are killed, but in the cases of homosexual prostitution considered here it was usually the 'client' who was the victim. These murders also often involved a theft. In some of the sexual murders, the male perpetrator claimed that he had responded to a sexual assault and tried to use the legal defense of a 'homosexual advance' which is no longer a legitimate legal defense but may still linger in the thinking of prosecutors and members of a jury. Accusations of pedophilia, whether true or false, were sometimes made by perpetrators who

32 Male–male murder – the evidence so far

tried to demonstrate a form of 'self-righteousness' and 'moral outrage.' Finally, we consider the very rare phenomena of sexual serial murder. As with all of the identified subtypes, sex-related murders sometimes involved a combination of hate, sometimes self-hate, and sometimes robbery of the victim.

Murders of older men

In much of the literature on violence and murder, it is often stated or implied that perpetrators are at risk of violence when they themselves are aggressors. While this may be true in some cases, it was very unlikely in the 40 (9%) cases of murder of older men over age 65. Across all of the types of murder, we consider the vulnerability of the victims and the potential threat the victim might pose to the perpetrator. On balance, older men were the most vulnerable of all the adult male murder victims. Most lived on their own, some were unable to defend themselves because of incapacities related to aging. The men who murdered older men were often among the most debilitated of the perpetrators, particularly with respect to the abuse of alcohol but also in terms of the highest levels of unemployment. Thefts and robberies of vulnerable older men were often associated with attempts to obtain resources to continue drinking. Three subtypes of the murders of older men included murders related to robbery, sex, and hatred of the elderly. Many involved attempts to obtain money to 'get back to the pub.' The sexual murders of older men mirror those presented in the earlier chapter focusing on sexual murders, with the additional element of the 'extra' vulnerability of the elderly victims because of their age. The third subtype, involved an apparent hatred and disgust of those who were old, and may help explain why some of the murders of older men were among the most vicious and brutal of all of the murders.

Summary

Following a brief review of some of the evidence and explanatory perspectives used in the study of violence and murder, it is clear that we the need a multi-level approach to the classification of cases of murder that use both quantitative and qualitive data in order to enhance the current level of knowledge about murders between men. In the following chapters, we present evidence from the Murder Study in our effort to extend what is now known about murders between men, and about the lives and orientations of the men who commit this crime. The Murder Study contained 424 cases in which men murdered men. From these cases, we developed a typology of 'Five Types' of male–male murder. We examine each of these types separately, using quantitative data to present the main patterns, and qualitative evidence to illustrate the nature of these patterns and the diversity within them. For each type of murder, we focused on the murder event, the situations and circumstances in which the murders occurred, the relationship between perpetrators and their victims, and the orientations and intentions of the perpetrators. After the separate examination of each of the Five Types of Murder, we turn to an examination of the life course of the men who committed these murders. In the last chapters, we focus on the lives of the perpetrators as children, as adults, and their life in prison after the murder. We explore how they adjusted to the daily routines of prison, their participation in prison programs focused on their offending behavior and responsibility for their crime, their expressions of remorse for the murder they committed and empathy for the person they killed, as well as how they viewed a possible future outside prison. We finish with an overview of the murder types and some thoughts on the problems associated with re-entering the world beyond prison once released.

Notes

1. For perpetrators' accounts of violence against women, see Dobash and Dobash, 1979, 1984; Dobash et al., 2000, Chapter 2; Dobash et al., 1998; Dobash and Dobash, 2011, 2015).
2. The 41 cases that could not be classified into one of the Five Types of Murder, were nonetheless included in the evidence about 'All' of the 424 male–male murders as shown in the Tables 7.1, 8.1 and 8.2.

References

Alcohol Focus Scotland, 2019. National charity working to prevent and reduce alcohol related harm [Accessed November 8, 2019].

Alcohol Change UK, 2010. Alcohol statistics [Accessed November 21, 2019].

Anderson, E., 1990. *Streetwise: Race, Class, and Change in an Urban Community.* Chicago, IL: University of Chicago Press.

Anderson, E., 1994. The code of the Street. *The Atlantic Monthly*, May, 81–94.

Archer, J, ed., 1994. *Male Violence.* London: Routledge.

Bandura, A., 1991. Social cognitive theory of moral thought and action. In W. M. Kurtines and J. L. Gewirtz eds., *Handbook of Moral Behavior and Development.* Hillsdale, NJ: Lawrence Erlbaum, 45–103.

Beeghley, L., 2003. *Homicide: A Sociological Explanation.* New York: Rowman and Littlefield.

Benson, D. and Archer, J., 2002. An ethnographic study of sources of conflict between young men in the context of a night out. *Psychology, Evolution and Gender*, 4 (1), 3–30.

Block, C. R., 1988. *Homicide in Chicago.* Chicago, IL: Loyola University of Chicago.

Block, R. and Zimring, F. E., 1973. Homicide in Chicago, 1965–1970. *Journal of Crime and Delinquency*, 10, 1–12.

Bourgois, P., 1995. *In Search of Respect: Selling Crack in El Barrio.* Cambridge: Cambridge University Press.

Brookman, F., 2003. Confrontational and revenge homicides among men in England and Wales. *Australian & New Zealand Journal of Criminology*, 36, 34–59.

Brookman, F., 2005. *Understanding Homicide.* Thousand Oaks, CA: Sage.

Brookman, F., (July 8, 2019). Written evidence submitted to the youth select Committee inquiry into knife crime. Available at: www.byc.org.uk/uk/youth-select-committee.

Brookman, F., Jones, H., and Pike, S., 2017. Homicide in Britain. In F. Brookman, E. R. Maguire, and M. Maguire eds., *The Handbook of Homicide.* Chichester: John Wiley and Sons, 320–344.

Bye, E. K., 2013. Alcohol and homicide in Europe. In M. C. A. Liem, and W. A. Pridemore eds., *Handbook of European Homicide Research: Patterns, Explanations, and Country Studies*. New York: Springer.

Carrington, K., McIntosh, A., and Scott, J., 2010. Globalization, frontier masculinities and violence: Booze, blokes and brawls, *British Journal of Criminology*, 50 (3), 393–413.

Cartwright, D. T., 1996. *Violent Land: Single Men and Social Disorder from the Frontier to the Inner City*. Cambridge, MA: Harvard University Press.

Cavanagh, K., Dobash, R. E., and Dobash, R. P., 2005. Men who murder children inside and outside the family. *British Journal of Social Work*, 35, 667–688.

Cavanagh, K., Dobash, R. E., and Dobash, R. P., 2007. The murder of children by fathers in the context of child abuse. *Child Abuse & Neglect*, 31, 731–746.

CDC, 2018. Quick stats: Number of homicides committed, by the three most common methods — United States, 2010–2016. *MMWR* 67 (29), 806. Published: July 27, 2018. DOI: 10.15585/mmwr.mm6729a4.

Cloward, R. A. and Ohlin, L. E., 1960. *Delinquency and Opportunity: A Theory of Delinquent Gangs*. Glencoe, IL: Free Press.

Cohen, A. K. 1955. *Delinquent Boys: The Culture of the Gang*. Glencoe, IL: Free Press.

Collier, D., LaPorte, J. and Seawright, J., 2012. Putting typologies to work: Concept formation, measurement, and analytic rigor. *Political Research Quarterly*, 65 (1), 217–232.

Copes, H., Hochstetler, A., and Forsythe, C. J., 2013. Peaceful warriors: Codes for violence among male bar fighters. *Criminology*, 51 (3), 761–794.

Daly, M., 2016. *Killing the Competition*. New Brunswick, NJ: Transaction.

Daly, M. and Wilson, M. 1988. *Homicide*. New York: Aldine De Gruyter.

D'Cruze, S., Walklate, S., and Pegg, S., 2011. *Murder: Social and Historical Approaches to Understanding Murder and Murderers*. London: Routledge.

Dobash, R. E. and Dobash, R. P., 1979. *Violence Against Wives: A Case Against the Patriarchy*. New York and London: Free Press and Open Books.

Dobash, R. P. and Dobash, R. E., 1983. The context-specific approach. In D. Finkelhor, R. J. Gelles, G. T. Hotaling, and M. A. Straus eds., *The Dark Side of Families*. Beverly Hills, CA: Sage, 261–276.

Dobash, R. E. and Dobash, R. P., 1984. The nature and antecedents of violent events. *British Journal of Criminology*, 24, 269–288.

Dobash, R. E., Dobash, R. P., Cavanagh, K., and Lewis, R., 2000. *Changing Violent Men*. Thousand Oaks, CA: Sage.

Dobash, R. P. and Dobash, R. E., 2004. Women's violence to men in intimate relationships: Working on a puzzle. *British Journal of Criminology*, 44, 324–349.

Dobash, R. E. and Dobash, R. P., 2011. What were they thinking? Men who murder an intimate partner. *Violence Against Women*, 17, 111–134.

Dobash, R. E. and Dobash, R. P. 2015. *When Men Murder Women*. New York: Oxford: Oxford University Press.

Dobash, R. P. and Dobash, R. E. (2018). When men murder children. In Brown, T., Tyson, D. and Arias, P. F. eds., *When Parents Kill Children*. Cham: Palgrave Macmillan, 81–102.

Dobash, R. P., Dobash, R. E., Cavanagh, K., Smith, D., and Medina-Ariza, J. J., 2007. Onset of offending and life course among men convicted of murder. *Homicide Studies*, 114, 243–271.

Dobash, R. P., Dobash, R. E., Wilson, M., and Daly, M., 1992. The myth of sexual symmetry in marital violence. *Social Problems*, 39, 71–91.

Dodd, V., 2019. Boy, 14, was knocked off moped and stabbed by rival gang, jury hears. *The Guardian*, January 9, p. 28.

Durkheim, E., 1951. *Suicide*. Glencoe, IL: Free Press. Original in French, 1897.

Eades, C., Crimshaw, R., Silvestri, A., and Soloman, E., 2007. *Knife Crime. A Review of Evidence and Policy* (2nd edition). London: Centre for Crime and Justice Studies.

Eisner, M., 2003a. Long-term historical trends in violent crime. *Crime and Justice*, 30 (1), 83–142.

Eisner, M., 2003b. The long-term development of violence: Empirical findings and theorical approaches to interpretation. In W. Heitmeyer and J. Hagan eds., *International Handbook of Violence Research*. London: Kluwer Academic Press, 41–59.

Elias, N., 1978. *The Civilizing Process: The History of Manners*. New York: Urize Books.

Elwert, G., 2003. The socio-anthropological interpretation of violence. In W. Heitmeyer and J. Hagan eds., *International Handbook of Violence Research*. London: Kluwer Academic Press, 261–291.

Fischer, D. H., 1989. *Albion's Seed: Four British Folkways in America*. New York: Oxford University Press.

Flewelling, R. L. and Williams, K. R., 1999. Categorizing homicides: The use of disaggregated data in homicide research. In M. W. Smith and M. A. Zahn eds., *Homicide: A Sourcebook of Social Research*. Thousand Oaks, CA: Sage, 96–106.

Forest, A., 2019. Global alcohol consumption has increased 70% in less than 30 years, new research shows. *Independent Premium* [Accessed November 20, 2019].

Freeman, J. B., 2018. *The Field of Blood: Violence in Congress and the Road to Civil War*. New York: Farrar, Straus and Giroux.

Ganpat, S. M. and Liem, M. C. A., 2013. Homicide in the Netherlands. In M. C. A. Liem, and W. A. Pridemire eds., *Handbook of European Homicide Research: Patterns, Explanations, and Country Studies*. New York: Springer Science, 329–341.

Gilbert, P. 1994. Male violence: Towards an integration. In J. Archer ed., *Male Violence*. London: Routledge, 352–389.

Gorski, P. 1993, The Protestant ethic revisited: Disciplinary revolution and state formation in Holland and Prussia. *American Journal of Sociology*, 99 (2), 265–316.

Hempel, C. G. 1961. Introduction to problems in taxonomy. In J. Zubin ed., *Field Studies in Mental Disorders*. New York: Free Press, 3–33.

Herzfeld, M. 1985. *The Poetics of Manhood: Contest and Identity in a Cretan Mountain Village*. Princeton, NJ: Princeton University Press.

Home Office, 2019. *Homicide in England and Wales: Year Ending March 2018*. London: Home Office, Office of National Statistics.

Homicide 2011, UNODC [Accessed April 27, 2013].

Homicide Index, Office of National Statistics 2019 [Annual rates of homicide rates for England/Wales].

Horowitz, R. and Schwartz, G., 1974. Honor, normative ambiguity and gang violence. *American Sociological Review*, 39, 238–251.

Hough, R. M. and McCorkle, K. D., 2017 *American Homicide*. Thousand Oaks, CA: Sage.

James, M. (2014). *A Brief History of Seven Killings*. London: One World.

Kaplan, A. 1964. *The Conduct of Inquiry: Methodology for Behavioral Sciences*. San Francisco, CA: Chandler.

Karstedt, S. and Eisner, M., 2009. Introduction: Is a general theory of violence possible? *International Journal of Conflict and Violence*, 3 (1), 4–8.

Killias, M., 1993. International correlations between gun ownership and rates of homicide and suicide. *Canadian Medical Association Journal*, 148, 10, 1721–1725.

Kuhn, T., 1962. *The Structure of Scientific Revolutions*. Chicago, IL: University of Chicago Press.

Lamnek, S., 2003. Individual violence justification strategies. In W. Heitmeyer and J. Hagan eds., *International Handbook of Violence Research*. London: Kluwer, 1113–1127.

36 Male–male murder – the evidence so far

Lazarsfeld, P. F. and Barton, A. H., 1964. Qualitative measurement in the social sciences: Classification, typologies and indices. In R. D. Lerner and H. D. Laswell eds., *The Policy Sciences*. Stanford, CA: Stanford University Press.

Lemos, G., 2004. *Fear and Fashion: The Use of Knives and Other Weapons by Young People*. London: Lemos and Crane.

Levoy, J., 2015. *Gettoside: A True Story of Murder in America*. London: Vintage.

Luckenbill, D. F., 1977. Criminal homicide as a situated transaction. *Social Problems*, 25, 176–186.

Manthey, J., Shield, K. D., Rylett, M., Ryle, M., Hasang, O. S. M., Probst, C., and Rehm, J., 2019. Global alcohol exposure between 1990 and 2017 and forecasts until 2030: A modelling study. *The Lancet*, 393 (10190), 2493–2502.

McVie, S., 2010. *Gang Membership and Knife Carrying: Findings from the Edinburgh Study of Youth Transitions and Crime*. The Scottish Centre for Crime and Justice Research. Edinburgh: Scottish Government Social Research. Available at: www.scotland.gove.uk/socialresearch.

Merton, R. K., 1938. Social structure and anomie. *American Sociological Review*, 3 (5), 672–682.

Miethe, T. D. and Regoeczi, W. C., 2004. *Rethinking Homicide. Exploring the Structure and Process Underlying Deadly Situations*. New York: Cambridge University Press.

Miles, C., 2012. Intoxication and homicide: A context-specific approach. *British Journal of Criminology*, 52 (5), 870–888.

Millon, D. H., 1991. Classification in psychopathology: Rationales, alternatives and standards. *Journal of Abnormal Psychology*, 100 (3), 245–261.

Morris, P. K. and Graycar, A., 2011. Homicide through a different lens. *British Journal of Criminology*, 51 (5), 823–838.

Nieuwbeerta, P. and Leistra, G., 2007. *Lethal violence. Homicide in the Netherlands 1992–2006*. Amsterdam: Prometheus.

Nisbett, R. E. and Cohen, D., 1966. *Culture of Honor: The Psychology of Violence in the South*. Boulder, CO: Westview Press.

Nud*ist/QS at www.qsrintertnational.com., see also Nud*ist/QS.

Oakes, J., 2019. The great divide. *New York Review of Books*, 66, May, 31–34.

ONS, Office of National Statistics, 2018, Statistic on alcohol. Gov.UK. Available at: www.statistics.gov.uk/hub/population [Accessed May 2014].

Peristiany, J. G., 1965, ed., *Honor and Shame: The Values of Mediterranean Society*. London: Weidenfeld & Nicolson.

Pitt-Rivers, J. A., 1954. *The People of the Sierra*. Oxford: Criterion Books. Note: now available online.

Pitt-Rivers, J. A., 1965. Honor and social status. In J. A. Pitt-Rivers, ed., *Mediterranean Country Men: Essays in the Social Anthropology of the Mediterranean*. Paris: Mouton, 18–77.

Polk, K., 1993. A scenario of masculine violence: Confrontational homicide. In H. Strang and S. Gerull eds., *Homicide*. Canberra: Australian Institute of Criminology, 35–51.

Polk, K., 1994. *When Men Kill: Scenarios of Masculine Violence*. New York: Cambridge University Press.

Polk, K. and Ranson, D., 1991. The role of gender in intimate homicide. *Australian and New Zealand Journal of Criminology*, 24 (1), 15–24.

Powdermaker, H., 1939. *After Freedom: A Cultural Study in the Deep South*. New York: Viking.

Pridemore, W. A., 2004. Weekend effects of binge drinking and homicide mortality: Preliminary evidence for the social connection between alcohol and violence in Russia. *Addiction*, 99, 1034–1930.

Pridemore, W. A., 2011. Poverty matters: A reassessment of the inequality-homicide relationship in cross national studies. *British Journal of Criminology*, 51, 739–772.

Scott, M. B. and Lyman, S. M., 1968. Accounts. *American Journal of Sociology*, 33 (1), 46–62.

Scottish Government, 2019. Homicide in Scotland 2019.

Short, J. F. and Strodtbeck, F. I., 1965. *Group Process and Gang Delinquency*. Chicago, IL: University of Chicago Press.

Silverman, R. A. and Kennedy, L. W., 1987. Relational distance and homicide: The role of the stranger. *Journal of Criminal Law and Criminology*, 78, 272–308.

Soothill, K. and Francis, B., 2013. Homicide in England and Wales. In M. C. A. Liem, and W. A. Pridemore, ed., *Handbook of European Homicide Research: Patterns, Explanations and Country Studies*. New York: Springer Science, 287–300.

Spierenburg. P., 1998a. ed., *Men and Violence: Gender; Honor; and Rituals in Modern Europe and America*. Columbus, OH: Ohio State University Press.

Spierenburg. P., 1998b. Masculinity, violence and honor: An introduction. In *Men and Violence: Gender; Honor; and Rituals in Modern Europe and America*. Columbus, OH: Ohio State University Press, 1–35.

Spierenburg. P., 2008. *A History of Murder: Personal Violence in Europe from the Middle Ages to the Present*. Cambridge: Polity Press.

Spiers, G., 2018. Celtic's painful Ireland legacy. *The Times*, November 24.

Sutherland, E., 1927. *Principles of Criminology*. Chicago, IL: J. B. Lippincott.

Sykes, D., and Matza, D. 1957. Techniques of neutralization: A theory of delinquency. *American Sociological Review*, 22, 664–670.

Tavuchis, N. 1991. *Mea culpa: A Sociology of Apology and Reconciliation*. Stanford, CA: Stanford University Press.

Thrasher, F. 1927, *The Gang: A Study of 1,313 Gangs in Chicago*. Chicago, IL: University of Chicago Press.

Toch, H. H. 1969. *Violent Men: An Inquiry into the Psychology of Violence*. Chicago, IL: Aldine reprinted in 2017.

UNODC, 2013. United Nations Office of Drugs and Crime "Homicide, 2011." Global Study on Homicide. Available at: www.unodc.org/documents/data-and-analysis/statistics//GSH2013/2014_GLOBAL_HOMICIDE_BOOK_web.pdf [Accessed April 27, 2019].

U.S. Department of Justice, 2017. UCR [Uniform Crime Report]. FBI, Criminal Justice Services Division. Available at: www.fbi.gov/.

Vandal, G. 2000. *Rethinking Southern Violence*. Columbus, OH: Ohio State University Press.

Weber, M. 1905. *Protestant Ethic and the Spirit of Capitalism [especially Chapter 5]*. Translated from German by Talcott Parsons in 1930, London: Routledge, reprinted 2001.

Weber, M. 1949. *The Methodology of the Social Sciences*. Eds. and Trans. E. Shils and H. A. Finch. New York: Free Press.

Wikipedia, *Chicago School of Sociology*. Summary of foundation of Sociology. Available at: https://en.wikipedia.org/wiki/Chicago_school_(sociology) [Accessed November 15, 2019].

Wilkinson, R. G., Kawachi, I. and Kennedy, B. P., 1998. Mortality, the social environment, crime and violence. *Sociology of Health & Illness*, 20, 578–597.

Wilson, A.V., 1993a. ed., Introduction. In A.V. Wilson, *Homicide: The Victim/Offender Connection*. Cincinnati, OH: Anderson Publishing, 1–19.

Wilson, A.V. 1993b. ed., *Homicide: The Victim/offender Connection*. Cincinnati, OH: Anderson Publishing Co.

Wolfgang, M. E. 1958. *Patterns of Criminal Homicide*. Philadelphia, PA: University of Pennsylvania Press.

38 Male–male murder – the evidence so far

Wolfgang, M. E. and Ferracuti, F., 1967. *The Subculture of Violence*. London: Tavistock.

Wood, G. S., 2000. An affair of honor. *The New York Review*, April, 47 (6), 67–72.

Wyatt-Brown, B. 1982. *Southern Honor: Ethics and Behavior in the Old South*. New York: Oxford University Press.

Zahn, M., 1991. The Wolfgang model: Lessons for homicide research. *Journal of Crime and Justice*, 14, 17–30.

2
CONFRONTATIONAL MURDER (FIGHTERS)

We characterize 'Confrontational Fighter Murders' as those linked to disputes involving the personal character and identity of perpetrators who show a willingness to use violence, and view fighting as a means of obtaining or maintaining respect and/or enhancing their reputation. For these men (37% of the 424 male–male murders) disputes arose in the contexts of perceived put-downs, humiliations, and displays of disrespect. Their aggression and violence often constituted 'performances' before an audience of others that are meant to display masculine qualities such as physical prowess, fighting skills, fearlessness, show a willingness to engage in fighting and a propensity to 'go all the way. The actual act of 'disrespect' may not have been directed at the perpetrator but rather a girlfriend, a friend or an associate. A few of the murders were not so much about direct individual 'injustices' but more about identity linked to a cause or a national 'organization' that must be supported and defended through violence. A small number of these murders involved bystanders who had nothing to do with any kind of dispute, but may have tried to intervene to stop a fight and ended-up being killed by an offender who appeared to define this as interfering in *his* dispute.

Confrontational murders may seem to be relatively spontaneous with a minimal build up. Some take place in the presence of others and involve multiple perpetrators and/or bystanders. Many take place in public locations near pubs, clubs, town centers, or in the homes of men who are drinking together. Most of the perpetrators and victims knew one another and alcohol consumption was usually involved. Something is said, something happens, or a previous dispute is revived. This sets off the event that begins with a confrontation which then turns into a fight and ends in a murder. Some scholars view this type of murder as primarily associated with notions about 'masculine honor' that are breeched and, then leads to an 'agreement' to engage in a 'fair fight' in order to resolve the dispute (Daly

40 Confrontational murder (fighters)

and Wilson, 1988; Polk, 1994; Brookman, 2005). While a few of the cases considered here appear to involve some form of 'agreement' to engage in a fight, a closer examination of the murder event as it unfolds often suggests otherwise. In some cases, the dispute may seem to be 'trivial' such as a casual 'remark' or a certain 'look,' such encounters may be far from trivial when they involve the individual's 'sense of worth and identity' (Walmsley, 1986, p. 8). At this point, the seemingly trivial look or comment becomes the source of the confrontation and violence.

Current research into this behavior often employs the term 'honor' or more recently 'code' to encapsulate these patterns. The term honor has been used for centuries to explain what we describe as confrontational murders. The core of these representations are attempts on the part of the perpetrator to 'live up' to his views of himself as seen through the prism of the assessments of others. The British anthropologist, Peristiany (1965), encapsulated this socio-cultural pattern in his early anthology, *Honor and shame: The values of Mediterranean society*, where 'honor is the value of a person in his own eyes, but also in the eyes of society. Honor, therefore, provides a nexus between the ideals of society and their reproduction in the individual through his aspiration to personify them' (Peristiany, 1965, pp. 21–22). This cultural pattern is not only apparent in Mediterranean cultures, research across time and in various countries have found a link between violence and men 'searching for respect.' These patterns persist, English ethnographers using recent research have produced evidence of the existence of a 'code' of respect revealing the importance of men's sense of self as anchors of violence. Masculine respect is linked to a 'moral order' that the men Ellis studied claimed made violence 'absolutely unavoidable' under certain circumstances (Ellis, 2016, pp. 105–124). The men he studied invoked the importance of violence for achieving and maintaining 'pride, self-dignity.' They felt entitled to recognition and respect and those who transgressed these 'demands' 'deserved punishment and violence.' Brookman and colleagues found similar patterns (Brookman, Copes, and Hochstetler, 2011). Their ethnographic research revealed that violence constituted a system that 'constructed self' going beyond mere ideals, they basically shaped 'evaluations of situations' and 'choices of lines of action' such as violence. The researchers found that the code provided 'scripts' dictating action, but also 'prescriptions and accounts' that validated justifications for violence (Brookman, Copes, and Hochsteler, 2011, p. 2). See Chapter 1 for the main body of research on violence, including the notion of 'respect.'

In the Murder Study, most Confrontational Murders reflected similar thinking and behavior. Men in the Murder Study, responded with violence to real and manufactured slights or insults that were interpreted by the perpetrator as offensive either to themselves or to something or someone of importance to them. Slights and put-downs may have been directed at the perpetrator, a friend, a group to which he belonged, or to some broader affiliation with which he identified such as a racial or ethnic group, a nationality, or a religion. When such slights are defined as 'morally offensive,' perpetrators may view their violent response as 'virtuous,' even view themselves as heroic. In so doing, many of these men viewed the murder they committed as a 'reasonable' and appropriate response to an unacceptable provocation, and saw their actions as upholding their own sense of what was 'right-and-wrong,' or what could not be 'tolerated.'

Initially, the term 'confrontational' was used by Wolfgang and other American social scientists to describe the context of violence in the early studies of gangs, and was later used to describe the contexts of homicide in the works of Daly and Wilson (1988), Polk (1994), and Brookman (2005). While our own classification follows much of this work, we have added the term 'fighters' because in most cases the murder was preceded by a fight or the murder actually occurred during a fight. Most of the murders did not take place in the context of a 'gang' although some of the face-to-face confrontations did involve other participants which more closely resembled a 'group' whose presence constituted what Toch described as 'a chorus,' a backdrop to the events as they unfold. In Polk's words, 'first to argue and then to fight.'

Main patterns – confrontational/ fighters and murder

The Murder Study contained 424 male–male murders, and 158 of (37%) them were classified as Confrontational Murders/Fighters. Here, we first use the quantitative evidence from the casefiles to describe the main patterns associated with 'Confrontational Murders.' Then, we use the qualitative evidence from the Casefiles and the Interviews to illustrate both the diversity and the dynamics within this type of murder. In order to do this, we have grouped the Confrontational Murders into six sub-types and each will be examined separately. We then compare the Confrontational Murders with Other Murders that were not of this type in order to examine similarities and differences between them (Table 2.1).

Background and relationship between and perpetrator and victim

Men who killed in the context of a confrontation (the fighters) were on average 27 years of age, and the average age of the victims was 33. Almost all of the perpetrators were 'working-class,' many were unemployed (59%) and those in employment worked in skilled or mostly unskilled manual jobs. About two-fifths of the perpetrators and victims were strangers, and all others were variously acquainted, although their relationships may not have been positive. In most cases, the men who were acquainted knew one another in the pub and/or neighborhood, and some were adversaries with a hostile relationship that might have persisted over a considerable period of time. 'Ongoing disputes' were common (46%), and the vast majority of the murders began with a 'confrontation' (83%) that then turned to violence.

42 Confrontational murder (fighters)

Conflicts, disputes and previous violence

Although the pub was often the *location* of confrontations, it was rarely the site of the murder since acts of physical violence were 'taken outside' into nearby streets, parks, and alleys. The majority of the murders took place in the home of the victim (56%) which constituted another location where confrontations and ongoing disputes were played out with deadly consequences.

Previous violence by the perpetrator against the victim was unusual but not unimportant (18%), as was previous violence by the victim against the perpetrator (16%). In addition, some of these cases also involved a previous incidence of violence by the victims against someone who was a friend or associate of the perpetrator (27%). In these cases, the murder may have involved acts of revenge or retaliation because of a previous incident in which the man who is killed had committed an act of violence against the perpetrator or one of his friends or allies.

Drinking, drunkenness and drugs

At the time of the murder, three-quarters of the perpetrators had been drinking on the day of the murder, and the same proportion of those who had been drinking were drunk when they committed the murder. Among the victims, just over half had been drinking at the time of the murder, and most of those who were drinking were drunk. In addition, one-quarter of perpetrators and victims had been drinking together at the time of the murder. Basically, whether the perpetrator or the victim had been drinking they were usually drunk. At the time of the murder, a few of the men had been drinking at home but most had also been drinking in a pub which constituted an important location for confrontations between men who were often in groups and were drunk. Around two-fifths of the perpetrators were using drugs at the time.

Murder event

Just over half (53%) of the confrontational murders were carried out by one perpetrator against a single victim, although a considerable proportion involved two or more perpetrators, and a few involved more than one victim. Witnesses were present in 56% of these murders, but many involved no witnesses. Witnesses were often friends or allies either of the perpetrator or the victim, or both. For the most part, witnesses did nothing either to assist or to deter the perpetrator. The lethal assault almost always included various types of violence, such as, punching, kicking and stamping (jumping up and down on the victim's chest and/or head), and many included the use of an 'instrument' such as a club that was used as a weapon. Nearly three-quarters (71%) of the victims suffered five or more injuries during the murder.

Cause of death

The cause of death was usually the result of a stabbing with a knife or sharp instrument such as a screw driver or a broken bottle (52%), and a few men (9%) were shot. While many stabbings were to the head, chest or back, some were directed at vital organs such as the lungs and heart which suggests the intent to do serious harm. In addition, 62% of the men brought some kind of weapon (usually a knife) to the scene which suggests a prior intention to do harm. Many of the men were angry (52%) at the time they committed the murder.

Other offense in addition to murder

Confrontational fighters were unlikely (25%) to have committed an additional offense such as a robbery or burglary as part of the murder.

Confrontational murders (fighters) – six subtypes

The 158 Confrontational Murders/Fighters, were grouped into six subtypes in order to focus on the different contexts of these murders, the orientations of the perpetrators, and the dynamic aspects of these events. The subtypes reflect different aspects of the confrontations and other characteristics of the murders.

> Confrontational murders (fighters) – six subtypes
> 1. Groups, conflicts and confrontations
> 2. Confrontations involving disputes and 'slights to self'
> 3. Confrontations involving disputes and 'slights against others'
> 4. The 'fair' fight – men agree to fight
> 5. Collateral victims: bystanders and displacement of violence
> 6. Confrontations involving allegiance with a wider group.

There is some overlap across these subtypes, as such the narratives may best be viewed as 'characterizations' that elaborate of the main elements of the subtypes.

Subtype 1. Groups, conflicts and confrontations

While some evidence suggests that gangs are a significant element in crime and violence in the US, does this apply to other countries? How useful is this as a general explanation of violence and murder? As discussed in Chapter 1, gangs appear to constitute an important aspect of some types of violence, particularly, in certain cities in the US, in some countries in Central and South America, and in some parts of Eastern Europe. This is often the case in locations linked to organized crime, drugs and other illegal activities.

In the Murder Study, we gathered information about the possible importance of 'gangs' in the perpetration of murder. Using a definition of gangs as groups of males with an identified leader, located in a specific location or neighborhood,

44 Confrontational murder (fighters)

and identified by a name, we found very few murders with these characteristics. Of the 424 male–male murders, only 13 cases (3%) were considered to be associated with gang membership, activity or animosity, and this corresponds with national crime statistics. For example, from 1997–2001, there were 4,123 Homicides in England/Wales and only 37 cases (1%) were judged to be a 'Gang Homicide' that involved a murder between males (Brookman, 2005, p. 314). Although gang-related murders are quite unusual, this type of crime receives a considerable amount of media attention and is a mainstay of popular literature, crime novels, films, and, television. In countries such as Britain and many European countries, there appears to be an inverse relationship between the amount of popular coverage given to 'gang' murders and the actual number of such events that are documented in national statistics. Gang membership was not generally relevant among the 'Fighters' in the Murder Study but belonging to a 'group' was often of great importance to many of these men. So, what is the difference? The distinction between a 'gang' and a 'group' was stressed by one of the men we interviewed.

> *And you were saying that when you were younger, you weren't in any gangs? So, when you were older were you involved in gangs?* No, it was a group of mates. We used to just hang around together. It was more like a group of lads. We'd all get together and go drinking and that.
>
> *(★736iv1.2.3)*

As shown in this statement, groups were usually based on friendship bonds. Many of these bonds were established in neighborhoods and schools when the men were boys. These bonds were sustained into adulthood particularly among those who remained in the same neighborhoods and sometimes involved men who supported the same football club, had the same sectarian affiliations, and other affinities of importance to them. Such bonds were also important in generating and sustaining animosities toward other groups of males that could prevail for many years, and might even have been 'inherited' across several generations (Fraser, 2015). The following cases illustrate the importance of the 'group' in events that began with a single confrontation or a series of confrontations and fights that ultimately ended with a murder. The first two cases clearly illustrate the importance of the 'group' and of ongoing disputes regarding the reputations of two warring factions of young men that had persisted for several months. While these cases illustrate the importance of group solidarity and action, they also involved young males who were acting to promote their own sense of self-importance.

In the first case, there were 40 participants in each group. This is very unusual, but what is not unusual is the context in which this murder occurred which involved extreme animosity between the two groups, and incidents of previous violence between them. Although the perpetrator in this case was only 15 years of age, we nonetheless included the case because it typifies a context of group rivalry and perceived insults and 'humiliations' that can lead to the killing of a

Confrontational murder (fighters) **45**

member of one group by a member of a rival group. The perpetrator was the leader of his group, and the most violent person among them. A melee occurred in a local park, the victim (age 17) was getting the most and the worst of the violence. The perpetrator assumed a primary role in the violence as he ran forward and stabbed the victim several times. Here, we present accounts from our examination of his Casefile and our Interview with him after he had been convicted and was in prison.

Ongoing conflict between two groups of young men

[Context – pre-trial probation report]
This event appears to be in direct retaliation for an earlier incident, assault, which took place about 7 days earlier. In this incident, a group of youths had been set upon by another group of youths who regularly visited the park. Friends and relations of the assaulted youths decided to go to the park and seek retribution for the attack. Recruitments were made from numerous locations for persons to attend. Word of this obviously reached the other school and there is little doubt that what could be described as a 'rumble' was to take place in the park on the night of the incident.

[Judge summary]
Murder by stabbing at least three times with an old-style long bayonet. His gang met up at a local supermarket and various 'satellite' locations – thus the attack seems to have been well organized on both sides. Some, but apparently not a lot of drinking was going on in both groups. The offense took place during a planned fight between gangs from rival schools [and neighborhoods] with approximately 40 boys on each side armed with knives, chains, coshes and pieces of wood taken from a fence. Some were wearing balaclavas. After preliminary skirmishing in the park, the deceased was set upon by a group of about 10 including the defendant, brought to the ground, kicked, punched and struck with various weapons. This was described by witnesses as 'like a pack of wild animals' and 'like a foxhunt'. He fought free of this group and broke away to run onto the grassed area near the path at the entrance to the park. The defendant then said 'move away', the group parted, he drew the bayonet and carried out the stabbing. All members of both groups then ran away. The defendants returning to their part of the city by bus. On the journey, the defendant showed the bloodstained bayonet to others and said, 'I just flipped my lid'. Some witnesses described him as acting like a madman, being 'off his head', and raving. Once arrested a search of his house found a sports bag containing a vast assortment of knives, other weapons and balaclavas, which included a bayonet.

46 Confrontational murder (fighters)

[Evidence of premeditation]
The defendant had been sharpening the bayonet saying that it was not sharp enough to do any good, and also remarked that 'You don't use fists anymore'. While admitting the offense to his friends, he consistently lied to the police but eventually made admissions to his solicitors and psychiatrists.

[Psychiatrist for the prosecution]
He had a severe conduct disorder but this did not constitute an abnormality of the mind.

[Psychiatrist for the defense]
The conduct disorder would, in an adult, amount to a personality disorder but this did not constitute an abnormality of mind which would substantially diminish his responsibility.

[Post-mortem]
He [victim] had sustained injuries consisting of two puncture wounds to his right side, the upper had penetrated the lung and the lower had penetrated the liver and severed a major blood vessel. There was a further puncture wound on his back which had penetrated a kidney and severed a major blood vessel.

*(*1176cf1.2.4)*

In our interview with him in prison, he accepted with some bravado, that he was looked upon by fellow students as being one of the hardest in the school. He recounted incidents demonstrating how he earned this reputation when, for example, he assaulted one of his fellow pupils with a baseball bat. This led to his exclusion from school although there was no official complaint made to the police. He also told us he always carried a knife or some kind of weapon. The animosity and fighting were ongoing, and was mostly about areas and reputations. It seemed that at the time of the murder he was proud of his reputation, although during our interview, it was clear he had come to see things rather differently.

In several cases, group membership, animosity, and actions aimed at boosting the killer's self-importance formed a significant part of the context in which the murder occurred. The next case involved rival groups of young men who had previously been engaged in a series of confrontations involving bravado, slanging matches, and violence. On the night of the murder, the victim's group travelled to the area of the rival group. Initially, there were several non-violent clashes, then the fatal encounter began as two perpetrators pursued members of the other group and attacked the victim who was on the ground.

Confrontational murder (fighters) **47**

Two groups clash, a slanging match, and a murder

[Context of the murder]
At this point the perpetrator [local youth] obtained possession of half of a snooker cue and a baseball bat. When the victim and his friends were refused entry to a disco, they began to make their way along the road. Co-accused and some others saw them, and insults and challenges to fight were exchanged between the two groups. The perpetrators and two friends then followed three of the men from the victim's group who turned into the park and armed themselves with branches. The co-accused and his friends then went into a chip shop to obtain rein-forcements. He then became the leader of a group of about 7–8 youths who returned to the street. At the same time, he and his friends emerged onto the road, the victims' group again began to shout at them.

[The murder]
The perpetrator (age 17) and his group began to chase the victim's group, but very quickly everyone desisted except the perpetrator and the co-accused. The two perpetrators chased the victim (age 16) and his group into a park, over a fence and across an open grassy area where the victim slipped and fell. He was then caught up with and beaten by the two perpetrators who left him on the ground. They then went to collect a friend and spent the remainder of the evening from about 10.30–2am in [pubs] and discos where they boasted of having battered a boy. Neither of the perpetrator's sustained any injuries.

[After the murder]
The victim was found in the park the following morning and when the perpetrators heard that he was dead, they collected the baseball bat and snooker cue which they had used and had been left in the bedroom of one of them. This perpetrator sawed them up, threw away the pieces, and bought a replacement bat and cue.

[The trial]
The perpetrators each gave evidence blaming the other. This perpetrator stated that he had struck two blows with the bat, one to the head and the other to the arm, and that neither of the blows were made with full force and that neither had caused the victim to fall down. He claimed that he then felt dizzy and used his inhaler for his asthma and had taken no further part in the assault using a baseball bat. His co-accused stated that all he did was kick the victim once before any blows by perpetra-tor with the baseball bat, and that when the perpetrator was hitting the victim with the bat, he was telling him to stop. Both perpetrator's stated

48 Confrontational murder (fighters)

that they had never seen the victim or his companions before and did not know them in any way at all. Both were convicted of murder.

[Post-mortem]
The post-mortem revealed that cause of death was blunt force head injuries and inhalation of blood. The victim suffered very severe injuries to his face and head with severe fractures of the skull. He also sustained severe bruising to his groin region and bruising to the chest and side.

*(*162cf1.2.4)*

The murder in the next case did not involve a long-running dispute. There was no antagonism between the victim and the murderer or indeed any member of the perpetrator's group. What was important was the context of group solidarity, a culture of binge drinking and 'fighting.' While this murder seems to 'come out of the blue,' further information about the activities of this man and of the group to which he belonged assists our understanding of the murder. Information about the offender indicates that he had a rather short but significant history of serious violence prior to the murder. In some respects, the perpetrator could be seen as a 'conventional' young man. He had no history of contact with criminal justice, and was a serving member of the armed forces in which he had a responsible job. Despite this, it seems his life was unravelling at the time with heavy bouts of binge drinking, drugs, and group fighting. The following account is primarily derived from the perpetrator's casefile but we also interviewed him. In the interview it was clear he had accepted responsibility and expressed considerable regret and remorse for the murder.

Group murder – on a 'dare'

[Police report]
A serving soldier (age 18), drinking and consuming drugs all day, killed a man (age 57) when friends with whom he had been drinking dared him to knock the man out. The perpetrator responded to this 'challenge' or 'dare' from the co-accused to attack the victim but denied any intention to cause serious harm. He has no real explanation as to why he had to respond to the verbal challenge of his friend beyond the fact that his judgement and perception were both seriously impaired by alcohol and amphetamines which he had used.

[Murder event]
The co-accused said, 'I dare you to drop the big bloke,' a man returning late at night from a guitar performance at a local pub. He attacked the victim from behind and 'punched him without warning.' He punched him to the floor and continued to punch and kick his face and body. The force of the blows rendered him unconscious, resulting in a fractured skull, his cheekbone was fractured in three places, a broken nose,

and extensive bruising and swelling to his eyes, face and abdominal areas. His injuries were so severe that he did not gain consciousness and died later in hospital.

[The day in question]
Earlier in the day he had been involved in another assault, and a heavy drinking session with five friends [3 co-accused and 2 others] throughout the entire day. He admitted to being extremely drunk at the time of the assault. The earlier assault, involved a grudge against the victim in relation to a quarrel over an ex-girlfriend. He brought this assault to an end when he became aware that the incident had got out of control. There would appear to be certain similarities in the circumstances of the earlier assault and the murder. Both were committed in the company of other young men in a precipitate and compulsive fashion following the consumption of a large amount of alcohol.

[Probation report]
It seems clear that alcohol has been a significant factor in this young man's offending. He described how initially his alcohol consumption began to escalate after he joined the Army at age 16. During the week, he was able to keep this under reasonable control, but a pattern soon developed of heavy drinking sessions when he returned home at weekends in order to see his family and friends. This was connected to his realization that he was unhappy in his career and was also miserable at being away from home. He described himself as feeling bored, unchallenged, trapped and homesick. He would drink to increasing levels in order to blot out his negative feelings about his situation, but also to mask his general unhappiness from his family and friends. In order to counteract the more depressive effects of heavy alcohol consumption, he began to use amphetamines as a way of maintaining his energy on the nights spent in the local pubs and clubs.

[Fights, fearlessness, commanding respect]
He had no problem with temper as confirmed by his parents who considered him 'to be an equable, even-tempered and amicable young man'. He had previously been involved in fights but he did not believe himself to be much different to his friends. However, he acknowledged that these fights often involved him going to the assistance of 'mates' and he described a strong need to appear unafraid and to be able to cope with threatening situations, also to command respect from others for not displaying weakness. He also described feelings of suppressed anger about having to return to a situation from which he saw no prospect of extricating himself and about which he felt unable to tell his parents

50 Confrontational murder (fighters)

[dislike of the army], because he was aware that they were proud of his being a soldier, and he did not wish to disappoint them.

(*1174cf1.2.3)

Subtype 2. Confrontations involving disputes and 'Slights to Self'

These murders involved confrontations usually involving perceived slights that the perpetrators 'considered' humiliating usually experienced in the context of sustained alcohol consumption. The combination of a culture of fighting, inebriation, and often the use of knives, characterized these murders. Some also included the presence of allies, some of whom participated in the murder. The presence of other men, even one other, constituted an 'audience' of spectators and witnesses, who may be important to the dynamics of the murder, particularly if they encourage or actually participated in the violence. Some of these confrontations were associated with men's attempts to enhance their own image by showing the victim and others that he was not a man to be trifled with. In the world of these men, 'violence commands respect' and constitutes a 'measure of personal worth' not only in his own eyes, but also in the eyes of others. In many ways, 'confrontational murderers' reflect the attributes of Toch's *Violent Men* (1969, reprinted 2017), that he described as 'self-regarding' and 'violent prone.' In the first case, the perpetrators had been drinking together for a long period of time before they joined forces and killed a stranger. This was an unprovoked attack on a man they claimed had 'stared' at them. The two perpetrators were clearly 'performing' for each other. They were trying to promote their own conceptions of themselves as men of some stature when, in fact, their actions demonstrated a reliance on subterfuge and a surprise attack as they inflicted serious lethal violence on a total stranger.

A stranger 'stares'

[Accounts from a second victim of assault, and a witness]
The victim (18) was employed as a fork lift driver. He was single and lived with his parents, had never come to the notice of the police or been in any trouble. He had spent the evening with his girlfriend, and about 10pm, he and his friend went to a pub and then on the street. The perpetrator (18) and his co-accused had been drinking since about 7.30pm, left the pub, and were on the opposite side of the road at a bus stop.

When the perpetrator and co-defendant saw the other two young men, they crossed the road and asked directions. As the victim began to answer, his co-defendant hit the victim's friend in the face. At the same time, the perpetrator attacked the victim, knocking him to the ground and began kicking him. The perpetrator then joined in on the attack on the victim's friend before they both ran off and tried to board a bus,

Confrontational murder (fighters) **51**

leaving the victim lying in the road and victim's friend, whose nose was fractured, staggering into the pub.

The fight was witnessed by a girl at the bus stop opposite who saw the perpetrator stamp on the victim's head. A woman in a neighboring flat called an ambulance, and the bus driver who refused to allow them aboard, alerted his depot by radio as they kicked his bus, jumped off and ran away. The perpetrator and the co-defendant went into another pub, and later went home by bus. The victim was taken to hospital where he died two days later.

[Statement to police]
The perpetrator said that he and his co-defendant had each drunk about eight pints of beer and rum. He said as they walked towards the bus stop near the pub, the other two young men (victim and victim's friend) had been walking towards them on the other side of the road and *had stared at them*. He and the co-defendant then crossed the road and co-defendant started the fight.

[The fight]
'So, I punched him [victim] about three or four times in the face. He went down, so I stuck my boot into his ribs and back. He tried to get up but he fell down again. The co-defendant was shouting, 'this is the hard one'. He was butting my pal in the face, so I went over and hit this kid in the face and kneed him. He went down and didn't get up'.

[Post-mortem]
There were 14 bruises and abrasions on his face and neck but no significant injuries on trunk or limbs. Fractures and other injuries to the face and head were consistent with blows from a shod foot – at least four kicks to the left side of face and ear and injuries to left side of neck were also consistent with kicking or stamping. Bruising around the mouth might have been caused by a fist or a foot. A considerable degree of force would have been required to inflict the injuries, particularly the fractures of the jaw bone and the temple bone. Death was due to pressure on the brain caused by bleeding within the skull in the left temporal region.

(*2007cf1.2.1)

In the next case, a man is killed after he admonishes two young men for taking advantage of 'free' pub food to which they were not entitled. At first, there appeared to be no lingering animosity between the men, but then the perpetrators responded to what they saw as a 'humiliation' by killing the man who scolded them for trying to take sandwiches that were intended for members of a darts teams. After leaving the pub, the perpetrators encountered him on the street, claimed that he had stared at them, then attacked and killed him.

52 Confrontational murder (fighters)

'Free' sandwiches, a stare, and 'people don't die from fights'

[Context/murder event]
The two perpetrators (both age 18) were in a pub where a darts match was being played. They weren't members of a darts team but when sandwiches were laid on for the darts players, the perpetrators helped themselves. 'In an authoritarian manner', the victim (age 31) questioned their right to the sandwiches. They apologized, and the matter seemed to end. After closing time, the victim walked alone to a bus stop. The two perpetrators walked past him, he stared [they claimed]. They asked why, they then punched him and he fell to the ground. Then they kicked him to death while he was on the ground. They left the scene and went to the nearby house of the co-accused. Later, they returned to the scene and saw the police cordon. When they were told that victim had died, there was disbelief, and the perpetrator said, 'but people don't die from fights'.

(*687cf1.2.3)

This case involved the murder of a publican whose actions appeared to humiliate and anger the perpetrator.

Murder in a pub – drunken man excluded, returns to pub and kills the pub manager

The perpetrator went into a pub and was ejected by the publican because he was aggressive and violent. He apparently felt humiliated, angry and vengeful, searched out a weapon, returned to the pub and stabbed the publican to death.

[Police report]
A drunken perpetrator (26) started a fight in a pub, was evicted, returned, and stabbed the pub manager (45) to death. The perpetrator was drunk and went into the pub for fags and more drink. He attempted to play dominoes with a group of men. They say no to him, an argument ensued, and a punch-up followed. He was ejected from the pub, went to another pub, got a flick knife [switch-blade] and returned to the original pub and stabbed to death the pub manager who had evicted him.

[Context]
He [perpetrator] was employed as a painter and decorator, married, but separated from his wife for five years, and resided with his parents. His wife had custody of their six-year-old daughter, and he had access at the weekends. The victim was employed as a manager of the public house and was married with two teenage sons. He had never met the perpetrator prior to the offence.

(*102cf1.2.3)

This murder involved two men who were long-term acquaintances involved in an ongoing dispute about the loan of a van and insulting remarks about the perpetrator's woman partner. A week of escalating animosity and more exchanges between the men, culminated in an unusual form of murder as the perpetrator set his victim on fire in a pub full of witnesses.

Grievance – murdered by a friend

[Context]
The perpetrator (39) poured petrol over the victim (37) and ignited him. In the week preceding the offence, there had been considerable antagonism between the victim and the perpetrator and his brother and nephew. A van had been loaned to the victim and not returned on time. Also, the victim had some days earlier made derogatory remarks about the perpetrator's partner calling her a 'fucking slag' – although this did not result in a fight at the time, they had exchanged words about this in the past. There was a week of culminating pressure and antagonism between his family and the victim and the perpetrator had some fears for his own safety. He responded to these feelings with violence.

[Murder]
On the evening of the murder, the perpetrator was working at the public house. He describes a series of events whereby he felt the victim was threatening him both verbally and by his actions [not confirmed by witnesses]. His feelings reached such a point that he went into the yard of the pubic house and collected some petrol he had previously used to burn newspapers. It was a gallon bottle previously filled with Bell's whisky but now contained petrol. He went into the pub, unscrewed the top of the bottle – walked across the dance floor of the bar where the victim was sitting and sprayed him with petrol. He then lit it and the victim was engulfed in flames. The victim ran toward the perpetrator who pushed him away with his foot to avoid setting the bottle of petrol alight which was still in his hands and shouted, 'Fuck off you daft bastard'. The perpetrator recollects pushing the victim away from him so that he would not get hurt by the flames himself and of passing a fire extinguisher as he made his escape from the room. He has experienced flashbacks of the victim burning and knows he may have prevented his death by assisting to extinguish the flames. The victim died of injuries eight days later.

(*873cf1.2.8)

Bragging about fighting skills

This is an example of the bravado associated with some perpetrator's interpretations of the murder. In our interview with this man, he recounted in great detail

54 Confrontational murder (fighters)

his version of the events that led to the murder. He gave a blow-by-blow account of his encounter with four attackers, including the victim. In highly exaggerated language, he recounted his knife fighting ability, his bravery, and claimed the murder was committed in self-defense. This account reveals his attempt to bolster his view of himself as a courageous and skillful fighter. He also appeared to be trying to impress the interviewer.

Bragging – an earlier fight, but not getting away with it twice

[Context]
So, I was going down the street to other pubs, and I was going past four guys who had battered me [30 minutes earlier]. So, they dragged me up there and it was kick, kick. Just the usual, and then they took off. So, I thought 'They're not getting away with it twice'. I chased them and we came to an alleyway that led to two streets and then it becomes a Close [dead-in] And they came at me.

[Murder]
'Here we go!' And the two came at me. One of them had a broken bottle. So, I said to him, 'You're getting it first because you can do the most damage.' And saying that, I pulled my knife. He pulled a knife out as well. So, I just punched him, kicked him, and he went down. And as he landed on the deck, he had his hand up like that, you know, so I jumped on him and smashed his wrist and broke it. But it started, and I take it [bottle] out his hand, and take the knife off him. I had my back to the wall. I couldn't go anywhere, and they kept threatening to punch or kick us. So, I thought, well I'd have to do something, so I swung the knife at them. As I swung, they were far enough away I wasn't going to hit them. I knew that for starters. I wasn't going to hit them. But as I swung the knife at them, the one with the bottle, he came up and tried to stick the broken bottle in the side of my face as I swung the knife at the three in front. It hit him, and it stabbed him in the chest, at his heart. He didn't die right away. I realized I'd stabbed him and I thought, 'Oh shit', and I dropped the knife. The one that broke his wrist [*note not the one who's wrist I broke*], he picked the knife up and disappeared and took it with him. The guy that died was only 18 years old but he was a big 18 year old! He was bigger than what I was, and the other two were reasonably big blokes, you know, and they just took off, and it left me and the guy who had been stabbed. He was laughing – okay, he'd been stabbed but it's not serious [he died].

(*738iv1.2.8)

What counts as an insult?

It is important to place these looks, apparent insults, 'slights' and the various perceived putdowns in the context of particular male cultures in which 'put downs' and 'slights' among friends are not generally considered to be an offense that requires a violent response, but are used to confirm allegiances and bonds when they are delivered within the context of men who are friends. In this context, such comments are viewed as a form of banter among friends that is not only tolerated but also enhances friendships. By contrast, the very same comments may be defined as a 'slight,' an 'insult,' or a 'humiliation' if delivered by a man who is not a friend, by someone who is outside of 'their' group. Among some working class African-American men, this is known as 'doing the dozens'; when one friend makes what would otherwise be seen as a derogatory comment about a man who is his friend. 'Doing the dozens' involves a sort of contest between friends who attempt to demonstrate their oral dexterity and wit by exchanging 'insults' in front others. Rather than being defined literally, and thus negatively, these exchanges are ways in which men who are 'insiders' can express friendship and bonds of affection. 'Doing the dozens' almost always involves an audience to the apparent 'insult' about family, friends, mothers, and, manhood. In some working-class communities in the west of Scotland, insults, a 'slagging,' are often exchanged between friends, but there is a fine line between the definition of a comment as 'slagging' between friends and an 'insult' delivered by an 'outsider' (Fraser, 2015, p. 172–173). In an interview with one of us, a man makes a fine distinction between the two.

'Slights' and 'insults' – context is everything

When you were doing this [responding to a slight] did it often lead to fights? Not necessarily. No, not necessarily, though later on my tolerance level did drop considerably. But in amongst my pals, I'd be in amongst my own, so if anyone is taking the piss, I know it's only in jest, so there was no threat. Sometimes, it would be a wind-up, they'd all join in. I never felt any threat in any way. Nine times out of ten, it would be a laugh and a joke sort of a thing. So, you don't fight, you know what I mean, because you are giving 'em a success basically [appreciation, status/respect]. But outside of our circle, my tolerance level dropped quite considerably. *What is it you didn't like, what is it you didn't tolerate?* People taking the piss [mocking or ridiculing]. People taking liberties, do you know what I mean? Towards me or towards anyone else.

(*876iv1.2.3)

Subtype 3. Confrontations involving disputes and 'slights against others'

The third subtype involved incidents in which the slights and insults were directed against someone or something that the perpetrator valued. The perpetrator

56 Confrontational murder (fighters)

deemed these actions worthy of a violent response and a confrontation ensued. The next two cases involved slights or insults that were not directed at the perpetrator himself but involved a girlfriend and a dog.

Insult directed at the perpetrator's girlfriend

[Context]
The perpetrator (28) and three co-accused went to a nightclub and then waited in the car park until it closed in order to purchase drugs from the DJ of the club (the victim, age 34). A few days earlier there had been a confrontation between the perpetrator and the victim about the perpetrator's girlfriend [the context was not clear but she felt insulted].

[Murder]
On the night of the murder, the four waited in the car and followed another car containing the victim and two of his friends until they reached the victim's house. There the perpetrator approached the victim and they discussed the purchase of cannabis from the victim. A confrontation began about a previous incident involving the perpetrator's girlfriend. Then a fight started between one of the co-accused and a friend of the victim. The fight between the perpetrator and the victim then started, and escalated when the perpetrator produced a three-inch knife and inflicted four stab wounds (chest-heart, slash across the victim's face from his left ear to left cheek). The others joined in the fight and the victim was pushed into a hedge. There was shouting, and the perpetrator and three co-accused got in his car and drove off. They were afraid the victim and his friends might pursue them and appeared to be unaware that he was fatally injured. At home, he washed his clothes and asked a neighbor to watch out for the police.

[Trial judge report]
He denied stabbing the victim, contended that during their confrontation the deceased had the knife and that he had only received a cut to the face as they struggled. I directed [instructed] the jury on 'self-defense' and 'provocation' although the defendant had not given evidence of either. Charges – Murder (the jury found him guilty and voted 11 to 1). He was also found guilty of Violent Disorder (the decision of the jury was unanimous). The defendant was an erstwhile heroin addict of bad character but with no previous violence recorded against him. He may well not have had the intention to kill.

(*871cf1.2.1)

The next case is rather convoluted. The victim was not involved in the initial confrontation but tried to intervene on behalf of his brother and was killed.

The perpetrator, his dog, and a murder

[Context]
At about 10.30 pm, three people and the perpetrator (16) had some drink. Then he and his dog left with his brother and another man. As they passed three men, the perpetrator accused one of them [brother of the victim] of trying to kick his dog.

[Murder]
The victim's sister who witnessed the incident from the window of her flat informed the victim (22) of these events involving his brother. Armed with a billiard cue, the victim went out to speak to the perpetrator who was then seen to assault, disarm [take the billiard cue] and stab the victim who attempted to escape the attack by running off, but eventually collapsed.

[After the murder]
The perpetrator was then joined by his brother and a friend, and all three made off to the perpetrator's home. At this point the perpetrator asked his friend to dispose of the billiard cue which was thrown into a garden.

[The victim]
Shortly after his collapse, the victim was found by two witnesses who had watched the assault from a window of their flat, as he staggered along the street. He was carried back to his home where he was pronounced dead by the police casualty surgeon.

[More assaults]
Following the assault on the victim, [same day] the perpetrator got into an argument with his brother, assaulted him and broke his jaw. During an attempt to prevent this assault, his friend and his mother were also assaulted and threatened by the perpetrator.

(*034cf1.2.4.)

Subtype 4. The 'fair' fight – men agree to fight

Accounts of violent encounters between males or groups of males often suggest that the offender and the victim 'agreed' that violence was an appropriate response to a slight or a provocation. We have long been critics of these assumptions with respect to men's use of violence against women and children. Evidence from our previous research does not support the notion that violent attacks by men upon women and children involve some kind of 'mutual' encounter, or a 'fair fight,' in which both individuals 'agree' to engage in physical violence (Dobash and Dobash, 1983, 2015; 2018; Cavanagh, Dobash and Dobash, 2005). But do these findings apply to violent encounters between men? Does the evidence from the Murder Study support the notion that violent encounters between men involve

58 Confrontational murder (fighters)

some form of mutual agreement to engage in a fight? We are skeptical of descriptions of male–male murder that view the perpetrators and victims as 'agreeing' to engage in a fight in order to settle a dispute or some kind of confrontation between them. We are also skeptical about the notion that these fights are based on explicit or implicit 'rules' (a code) about what constitutes a 'fair fight,' and that these rules are adhered to. Of the 158 Confrontational Murders/Fighters, very few fit the conception of encounters based on an agreement to 'fight,' or that the resulting fight was fair. Instead, most of these murders were much more 'one-sided.' At the outset of a murder event, our evidence suggests that the victims rarely 'agree' to a potentially lethal fight. Additionally, the victims were often vulnerable by virtue of age, size, physical prowess, etc. Then, the fight was often not 'fair' as perpetrator/s attacked without warning, were joined by others and/or produced a weapon.

These issues are illustrated in two cases. In the first, following a series of confrontations, the perpetrator and the victim appeared to have reached a mutual agreement to engage in a 'fair' fight, with the implicit assumption that it would involve only fists and feet. However, the murderer very quickly broke the 'rules' by introducing a weapon into a fight that then turned into a murder. In the second case, in the interview the murderer rationalized his use of violence by claiming that the victim had insulted him, had 'taken liberties.' The perpetrator and the victim each had two friends, and the perpetrator claimed that all of these men had agreed to have a 'fair fight.' Despite this supposed agreement, the perpetrator quickly introduced two weapons, a knife and a gun, and the fight became a very one-sided encounter that ended in a killing. Another factor that seemed to be involved was racism. The three the men in the victim's group were Sudanese, and all of the men in the perpetrator's group were white. In both of these murders, the perpetrator's use of violence can be seen as promoting their self-image as dangerous, violent men who deserve respect.

Bouncers and a 'fair fight'

Two groups of door men, 'bouncers,' who worked in the same club were engaged in an ongoing conflict. The context leading to the murder involved only two of these rivals. The perpetrator was seriously annoyed by the actions of a member of the other group of bouncers. This ultimately led to what at first appeared to be a classical 'square go' with both men agreeing to a fight involving fists and feet, but very quickly escalated when the perpetrator produced a weapon.

Men agree to a 'fair' fight

[Context]
This male perpetrator (age 33) and the victim (30), both worked as bouncers in the same club, and arranged to have a 'square go' after an incident in a local nightclub the previous evening when the perpetrator punched the victim after being told that he had been the man who, several weeks earlier,

had phoned his home in the middle of the night asking for drugs [while this seems the main issue, other evidence suggests previous antagonisms].

[Murder event]
When the perpetrator, apparently for the first time, met the deceased in the early hours of the morning in a nightclub, the two proceeded to the foyer where the perpetrator punched the deceased once on the face causing him to fall and strike his head and cutting it in such a way that two stitches were required. An arrangement was then made between the deceased and the perpetrator to meet later that day near a shopping centre. Although there was some evidence to suggest that they intended to talk over their differences, the weight of the evidence indicated an arrangement for the two of them to have a 'square go.' Each went by car accompanied by three or four friends. The evidence — which the jury by their verdict must have accepted — indicated that the deceased and the perpetrator first engaged in a fight involving fists and feet.

Then, the perpetrator pulled a combat style knife with a blade about seven and a half inches long from the inside pocket of his jacket and stabbed the deceased at least two times. One penetrating to a depth of about three inches in the region of the left armpit, the other (the fatal wound) entering the left side of his chest and passing from left to right backwards and upwards extending to a depth of 7.3 inches and effectively penetrating the whole of the width of the deceased's body and fracturing a posterior rib. The pathologist's view was that a forceful thrust with a significant amount of momentum was required as the knife was embedded to the hilt. Death, was quick and inevitable.

[After the murder]
He quickly departed the scene, dumped the car in which blood was later found, removed and washed the clothes he had been wearing, cleaned and then threw away the knife. He then, in the company of his solicitor attended the police station where, in the course of interviews extending over two-and-a-half hours which were videotaped and played to the jury, he made a statement to the effect that he had thought that the deceased had had something in his hand when he came at him [not confirmed by witnesses], and that he had had no knife with him, and [he boasted] that being an ex-Army man with undercover service he had contempt for those who carried knives. He stated that he had defended himself by grabbing the victim's hands and arms, crossed them over, and pushed them backwards during which any injuries must have been sustained.

(*287cf1.2.3)

In our interview with the perpetrator in the next case, he bragged about belonging to various motorcycle gangs, and spoke of his reputation for being an aggressive

60 Confrontational murder (fighters)

and violent character. After a night of serious drinking and the use of illegally acquired prescription drugs (Temazepam and Valium), he was returning from the pub with friends when he passed three Sudanese University students. He (age 26) claimed that one of them brushed against him which made him angry. He saw this as an 'insult,' and claims that they then agreed they would 'take the dispute elsewhere.' When they arrived at a separate location off the street, a fight began. At this stage, he produced a knife and a gun, and shot and stabbed one of the students to death (age 24). The following account comes from our interview with him.

Perpetrator claims he was insulted and they agreed to fight

[Context – the insult]
And you saw this as what, a challenge? I saw it as taking a liberty. *A liberty?* A fucking liberty, you know what I mean. Yeah, it was a blatant fucking taking the liberty because I had moved out of their way. I'd made myself as small as I could, do you know what I mean? And the way I saw it, he was trying to 'give it big' in front of his pals, and I'm not fucking having it. *You mean you hadn't said anything to them to begin with?* No [the evidence suggests he may have deliberately bumped into the victim in order to provoke a response and/or to provide him with an excuse to use violence].

[Murder event]
You could see it [attempted punch] a mile away. I blocked it, stabbed him once, but I had to reach forward [with the gun] because he was trying to get out of the way and the shot went low, and it punctured the heart. I wasn't aware of this at the time. I still assumed that I'd got him in the shoulder because that's where I was aiming. Yeah, and he sort of froze and fell back as if someone had tied a board to his back. He just, whoosh, do you know what I mean? I knew it was bad. I'd never seen anyone fall like that before. *Who were the victims?* They were Sudanese. He was a black guy, but so was the three of them.
[He then defends his actions by citing 'rules' for fighting]
Do you mean there are rules? Yeah, there is. There's unwritten rules, yeah. A knife fight is a knife fight, do you know what I mean? A gun fight is a gun [fight], a bottle fight is a bottle [fight]. If he's got nothing, you don't use anything. Right, do you know what I mean? *Yeah.* That's why I put the knife away when I fought the other two. *You didn't use it anymore [after stabbing him]?* Yeah, that's right. He had a knife [not confirmed by evidence], I had a knife. If he hasn't got a knife, I won't use a knife. *[Note. He cites 'the rules,' but fails to mention his use of a gun].*

[After the murder]
So, the police got you about 10 days afterwards? Like I said, they'd like went to town, because I was a known villain. I was known for my villainy. And

Confrontational murder (fighters) **61**

when they [police] turned up, there was a couple of hundred of 'em – no exaggeration. I remember seeing it in the paper, a couple of hundred of 'em. They was firmed up, you know, they was expecting the off [violence], and yeah they was all going for it alright. They was all going for it. That's about the best way I can explain it. *Did you plead guilty to manslaughter?* No, what it was, my argument was that I didn't leave with the intention of killing anyone. I didn't go down there with the intentions of killing him, it was a fight that just went drastically wrong. I went over the top. Do you know what I mean?

*(*876iv1.2.3)*

Notions about the 'rules; of engagement, the belief in the concept of a 'fair fight' seem to have played a part in these murders, at least in the minds of the perpetrators. Even as they violated the 'rules' of fair fighting, they simultaneously upheld the notion of these rules as expressed in this interview, 'it was a fight that just went drastically wrong.' What is clear, is that these encounters did not follow the 'rules' of a 'fair fight' that was 'agreed' upon by all concerned. Perhaps fighters simply use the notion of the 'fair fight' as a ruse to engage others into a violent encounter in which they do not expect to follow these rules.

Subtype 5. Collateral victims, bystanders and displacement of violence

In 'collateral murders,' someone is killed who was not involved in a confrontation that had taken place between the perpetrator and someone else. Following an unrelated dispute, the perpetrator takes out his rage on someone else, anyone else, the next person he sees, the stranger on the street. The victim may be acting as a 'good citizen' trying to assist someone who is being attacked, or they may simply be walking down a street or waiting at a bus stop when they become the target of an attack that simply comes 'out of the blue' as an enraged stranger attacks them. Three cases illustrate this subtype of confrontational murder that involved the killing of someone who was not party to a dispute. The first case took place in a nightclub and involved the killing of a man who tried to stop a fight in which a shotgun was being brandished. The second case involved the killing of a good citizen who was trying to stop a fight between two friends as one of them threatened the other with a machete. The third case involved two drunken men who had been evicted from a pub for fighting and then took their anger out on a total stranger who was walking along a public footpath.

Killed in a nightclub while trying to stop a fight involving a sawn-off shotgun

[Context]
This 23-year-old man stabbed a male stranger (26) who attempted to intervene in a fight in a nightclub between people who were unknown

62 Confrontational murder (fighters)

to him. The murder involved the public-spirited actions of the victim who tried to stop a brawl. The perpetrator was single unemployed and lived with his father. The victim (26) was employed, lived with his wife and two children, and was not known to the perpetrator.

[Murder]
In the late evening, the victim accompanied some friends to a nightclub. A squabble developed between two groups [one of which] included the perpetrator and members of a notorious family. A member of the family left for his home and returned with a sawn-off shotgun. It appeared he intended to use it in the disco to shoot a person in the rival group. The deceased was one of those who intervened as the gun was pushed into the air at the time it was fired. A fight broke out, and the perpetrator who was a close friend of the man with the gun became involved. He was seen to pull out a knife and stab the victim in the course of a general fracas. The victim managed to find his way into a corridor where he subsequently died. Although the police arrived at the scene at 1:45 am, the victim's body was not discovered until 10 hours later behind a cellar door.

[Trial judge report]
The death of the victim arose from a deliberate attack on him with a knife. There was no suggestion that the victim or the perpetrator knew each other or that the reason for the perpetrator's attack was related to anything other than the public-spirited actions of the victim in seeking to prevent serious injury being inflicted on someone by the perpetrator's friend.

*(*01cf1.2.3)*

The next murder involved displacement of violence when perpetrators who were angry with someone else, took their feelings out on a victim who had nothing to do with the dispute but nonetheless became the focus of their rage. This 'collateral murder' took place when the perpetrator and his friend, both drunk and high on drugs, were engaged in a dispute on the street involving a machete. When a passerby, who was accompanied by his son, tried to stop the fight, the perpetrators seemed to view this as an unwarranted intervention into 'their fight,' joined forces, turned on the 'good citizen,' and killed him in front of his son. In our interview with the perpetrator, he recounted the events of that night when, in a drunken stupor, he and his friend committed murder.

Bystander intervention on the street leads to murder of a stranger

[Murder]
Can I ask then about the murder, who was the victim? A bus driver. I didn't know him. It was the first time I'd seen him, even though he lived in my area. I'd been drinking all day, from about 11 o'clock or something.

Smoked cannabis, taking tablets, and all that. It made me confused. Then, there was an argument between me and my co-accused. He wanted to get a taxi and go to another pub, but I wanted to go straight home to my girlfriend's. We were arguing in the street, and he's got a big machete, and I'm saying 'put the knife down' and he wouldn't. He wouldn't put the knife down, and he's pointing it at me. And this man came round the corner with his son, seen him with the knife and said something like, 'put it down' or something. Then my co-accused starting fighting with him. The two of them started fighting [the victim was probably trying to defend himself].

At first, I never did anything. And then I did, I started. *And the gun?* Somebody, I don't know where I got this gun from, I think I got it from one of his [co-accused] friends. And I pulled the gun, shot the geezer, but my co-accused slashed him first with the machete. *Slashed him?* I couldn't really remember much because I was that high on drugs. *When, did you shoot him twice? Two straight after each other?* Aye, in the chest. I didn't mean to shoot him in the chest, but with being in that much of a state I did it. I think I was going to shoot him in the leg or something.

(*631iv1.2.3)

The last of these cases, involved the killing of a man who was not a bystander, not a witness, and not involved in any capacity. The victim was a total stranger who had absolutely no involvement in any aspects of the confrontation.

Drunk and high, ejected from a pub, kill a stranger walking on a footpath

This perpetrator (21) and his co-accused (17) both drunk and on drugs, killed a male stranger (39) who was going about his ordinary business at night. At the time, the perpetrator was living with the brother of his co-accused and his wife. He had been drinking on the day. He had consumed ten cans of lager before lunch, smoked cannabis and continued to drink the remainder of the day but described himself as, 'not really drunk.'

[Murder]
The co-accused and another male called for the perpetrator about 6.30 pm, and they spent most of the evening drinking in a pub. During the evening the perpetrator says he was the subject of racist abuse from a group of young males in the pub. This developed into a fight which led to the perpetrator, his co-accused and a male friend being barred from the pub. They felt aggrieved and wanted to fight but left, throwing a beer glass at a parked car, the alarm sounded and all three of the men ran off.

The co-accused saw the victim [a stranger] walking along a path near the river, and began to 'push' the victim, dragged him some way along

64 Confrontational murder (fighters)

the path, and began to kick him. The perpetrator described a situation which he agrees was frenzied. He joined in the assault by kicking the victim. He denies stamping on him but claims that the co-accused did so. The perpetrator says that, at this point, he became scared and thought that the victim could perhaps be dead. They then dragged the victim onto the dirt track where attempts were made to throw him into the river. They failed, and left the body on the track, where he was discovered two hours later and pronounced dead.

[Injuries]
They kicked him repeatedly about the head, and stamped on his face and head. His injuries were so severe that he suffered massive head injuries. Shoe marks were visible on his face, and he was so badly disfigured that his own father had to view the victim's tattoos to enable him to identify him.

(*205cf1.2.4)

These cases illustrate how men can be killed in the context of a confrontation in which the victim was not directly involved as a participant.

Subtype 6. Confrontations involving allegiance with a wider group

Some conflicts and disputes focus on various forms of allegiance to a wider entity that involves allegiances and rivalries. Ethnicity, religion, nationality, and even sports rivalries can become the source of conflict that is expressed in acts of aggression, violent encounters, and even murder. Two cases illustrate murders that were associated with one-sided confrontations between individuals that were conducted against a backdrop of competing sports and political groups. The first involved supporters of two sports clubs. There is a long history of conflicts and violence associated with football rivalries in Britain and in many countries in Europe (see Williams and Taylor, 1994). Some rivalries between the supporters of different football clubs also reflect wider sectarian divides such as those between Catholics and Protestants and between cities and nations.

In the first case, after a match the victim was leaving the stadium wearing a scarf displaying the colors of his club. The perpetrator, who supported a rival football club, demonstrated his negative feelings about the opposing club in an aggressive manner seemingly intended to demonstrate loyalty to his own team. In the presence of other like-minded fans, he attacked a total stranger who was wearing the 'wrong' colors. The innocent victim had done him no harm and had not engaged in any exchanges, but was simply wearing the colors of the other club.

Confrontational murder (fighters) **65**

'My' football club – killing a supporter of the 'other' team across a sectarian divide

This perpetrator (22), stabbed the victim (16), a school boy [a stranger] and a rival football supporter on his way home from the football match after having been identified by his football scarf as a supporter of the other team.

[Perpetrator's account]
He states it was Saturday afternoon and he had been doing all the usual things he normally did on Saturday such as visiting the local bookmakers [betting shop] and socializing with his friends until a girl he knew asked him if he would escort her to the bus stop opposite the football match which had just ended. Supporters usually walked along this road, and he said she found it uncomfortable to stand at the bus stop with so many people.

He escorted her over and noticed a fight breaking out that involved a few of his friends so, 'I did what anybody would do and ran over to assist my friends out of loyalty.' It was a sectarian attack. As he arrived at the fight scene, he started exchanging punches and kicks with the opponents. He then saw the victim and took a knife from his pocket that he always had for defense reasons [note: the victim was not involved in the supposed fight].

[Murder]
He pushed the knife towards the victim's face and slashed him. At that moment, there was a lot of shouting and the fight broke up and everybody fled the scene. He returned home thinking nothing serious had happened and basically continued to do what he normally did on a Saturday evening. After dinner, he got ready to go out for the evening. Later that evening while out with his friends, he phoned home, for whatever reason he cannot remember why, and it was then that his mother informed him that the police had called at the house to question him. He then contacted his lawyer suspecting it was for the earlier slashing and arranged to meet him at his office. Once at his lawyer's office, they contacted the police and arranged to go to the station the following day where he was questioned, charged and held in custody. He later described the murder: 'I ran along and had a bit of a roll about, 'chibbed' the cunt, fight broke up, and that was it.'

[Coroner's report]
Death was caused by a single deep incised wound of the neck which severed the right internal and external carotid arteries and the internal jugular vein. The cause of death was exsanguination [loss of blood]. The victim was a complete stranger to the perpetrator, and was identified solely by the football scarf he was wearing.

(*289cf1.2.3)

66 Confrontational murder (fighters)

Superficially, the immediate context of this murder appears to be restricted solely to a rivalry between the fans of opposing football teams, but the wider context reveals that each team was strongly identified with different religions. In the eyes of the perpetrator, the color of the scarf represented a host of issues about his own social identity and the identity of his victim that were oppositional and, in his view, 'warranted' violence.

The next case involved violence and murder by a member of a dissident group in conflict with the British state in the long-standing violence in Northern Ireland known as 'The Troubles.' The IRA planned and executed numerous bombings and killings within Northern Ireland and on the mainland of the United Kingdom.

Sectarian murder by nationalist – the IRA

The perpetrator (37) was active in [Big City] bombings during the 'troubles', and had placed nineteen explosives that had failed to detonate. He was apprehended when a bomb exploded prematurely on a train. In trying to escape, he shot dead the train driver (40) and shot at, but did not injure, an engineer and two police constables. When the police net closed, he shot himself in the chest but emergency surgery saved him. He is fiercely political and considers himself a prisoner of war (something of a hero). He did not recognize the court [as valid], was found mute by police and refused to plead.

[The context]
Two men and a woman were travelling in the leading train carriage when a man entered the train carrying a duffle bag. It began to smoke. The perpetrator (37) immediately threw it to the ground and within seconds it exploded. The blast blew the woman out of the carriage and one of the men was knocked unconscious by debris. The [perpetrator] who had been carrying the bomb had cuts to his face and left arm, but no-one was killed.

[Murder]
As the train stopped 200 yds from the station, the perpetrator produced a gun and jumped down onto the track. The driver, got out to examine the damage. He walked towards the back of the train and the gunman walked towards the front. As they confronted each other, the gunman fired two shots and the victim (40) fell to the ground. The subsequent post-mortem revealed that a bullet had entered his body below the right collar bone and ruptured the heart.

Meanwhile an engineer who happened to be at the Station at the time of the explosion, ran along the track and arrived just after the shooting. He came face to face with the gunman and said, 'Not me mate, I have a

Confrontational murder (fighters)   **67**

wife at home. I have come to help those injured people.' He was immediately shot in the chest and lost consciousness, but subsequently recovered after emergency surgery.

In the chaos following the explosion, the gunman became confused as to direction the train was travelling and walked back and forth alongside the train. By this time, a Police Constable (PC) had arrived, parked his car level with the train, and heard someone shout, 'He has a gun and shot the guard.' The gunman fired at the unarmed officer who heard the sound of the bullet going over his head. The PC returned to his car and peered over the boundary wall of the railway track. The gunman spotted him, took deliberate aim with both hands and fired another shot which missed.

Several people assumed he was one of the injured passengers until they saw the gun in his hand and backed away. One rushed back to the station platform to warn others to stay out of his way. The gunman then climbed onto the platform and left the station exit where police were waiting to follow him. A PC called out, 'Don't be stupid,' and the gunman fired at him and missed. He purposefully took aim again, but this time there was a blank click.

Clearly the gun had only misfired, because the gunman then turned the gun towards his chest and shot himself. He fell backwards but rolled over onto his stomach holding the gun in front of him. Suddenly he got up, walked down the road, and turned into a factory yard where he laid down. A PC approached him from behind, knocked him over the head with a truncheon and seized the gun.

[After the murder]
On the way to the hospital, the gunman gave a false name. On arrival, it was found that the bullet had passed right through his chest and lodged in the back of his shirt. He received emergency surgery, was detained in hospital, and was subsequently identified.

[Trial and convictions]
There were four co-defendants in the trial. All remained silent, were found 'mute by malice,' and the Court entered pleas of 'not guilty' on their behalf. The perpetrator was convicted on seven counts. Two male co-accused were convicted on three counts, and a female co-accused was acquitted [Tariff 30 years].

*(*857cf1.5)*

These extended narratives from the casefiles and interviews of real-life murders has enabled us to take a closer look at the diversity within 'Confrontational Murders' and the dynamic elements involved as fighters engage in fights that they take all the way. Confrontational murders were grouped into six subtypes. Some of the

68 Confrontational murder (fighters)

confrontations involved disputes between different groups and perceived 'slights' directed at the perpetrator or others of importance to him which formed the beginning of a fight that ends with the death of one or more of the combatants. Some of these murders did not involve a confrontation between the perpetrator and his victim but, instead, originated elsewhere when men who had become angry about something took it out on a total stranger, a passerby, or a good citizen. Lastly, for some perpetrators the identification with a wider group such as a football team, or religious or political group may mean they view those identified with 'other' groups as 'the opposition' and worthy of a fight, even to the death.

Comparisons of Confrontational.Murders/ fighters and Other.Murders

We return to all of the 158 'Confrontational Murders' in order to compare this type of murder with Other.Murders that were not of this type. We ask how are these murders similar, and how do they differ? What are the distinct characteristics of confrontational murders? The comparisons include the background of the perpetrators, the relationship between perpetrators and victims, conflicts and disputes prior to the murder, and drinking and drugs. Various elements of the murder event include the location, number of perpetrators, witnesses, injuries, the cause of death, and whether another offense such as robbery was committed at the time of the murder. Here, an asterisk★ indicates differences that are statistically significant, but all percentages and specific levels of significance are shown in Table 2.1 Murder Event – Confrontational.Murders and Other.Murders.

Background and relationship between perpetrators and victims

The Confrontational.Murderers and Other.Murderers were of a similar age (27 years), but the average age of their victims differed as Fighters killed men who were closer to their own age compared to the victims of Other.Murders who were around ten years older (33 years vs 44 years★). The majority of the 'Fighters' were mostly unemployed, but this was more likely among those who committed other types of murder (59% vs 73%★). Perpetrators of Confrontational.Murders were less likely than Other.Murderers to have killed a stranger (26% vs 34%).

Conflicts, disputes and previous violence

While most of the confrontational murderers knew their victim, many were not on friendly terms. Before the murder, nearly half of the Fighters were engaged in an ongoing dispute with their victim, compared with about one-fifth of Other. Murders (46% vs 22%★). In addition, confrontations at the time of the murder were far more likely among the 'Fighters' than Other.Murderers (83% vs 55%★).

The evidence presented in the qualitative accounts suggests that Fighters viewed these confrontations as 'provocations' that set things off and began the violent event that ended in murder. In many cases, the issue at stake involved an ongoing dispute between the men but, in others, it was not. And as shown in the qualitative evidence, what counted as 'contentious' may have been something that others would define as 'trivial,' but these men viewed them as 'insults,' as 'taking liberties,' as challenges to their sense of self-worth and/or their individual identity that must be defended and in their view, 'required' a violent response. A few of the 'confrontational murders' were retaliatory and occurred in the context of previous insults, aggression, and/or violence against the perpetrator or his friends or allies. The latter, further emphasizes the importance of the group in this type of murder.

Drinking, drunkenness and drugs

The majority of all the murder events were fueled by drinking and drunkenness among the perpetrators, and sometimes among the victims. Drinking was more likely among the Fighters than Other.Murderers (77% vs 62%*), and in both groups of murderers, most of those who had been drinking were drunk (77% vs. 70%). A fair proportion of the victims had also been drinking on the day they were murdered, and this was more likely among the fighters (57% vs 41%*). Those victims who had been drinking were also likely to be drunk (73% vs 71%), and a few perpetrators and victims had been 'drinking together' before the murder (24% vs 33%). Some perpetrators had also taken drugs at the time of the murder (18% vs 20%).

Murder event

The home of the victim was *less likely* to be the scene of the crime among Fighters' than the men who committed 'Other.Murders' (41% vs 56%*). Confrontational murders were much more likely to occur in a public location, such as parks, streets, wastelands, or near pubs where the men were drinking. About half of all the murders were committed by only one perpetrator (53% vs 61%) who was likely to be angry, although this was more likely for confrontational murderers (52% vs 34). As Table 2.1, shows Other.Murders did not usually involve witnesses, whereas, confrontational murders were much less likely to be committed in the absence of witnesses to the murder event (44% vs 69%*). This suggests the importance of the group in these violent encounters. Whatever the orientations or actions of these witnesses, the evidence suggests they often constituted an 'audience' for the perpetrator(s). Although most witnesses did nothing, a few participated in the attack, a few tried to intervene, and a few phoned emergency services for the police. The presence of witnesses and their effect upon the murder event varied. In some cases, their presence appeared to act to deter or curtail the violence but in many cases the presence of witnesses served as a 'chorus' for the murder event itself.

70 Confrontational murder (fighters)

Cause of death

The usual attack involved the use of fists, feet, clubs and knives. But stabbing was the most common cause of death among Confrontational.Murders and Other.Murders (52% vs 45%). This often involved 4–5 wounds but as many as 10 or more wounds was not unusual. While the use of a knife/sharp instrument occurred in many of the murders, what differed for the 'Fighters' was the number and the location of stab wounds. Stab wounds to the neck, chest and extremities (arms and legs) were not uncommon, but 'Confrontational Murders' were more likely to involve stab wounds to vital organs in the middle of the body such as the lungs and heart (not in Table 2.1) which may be an indicator of the intention to inflict more serious harm. The use of a firearm was unusual in both groups (9% vs 12%), as was strangulation (2% vs 10%).

Other offenses in addition to murder

Only one-quarter of the confrontational murderers committed a second offense along with the murder, compared with nearly one-half of Other.Murders (24% vs 48%*), which suggests the centrality of 'the confrontation' and that these murders were not usually an element of another offense such as a robbery or burglary although this did characterize nearly three-quarters of Other.Murders (24% vs 71%*).

Summary and conclusions

As shown in Table 2.1 comparisons of Confrontational.Murders and Other. Murders' not only illustrates some of the differences and similarities between these different types of murder, but also helps clarify the *main* characteristics of Confrontational.Murders. These include: ongoing disputes prior to the murder; a confrontation at the time of the murder; as well as drinking and drunkenness among the perpetrators and among some of the victims. Many of the perpetrators were angry or in a rage. Confrontational murders were more likely to take place in a public location and include witnesses who might constitute an audience. The most common cause of death was 'stabbing,' and most deaths involved 'five or more injuries.' Confrontational murders rarely involved another offense such as robbery.

Many of the men who committed Confrontational.Murders were sensitive to 'slights' or humiliations directed at them or at others of importance to them. They considered these actions as challenges that must be redressed, and justified their use of violence. In some cases, the violence constituted a performance for others that, in the eyes of the perpetrator, confirmed their prerogative to judge 'what was right or wrong,' what could or could not be 'tolerated,' what constituted 'taking a liberty,' or when someone was 'taking the piss.' The use of alcohol and drunkenness were important, and Confrontational murders were often preceded by men

Confrontational murder (fighters) **71**

TABLE 2.1 Murder Event. Confrontational.Murders and Other.Murders

MALE–MALE MURDER	*Confrontational.Murders*	*Other.Murders*
	n = 158	*n* = 266^
	(%)	(%)
BACKGROUND		
– Age:		
– Perpetrators	27 yrs	27 yrs
– Victims	33 yrs	43 yrs★★★
– Unemployed at murder	59%	73%★★
RELATIONSHIP BETWEEN PERPETRATOR and VICTIM		
- Stranger	26%	34%
CONFLICTS and DISPUTES		
– Ongoing Dispute	46%	22%★★★
– Confrontation at Murder	83%	55%★★★
– Prev.viol; Perp.against.vic.	14%	10%
– Prev.viol;Vic.against.perp	16%	7%★★
DRINKING and DRUGS		
– Perp. Drugs	18%	20%
– Perp. Drinking	77%	62%★★
– if perp. drinking, Drunk	77%	70%
– Drinking 3–6hrs	37%	42%
– Drinking all day	17%	24%
–Vic. Drinking	57%	41%★★
– if vic. drinking, Drunk	73%	71%
– of those drinking, drink together	24%	33%
MURDER EVENT		
– Home of victim	41%	56%★★★
– One perpetrator	53%	61%
– No Witness	44%	69%★★★
– Perpetrator [angry, rage, indignant]	52%	34%
– Injuries = 5 + injuries	71%	71%
CAUSE of DEATH		
– Strangle	02%	10%
– Stab	52%	45%
– Beat w/object/instrument	17%	19%
– Beat w/hands/feet	21%	15%
– Shot	09%	12%

Continued

72 Confrontational murder (fighters)

TABLE 2.1 continued

OFFENSE/s		
Murder + 2nd offense (yes)	24%	48%**
– if 2nd offense 'property offense':	24%	71%***
statistically significant: *$p < .05$, **$p < .01$, ***$p < .001$		
^ numbers vary when: not applicable and/or missing data		

drinking together in pubs and public locations such as parks and streets as well as in their homes where conflicts occurred.

Antagonisms and posturing often took place in the same or adjoining neighborhoods which had the effect of sustaining and amplifying previous disputes and grievances. What was fundamentally at stake was the individual's desire to demonstrate their prowess in order to enhance their own standing to themselves and/or to others. When others were involved these men are best described as a 'group,' rather than a gang, in which personal as well as group identity was of importance. In contrast to some claims, very few of the murders were strictly spontaneous, nor could they be defined as 'fair fights' that involved implicit 'rules' as well as a mutual agreement between perpetrators and victims to engage in potentially lethal violence. Instead, it appears that either from the onset of the confrontation, or sometime during the violent attack, the victims were disproportionately disadvantaged and made vulnerable by perpetrators who came equipped with a weapon such as a knife, brick or club, and were willing to inflict serious injury upon their victim, even to the point of killing them.

References

Brookman, F., 2005. *Understanding Homicide*. Thousand Oaks, CA: Sage.

Brookman, F., Copes, H., and Hochstetler, A., 2011. Street codes, accounts, and rationales for violent crime. *Journal of Contemporary Ethnography*, 40, 397–424.

Cavanagh, K., Dobash, R. E., and Dobash, R. P., 2005. Men who murder children inside and outside the family. *British Journal of Social Work*, 35, 667–688.

Daly, M. and Wilson, M., 1988. *Homicide*. New York: Aldine De Gruyter.

Dobash, R. P. and Dobash, R. E., 1983. The context-specific approach. In D. Finkelhor, R. J. Gelles, G. T. Hotaling, and M. A. Straus eds., *The Dark Side of Families*. Beverly Hills, CA: Sage, 261–276.

Dobash, R. E. and Dobash, R. P., 2015. *When Men Murder Women*. New York and Oxford: Oxford University Press.

Dobash, R. P. and Dobash, R. E., 2018. When men murder children. In Brown, T., Tyson, D. and Arias, P. F., eds., *When Parents Kill Children*. Cham: Palgrave Macmillan, 81–102.

Ellis, A., 2016. *Men, Masculinities and Violence: An Ethnographic Study*. London: Routledge.

Fraser, A., 2015. *Urban Legends*. Oxford: Oxford University Press.

Peristiany, J. G., 1965. ed., *Honor and Shame: The Values of Mediterranean Society*. London: Weidenfeld & Nicolson.

Polk, K., 1994. *When Men Kill: Scenarios of Masculine Violence*. New York: Cambridge University Press.

Toch, H. H., 1969. *Violent Men: An Inquiry into the Psychology of Violence*. Chicago, IL: Aldine reprinted in 2017.

Walmsley, R. 1986., *Personal Violence*. Home Office Research, no. 89. London: HMSO.

Williams, J. and Taylor, R., 1994. Boys keep on swinging: Masculinity and football culture in England. In T. Newburn and E. A. Stanko, *Just Boys Doing Business*? London: Routledge, pp. 214–233.

3

MURDER FOR MONEY/ FINANCIAL GAIN

Of all the 424 male–male murders, 81 (19%), were related to money or some kind of financial gain. Most occurred in the context of burglary or robbery but there were other subtypes. Financial issues and money were at the core of the murders associated with disputes regarding illegal drug dealing focusing, for example, on procurement, distribution and profits. Other murders in the context of criminal activities were associated with the 'share-outs' of goods/money from proceeds of crime. A few murders did not involve illegal activities, but were associated with disputes regarding informal, personal loans. Men were also killed in attempts to monopolize access to legal or illegal activities, such as, groups of 'door men' fighting over the 'contract' to provide security at leisure locations such as pubs. A few murders occurred during conflicts with government agencies, where the state was responsible for overseeing the activities of the perpetrator. Here, the issue was unlawful behavior that was under scrutiny of the state and the perpetrator killed agents of the government who were investigating this activity, such as the operation of an unregistered auto repair shop. The last example of killing in this chapter is a contract murder where the killer was paid by a third party to murder a 'targeted individual.'

Much existing research would characterize many of the murders considered in this chapter, instrumental, committed primarily or solely in an attempt to obtain money or resources where there appears to be an absence of strong emotions. By contrast 'expressive' homicides involve emotions such as anger and rage (see Block and Block (1991) for a classic interpretation). While the definition of 'instrumental' has expanded to include murders linked to attempts to improve 'one's social status' and those including an additional crime, the term is not particularly meaningful when applied to actual murders. Miethe and Drass (1999) have noted that a sharp distinction between instrumental and expressive murder cannot be sustained nor seen as discrete entities. We agree, and rather than employ the term here we prefer to consider all murders broadly instrumental in that they are purposeful in intent to inflict serious injury and to kill (Tedeschi and Felson, 1994; Levi and Maguire, 2002). As demonstrated in this chapter, many of the murders that seemed to be committed for purely financial reasons, often involved additional intentions such as retaliation and retribution linked to strong emotions. In order to consider the types of murders related to money, we begin with a quantitative overview of the entire sample of this type of murder, $n = 81$, focusing primarily on the context, circumstances and the specific nature of the murder. Employing qualitative evidence, we then demonstrate the diversity and dynamic aspects of the murder events we have included in this category.

Main patterns – murder for money

Background and relationship between perpetrators and victims

At the time of the murder the perpetrators were in their late twenties, average age 27, but the victims were much older, average age 42. Around two-thirds of the perpetrators were unemployed at the time. If employed, they were usually working in skilled or unskilled manual jobs. Considering the murder itself, many of the victims were killed by a stranger (41%) or an acquaintance (23%) but the third largest category (14%) involved the murder of a 'business' associate involved in the illegal drug business (see Table 3.1 for the specifics of these murders).

Conflicts, disputes and previous violence

Around two-fifths of these relationships involved an ongoing dispute between the victim and perpetrator, with some extending over a considerable period of time. Verbal confrontations at the outset of the violence occurred in around two-fifths. Previous incidents of violence between the victim and perpetrator were rare. Only 5% of the cases involved previous violence by the perpetrator against the victim 4% involved previous violence by the victim against the perpetrator.

What was especially distinct about these cases was the deliberate and often pre-planned nature of the attack and murder. Many of these men were acting in a concerted and 'level-headed' manner that did not appear to involve intense emotions. Only 25% could be described as angry or in a rage during the murder. These data support the interpretation of the 'rational' and deliberate nature of many of the men who murdered for money, resources, or commodities.

76 Murder for money/financial gain

Drinking, drunkenness and drugs

The evidence suggests that 44% of the perpetrators and 34% of the victims had been drinking on the day of the murder. A majority of the perpetrators and victims who had been drinking were drunk (72% vs 64%). Drinking and drunkenness appear to be a common past-time of perpetrators. A reasonable proportion of the perpetrators, two-fifths had been drinking for 3–6 hours and one-fifth had been drinking all day. This suggests that when drinking the perpetrators generally devoted a considerable amount of their time to this 'leisure' activity. On the day in question around two-fifths of the perpetrators had consumed drugs.

Murder event

Just over one-third of the murders occurred in the home of the victim, another third occurred in a workplace or commercial location and a third were committed in a public location such as a street or park (not in Table 3.1). Just under two-thirds of the murders involved more than one perpetrator. Most of the murders (69%) were not witnessed. While bodily violence, hands and feet, were often used in the murder, the use of a weapon, such as a club, and/or a knife/sharp was common, 90%. A considerable proportion (69%) of these weapons and bodily violence resulted in five or more injuries. Firearms, usually a handgun, were used in just under two-fifth of the murders.

Cause of death

In most cases, 43%, the victims died from a stabbing but beating with an instrument and or bodily violence were contributors.

Other offenses in addition to murder

A considerable proportion of these murders, 68%, included one our more additional offenses, primarily a theft (91%).

Murder for money – seven subtypes

As noted earlier, there is considerable variation in this type of murder and we have distilled them into seven subtypes. However, of the 81 cases one dominated: killing in the context of burglary or robbery. The second largest category involved murder in the context of illegal drug dealing. While a considerable proportion of the financially based murders are encompassed by these categories, disaggregation into additional types provides enhanced knowledge, and thus enhanced understanding, than an aggregated approach to this overall type of murder would provide.

Murder for money – seven subtypes
1 Thefts, burglary and robbery
2 Drug dealing, disputes and murder
3 Criminal activity, 'share-outs' and murder
4 Personal debts, disputes and murder
5 Gangs, conflict over control of territory and resources
6 Unlawful activity, disputes with officials and murder
7 Contract to kill.

Prevalence and nature of burglary and robbery in UK and USA

The world over burglary and robbery are considered serious crimes. In the case of burglary, the crime involves an intrusion into a private and safe location that is meant to be a haven from the outside world. Breaking the boundaries of the home is a grave intrusion and violation of an idealized location. There is considerable evidence regarding burglary and robbery but much less about murders committed in the commission of burglary or robbery. Burglary and robbery are almost exclusively committed by males. In 2012 in the US 87% of robberies and 84% burglaries were committed by males (US Department of Justice, 2012). In England/Wales, 89% of burglaries and 94% of street robberies were committed by men and in 76% of the cases of robbery, the victims were men (Brookman et al., 2007, p. 861).

While the specific legal definitions of burglary and robbery vary across jurisdictions, the fundamental aspects of these crimes are similar. A burglary is theft preceded by forceable entry to a residential or commercial property. In England/Wales a burglary is defined as stealing or attempting to steal something from a residence or business (Elkin, 2017). Most definitions also include entry obtained through deception or the compliance of the property owner or renter. These circumstances usually involve neighbors, friends or relatives who allow access. Robbery does not usually involve a break-in but does include theft accompanied by coercion and/or violence usually in a public location, such as, on the street. In some jurisdictions both types of theft using a *weapon* is considered most grave and can lead to a charge of *aggravated* robbery which in England/Wales can result in a more substantial sentence, up to 25 years. When successful, burglary in England/Wales, usually results in the theft of purses, wallets, money, jewelry, and computers (Elkin, 2017). Seventy percent of burglaries occur during the working week and in half of the cases someone was at home, thus potentially increasing the risk of violence. Those most at risk of burglary in the UK are women living on their own with a child in a rental property in an urban setting. Higher income individuals have the lowest rates of both crimes. There has been an overall reduction in burglary during the twentieth century. In England/Wales in 1993, there were 2,455,000 reported burglaries whereas in 2017 there were only 650,000

78 Murder for money/financial gain

(Elkin, 2017). Today and in the past incidents of homicide associated with burglary or robbery have been quite low. According to Brookman (2005, p. 314), in England and Wales, during the years 1997–2000, there were 4,123 homicides, of these 294 occurred in the 'course of another crime' with around 200 male–male homicides committed in the context of burglary or robbery.

In the US, there has been a move to change the nomenclature of burglary. In a Special Report of the US Bureau of Justice Statistics, Catalano (2010) considers the development of the term 'Home Invasion' to encapsulate crimes of burglary. She notes the term has recently become a sort of catch-all for these types of crimes despite the imprecision associated with the term. Catalano notes 'Home Invasion has become used widely to describe an array of victimizations' and Catalano distills these definitions into various dimensions, including: 'unlawfully entering a residence while someone is at home' and 'an offender forcibly enters an occupied residence with the specific intent of robbing or violently harming those inside' (Catalano, 2010, p. 2). While this attempt to distinguish between burglary and 'home invasion is useful,' as our data suggest, establishing specific intent and distinguishing between those burglaries characterized by the intention of 'violently harming' someone is very problematic. In order to simplify the investigation of these murders we will adhere to the English/Welsh definitions discussed above. In our data some burglaries, involved the use of force to gain entry and in a few the burglar was intent on committing violence. But in most cases the attack was more circumstantial as, for example, when the victim reacted to the perpetrator by remonstrating with him or unusually by physically responding to the intruder while attempting to stop a theft. This characterization applies to a considerable proportion of the murders that occurred in the context of a burglary and in some cases of robbery. However, as indicated earlier, in many cases of burglary the intruder did not need to use force or violence to enter the home of the victim, since the relationship between the offender and victim was such that entry was either with explicit or implicit consent.

Catalano's Special Report for the US Bureau of Justice Statistics while attempting to clarify various definitions of burglary and robbery also reports findings regarding the context and nature of these crimes. Using the National Crime Victimization Survey of nonfatal crimes involving burglary from 2003 to 2007, Catalano distinguishes between burglaries that occurred when someone was at home and those that occurred when no one was in at home. The national victimization survey indicates that of the 3.7 million burglaries during the time period, in 28% of the cases someone was at home at the time, thus 'at risk' of a violent assault. In these cases, 65% of the victims knew their assailant, with strangers accounting for 28% with the remaining 7% not identified. It seems that those who break-in to people's houses target certain types of households with the most vulnerable at greatest risk. The evidence gathered in the US victim survey reports very similar patterns to those reported for England/Wales. In the US, women living on their own with children were the most likely victims in occupied residences. Additionally, levels of income make a difference: the poorest have the highest rates of victimization, and the wealthiest the lowest. Around 30% of those residents who were at home experienced some form of violence including, assault, serious assault, rape and sexual assault. The majority of these attacks did not result in any injuries or only minor ones, whereas 9% involved serious injury. During the period of reporting – 2003–2007 – the FBI's Supplementary Homicide Reports, recorded 430 burglary-homicides, less than 1% of all homicides. Of the 2.1 million household burglaries where someone was in residence and at risk, fewer than 1% involved a homicide. These data and others indicate that the risk of assault and injuries during a burglary appear rather low and the risk of a homicide very low. Of course, this should not lead to the conclusion that such violence and murders are less important than other types or that they have little to no impact on the survivors and the communities in which they occur.

The research findings regarding the motivations and context associated with robbery in the US and UK are generally consistent. Qualitative-based interviews with convicted burglars leads to a rather straight-forward and predictable conclusion. Burglars tell interviewers they commit robbery because they need money or goods to buy drugs and alcohol in the context of a subculture of crime and aggressive/violent theft (Brookman et al., 2007). Robbery is a hostile crime in that the victim is threatened with or actually suffers violence. An intimidating demeanor and a viable threat are often used, such as showing a weapon. In the US this is usually a gun. In Britain it might be a knife, but it is usually an instrument wielded as a weapon. As well as money for 'desperate partying,' robbers seek other outcomes: the 'buzz' and excitement of provoking fear in the victim, status enhancement as a man who is not 'to be messed with' and revenge linked to street justice. Perpetrators' generally seek to minimize risks to themselves by identifying and attacking vulnerable targets, such as, a stranger who is on his own, on the street late at night, and drunk. Also, a vulnerable man is one who also looks likely to have something worth stealing. Money was not the only purpose of the attacks. In interviews, some men admitted they enjoyed beating-up the victims and for some this was central to the crime. Dangerous behavior that might very well result in murder. The existing evidence establishes a clear link with violent thefts and a masculinity expressed through 'aggressive displays of toughness' and violence.

Subtype 1. Thefts, burglary and robbery

In this section we begin our analysis of murders linked to money, by presenting the qualitative evidence of murders involving burglary and robbery. In some cases, the narratives are similar to those considered above. Many of the circumstances of the murders parallel the assaults found in research in the US and UK. However, the evidence from the Murder Study differs in terms of the objectives of these two crimes. As in the research on assaults and robbery, the murders analyzed here were connected with efforts to obtain money for drugs and alcohol. But we found

80 Murder for money/financial gain

little evidence of a lifestyle of 'partying' and pleasure and the victims were not always strangers, indeed, murders of complete strangers were rare. Rather victims were often known to the preparator as friends, relatives, and neighbors. We begin with cases involving these types of relationships.

Three cases demonstrate the strategies used in cases involving burglary and murder that did not include 'forced entry'. What they did include was violence and thefts committed against vulnerable men who lived alone and were acquainted with the perpetrator.

Burglary and murder of a man who had given the perpetrator considerable assistance

A 21-year-old chronic alcoholic, usually homeless, mostly unemployed, man, killed an elderly (64-year-old) hotel owner who came to Britain as a child escaping from Poland during WWII. At times the victim gave the perpetrator jobs in his small hotel. Once a week he played cards with friends and often carried as much £2,000 for the game. The perpetrator and another man went to his apartment to rob him but were caught in the act by the victim who challenged them. The perpetrator had brought a stolen kitchen knife to the scene and stabbed the victim 74 times. When asked why so many times, he said 'Because he wasn't dead yet'.

(★801cf1.2.2)

Preying on the most vulnerable – victim known to perpetrator

Robbery and killing of a single, reclusive man (54) who lived in in the same building as the perpetrator (35) with whom he was acquainted.

[Trial judge]
The victim suffered from schizophrenia and lived as a recluse in a bedsit [studio apartment]. The perpetrator lived in the same building as him and he was known to have cash in his room. The perpetrator may have stolen money from him in the past. He was short of money – he needed to visit a cousin to whom he had taken a fancy. The victim was brutally killed by a series of blows to the head with an irregularly shaped heavy blunt instrument such as a wrench or claw hammer (weapon was not recovered). After the killing, the perpetrator had around £5,000 which he had probably stolen from the victim. The circumstantial evidence against him was strong and he admitted to a friend that he, 'didn't mean to go that far.' I do not think the perpetrator went to the victim's room intending to kill. He went to steal or rob. The venture got out of hand and he killed perhaps because the victim surprised him or because he refused to hand over the money. He has a record of dishonesty and some violence but nothing very serious. However, in view of the brutality of the killing he is a dangerous man.

(★253cf1.2.2)

Murder and stealing money from a savings account

This 25-year-old male neighbor battered this 63-year-old man to death in order to steal his Building Society documents and pin numbers for two accounts. The motive was to obtain the money for amphetamines; £10,600 was subsequently obtained, leaving £5 in his account. Fifteen-year tariff.

(*10301.2.2)

This case also involved murder and money to be used for drugs. The victim was a young man who had served a prison sentence, was recently released and by all accounts was attempting to start a new life. At the time of his death he was living in a probation hostel for the rehabilitation of offenders but his efforts to move beyond his sentence were cut short by his death at the hands of two drug users who were also living in the hostel and 'needed' money for drugs.

Murder of a young man 'trying to get his life back together' – known to perpetrator

[Context of murder]
Two 28-year-old men were both found guilty of murder. They were heroin addicts and they stabbed to death a lodger in a NACRO [National Association for the Care and Resettlement of Offenders] hostel [for prisoners after release] where they were all staying. His body was buried under the floorboards. The victim (22) was an innocent young man trying to get his life back together. After the murder the two men got access to his bank account, obtained all his cash and sold all his goods to get money for smack. Each claimed the other had committed the murder, and that their own part was only helping the other get the body under the floorboards. This was a typical drug-driven murder in the twilight zone of the city. Young men groomed on cannabis turned to heroin and killed an innocent young man who was himself a 'lifer' trying to go straight.

[Discovery of the body]
A health and safety maintenance worker called at the house because of the foul smell, and thought it was a dead animal. The body was found [under the floorboards] in an advanced state of decomposition. There were 23 knife wounds with 2 weapons. The victim had gone missing from the hostel sometime earlier in the year. There was a long history of harassment of the victim by the two perpetrators for money and there was lots of physical aggression to the victim. The victim's family phoned the hostel to say they were worried because they hadn't heard from him. They spoke to the perpetrator who said he had decided to go and stay in another country. He [the victim] had missed a probation visit which he

had never done and police called round at the hostel to investigate and were shown round by his co-accused. At the end of March both defendants left the hostel. Throughout this time, they were dealing in crack. The perpetrator began drug use with cannabis at age 11.

(*249cf1.2.2)

Not all of the burglary murders occurred in a domestic dwelling some took place in a commercial or industrial building as in the following examples. The first involved a perpetrator who knew the victim who was his former work supervisor and was known to carry a fair amount of cash. In this case the perpetrator attempts to implicate a gay man by rearranging the victim's clothing to suggest a sexual attack. Not believed.

Robbery murder of former workmate

This male perpetrator, 27, was drinking in a pub, leaves with no money, follows his former work supervisor, victim, 38, who had been in the pub flashing his money and robs and stabs him.

[Context]
This is a very violent man with a long criminal history of violence. He was drinking and drug taking in the pub. When he has no more money he leaves and passes his former workplace and notices the door was open and goes in. Or rather he follows the foreman who had been in the pub when he was there. He has an argument with the victim and stabs him and takes his money.

[Murder]
The victim was found at 7 am the following morning. His trousers and underpants had been pulled down to his knees and one of his trouser pockets had been turned inside out in an attempt to give the impression of a homosexual attack.

[Cause of death]
The PME [post-mortem examination] revealed the cause of death to be multiple stab wounds to the chest and abdomen. There were penetrating wounds involving the heart, both lungs, the liver, and the roof of the mesentery [tissues dividing the organs of the body]. In addition, there was a neck and throat wound which appeared to have been inflicted after the death of the victim who also suffered self-defense type injuries to the upper limbs.

[Trial judge]
The accused admitted that he had done the murder and pulled the victim's trousers down to make it look like a homosexual incident. The

Murder for money/financial gain **83**

accused is a stocky and very powerful man. In the witness box he showed very little sign of feeling except when he put forward the view that no one could ever impute homosexuality to him. The circumstances alone indicate to me that the accused would not be an appropriate candidate for any program for early release.

[Pre-sentencing psychology report]
When he recounted the offense, the writer felt that he was describing an everyday occurrence and not taking the life of another. He appears to be a reasonably intelligent street wise man who shows no remorse and has developed a totally distorted sense of right and wrong.

(*056cf1.2.2)

In the following examples the victim was a stranger. These murders often involved commercial locations and in one example an attack on the street. They also seemed to involve considerable violence as the perpetrator had to overcome the victim who most likely resisted the violence and attempted theft.

Firearm robbery/burglary of a factory – strangers
Three men plan a robbery of a factory using guns. This perpetrator (34) and his two co-accused, set up a robbery, in the course of which, he shoots the face off the factory owner (42) with a sawn-off shotgun. The co-accused are not happy about this as they are implicated. The perpetrator goes on the run for seven months, and one of the co-accused informs on him. At the trial he is found guilty of murder and robbery while the co-accused are found guilty only of the robbery.

(*274cf1.2.2)

Burglary/robbery in a hotel – staff member killed by strangers
Three men stab to death a hotel barman who tries to stop them from stealing money from the till.

[Context and murder]
At the time of the offense the perpetrator (17) had absconded from prison having escaped whilst in transit to the court. Prior to his imprisonment, he was single, unemployed and living with his mother and younger brother. The two-male co-accused were 19 and 20. The victim was 22, single and lived with his parents. He was employed as a barman in the hotel where the murder took place.

[The murder]
The perpetrator and two other youths entered the hotel around 10pm. The co-accused made a telephone call from a public telephone in the reception area, and the three men then left but returned about 11pm.

84 Murder for money/financial gain

The co-accused made another call and while doing so the perpetrator attempted to steal from behind the reception desk a handbag belonging to the manageress. She told them to leave the premises. At this stage the victim, who was a barman in the hotel, came from behind the bar into the foyer and stood beside the manageress. The perpetrator and the two-co-accused stood on the outer side of the glass door entry to the hotel while the manageress and the victim stood just inside the door in the hotel foyer itself. At this point, one of the co-accused was striking the door with his fist, and then produced and opened a knife. Behind him, the perpetrator was observed to make a movement suggesting that he too had a knife. Together, they rushed through the foyer and cornered the victim. The co-accused was observed trying to strike the victim while the perpetrator stabbed him on the body with the knife. Both men then ran away from the hotel.

[Trial judge]
The terms of the pre-sentencing probation report on the perpetrator suggested that he is presently out of control and this is reinforced by the nature and extent of his criminal record. While his involvement in the drug scene suggests this may explain to some extent the reckless and inexcusable conduct in which he indulged at the time of the crime. He had already shown a propensity to carry a knife and was obviously pre-pared to use it if he thought fit. These two factors make him, at present, a clear danger to the public at large. Any period of incarceration would require to be long enough to make certain that such danger is removed.'

*(*145cf1.2.2)*

Robbery and murder in a jewelry shop
This 36-year-old man kills the male owner (50) of a jewelry shop with a sawn-off shotgun in the midst of armed robbery.

*(*635cf1.2.2)*

Robbery and murder on the street
The perpetrator attempted to rob victim (jewelry shop owner) who was carrying a reasonable amount of jewelry. When the victim resisted, he stabbed him several times and made off with only a few second-hand watches.

*(*872cf1.2.2)*

The next robbery occurs in a very unusual location: a holiday campsite. Exceptionally, it involved the murder of a foreign tourist, and serious injuries to his wife and children. While the murderer sought to stress his political associations as important to the murder, this was probably unlikely. Instead it seemed to be an opportunistic attempt at robbery of a family that may have appeared to be affluent.

Firearm robbery and murder at a campsite – strangers

At a holiday campsite, a 53-year-old man robs and shoots a male tourist from a foreign country and attempts to murder his wife and two children.

[Context]
On the day of the offense the tourist family had spent the night in their campervan and were preparing to depart the campsite when the perpetrator approached the van carrying a .45 caliber revolver and a kitchen knife. He confronted the victim demanding money. When the victim attempted to speak to the perpetrator, he shot him twice, and then proceeded to shoot the victim's daughter, son, and wife and also stabbed her in the chest [they all survived]. The perpetrator claims IRA connections, and maintains he was trying to move explosives. He says he thought the victim was photographing him, and so asked him for money then shot and stabbed him, his wife and their two children.

[Trial judge]
In view of the unprovoked and sustained attack on an innocent family who were in the words of counsel 'in the wrong place', I consider that nothing less than two life imprisonments was appropriate in response to the charges of: murder, attempted murder, robbery and contravention of the Firearms Act. In making the recommendations as to the minimum period that should elapse before the accused was released (20 years), I was particularly influenced by the extreme brutality and violence of his conduct.

*(*129cf1.2.2)*

The above examples demonstrate that burglary and robbery vary across different types of relationships and can involve the use of considerable violence to subdue the victims in order to gain access to their money and/or goods. While some of these murders were not associated with the explicit intention to kill, the actual violence inflicted on the victim was usually brutal. In the next example recounted in one of our interviews, a young man describes his violent response to being disturbed in the home of a man during a burglary. The interview was particularly disturbing because the man appeared to revel in his marital arts response and skills using various and numerous serious blows to inflict fatal injuries. In claiming that his response was one of a man trained in the martial arts he clearly failed to understand and embrace the philosophy and discipline of the martial arts which emphasize mental and physical control and the use of the 'arts' in self-defense against stronger aggressors rather than attacks on the weak. He also failed to express any form of remorse or empathy and clearly lacked insight into his violent behavior.

Murder and the martial arts

Oh, it's so fucking crazy now! The guy (37) walks in and I'm (22) ransacking his bloody desk doors and stuff. I'm going through his stuff, in his living room. And I actually heard something, but I didn't know what he was doing – it never seemed to register with me. I just kept doing what I was doing and I heard him shouting. He's came at me and he's whacked us with a bottle. Now, by rights I should have been knocked unconscious and blood pouring out me but I don't know why but it wasn't. And I just – it didn't seem to go down, it didn't seem to register – what was registering was defend yourself properly. And I'll tell you what I distinctly remember of that night was, in my head I was hearing voices. Like it was like my commander, my instructor of karate would say the names of various punches, kicks, etc. – and it was actually as if it was him, I could hear – obviously it wasn't. But the next thing I know I've just exploded. I've threw – I know [because] it's on the Coroner's reports – and he said it was 7 or 8 punches landed, every one with extreme force. I reckon about 9 to the head and the body and the next thing the guy's spilled on the deck and that's it!! That's it literally. I never touched him again after that. And the man died. And he had 27 broken bones in his head – and all but one was various facial bones – and I had actually fractured a part of his skull, broken several ribs up each side and I cracked his sternum and his jaw, his cheekbone – I'd just exploded! I think everything that had been waiting to come out had just finally came out that night, it just went – bang!! And my whole body just went – I had been trained to such a level where that happened, some poor person, you know, somebody was really going to suffer and that's what happened. The guy died [NB: *not I killed him*]. He died from massive hemorrhaging inside due to his injuries that I'd taken off him.

(*293iv1.2.2*)

Subtype 2. Drug dealing, disputes and murder

The following subtype involving murder and money, is related to conflicts linked to drug dealing. The procurement, distribution, and sales of illegal and illegally acquired prescription drugs, is a multi-million-dollar industry spanning numerous countries, corrupting the lives of millions of citizens, and in some locations officials of the state. While not all drug dealing involves violence, contemporary and historical evidence suggests that it is a pervasive aspect of the illegal drug industry (European Monitoring Centre for Drugs and Drug Addiction, 2018). The world, especially Central America and the Caribbean, is replete with reports of violence, often lethal, committed by drug 'gangs' against citizens, members of other gangs, law enforcement agents, government officials and journalists. The violence reflects conflicts and disputes over territory, deals gone bad and attempts to impede or completely destroy the state's response to illegal activity. The extremely high rates of homicide in these areas are mostly driven by such violence.

This is aptly illustrated in innumerable popular films, books and American and British TV programs such as 'The Wire,' 'Breaking Bad,' and Netflix's, 'Narcos Mexico' and in the UK 'Top Boy.' Films such as 'No Country for Old Men,' 'Trainspotting,' 'Human Traffic,' 'Gomorrah and Blow' (actually too numerous to list) reflect the serious violence associated with drug dealing. Books include, for example, *A Brief history of seven killings* which portrays the extreme violence related to the illegal drug business in Jamaica. While these depictions may exaggerate the extent and nature of the violence, it is clear that the illegal drug business is implicated in many homicides across the world. While the majority of victims are male this is not always the case – as, for example, in Cuidad Juarez, Mexico where the murder of many women has been linked to drug cartels.

The cases considered here are examples of conflicts that are outside the reach of legal dispute resolution and criminal justice interventions. Of course, the issues they encompass are often encountered in legitimate businesses, such as, disputes over pricing, supply, delivery and distribution but in the legitimate world, resolution of contractual disputes do not generally lead to murder. While financial issues are central to the illegal drug market, it is also the case that more is involved in many of these violent encounters and murders. The perpetrator and the victim are often engaged in a contest of will and reputation, as in, 'no one can get one over on me,' 'no one treats me like a punk/mug and gets away with it.' Topalli and Wright (2015) interviewed street drug dealers who had experienced a theft and/or an assault from another dealer and asked how they responded to these crimes. None of the 'victims' mentioned the formal system of justice, rather they invoked personal justice. The dealers detailed various aspects of their responses. The first reaction was intense anger and the preferred response was 'direct violent retaliation.' The aims of these responses were reparation of their reputation, recovery of money or goods and vengeance. The main intention was 'getting even.' The dealers told the researchers, 'you live and die by your reputation' and you 'must maintain a street reputation.' Thus, the best response was violent retaliation. The cases presented here reflected these sentiments and while murder was the final outcome, in some cases there were attempts to recover 'goods' that failed. Below we provide representative examples of the violent 'settlement' of disputes within and across drug suppliers. In several ways, drug-dealing related murders are quite distinct. As the examples indicate the murders often involved more than one perpetrator, the violence was particularly brutal, and in some cases the perpetrators invested considerable effort in attempting to obliterate all evidence of the murder by destroying the bodies of the victims.

Two rival groups of drug dealers engage in a dispute
A 20-year-old heroin dealer, with five others, attacked rival drug dealers: one died (age 20) and two others were seriously injured but survived.

88 Murder for money/financial gain

[Context and circumstances]
Five days before the murder, the perpetrator and his drug dealing associates, with the 'enforcer', went to the house of the rival dealers and attacked them with baseball bats and a hammer. A few days later, the perpetrator and co-accused, under the pretense of walking with two of the rival drug dealers to a pub to discuss a trading dispute, lured the victims into an ambush, and four–six men attacked them with knives and baseball bats. The murder victim was struck with a bat, stabbed, and died. Trial judge regards all three [perpetrators] as equally culpable although there is evidence that the defendant stopped a passing police car and drew attention to the fatally injured victim.

[Psychologist report shortly after sentencing]
His story is that the victim and the other drug dealers pressured him to sell drugs for them. He did for a while, then refused to continue. There were various verbal and physical altercations due to this. He claims he was walking down the road when a group of men attacked him and another drug dealer [co-accused], and they ran in different directions. He claims he had nothing to do with the attack.
(★683cf1.2.5)

Welshing on a drug deal – failure to supply

[Context]
The perpetrator (age 22) gave the deceased (27) a large sum of money to buy cannabis and expected to receive the drugs on the same day. Instead, the victim failed to produce the drugs and did not return the money. During the few days that followed, the defendant made many attempts to obtain the money or the drugs but to no avail, and the victim avoided contact with him as time progressed. A few days later, the perpetrator spoke to his ex-girlfriend who had loaned him some of the money to buy the drugs, and told her that if he did not get either the drugs or the money, he might use a knife on him [victim].

[The murder]
The next day he went to a shop and bought the knife, and then went to where the victim lived. When the victim emerged from his flat with his common-law wife's young daughter, he demanded the money and told the victim he had a knife. The victim drove off but returned after delivering the child to school, and was again confronted by the perpetrator who stabbed him in the shoulder and in the back. The victim was trapped in an area from which he could not escape and tried to face the perpetrator. He was then stabbed in the groin and twice in the chest, one blow penetrating the heart. The perpetrator left and went to

Murder for money/financial gain **89**

[a local city], and later that evening went to hospital in a distressed state. The police were called and he was arrested.

[The victim and perpetrator]
Everybody was telling him [victim] to do something, but he was dithering. He knew the reputation of the perpetrator, and he feared him as many people did. The perpetrator says he didn't know what to do and felt harassed by others telling him to do something and not let him [victim] get away with it. He says, the victim threatened him with a stun gun and also threatened to do his younger brother. He followed him into a courtyard off the street and killed him.

(*245cf1.2.5)

The next cases represent the brutality of murders associated with drug dealing based disputes and the extensive and horrific attempts to destroy evidence by obliterating the body of the victim. This is especially the case in the last example where such efforts were carried out over a number of months.

Drug dispute – burning the body
The defendant with another, inflicted multiple stab wounds on the victim and set his body on fire. They are all drug dealers and the killing results from a drugs dispute.

(*724cf1.2.5)

Stealing drugs from a 'supplier,' murdered him, body never found
Drug dealer (25) and two co-accused, took a drug supplier (victim) out to a woodland with two others, stole the drugs, shot the victim, and *dismembered and buried the body which was never found.* The perpetrator had a history of supplying and dealing drugs but had few charges. He was travelling on a foreign passport at the time.

(*014cf1.2.5)

Two murders – victim failed to deliver – bodies dismembered and buried
Perpetrator (age 20) shoots an associate (24) involved in the illegal drug business and also kills his girlfriend. Killings related to large-scale ecstasy dealing – victim failed to deliver.

[Trial judge summary]
Male victim was a middleman between drug importers from another country. The perpetrator and his brother, co-accused, lured him to an isolated place and shot him with a borrowed shotgun. The perpetrator's girlfriend happened to come along and was also shot. *They then dismembered and burned their bodies on a bonfire.* The perpetrator was the instigator and leader and is a very dangerous man who was handcuffed in the dock

90 Murder for money/financial gain

because of the risk of violence and escape. He has many convictions and escaped from custody on three previous occasions. He had absconded from prison while on home leave at the time these crimes were committed. Both men are without morals and would plainly be likely to re-offend without compunction.

(*665cf1.2.5)

Drug deal, horrific murder and gruesome disposal of the body. This case is another example of drug dealing gone wrong. The victim was murdered in a horrific manner and his body disposed of in an attempt to erase all physical evidence of the murder. After many months the perpetrators were caught and tried and although the body was never recovered, a fragment of bone was found and used to establish the victim's identity. The perpetrators were sentenced to life with tariffs of many years. The main perpetrator was found guilty, appealed the conviction and the long sentence. The appeal was summarily dismissed.

Drug murder – attempt to completely obliterate all traces of the murder and dispose of the body by destroying all traces of the corpse

[Context]
The victim (35) was a drug dealer who acted as a link between the suppliers in two major cities. At the time of his death, the perpetrator (37) owed the victim a serious amount of money [£75,000] and he was short of money to pay off the debt. After a pre-arranged meeting, the victim was killed in the kitchen of the home of the co-defendant. The killing may have been pre-planned, the meeting certainly was. The means of death are not certain because of the disposal of the body.

[Murder]
He probably battered the victim with a hammer and choked him with an electric cord, there was certainly a violent struggle in which the victim was outnumbered

[After the murder]
The body was taken to a remote hillside and buried in a shallow grave. It was dug up and reburied in a concrete tomb for extra security and finally, the perpetrator alone incinerated the body in the concrete pit for many hours, the bones pulverized and reburied. Only a fragment of skull bone was ever recovered, this proved sufficient for DNA profiling. The killing would have been unsolved had not the co-accused gone to the police sometime later and told them of the burial which he claimed was his only part in the crime. He was at the time seeking a cash reward and a [supportive] letter from the police to a judge who was about to sentence him for drug offences. Perpetrator and second defendant blamed each

Murder for money/financial gain **91**

other for the murder. This man [main perpetrator] boasted of the scale of his drug dealing and six months prior to the murder had pleaded guilty to an offense of supplying 180 kilos of cannabis.

[Trial judge]
He is a long-term offender and informer and very greedy. I felt he was not wholly in touch with reality. The method of disposing of the body was chilling and recounted without a flicker of emotion.

[Previous offences]
35 including burglary, theft, handling stolen goods, drugs, insurance fraud plus rape of 16-year-old girl when he was 20.

(1001cf1.1.2.5)

Subtype 3. Criminal activity, 'share-outs' and murder

In the drugs and murder section, we analyzed cases involving murders that occurred in a context of money or resources in unlawful circumstances where both the perpetrator and the victim were usually implicated in criminal activities. Disputes related to 'share-outs' of money or goods associated with criminal activity, usually theft, do not make up many of the cases of murder for money, but such circumstances are not unusual. The following two examples illustrate these circumstances.

Illegal activity – money owed victim – dealt with by his murder
Three men, drug dealers and petty thieves, argued with the victim over proceeds from a scheme they ran together using stolen cars.

[Context]
The perpetrator (25) a drug user and petty thief, and two co-accused (male friends, age 20s) were in the perpetrator's flat which he shared with his co-habitant. There was an argument with the victim (27) who had turned up [just released from prison] seeking proceeds from thefts that had been part of illegal activity involving the three men stealing cars and using them to conduct raids on local premises.

[Murder]
The men moved outside. The perpetrator took a baseball bat and hit the victim on the back of the head. He then threw a television on his head while he lay on the ground. The three men brought him back in the house to give him a cup of coffee, but he was dead from 30–40 blows. They then put him in the boot of a car, and threw the body over a motorway bridge into a canal. Drugs and alcohol were problems outside and inside prison.

(*1067Cf1.2.5)

Two thieves dispute over money

A 22-year-old man kills a 27-year-old – they were partners in thieving and were having a dispute about stolen property.

[Murder]
It happened three weeks after their [near simultaneous] release from prison for crimes of conspiracy to abduct women, robbery and rape. The victim and perpetrator were partners in crime at one time, had a serious argument about the division of stolen property, and one of them killed the other.

(★702cf1.2.5)

Subtype 4. Personal debts, disputes and murder

Informal debts between individuals, often friends and relatives can sometimes become the focus of intense disputes involving issues: such as, denial of loan/debt; the size and nature of the original loan; schedule of repayment; and agreed date and method of repayment. Unlike the debts considered above, these debts were not associated with any illegal activity but, rather, were entered into in the course of normal informal business arrangements, personal loans, and the like. In the first case the perpetrator attempted to avenge a debt owed to his brother by killing his own friend. While the violence was particularly brutal it seems, the perpetrator was a relatively conventional man with a troubled background.

Murder of a friend related to informal business debt

Single man (22), killed a 22-year-old friend because of a business debt between his brother and the victim. The perpetrator was born in Pakistan where he had been tortured by police for his political beliefs, but when he was 19, he came to England as a political exile. His brother and the victim bought a cash-and-carry, which dissolved after a few months. There was an agreement to repay the original share to the brother of the perpetrator. The debt was being renegotiated, but was disputed. After meetings with the community elders the previous night, the perpetrator met his friend in an amicable fashion. Then a disagreement began in which the victim called the perpetrator's family names, and he (normally a peaceful man) went berserk and stabbed the victim 15 times (heart, armpit-lung, knee-artery, etc.) in front of 46 witnesses with a knife he had purchased earlier saying, 'I wonder what life is like in English prisons'? The perpetrator claims self-defense and that the victim started it by going to his car and pulling out a knife. He also claims [at the time] he was less able to handle stress because of his earlier experience of political torture. He expresses no remorse and blames the victim.

(★807Cf1.2.5)

Murder for money/financial gain **93**

An informal debt between friends, not paid and the perpetrator kills his friend in a casual − off handed manner. An attack that reflects a man familiar with violence.

The perpetrator (42) and victim (34) were friends. The victim owed the perpetrator money. The victim's partner had a baby and the perpetrator, the victim and their girlfriends go out for a drink to celebrate. The women went home, and the perpetrator [a hard man] asked the victim when he is getting his money back and says if not soon, he will have him beaten up. Perpetrator goes to the toilet and when he returns calls victim's partner a 'tart' and stabs and kills him.

(*117cf1.2.5)

Subtype 5. Gangs, conflict over control of territory and resources

The following cases involve violence intended to defend and expand territory linked to illicit and lawful activity. In the first example a gang seeks to expand its territory by murdering the leader of an opposing gang that controls the 'disputed' territory. In the second case the 'territory' includes two rival groups of bouncers engaged in a struggle to monopolize the lucrative business of security at a club. The first example demonstrates a rare type of murder in the UK, involving two organized gangs with one carrying out an intricately planned murder in an attempt to expand their territory and influence. It is particularly unusual because of the use of a firearm, extended conflict between two organized gangs across two major cities, and the context involving an explicit attempt to take over the territory of another gang in order to expand and monopolize a large-scale protection racket. The murder was planned and organized by the gang's leader, an apparently powerful individual who directed and probably intimidated a number of younger men who belonged to the gang. The leader planned the execution but as the judge said he 'did not pull the trigger,' rather using a sawn-off shotgun it was carried out by one of the other co-defendants. We interviewed one of the perpetrators who, before the murder, was, like all of the defendants, a relatively conventional young man with no history of criminal offending. When we interviewed him, he told one of us he played only a minor role in the killing, appeared to be very remorseful and noted − for him the murder happened because 'I Lost my focus.'

Territory − gangland killing

Gangland killing − Ethnic Chinese Protection Racket − five co-defendants − one interviewed for the research − what follows is from his casefile.

[Context]
An ethnic Chinese gang (probably Triad) from [Big City]) killed a member of rival Chinese gang. The deceased victim male (20), was shot in

his fish and chip shop with a sawn-off shotgun. Five co-accused – leader (age 28) of the gang did not pull the trigger. An additional four young men (ranging in age 16–19) were convicted under the 'joint enterprise' rule and sentenced to life imprisonment.

[Murder]

The leader gave precise instructions as to the manner in which the murder should be carried out. But the initial plan was not carried out when one of the co-defendants who was to carry out the shooting, lost his nerve. The gang leader then ordered another of the co-defendants to carry out the killing, which he did. After the murder the five men met up at a service station on the motorway. They all then went to ground, having hidden the car and buried the gun somewhere in the countryside. The gun was never recovered.

[Trial judge]

The leader and co-defendants initially claimed the victim had beaten up one of the younger members of the group and that the killing was in retaliation. As the trial progressed, it emerged that far from being a wholly disproportionate response to a fist fight, the killing was related to a much more sinister motive. It was alleged in the course of the trial that the gang leader intended to take over the Triad organization of the Chinatown of another [big city]. The killing was a move to impose [gang Leader's] prowess upon the local community and to 'bring down' the current [Big City] Triad bosses. The murder was, in fact, as I said in my sentencing remarks, a cold-blooded execution. The gang boss denied any Triad connection, all knowledge of the killing and all responsibility for it, whilst agreeing that he was present at the time of the proposed planning by the other defendants. He stuck to his story that the plan was to enter the chip shop and discharge the gun so as to frighten the victim, but claimed he had no knowledge that his car was to be used in the murder.

[Gang leader]

The leader was an older man and the brains and driving force behind the whole enterprise. There is no doubt that these other younger defendants were in awe of him. One co-defendant admitted that he had become a 'follower' of the gang leader in order to become a Triad member. The gang leader was fully prepared to enter into the work of building an expanded gang and has demonstrated himself to be a ruthless and capable criminal. In his case there is a high likelihood of future re-offending but it must be borne in mind that he, like all the other defendants, was a man of good character.

*(*883cf1.2.4)*

Before and during the period of the Murder Study there was an established although often unregulated, business in the provision of security at leisure locations in Britain, including pubs, clubs and strip clubs (for a definitive account see, Hobbs et al. (2003)). A burgeoning nighttime economy meant there was a need for regulation at such venues, particularly since they usually catered for intoxicated and violent young men and 'disorderly' women. Much research has been devoted to this development and the culture of regulation it created, particularly the orientations and behaviors of the bouncers who were hired to deal with 'trouble.' They acted as a police force which was not sanctioned to use violence. However, aggression and violence were central features of the actions and reputations of bouncers. While some doorman attempted to deal with disruptive, aggressive and usually intoxicated people without the use of force – violence was often employed. Indeed, bouncers needed to convey a reputation for using serious violence, which coupled with a formidable physique and commanding demeanor might deter aggressive patrons. This pattern of male behavior is deeply embedded in a culture of masculinity, particularly one that appreciates and admires aggression and violence coupled with heavy drinking. The culture of bouncers was generated from general and specific reputations and actions that were circulated in the nighttime economy. All of this was reinforced by the group culture of bouncers. While there is a considerable and long history of the use of 'guards' and 'stewards' at pubs and 'leisure' locations, these new 'businesses' involved the infiltration of existing and newly established 'gangs.' Competition for business was often fierce and resolutions of disputes between rival groups sometimes violent. Murders of a bouncer were rare, but violence was not and the following example presents the lethal outcome of an ongoing dispute regarding a contract to provide security at a pub.

Criminal gangs fight for 'contracts' as 'doormen' – security guards at a pub

[Context]
The perpetrator (32), fueled by alcohol and drugs, stabbed a doorman (age 39) during a brawl in retaliation for a previous violent incident between the perpetrator's brother and the victim which had been followed by threats to the perpetrator. While this may have been a personal dispute it most likely also involved competition for the security business at a pub.

[Murder]
When the perpetrator's party was excluded from the nightclub, a row erupted. The perpetrator was struck by a doorman at whom a bottle had been thrown (although not thrown by perpetrator), and a scuffle ensued between the doormen and the defendant's allies. The perpetrator and victim were not involved in the scuffle, but the perpetrator drew

96 Murder for money/financial gain

a knife and stood waiting. It was a vicious 'throwing' knife, which he either brought to the scene or acquired from someone there [he said in our interview it was given to him there]. The victim approached him, unarmed, and was deliberately stabbed in the stomach. The perpetrator then stabbed the original doorman in the buttock.

[Trial judge]
Both the perpetrator and the victim had substantial criminal records. The victim was on bail for affray [fight] at the time of his death but his other convictions were over ten years old. The jury had been given evidence (by defense) of a series of club/pub-based episodes of violence involving rival groups of bouncers. I doubt whether the defendant's presence at the club/pub on the fatal night was 'chance' – his brother had been ousted from control of the club's security. The killing and the accompanying [stabbing] of another doorman appear to have been part of an ongoing culture of violence imported from [Two Big Cities] where both men originated. It has some connection with control of 'door security' in clubs/pubs. This defendant is part of a criminal clan but is not, on his record, habitually violent.

(*1097cf1.2.5)

Subtype 6. Unlawful activity, disputes with officials and murder

These cases represent examples of the murder of government officials who were investigating and attempting to enforce legal orders of local and national agencies. The perpetrators were engaging in unlawful activity. In one case the use of unlawful certificates for carrying out motor vehicle inspections (MOTs) and in the other the perpetrator had unlawfully erected buildings that were the subject of a demolition order. In these cases, it was clear that the murders were linked to resentment, hatred and an intention to kill based on a long-standing sense of victimhood. The two examples illustrate the responses of men who held grievances against institutional authority, felt they had been victimized and targeted those who were attempting to enforce the law. The cases are explored in some detail, demonstrating the responses of men who knew they were acting illegally, but refused to accept the government decisions regarding those activities and carried-out deliberate violence with explicit intentions to kill. Both cases involved the use of a firearm, which is rare in Britain.

Auto repair shop owner shoots and kills two government officials

[Context]
This garage owner (32) killed two MOT (Ministry of Transport) inspectors (56 and 28) who were visiting his [car repair] garage to investigate

irregular uses of MOT certificates. He had connections with four other similar garages, one went into liquidation and the MOT authorization [for testing cars for safety, road worthiness, etc.] was withdrawn from the relevant garage. Upon a query from the MOT office, a certificate was produced from one of the other garages that did not apply to the one in question. The perpetrator was enraged by the Inspectors investigations and wrote an aggressive letter through his solicitor. Two inspectors visited his garage in order to investigate the legality of the certificate. After considerable planning, he waited for them to arrive and enter his office where he was heavily disguised [Halloween mask and dark clothing] and, from a distance of two feet, shot and killed both inspectors in the head with a sawn-off shotgun.

[Trial judge]
The witnesses were clearly terrified of him. While apparently of good character, it's clear the defendant is a frightening man with ready access to guns. He had earlier gone with weapons with another person (now prosecution witness) to the Department of Transport Office intending to fire at the officials' cars in order to frighten them off. He showed no remorse or regret. In my view, he is an exceptionally dangerous man who can kill two persons in those circumstances in cold blood and after considerable planning simply because they were performing their duties as civil servants. Many of the witnesses spoke of the fear they felt from the defendant, and none of the principle witnesses initially told the truth, each [eventually] saying that they failed to do so through fear of the defendant and his associates. Before and during the trial he attempted to intimidate witnesses, and a contract was taken out on the main witness. During the trial, a handgun and ammunition were found in the Prison [in which he was being held], and it was suspected that it was there in order to facilitate his escape.

*(*615cf1.2.5)*

This murder of an agent of the government was notorious and related to a long-running dispute between a property owner and the local authority which was the focus of national public and media attention. While the type of dispute – regarding the erection of a building on private property without consent – is probably not all that unique, its resolution ending in murder certainly was. For various reasons, the entire context and actual murder are very unique, first because the perpetrator was an apparently conventional citizen with no known history of violence or criminal convictions and because it involved the use of a firearm resulting in the death of one person and serious injuries to two others. Coincidently, we obtained information from both the casefile of this man and through an interview with one of us. At interview, he proved to be a very forceful and obsessional man who believed his violence was justified, this after a considerable period

98 Murder for money/financial gain

of time in prison. The interview which began with an interrogation of the interviewer 'You a psychiatrist, psychologist, Mason, Jew' was difficult, but revealing. The following while informed by the interview is based on casefile information.

Dispute over illegal construction of buildings and murder

Murder in the context of a dispute over the perpetrator's construction of illegal buildings resulting in the murder of local authority [county] official. This 52-year-old man kills district council (46) [local government] planning officer and shoots a policeman and TV cameraman in a one-off incident after a long-running dispute over the construction of illegal buildings.

[Context]
A number of years prior to the murder the perpetrator acquired land in a local beauty spot located in a protected area. He then proceeded to erect outbuildings comprising workshops, greenhouses and a garage, together with a static caravan. A few years later he commenced building a dwelling on the land which he referred to as his 'summerhouse' and had stated his intention of taking up residence in it with his elderly mother and brother. He subsequently became involved in a long-running dispute regarding the prohibited construction of two of these buildings for which he had not obtained building permits. While he claimed no premeditation, he had been threatening violence to the local authority and its officers for some months. He had prepared firearms and ammunition in advance to use if the enforcement order went ahead. After the murder a search of his property revealed 'massive' quantities of unlawful firearms, ammunition and component parts of firearms. The long-running dispute had obtained local and even national notoriety and on the day in question a considerable number of his supporters had gathered and the incident was recorded by BBC and local authority camera crews.

[Murder]
At a public enquiry the council requested the removal of the buildings and the request was granted. After an additional prolonged and involved dispute the local authority instigated an enforcement notice in order to demolish the buildings. The perpetrator was on site when council officials and building contractors arrived to demolish the buildings. After a short discussion between the perpetrator and the solicitor instructed by the council, preparations were made for demolition contractors to forcibly enter the site with machinery. As the machinery moved in, he retired to the caravan [trailer] on his land and returned armed with a .455 Enfield Revolver with which he proceeded to shoot the council official in the chest. He died instantly. He then fired at the solicitor

representing the local authority intending to kill him but seriously wounded a cameraman and police officer. He also shot up vehicles. He then discharged two further shots into the council officers' body, one in the chest and the other into the brain. In all, he fired a total of 26 shots at people and vehicles he connected with the local authority. Criminal charges included: murder, attempted murder, two charges of wounding with intent – convicted of all four.

(*1182cf1.2.5)

Subtype 7. Contract to kill

While contract killings are the focus of much fictional representation and public fascination, reliable evidence from the US suggests they account for no more than 5% of all homicides and are often related to attempts to obtain insurance money. Evidence collected in our Murder Study revealed very few such killings. In most cases these were murders of a woman intimate partner of a man who wished to eliminate her in order, for example, to profit from the proceeds of her life insurance and/or because she was an impediment to his affair with another woman. The following example taken from one of our interviews involved a perpetrator who told us he was reluctant to kill but was pressurized by a husband to kill his wife but resulted in the murder of the woman and her adult son. The second case while involving a contract to assault two men did not result in their murder but rather the murder of the two hired killers who failed to complete the contract.

> ### Contract to kill a wife, but also killed her adult son (perpetrator age 30)
> *So, tell me what happened?* It was a contract killing. And what happened was there was a fella I was working with, and I mean he had the lot on me [burglary and robbery], he knew about us, and, he wanted to get rid of his wife (48). He tried to kill her before but he come to me and offered me money and I've tried for about four months to put him off. But, in the end because he had that much on me, I gave in, and sure enough I done it.
>
> *No!* Never committed violence of any sort, and as I say, when I actually committed the murder, it wasn't like doing it was myself, it was like an out of body experience really, because it wasn't like I was pulling the trigger, it was like someone else was doing it and I was standing there watching it. *You were distanced from it?* Yeah. That's how it seemed, I've never used a gun before, although I'd had one. And, so you feel that detached, well it's not like a hands-on thing, like where you strangle someone, you are detached from it because you are using something to do it for you. *How much money did he offer you?* He offered me £20,000 but no money ever changed hands. He'd offered the money cause he was having an affair with a woman.

100 Murder for money/financial gain

So, it happened at night? Yeah, about half eight in October. Went to the house, I was supposed to be taking some stuff round there, and, what happened was his son (age 26) was there. Because it was two murders, it wasn't one, it was two murders, he wasn't supposed to be there, but he was. *Right.* So, I got into the house, I had a shotgun in a bag, and, it was a sawn-off. I went to the house; the son was messing with a radio and he was leaning down on the floor looking at the radio and I shot him. I shot him first and then his wife, I shot her. After that, got in my car, stopped on a bridge and slung the gun in the river and then I drove down to see him [husband who contracted the murders] at our place of work.

I went in and said, look it's done, so he knew what had happened. And, what happened he went home and he found the bodies, so he phoned the police, they thought it was a burglary gone wrong, they didn't have a clue. He was staying with his friend, so he'd let out inadvertently what had happened thinking that his friend would be okay. And his friend was frightened, panicked, went straight to his solicitor, solicitor got onto the police. And I got arrested two weeks later. When they arrested me, he'd already made statements, it was like an open telephone book, that was it, the game was up.

And did he get charged with murder as well? Yeah. *And you both got convicted?* Yeah. *And what were you thinking, feeling at the time? When it happened?* I just didn't think I could do it, I'll be honest I didn't think I could do it, even right up to the moment when I went in the house, I still didn't believe I could go through with it especially when I knew there was two people there, there was only supposed to be one. And it didn't dawn on me until afterwards that he'd put his son there to be shot. *So, he manipulated the situation?* Well of course, yeah, he did. His son knew he was having an affair. I mean this come out at the trial, a lot come out at the trial that I didn't half know about, as I say when he tried to kill his wife before she'd already sworn out an affidavit to a solicitor saying, if anything happened to me it was down to my husband. He [her son] should never have been at the house but he put his son there to kill his family in one swoop, and then he's free to do what he wants to do.

(*830iv1.2.9)

Murder about a fence

The murders described below involved a contract to assault two neighbors because of a dispute over a fence. The contract was *NOT* carried out and the perpetrator who ordered the assaults killed the 'contractors' for failure to complete.

[Context]

The perpetrator (37) paid two men to beat up his two male neighbors over a dispute about a fence between their houses. He had made an advance payment of £3,000 but the contract was not fulfilled and the money not returned.

[Background and circumstances]
The perpetrator with his girlfriend bought a house and two years later, two gay men (partners) bought the house next door. Initially relations were good, but they became acrimonious due to an argument about a garden fence which was blown down in a storm. The neighbors paid to have it re-erected, but he disapproved of the standard of work and felt it encroached on his property. He dismantled the fence. This led to court proceedings, and the neighbors sought an injunction to keep him and his girlfriend off their property. The court ordered the perpetrator to pay damages and costs totaling a fairly large amount – £25,000. He was unhappy about this, didn't pay, and consulted solicitors with a view to taking proceedings against original solicitors for negligence. He and his girlfriend sold the property, their relationship broke down, he was bitter and confided in a friend that he wanted the neighbors 'slapped'. The friend got him the phone number of a man who could do the job.

[Murder]
He met the two men (eventual victims 25, 32), arranged to have them beat up the neighbors, and paid a cash deposit in advance, but they did not carry out the attack and he demanded his money back. The evidence suggests that the victims were in fear of their lives during the month of the murder. [They changed their phone number], installed security lights, tried to get a loan to repay the advance, and asked their women partners to leave the house with no explanation of why. He went to the housing estate where the two men lived and killed them at close range with a sawn-off shotgun while they were sitting in a car outside the house of one of the victims.

[Trial evidence]
He blamed his neighbors for causing the souring of his relationship with his girlfriend and the loss of contact with his daughter [court ordered]. His girlfriend describes him as very uptight, stubborn, couldn't argue with him as he thought he was always right, and couldn't accept someone else's view [orientations frequently displayed in prison].

*(*619cf)*

Comparisons of Money.Murders and Other.Murders

The 81 murders examined in this chapter were generally motivated by the desire to illegally obtain money and/or resources primarily through burglary and theft.

102 Murder for money/financial gain

Some involved settling disputes regarding resources and commodities such as drugs. Comparisons of the Money.Murders and Other.Murders are shown in Table 3.1 and suggest important similarities and differences between these groups of murderers (significant differences are identified by a single asterisk★ in the text with precise levels shown in the table).

Backgrounds and relationships between perpetrators and victims

The average age of the men in both groups was almost identical (27 for Money-Murderers vs 28 for Other.Murderers). Victims were much older and similar in age (42 vs 40). Perpetrators in both groups were about equally likely to be unemployed at the time of the murder (66% vs 74%). Murders associated with money were significantly more likely to involve a stranger than was the case in all Other.Murders (41% vs 23%★). As the qualitative evidence suggests, burglary and robbery, which constituted a significant proportion of the financially based murders, were often perpetrated against strangers.

Conflict, disputes and previous violence

Ongoing disputes between the perpetrator and the victim were much less apparent in the money group than in Other.Murders (19% vs 32%★). Confrontations at the time of the murder, involving, for example, an argument and verbal and physical aggression, were also significantly more likely in the Other.Murders (47% vs 60%★). However, confrontations occurred in about one-half of all the Money murders. The comparisons also reveal that the levels of previous violence between the perpetrator and victim in both comparison groups, while different, was very low, especially among the Money group (5% vs 12%). There was a similar level for previous violence by the victim against the perpetrator (4% vs 12%). The very low levels in the money group reflect the fact that many (41%) of the men they killed were strangers.

Drinking, drunkenness drugs

While a reasonable proportion of the perpetrators in both types had been drinking on the day of the murder this was significantly less likely for the men who murdered in a context involving monetary motives (44% vs 73%★), but what was similar were the levels of drunkenness. If drinking, perpetrators in both comparison groups were equally likely to have been drunk at the time (72% vs 74%). Although victims in the money type were significantly less likely to have been drinking before the murder (34% vs 50%★), if they were drinking, they were about equally likely as Other.Murders to be drunk (64% vs 73%). Around one-third of the victims in both categories had been drinking with the perpetrator before the murder. Drinking in moderation seems unusual among these men and the evidence indicates that both types had spent considerable amounts of time drinking on the day of the murder, ranging from three hours to all day (65% vs 58). The data further suggest a similar pattern for the victims. On the day, drugs had been used by a reasonable proportion of men in both groups (22% vs 19%).

Murder event

The home of the victim was less likely to be the location of Money.Murders than Other.Murders (31% vs 55%*). Fewer than half involved only 'one perpetrator' (41% vs 61%*), and most were not witnessed by anyone apart from the other perpetrators involved in the murder (69% vs 57%*). The group element of Money. Murders is shown in the narrative accounts, and involved friends, associates, and accomplices most of whom joined together in a robbery. Strong emotions such as 'anger, rage and indignation' were significantly less likely among Money.Murders than Other.Murders (25% vs 43%*), which might be expected as these murders involved the relatively 'cool business' of theft rather than the 'hot emotions' associated with some other types of murder.

Cause of death

Most of the murderers involved five or more injuries (69% vs 71%), and the most likely 'cause of death' was by stabbing (43% vs 48%), followed by beating with an object or instrument (18% vs 17%), and beating with hands and feet (13% vs 17%). While the use of firearms is relatively rare in Britain, it is notable that Money. Murders were more likely than Other.Murders to involve 'shooting' (17% vs 9%). Again, the larger percentage of deaths caused by shooting in murders related to money (along with the 'cooler' emotions of the perpetrators) no doubt reflect the more 'business-like' nature of these murders.

Other offenses

Another distinctive element of Money.Murders is the large percentage that involved the commission of another offense in addition to the murder (68% vs 32%*), almost all of them were thefts (91% vs 48%*) Table 3.1.

Summary and conclusions

Most male–male murders involving money or financial gain were burglaries or robberies. While nearly half of the perpetrators were drinking at the time of the murder (and most of those who were drinking were drunk), this pattern was much less likely among Money.Murders than Other.Murders (44% vs 73%*). In addition to thefts, other financial issues at stake involved failures to repay a debt,

104 Murder for money/financial gain

TABLE 3.1 Murder Event. Money.Murders and Other.Murders

MALE–MALE MURDER	*Money.Murders*	*Other.Murders*
	n = 81 (%)	*n* = 343^ (%)
BACKGROUND		
– Age:		
– Perpetrators	27 yrs	28 yrs
– Victims	42 yrs	40 yrs
– Unemployed at murder	66%	74%
RELATIONSHIP BETWEEN PERPETRATOR and VICTIM		
– Stranger	41%	23%★
CONFLICTS and DISPUTES		
– Ongoing Dispute	19%	32%★
– Confrontation at Murder	47%	60%★★
– Prev.viol: Perp.against.victim	05%	12%
– Prev.viol.:Victim against.perp	04%	12%★
DRINKING and DRUGS		
– Perp. Drugs	22%	19%
– Perp. Drinking	44%	73%★★★
– if perp. drinking, Drunk	72%	74%
– Drinking 3–6hrs	42%	37%
– Drinking all day	23%	21%
– if Vic. Drinking	34%	50%★★
– if vic. drinking, Drunk	64%	73%
– of those drinking, drink tog.:	32%	29%
MURDER EVENT		
– Home of victim	31%	55%★★★
– One perpetrator	41%	61%★★★
– No Witness	69%	57%★
– Perpetrator [anger, rage, indignant]	25%	43%★★
– Injuries = 5 + injuries	69%	71%
CAUSE of DEATH		
– Strangle	09%	07%
– Stab	43%	48%
– Beat w/object/instrument	18%	17%
– Beat w/hands/feet	13%	17%
– Shot	17%	09%

OFFENSE/s		
Murder + 2nd offense (yes)	68%	32%★★★
– if 2nd offense: 'property offense':	91%	48%★★★

statistically significant: *p < .05, **p < .01, ***p < .001
^ numbers vary when: (not applicable) and/or (missing data)

and other financial disputes. Some perpetrators rationalized their use of violence because of financial exchanges gone wrong, a sense of having been 'cheated' or 'bested' that 'justified' some form 'retribution' that 'justified' their act of murder. Strangers were more likely to become the victims of Money.Murders and while more than one perpetrator may have been involved, these murders often differed from Confrontational.Murders where additional perpetrators seemed to be providing support or encouragement – acting as a 'chorus' in the violence. In some cases, the additional offense of burglary appeared to be the main stimulus for the lethal actions of the perpetrator/s. Lethal violence may have been used as the perpetrator responded to being interrupted during a burglary. In such circumstances, the perpetrator may have seen the victim as an irritant to be dealt with through violence or violence may have been used to eliminate a witness to his theft. The exception to this pattern of 'circumstantial' murders, were the disputes and murders associated with drug dealing and legal activities regulated by the state where the perpetrator objected to government interference in his affair. In these cases, it was clear that the principle intention was murder. While we considered the similarities across the seven subtypes one of the very strong and important differences was associated with the aftermath of drug-related murders where, exceptionally the perpetrators sometimes acted in an extremely deliberate manner when attempting to eliminate all evidence of the killing by disposing of weapons and obliterating the body of the victim.

References

Block, R. L. and Block, C. R. (1991). Beginning with Wolfgang: An agenda for homicide research. *Journal of Crime and Justice*, 14, 31–70.

Brookman, F., 2005. *Understanding Homicide*. Thousand Oaks, CA: Sage.

Brookman, F., Mullins, C., Bennett, T., and Wright, R., 2007. Gender, motivations and accomplishment of street robbery in the United Kingdom. *Criminology*, 47, 861–884.

Catalano, S., 2010. Special report: Victimization during household burglary. Bureau of Justice Special Report, US Department of Justice, Office of Justice Program, Bureau of Justice Statistics. Washington, DC.

Elkin, M. (2017) Overview of burglary and other household theft: England and Wales. Office for National Statistics, Crime and Justice, statistics@ons.gov.uk [Accessed August 12, 2019].

European Monitoring Centre for Drugs and Drug Addiction, 2018. Drug-related homicide in Europe: A first review of the data and literature, EMCDDA Papers, Publications Office of the European Union, Luxembourg.

106 Murder for money/financial gain

Hobbs, D. Hadfield, P., Lister, S., and Winlow, S., 2003. *Bouncers, Violence and Governance in the Night Time Economy*. Oxford: Oxford University Press.

Levi, M. and Maguire, M., 2002. Violent crime. In M. Maguire, R. Morgan, and R. Reiner (eds.) *The Oxford Handbook of Criminology* (3rd edition). Oxford: Oxford University Press.

Miethe, T. D. and Drass, K. A., 1999. Exploring the social context of instrumental and expressive homicides. *Journal of Quantitative Criminology*, 15 (1), 1–15.

Tedeschi, J. T. and Felson, R. B. (1994). *Violence, Aggression and Coercive Actions*. Washington DC: American Psychological Association.

Topalli, V. and Wright, R., 2015. Drug dealers, robbery, and retaliation, vulnerability, deterrence and contagion of violence. *British Journal of Criminology*, 42 (2), 337–351.

U.S. Department of Justice, 2012. Crimes in the US: Offenses charged, Table 42. FBI, Uniform crime report.

4

MURDER BETWEEN MEN IN THE FAMILY

In many ways, the family and the wider kinship network resemble a microcosm of the wider society in terms of the diversity of members by age, generations, and gender but also in terms of the nature and complexity of interpersonal relations, emotional attachments, competition, conflicts, love, affection, hatred and violence. Within the family, murders between males have long been depicted in myths, religious texts, plays, novels, music and art. Fathers kill sons, sons kill fathers, brothers kill one another, and so do cousins and brothers-in-law, and sometimes brothers band together to kill outsiders of whom they disapprove. Stories of conflicts between junior and senior members of families include the killings of grandfathers or fathers that are likened to the killing of a king with the obvious differences in hierarchical status of the men along with conflicts about wealth, property, and other issues of importance to both sides of the generational divide.

Conflicts between similar aged family members, particularly brothers and male cousins, have also been the subject of legend, myth and popular literature, with accounts of brothers killing brothers, murders between envious and aggrieved siblings, and killings related to feuds between families have been told for all time and in virtually every country in the world. These stories often mirror real-life conflicts, violence and murder within the complex world of family relations, and we will refer to a few of them as we examine real-life cases of Family Murders. One murder between brothers has famously been portrayed in the Biblical story of Cain and Abel, the first sons of Adam and Eve. It is a story of sibling rivalry and jealousy between brothers in which Cain kills his brother Abel, and is then exiled by God to the land of Nod and a life of wandering. In Genesis, Cain was the first human to be born and Abel was the first human to die. It is a moral tale about sibling jealousy, rivalry, and violence, as well as a tale about punishment for the first act of murder.

(*Cain and Abel*, the first murder)

108 Murder between men in the family

In everyday life, conflicts and disputes within the family are often intense. Issues of power and authority may characterize contests and struggles between older and younger men when grandfathers, fathers or uncles attempt to direct, manage, control, correct or chastise younger men within the family unit. Younger men may challenge such efforts, and view them as inappropriate or completely unacceptable. They may fight to assert their independence and deny the authority of the older male relative be he a grandfather, father, uncle, or older brother. Patricide (the killing of one's father), or other 'senior' male relative involves hierarchies of age and status, with associated claims of authority and corresponding acts of control embodied in notions about the relationships between such members. Even when there is no hierarchy of the old against the young, brothers and cousins of similar age and status may compete with one another, and disputes about any number of things may spiral out of control and become lethal.

Main patterns – men murder men in the family

Of the 424 male–male murders, 72 cases (17%) were in the family. We use the term family in a broad sense including the immediate family of grandparents, fathers, mothers, children including step-children, siblings and other kin. We also include those related by marriage or cohabitation, and same-sex intimate relationships. Using the quantitative evidence from the Murder Study, we first illustrate the 'main patterns' associated with the 72 murders committed by men against other men within the context of the family, then turn to the qualitative accounts from the case-files and interviews in order to illustrate the nature and diversity of these murders. What kind of murders occur within and between families? Who is involved? What is happening? And why? In addressing these questions, we first present the 'main patterns' that characterize all 72 male–male murders committed within the context of the family. Then, we use textual accounts to illustrate the nature and diversity of these murders which we have classified into five subtypes of family murders. Lastly, we return to all 72 Family Murders and compare them with 'Other.Murders' that did not involve the family and consider how they are alike and how they differ.

Background and relationship between perpetrators and victims

At the time of the murder, the average age of perpetrators was 29 years, and the average of their victims was 40. The majority of perpetrators were unemployed (60%).

Conflicts, disputes and previous violence

Slightly less than half of the family murders (46%) involved an ongoing dispute between the perpetrator and the victim, and two-thirds of these disputes were long-standing. A few cases (15%) involved previous violence by the perpetrator against the victim, and 21% involved previous violence by the victim against the perpetrator. Some were 'collateral murders' in which a male victim was killed while protecting a woman from domestic violence. This included fathers protecting their daughters, male neighbors, and new male partners.

Drinking, drunkenness and drugs

At the time of the murder, 71% of perpetrators and 51% of the victims had been drinking, and the majority of them were drunk. Only 14% of the perpetrators were on drugs.

Murder event

Most family murders (81%) took place in the family home or the separate residences of the victim or the perpetrators. There was usually only one perpetrator (78%), and no witnesses (72%). The majority (63%) involved five or more injuries. Half of the men (51%) were described as angry, enraged or indignant when they committed the murder.

Cause of death

The most usual case of death was by stabbing (54%), followed by beating with an object (17%) and shooting (16%). Few were beaten with hands and feet (9%), and strangling was rare (4%). and no other offense was usually involved, although about 20% of the murders of family members also involved some form of theft.

Other offenses (in addition to murder)

Only 30% of these murders involved a second offense, and 71% of them involved a property offence (Table 4.1 Murder Event. Family.Murders and Other.Murders).

In brief, most family murders were committed by one man against a single victim in the context of a confrontation at the time of the murder, and often against a backdrop of previous disputes, most long-standing. A few family murders involved previous violence by the victim against the perpetrator, and *vice versa*. The majority of perpetrators and half of the victims had been drinking at the time, and most of them were drunk. Most family murders took place in the victim's home, and stabbing was the usual cause of death.

Family murders between men – five subtypes

The following murders committed by men against other men within the context of the family illustrate different relationships between the perpetrators and their

110 Murder between men in the family

victims, the diversity of the contexts and circumstances at the time of the murders, the dynamic elements as the murder events unfold, and details of these murders including the nature of the attacks and the type of injuries. In dealing with this diversity, we grouped these murders into five subtypes. For those within the family, we begin with the closest family relations involving murders between men *related by blood*. Within the context of marital relationships, we examine murders between male intimate partners or cohabitants. *Collateral murders* involve conflicts that begin with issues between men and women partners but end with the murder of a man who may be her father, brother, or another man acting as her 'protector,' or a man who becomes her new male partner. *Feuds within and between families* can be complex, long-standing, involve the killing of many individuals, and last for years. Finally, we examine murders involving *brothers who band together* to kill an outsider they view as having caused some offense or belongs to a group against whom they are prejudiced. Elsewhere, we have examined cases from the Murder Study that involve the murder of children (Cavanagh, Dobash and Dobash, 2005, 2007; Dobash and Dobash, 2018), but for another approach to classification of family homicides, see Liem and Koenraadt, (2018). Here, our focus is only on murders involving males who are aged 16 and older.

> Family murders between men – five subtypes
> 1   Blood relatives
> 2   Gay intimate partners
> 3   Collateral intimate partner murders – male victims
> 4   Family feuds and feuding families
> 5   Brothers against others.

Subtype 1. Blood relatives

We begin at the 'top' of the family tree when the oldest men in the family, grandfathers, are murdered by their grandsons, then move down the family tree to include fathers killing sons, sons killing fathers, and brothers killing brothers. In many cultures, grandfathers traditionally occupy a position of some reverence and respect by virtue of their age and status as the oldest men in the family, and reverence and respect usually remain even when they are diminished by extreme age or infirmity, and often in spite of flaws in character or previous bad behavior toward family members or others. While a grandfather may be respected, revered and loved by some, others may view him as just an old man, or a person with money or possessions that might be stolen with ease by a younger relative who, by virtue of their relationship, can freely come and go within his house, rifle through his wallet or steal his bankbook. A grandfather may be viewed as having valuable assets that might be taken and sold, food and alcohol that might be consumed, or a house that might be used for parties or occupied without the permission of the 'old man' and/or in opposition to his wishes.

Grandsons kill grandfathers

This grandfather was killed when he accused his grandson of stealing from him, and this was compounded by the fact that the grandson had, without permission, been using his grandfather's house as a place to stay over the Christmas holiday.[1]

Grandson kills his grandfather

A grandfather is robbed by his grandson who beats him beyond recognition and leaves his body under the bed for six days during which time he returns to the house and sleeps with his girlfriend on the sofa in the living room while his grandfather is lying dead in the bedroom. The 19-year-old man who was homeless, unemployed, and living rough, killed his 77-year-old grandfather who accused him of stealing his money. He beat his grandfather with the butt of a gun until his face could not even be identified when the body was discovered by a social worker six days later. During that time, he returned to the house a few times, once to tie up the body, and another time to sleep overnight with his girlfriend.

[Murder – Statement to police]
I went to my grandfather's house on Christmas probably around 10pm. We sat and talked for about half an hour, then he started playing hell with me. It was about myself. I was supposed to have stolen some of his money, and he was shouting and I got mad and told him to sit down but he wouldn't, so I got up and I hit him with my gun. I just kept hitting him, I don't know how many times. The gun butt broke. I kept hitting him on the head. He fell down on the carpet, and there was a lot of blood about. He was unconscious but I didn't know whether he was dead or not, so I left him lying on the carpet and I left the house. I went back the next norming and he was still lying there, so I tied his hands and his feet and I put something around his mouth. I used some of his ties to tie him up. Then I took him in the bedroom. I put him under the bed. There was some blood on the television, so I covered it up with some newspaper. I left after this. I have been back a few times since. The last time was New Year's Eve morning.

[After the murder]
The body was not found for six days, and was only discovered when a social worker who tried to visit became concerned and alerted the police. The body couldn't be facially identified because of the extensive head injuries. A twenty-year-old witness [the perpetrator's girlfriend] said that two days after the murder she had spent the night with the killer at his grandfather's house but that they slept on the settee and didn't go into the bedroom.

112 Murder between men in the family

[Pre-trial report]
He was completely remorseless and had no contrition. In general, from his manner and behavior, I could sense a disguised and hidden arrogance. He is an irresponsible, immature, insouciant man, evincing psychopathic traits and unable to profit from experience.

(★641cf1.2)

The next grandfather was a man of faith and a highly respected member of the community who was trying to assist his grandson overcome an addiction to alcohol, who became resentful and enlisted a male relative to help him kill his grandfather. The family was part of a wider faith community that respected their elders and did not believe in drinking alcohol. The violation of these and other fundamental principles of the community was so extreme that the trial judge expressed concern should, at some future date, he be released from prison.

A grandfather who was trying to assist his grandson overcome an addiction to alcohol was strangled by his grandson and another male member

In a premeditated attack, a 27-year-old man and his male relative strangled his 75-year-old grandfather, a highly respected man in the community who was trying to assist his grandson to overcome alcoholism.

[Context]
The perpetrator had been married for four years but the relationship had broken up because of threats to his wife and his problem with alcohol. He had twice failed as an in-patient at a local alcohol addiction unit, and went to stay with his grandfather who was very supportive of him. In trying to help, his grandfather took a strict approach to his recovery that included monitoring his visits to the doctor and ensuring that he took his prescribed medications. He also tried to monitor his movements and stop him seeing friends who might give him alcohol or encourage him to drink. He deeply resented his grandfather's efforts, particularly when he managed to get alcohol and was drunk.

[Murder]
On the morning of the murder, his grandfather took him to the doctor who was treating him for alcoholism. Later that day, he and a male relative, both got drunk, planned to kill the grandfather. They went to his home, strangled him to death, stripped his body and put it in a large hold-all. Afterwards, they returned to a park where they had been drinking and tried to get the help of a taxi driver to get rid of the body. They both continued drinking, and in the evening the perpetrator reported to another man that his grandfather was sick and that he wished the police to be called.

Murder between men in the family **113**

[He said]
Over time, he made several different statements beginning with, 'The police said it was premeditated which I deny. It was an accident'. Sometime later, he declared, 'I think God made me do it'.

[Trial judge]
The strange feature of this case is that the *Sikh's customary respect for elders* was overcome in both men so that they attacked the grandfather. When their release comes to be considered, it seems to me that the feelings of the Sikh community about a case of this kind are of great importance. It was a brutal attack upon an elder, intending to kill him. Respect for elders is, I understand, a strong tenet of Sikh ethics. Moreover, it was *premeditated* under the influence of drink and Sikhs, as I understand, deplore alcohol.

(*612cf1.2.7)

Sons kill fathers and brothers kill brothers

Sons kill fathers and fathers kill sons for reasons related to the authority and control of younger men by older male relatives, financial issues, and the like. The issues at stake vary and may include theft, drunkenness, inheritance, previous physical and/or sexual abuse, and others. A combination of factors might involve unresolved conflicts that are relatively minor but over time or in combination with other issues become toxic. Physical violence or sexual abuse may have been perpetrated by a father against his son or against another member of the family including a mother or sister. Sons may kill fathers in an effort to protect such relatives from further harm, as acts of revenge for abuse, or both. Sons may kill fathers while stealing from them, because of unpaid debts, or failed business ventures. Most act alone, although some involve others in the murder (on *Parricide*, children killing their parents, see Heide (2013) and Ewing (1997, pp. 100–114)). In this case, a son and companion kill his father in the context of a theft in order to buy drugs. They inflict over 50 injuries by kicking and hitting him with a baseball bat which far exceeds any level of force needed to steal his money, and raises the question of what else might be going on.

Son beats father to death with a baseball bat
The perpetrator (16) and co-accused murder his father (58) while robbing his flat.

[Context and murder]
He had no money and needed money to buy drugs at a rave on New Year's Eve. He knew his father kept large sums of money in his flat, decided to rob him and persuaded the co-accused to join him. They went to his father's flat, beat him up using their feet and a baseball bat, inflicting 50 separate injuries including a fractured skull which caused his death.

114 Murder between men in the family

[Trial judge report]
I have no doubt that the perpetrator was the leader. He had four convictions for dishonesty, and I regard him as a wholly amoral, self-centered and dangerous young man who will easily manipulate others for his own purposes. There is a history of violence and abuse by his father, and he believed his paternal aunt was actually his mother.

(*201cf1.2.7)

Son kills father and blames his mother
The son (28) battered his father (63) to death, buried his body, and blamed his mother until he finally confesses to a prison psychiatrist after 14 years in prison.

[Context]
He lived with his father and mother who were both heavy drinkers. On the eve of the murder, his father and mother each drank about one litre of sherry. During the night, he battered his father with a hammer 12 times. After the murder, he took the body out of the house and buried it. The next day, his mother reported the victim missing, saw bloodstains on the stairs, talked to her other off-spring, suspected the perpetrator, and called the police. The police questioned him. He said he wanted to show the police the body. While being driven in a car by one officer, and followed by another, he pulled a knife on the police officer, threatened to kill him and tried to escape. For this, he was charged with the additional offense of Grievous Bodily Harm.

(*714cf1.2.7)

Brother kills brother
There was a lot of 'aggro' between the perpetrator `(37) and his brother (30), who had been arrested and sentenced to 60 days after a poaching incident. He knew his brother would come after him when he got out of jail, so he armed himself with a sawn-off shotgun. Both brothers happened to visit a scrap yard, some 'aggro' ensued, and the perpetrator says he shot his brother in self-defense as he thought he was going to do something to him.

(*112cf1.2.7)

In cases not reported here, other murders between male relatives involved a fear of one another or a mutual hatred. Ohers were more neutral with respect to such emotions and were more closely associated with issues involving money, property, business ventures, and debts.

Subtype 2. Gay intimate partners

Murders between same-sex male partners, may share some similarities with heterosexual relationships, including conflicts about jealousy, possessiveness,

Murder between men in the family **115**

separation and new partners. As discussed in Chapter 5 about sexual murders, there is a growing body of research on violence in the LBGT community, but much of this is about violence directed at gay men and less about violence between gay men. These cases from the Murder Study provide a glimpse into this subtype of Family Murder. Men who are being abused in a same-sex intimate relationship may be unwilling to report abuse or seek assistance when neither is available. They may be reluctant to expose themselves or the gay community to censure, and some may fear being 'outed' or otherwise identified. For these and other reasons, less is known about cases of abuse in same-sex relationships. Sometimes, details about conflicts or abuse are only revealed after a tragic event such as a murder, and may only become known during a legal trial and recorded in a casefile after one of the men has been murdered by the other such as some of the cases in the Murder Study that are recounted here. When conflicts between men who are intimate partners end in murder, issues of possessiveness, jealousy, separation, desertion, retaliation and revenge often form part of the contexts in which these murders occur. It would be wrong to assume an identical correspondence between the issues involved in same-sex and heterosexual relationships, but there may be some general similarities between them. The first case involved male partners with a history of alcohol abuse and violence throughout their long relationship. In a drunken fight, one man fatally stabbed the other as they grappled for a knife.

> ### Same-sex, intimate partners for 16 years, alcohol and previous violence
> Gay partners for 16 years, one stabs the other in a row [argument]. There is a history of violence and alcohol abuse. The perpetrator (48), a gay man, and the victim (31) who was also gay had been partners for 16 years in a homosexual relationship. They went out for a drink, came home early in the evening, had an altercation which developed into a struggle. The perpetrator had a kitchen knife with a 5½ inch blade. During the struggle, both men fell to the floor, and the victim was sitting astride the perpetrator who was trying to pull the knife from his hand. The perpetrator could no longer resist the pull of the victim's arm and let his resistance go at which point the knife came forward and struck the deceased in the left side of his body. When the paramedics arrived, they took the victim to the hospital where, after one hour, he was declared dead. He died of a hemorrhage from a stab wound to the left side of his back. The victim and perpetrator had carried out violent assaults upon each other during the past few years during domestic disagreements and while under the influence of alcohol.
> (*1027cf1.1.5)

In the next case the men were long-term partners in an on-and-off intimate relationship that lasted for many years. It was eventually complicated by an

116 Murder between men in the family

extreme form of alcoholism, financial insecurity and an unseemly episode that resulted in a killing while both were drunk that was deeply regretted by the victim's male partner. The extreme state of remorse and regret was acknowledged by the trial judge who gave the perpetrator the shortest possible sentence for this offense.

Alcoholic partner, human faeces on the floor, and stabbed to death

A gay couple with both, but especially the victim, very addicted to alcohol. They appear to have had a serious dispute ending in a stabbing that resulted in death. The victim (38) was a professional who was killed by his homosexual partner (37). The couple had lived together for various periods of time and, in the last instance, for a period of 18 months.

[Murder]
The perpetrator phoned the emergency number at 1:00am, and reported that he had stabbed his co-habitant and that he was 'bleeding to death'. He again rang ten minutes later and stated that he had just killed him. On arrival, blood was seen to escape the body from a puncture wound in the chest. A knife could be seen protruding from the left side of his neck and was deeply embedded in the wound. Another three knives were found on the floor next to the body. The perpetrator was still present in the flat and was arrested. He was distressed, disturbed and agitated. The examination of the body revealed six stab wounds. Both lungs had collapsed, the chest cavity had filled with blood, and the heart had been punctured.

[Context]
He stated he returned to the flat from a night out with two cousins. On entering the flat, he had seen marks on the carpet which appeared to him to be human faeces. As the victim was an alcoholic, he had caused a mess like this on previous occasions which the perpetrator had had to clean up. He stated that he just flipped. He got knives from a drawer in the kitchen and was just 'slashing' at him.

The couple had been together for a number of years in the past and had 'broken-up' but had re-established the relationship 18 months before the murder. They first met when the victim was working in a professional capacity and the perpetrator was a 'client'. Within a few months, a homosexual relationship developed and they began living together. After about ten years together, the victim got a girlfriend, a woman who worked for him, and asked the perpetrator to leave. Sometime after this, the two men resumed their relationship which was not unproblematic.

Previous domestic violence incidents had occurred between them, and the victim had previously been stabbed in the thigh. After the stabbing that resulted in the murder, the perpetrator took the contents (about 30 tablets) of a bottle of Diazepam but then vomited in the sink prior to the arrival of the police [which he would have known was imminent]

[Trial judge]
The defendant is aged 37 and has no history of violence. The deceased was the love of his life.

(*1004cf1.1.5).[2]

The next case received wide public attention because it involved several murders committed over a period of time and in different locations including inside a prison for the criminally insane. Here, we include only the first murder of his gay lover. The others involved hostage taking, torture, the killing of male inmates in two different prisons, and a failed plan to instigate his own death at the hands of correctional staff. He had a long history of problems including mental illness and a desire to kill himself and others.

Multiple murders, hostage taking and a desire to kill himself and others
At a young age, he killed his gay lover and was sent to [a prison for the mentally ill]. While there, he and another man took a patient hostage and tortured and killed him. For this offense, he was sent to a penal institution where he killed two inmates in the space of two hours in two separate incidents.

At the time of the first murder, he had been living an unsettled life style in his home in [City] and survived by stealing. He formed a homosexual relationship with a man who was 40 years old, and they lived together until he killed him and was committed to [institution for the mentally ill]. He said, 'He is the only one who ever showed any feeling towards me. I felt like a son'. When his friend was away working, he frequented [area] where he earned a living as a male prostitute, but he also engaged in heterosexual activities. He had never had an exclusive relationship with one person, drank heavily, took drugs and, from time to time, experienced urges to kill himself and others.

[Murder #1]
He armed himself with a knife and killed his homosexual partner. He then telephoned police to confess and was soon arrested. He had urges to kill people, moods of depression, suicidal tendencies, a paranoia about people watching him. He was judged to be grossly impaired and was convicted of 'manslaughter on the grounds of diminished responsibility'. [Murder #2–4 and attempted murder #5, which is not presented here.]

118 Murder between men in the family

[Trial judge]
'Wherever he may be placed he will constitute a continuing threat to the safety of any person in whose presence he may come'.

(*1146cf1.1.5)

Subtype 3. Collateral intimate partner murders – male victims

When conflicts between intimate partners end in murder, the victim is usually a woman partner who is killed by her male partner, and a few involve men killed by their male intimate partners as shown above. Here, we focus on cases that begin with conflicts/abuse of a women partner but end with the murder of a man. We use the shorthand, 'Collaterals,' to describe 'intimate partner collateral murder' (IPCM). How does this happen? Who is murdered? These murders take place in three general contexts.

Collaterals – male protectors and allies (of the perpetrator's woman partner)

These murder victims include men who intervene during an ongoing assault by a man against his woman partner and are killed by her male partner. These male victims include male relatives, friends, neighbors and bystanders in the context of intimate partner abuse/violence, and are themselves killed by the abuser.

Collaterals – male assistors (of the perpetrator's woman partner)

These murder victims include men acting in their professional capacity to help or assist a woman, (e.g. a lawyer, police officer, male neighbor is murdered when providing some form of assistance to the perpetrator's woman partner who is either abused by the perpetrator or seeking a divorce from the perpetrator, etc.) who kills the man from whom she is seeking assistance. These victims include police officers, lawyers, social workers, male neighbors, neighbors and others.

Collaterals – New male partners (of the perpetrator's woman partner)

These murder victims include men who become new boyfriends, husbands, or lovers of the perpetrator's woman partner once she has left the perpetrator for another man, and he kills her new male partner.

'Intimate partner collateral murders' can best be understood in the context of perpetrator's previous abuse of his woman partner or in the context of conflicts involving separation, divorce and custody of children. These circumstances form the background of the lethal violence he unleashes against a man who intervenes in an effort to stop an ongoing violent attack against 'his' woman; a man who tries to assist a woman who is trying to leave a relationship with him; or a man who becomes the new male partner of 'his' woman. Elsewhere, we have examined other victims of 'intimate partner collateral murders' including children killed in acts of vengeance by their father against their mother, and women friends, neighbors or professionals killed by abusive husbands/partners while providing some form of assistance to the perpetrator's wife/cohabitant/girlfriend (for 'Intimate Partner Collateral Murders' when women or children are killed, see Cavanagh, Dobash and Dobash (2005); Dobash and Dobash (2012); Dobash and Dobash (2015, p. 332, also see Index entry for 'collateral murders'); Dobash and Dobash (2018). Here, we focus only on cases of intimate partner collateral murders (IPCM) of men.

Collaterals – male protectors and allies (of the perpetrator's woman partner)

Men killed while acting as protectors of women who are being abused, are often close relatives, particularly fathers and brothers, and this may also be the fate of mothers and sisters. Men killed while attempting to get the man to stop using violence against his woman partner included his friends and acquaintances.

Father killed by his daughter's former partner

The perpetrator (24) had previously lived with his former cohabitee and her father (53), the victim. There had been no reported problems between the two men during that time. Two years before the murder, he/perpetrator and his cohabitee separated but he sometimes visited the family home of his 'father-in-law'/victim to visit his three-year old daughter who resided there with her mother/his former cohabitee. His relationship with his former partner was fraught, and he describes feeling 'devastated' when she told him to leave because of his violence to her, and his alcoholism. Immediately before the murder, he learned that his daughter was referring to the new partner as 'Daddy', and this annoyed him. She was 3-yrs-old when her father murdered her grandfather.

[Murder]
At the time of the murder, the perpetrator's ex-partner was away camping with her new boyfriend/partner to celebrate her 21st birthday. In a jealous rage, he went to her house (shared with her new partner) to destroy her possessions and clothing while she was away. While in the house, he was disturbed by her 53-year-old father (his former father-in-law and grandfather of his daughter) who had gone to his daughter's house at 9pm to check the property and turn on the lights. Upon entering, he disturbed the perpetrator, a confrontation occurred, and the perpetrator stabbed his former 'father-in-law' 25 times in the neck,

120 Murder between men in the family

chest, and back which caused his death. He then went to the pub/club where he was reported to have been undisturbed.

[Police interview]
'He said that once he started he had to 'finish the job'.

(*109cf1.1.2)

Both parents were killed while trying to protect their daughter from an aggressive male partner who saw them as interfering in 'his' life as they tried to shield their daughter from further violence. He would not be thwarted in his violent treatment of 'his' woman partner, and killed both her parents for trying to help their daughter.

Shot and killed his father-in-law and mother-in law for protecting their daughter from his violent attacks against her

He (27) became convinced that his in-laws were interfering too much in his life. After a quarrel in which he struck his woman partner, she took the [new born] baby and returned to her parents. She cleared out her and the baby's clothes. He said, 'Basically, I knew that she had gone for good'. He phoned his father-in-law who told him he was fed up with him always knocking his daughter about. He subsequently visited their farm and had a violent argument with his father 'in-law' (47) and assaulted and bruised his mother-in-law (44).

[Double murder]
The morning of the offense, he went to their farm/house, left the car at the bottom of the drive, walked up, loaded the shot gun and walked into the house where he shot his father-in-law. He then reloaded the gun and shot his mother-in-law.

(*1178cf1.1.2)

Other collateral victims included the perpetrator's friends, the man next door, or bystanders who tried to persuade him to 'calm down,' or to stop during an attack on his woman partner.

Drunk, assaulted his wife and killed his friend

He was drunk and assaulted his wife in front of his friend who then intervened in an attempt to stop the assault. He responded by stabbing his friend to death.

(*051.cf1.1.2)

Collaterals – male assistors of the perpetrator's woman partner – professionals and first responders

Other male assistors were killed while acting in a professional capacity including first responders called to incidents of domestic violence, lawyers involved in divorce or child custody cases, and others. While fulfilling their professional duties as police officers, social workers, lawyers, or others acting in an official capacity these men were placed between a violent man and the woman partner he victimized. Some professionals, such as police officers, were directly involved during or immediately following a violent attack. Others, including lawyers, were involved at other stages in 'marital' conflicts involving restraining orders, legal separations, divorce and child custody. Once again, the main issue involved the intimate relationship between the male perpetrator and his woman partner, and these men became 'collateral damage.' Two cases illustrate men who were killed while acting in a professional capacity including a police officer acting as a first responder at a scene of a 'domestic assault,' and a divorce lawyer acting for a woman seeking to leave her husband.

Police officer killed while on duty responding to a call about domestic violence

A police officer on duty was murdered while responding to a call involving a domestic disturbance at the house of a former girlfriend [intimate partner] of the perpetrator who was drunk and on drugs. He beat the officer with a wooden stake ripped from a fence, and he also had a knife.

[Context]
A 25-year-old man and his 16-year-old co-defendant killed a 40-year-old police sergeant while he was on duty. Both the perpetrator and his co-defendant drank a considerable amount of alcohol, sniffed lighter fluid, and took temazepam, then caused a disturbance at the home of the perpetrator's ex-girlfriend/intimate partner. She was going out with a new guy. He was angry about this and tried to pick a fight with the new boyfriend. The perpetrator and co-defendant then broke a window at the home of his former girlfriend.

[Murder]
The victim, a police sergeant, and a young police constable were investigating a complaint about the window, and the perpetrator and co-defendant verbally taunted them. The police left, but within minutes they radioed twice for help, and the second call was an emergency. The perpetrator and his accomplice attacked the police officer with barriers torn from a fence, and also produced a knife. Local residents and passers-by witnessed or heard the assault. There were multiple stab wounds and severe bruising. It was thought that the perpetrator was much more responsible for the death than his 16-year-old co-accused who was deemed to be an immature, insecure and inadequate young man of limited intelligence.

(★661cf1.2.5)

122   Murder between men in the family

This male solicitor (42) was murdered while acting on behalf of a woman seeking a divorce from her unfaithful husband. The perpetrator viewed this as an affront, and responded with lethal violence.

Successful man stabs and kills his wife's divorce lawyer

[Previous social history]
At age 20, he joined the Army, met and married his wife, and after three years bought himself out of the Army. He later became very successful in the building trade. At the time of the murder, he was 39 years old and a successful man able to buy an expensive house and enjoyed a high income.

[Murder – police report]
At about 1:30 pm, he went to the victim's office building (his wife's divorce lawyer) and was told he wasn't there. He later phoned and established that he was in the office, went back to the premises, immediately ran upstairs into the victim's office, threatened him, and demanded the letters [evidence of the perpetrator's affair to be used in the divorce case]. He then produced a sheath knife and repeatedly stabbed the victim in the face and body. He was disturbed by one of the victim's female employees, and ran from the premises discarding his bloodstained jacket in the hallway. As a result of police enquiries, he later surrendered himself at the police station.

[Police interview]
'Yes, I stabbed him with that knife. I lost my temper. I just blew up. I just wanted him dead.'

[Context]
He separated from his wife and went on a drinking binge. Once he returned, he admitted to having had an affair and that he was uncertain whether he wanted to live with his wife or his new lover. His wife started divorce proceedings, found letters he had written to his lover and gave them to her solicitor for evidence. He says that after the break–up, he was hounded by his wife's solicitor who seemed to take delight in making him suffer, and that this went on for 12 months.

[Pre-sentence report]
The offence seems to have arisen out of his perception that his victim (wife's solicitor) held him in contempt and was out to cause him as much trouble as possible. The one consistent thing he has said about his offence is that the solicitor patronized and humiliated him.

[Trial judge]
'Murder' was the only right verdict, and this was a peculiarly vicious and brutal one'.

(★643cf. 1.1.2)

Collaterals – new male partners

When a woman leaves her intimate partner and establishes a relationship with a new male partner, everyone may be in danger. The woman, her children, a man or woman who offers her protection or assistance, and the man with whom she begins a new relationship. New male partners are often the subject of extreme jealousy by former partners/perpetrators who view new male partners as having 'stolen' his wife (and children), and thus 'fair game' for any form of harassment or violence the perpetrator wishes to inflict upon him. However badly the perpetrator may have behaved toward his woman partner concerning infidelities, drunkenness, maltreatment of her or the children prior to a separation or divorce, many of these men feel that it is they who have been victimized and may go to great lengths to make others pay.

In the first case involving the killing of a new male partner, the perpetrator clearly states that the killing is 'her fault' and that the man would be alive if she had not established a relationship with him. Other cases involved histories of violence prior to separation and the formation of a new relationship. An obsession with the new relationship, jealousy, anger, stalking, and ongoing threats were commonly directed at the ex-woman partner and her new male partner prior to the murder. In some cases, ongoing threats and harassment persisted for several years after the woman had left the perpetrator and established a new relationship. In others, the new man was murdered within a very short period after the new relationship had begun.

'She made me do it'

He (26) killed the new male partner (37) of his ex-girlfriend/partner. The victim was very seriously injured with 16 fractured ribs and several internal injuries. In evidence, the defendant said that he caused the injuries by jumping and stamping on him. He admitted that his 'girlfriend' had broken off the relationship two weeks earlier, and that she had taken up with another man. When confronted, he [eventually] admitted to 'slapping her' 'but said that she asked for it by showing me up in front of other people, 'She made me do it'. She regularly went to Women's Aid refuges.

[Report]
He said he doesn't like to be told what to do by a woman. Clearly, he has misogynistic ideas and attitudes. He blames the killing on his woman partner, 'If she didn't do what she did [leave him for another man], the geezer would be alive today.'

(★270cf 1.1.2)

124 Murder between men in the family

Stabbed new partner with bayonet in a drunken and frenzied attack

He (47) had lived with his partner and her young son for two years, but the relationship deteriorated because of his aggressive behavior. There were numerous police visits, and she eventually left him. Because of continual harassment and violence, she had to change the locks and obtain a non-molestation order against him. He brooded for some six weeks, drinking to excess and uttering threats against her and the deceased [her new partner]. On the night of the murder, after an evening of drinking in a pub, he lay in wait for the return of her new partner, and stabbed him to death in a frenzied attack with a bayonet he had obtained from the territorial Army.

(*992cf. 1.1.2)

Married seven years, divorced three years, kills new male partner who was a police officer

[Trial judge]
He had an obsessive and possessive love for his former partner. They were married for seven years, and he became increasingly jealous and constantly pestered and harassed her. Three years after the divorce, his former wife met and married the deceased [a police officer]. Having learned of this, he was very distressed. Learning that the couple were living at his former matrimonial home, he went there in the early evening armed with a knife and stabbed her new husband to death by inflicting 28 stab wounds on his body. Throughout their association, he had been violent to his former wife, and just before the murder he had cut the telephone wire on three occasions and broken 14 windows at her/their house. He had a history of previous serious violence to co-habitants and attacks on various other partners.

(*934cf. 1.1.2)

This lengthy account of the murder of a new male partner follows the event as it unfolds with witnesses shouting and trying to stop the fast-moving action as the perpetrator defiantly declared his intention to kill, and was indifferent to pleas to stop the attack as he went on to finish what he had come there to do.

Before witnesses, man kills the new male partner of his former woman partner who left him five weeks before the murder

Man (40) killed the new male partner (20) of his former woman partner who had left him five weeks before the murder.

[Context]
At the time of the murder, he was a 40-year-old alcoholic and binge drinker with a long-standing alcohol problem that began when he was only 14 years old. Two years previously, at the age of 38, he met an

Murder between men in the family **125**

18-year-old girl and began a relationship with her during which they had two children. But after two years together, she left him because of his violence and alcoholism. This was five weeks before the murder.

After leaving him, she became re-acquainted with an old school friend, a 20-year-old male, and they had begun to cohabit. During this time, the perpetrator had numerous contacts with his former partner and asked her to return. There was some reconciliation between them, but she remained with her new partner.

[On the night of the murder]
The perpetrator had been drinking all day, and arrived drunk and aggressive at the apartment of her new male partner. She and her new male partner were playing Scrabble with three friends (no alcohol was consumed, all were blood tested). Soon after he arrived, she left to contact the police as she was concerned for her own safety. A friend of the couple asked the perpetrator to leave, but instead of leaving, he went to the kitchen, got a kitchen knife and stabbed her new partner twice in his back and neck which struck an artery.
The victim ran into the street where he fell down and died.
[One of the witnesses] shouted at the perpetrator and tried to stop his attack, but it was all very quick.
[Another witness] shouted, 'You have killed him. Where is the knife?'
[Perpetrator] 'The knife is on the floor. I've finished with it'.
[Witness] 'Do you realise what you have done?'
[Perpetrator] 'I don't give a fuck'.
[Witness] 'He's dying and you're going away for a long time'.
[Perpetrator] 'I've done what I came to do, and you can fuck off'.
The witness then struck the perpetrator on the head with his fist and punched his face.
The police arrived and cautioned the perpetrator. He made no reply, and was taken to the police station and charged. During the first two police interviews, he tried to claim that he didn't remember anything because of the alcohol. Then, he admitted responsibility for the death but said he did not intend to kill the victim just to frighten him. The victim died at the scene.

(*811cf1.2.2)

In brief, men who become collateral victims of intimate partner conflicts, are killed in three general contexts: 1) men acting in a personal capacity as 'protectors or allies' of women who are being abused or separating from their male partner, particularly fathers, brothers, as well as male friends and others; 2) men acting in a professional capacity related to domestic violence and/or marital separation including police, lawyers, social workers, medics and others; and 3) new male

126 Murder between men in the family

partners of woman after they leave the perpetrator who responds by killing the new man for 'stealing his woman.'

The killing of the entire family, known as 'Familicides,' are very rare, but those that do occur usually receive extensive news coverage, and often engender a great deal more public shock, horror, and outrage than the other types of collateral murder mentioned above (for cases see Websdale (2010)). There was one familicide in the Murder Study that involved the murder of the woman partner and their children. It is not included here because our focus here is on adult male victims over age 16, and this male victim was a younger child.

Subtype 4. Family feuds and feuding families

Some family murders involve feuds between families with ongoing conflicts, disputes and fights that may result in a death. One death may not end the feud but signal the beginning of future events in which other family members become involved and still others are killed. Fights between feuding families are the stuff of legend and drama. One of the most enduring tale of a family feud is Shakespeare's 'Romeo and Juliet.' Written in the 1590s and set in Italy, this classic has been performed thousands of times all over the world and inspired modern versions for stage, ballet, art, music, and films. The backdrop is a long-standing feud between two families. The immediate context is a street-fight between young men from both sides during which a weapon is drawn and one young man is killed. In response, his kinsman draws a weapon and kills the perpetrator, and 'So begins the tale of woe of Juliet and her Romeo.' Shakespeare's tragic tale of the young lovers, begins with a street fight and a double murder between two feuding families, then focuses almost exclusively on the forbidden love affair across the family divide, and ends with the deaths of both young lovers. We recount the events in the same format as a casefile from the Murder Study.

In this 'tale of woe of Juliet and her Romeo,' audiences focus on the tragic love story of two young lovers from families whose feuding prohibits them from marrying, but with the help of a friendly priest, they hatch an elaborate (and dangerous) plan so that they can escape their warring families and wed (*Romeo and Juliet*).

Romeo and Juliet die

[The plan]
Juliet drinks a potion that will for a period of time make her appear to be dead during which time her family will mourn and bury her in the family crypt where she will later recover from the coma-like-sleep, and she and her Romeo will reunite and escape together. Sadly, the message about the plot is not delivered to Romeo, who he hears of her death, buys poison, goes to the crypt where she is lying 'dead', and kills himself by drinking the poison. Juliet awakes, and finding Romeo dead by her

side, uses his knife to kill herself. Both families suffer the loss of their beloved kin and, in the final words of the ruling Prince of Verona, everyone is punished in this needless feud between these two families.

[Postscript]
In the end, Romeo and Juliet are collateral deaths of a family feud.

In the Leonard Bernstein's musical, 'West Side Story,' the feuding families are located to 1950s New York City with the feud involving newly arrived immigrants from Puerto Rico and a local gang of 'Anglos,' the 'Sharks' and the 'Jets.' The two groups of young males prepare for a fight on the street, singing, 'there's going to be a rumble tonight' (West Side Story). During the fight, someone is killed by the 'nice guy' Tony who is trying to stop the fight. Maria 'belongs' to the other side, but they fall in love and try to find a way to escape the feuding sides in order to be together. They fail, and in the end Tony is killed. As in Romeo and Juliet, everyone is punished because of a futile family feud. The universal appeal of the story lies in the beauty and romance of young love, and in the heart-breaking tragedy of the death of the young lovers. The final message delivered to everyone is about the potential dangers of feuds between families and other groupings. Both stories begin with a murder in which a man from one family/group kills a man from the other. As we are caught up in the love story, something important is forgotten.

Romeo is a murderer (and so is Tony)

[Report]
Although he is a gentle soul, he was inadvertently drawn into a 'contest' between young men on both sides of two warring families. In a street fight, one young man is killed and Romeo responds by killing another.

This fictional tale begins with a murder that is overlooked as we become captivated by the magical love story and the tragic ending. The fact that Romeo (and Tony) commit a murder is either completely forgotten or completely forgiven, perhaps because he is viewed as a nice guy, or because he is young, good looking and in love with an innocent beauty. In 2020, this timeless tale was released yet again in a new play on Broadway (@Westsidestorybway.com), and a new film by Stephen Spielberg (West Side Story).

Tales of family feuds date back to antiquity and resemble 'real life' murders involving real-life families at war. Unlike the killings committed by Romeo (and Tony) in the context of these fictional tales of feuds in which they killed in the heat of the moment and without a previous plan to kill, some encounters are planned and begin with a clear intention to kill. One infamous example of multiple murders between feuding families involves the true story of the Hatfield-McCoy feud in rural West Virginia and Kentucky between 1880–1891,

128 Murder between men in the family

that reached a final death toll of four Hatfields plus four of their supporters, and seven McCoys. In the end, nine Hatfields were imprisoned (seven for life) and one was executed. How did all of this happen? Again, we recount the events using the same format as for the casefiles and interviews in the Murder Study.

Hatfield and McCoy family feud

[Characters]
- William McCoy, head of his family, born in Ireland about 1750, many ancestors came from Scotland where feuding clans were endemic – lived on the Kentucky side of the river.
- William Anderson 'Devil Anse' Hatfield (and family) – lived on the West Virginia side.

[Context]
Most men from both families fought on the Confederate side in the American Civil War except Asa Harmon McCoy who fought for the Union and was killed by a group of Confederate Home Guards. The Hatfield's were implicated.

[Ongoing disputes]
Between 1880–1891, a long-running dispute began over the ownership of a hog and disputes about inter-clan 'marriages'.

[Several murders]
There were several brutal revenge killings, and a 'massacre' including women and children.
The two families killed more than a dozen people, wounded others, houses were burned, people were imprisoned and hanged. Many sheriffs, lawyers and courts were involved, with the last of several trials in 1901.

A legacy of 'never forgetting or forgiving' was accompanied by ongoing encounters that lasted for years, crossed over into the next generation, and into families well beyond the lifespan of the original participants to the conflict (Hatfield-McCoy, family feud and multiple murders).

[Postscript]
- June 14, 2003, descendants of the Hatfield and McCoy families declared an official truce, and signed a proclamation of peace.
- 2011, a musical comedy, 'The Hatfields and McCoys Dinner Show' opened near the entrance to the Great Smoky Mountain National Park.
- 2016 *Hillbilly elegy* by J.D. Vance, a descendant of the Hatfield clan, wrote *Family Feud*.

- Now, 'Hatfield & McCoy Reunion Festival & Marathon is held annually, with the theme 'no feudin', just runnin'.

(Hatfield–McCoy Feud)

Feuding families in the Murder Study

The Murder Study contained several real-life examples of murders associated with family feuds and feuding families. The issues at stake varied from past grievances associated with personal conflicts, money and debts, and love matches that were disapproved of by the wider kin groups. Insults, money, crime and love all figure in the contexts of these murders which, for the most part, were perpetrated by two or more individuals rather than by a single man as in most of the other subtypes of family murders. The fact that several men are involved, whether as perpetrators, victims or both, forms an important part of the dynamics of the events that end in one or more deaths. These cases involved feuding families, street fights, thefts, and murders on one or both sides.

Feuding family street 'rammy' resulted in 17 charges and 2 murders
The perpetrator (21) had just been released from serving a sentence in a Young Offender's Institution, YOI. Soon after arriving home, he became embroiled in a street fight between his family and a neighboring family. The feuding family street 'rammy' (fight) involved many men from both factions. There was a lot of violence on both sides. In the end, seventeen charges were brought against several men, and the perpetrator was charged with two murders of men, both in their thirties. The perpetrator admitted to having committed one of the murders but not the other.

*(*141cf1.2.4)*

Gangland killing – feuding families, and revenge for a previous stabbing
This was a gangland killing between two feuding families.

The perpetrator (26) and two brothers from one family were in the pub when the male victim (29), a member of the other family, came in. A fight started and the victim was stabbed to death. The perpetrator was employed as a labourer with a local building firm and lived with his common-law wife. The victim also lived with his common-law wife in the same city.

[Context]
There was animosity between both families because of an incident that occurred about two years before the murder. The previous incident involved a stabbing of the brother of the perpetrator who appeared to have taken revenge upon his brother's attacker by stabbing him to death

130 Murder between men in the family

in the same pub were the original took place. That incident started the feud between the two families.

(*100cf1.2.4)

Rival families in the same housing estate – revenge for a theft
The perpetrator (31) killed a male member of a rival family living in the same public housing scheme. There was some conflict about a theft from the perpetrator's home by a relative of the victim, and the murder appeared to be an act of revenge for this. The perpetrator went to the victim's home after drinking at home with his brother, and stabbed the victim to death. He continues to deny the murder even after being convicted of murder and having spent eight years in prison for that offense.

(*078cf1.2.4)

An ongoing family feud heated up at a family wedding five months before the murder. There was an assault, an arrest, and a court case that 'went the wrong way.' Then, the previous victims of the assault took matters into their own hands and killed one of the original attackers.

A family wedding, an assault, a court case, and a murder five months later

[Five months earlier – a wedding and an assault]
A male member of one of the feuding families (26) had organized the large and lavish event. Everyone was dressed in their finest clothes and lots of food and beverages were provided for all the guests including members from both families who had previously been in dispute. Everyone was there to celebrate the marriage of two members of the community and not worry about past grievances.

[Assault]
On the way home from the wedding, there was an assault involving several men from the disputing families. From one side, a young man (19) along with several kin and friends attacked four men including the man who had organized the wedding, inflicting quite serious injuries to the head of one man and gave another a black eye. The Police were called, the attackers were arrested, the victims brought a formal complaint against the assailant (19) and his kin/friends.

[Five months later – the court case]
The law was taking its course at the local magistrate's court when something was done or said that seemed to have stirred the defendants up and rekindled their animosity.

... and the previous perpetrator of the assault became the victim of murder...

[Murder]
Things had gone wrong in court. Someone refused to give evidence, and the case did not/could not proceed as they (victims of the original assault) expected. The men spent the next eight hours drinking and brooding over their wrongs. Finally, they all went to the pub where they had reason to think the [original attacker in the wedding assault] (19) would be, and after heated abuse, the perpetrator (26) stabbed the victim (19) in the flank (a trace of the wound went more than half way through his body). As the victim was trying to escape, the other co-accused plunged the knife into his heart. After the victim had collapsed onto the floor, the perpetrator and co-accused shouted, 'Get up now you bastard'. The police were called and arrested all four defendants. The victim was taken to hospital, and after efforts to resuscitate him had failed, he was pronounced dead at 10:30 pm.

[Immediately after the murder]
After the stabbing, the perpetrator ran out of the pub, waited for a short period and then walked back into the pub and continued drinking. He maintained that he was scared at this point. He said he was not 100% sure that he had stabbed the victim. He maintained that he was concerned about the safety of the victim but did not appear to do anything to help him. It was not immediately apparent to the perpetrator that the victim had been fatally wounded, and he said his memory of events following the stabbing was poor. He said, 'There is no doubt I did want to hurt him physically. It wasn't an accident. I didn't want to murder him. I did want to hurt him. How I managed to do it was a combination of anger built up from the past. Drink also played a part'.

[Trial judge]
Commented on the degree of dangerousness of the four men who committed the murder: The perpetrator (26) had five previous convictions for assault; the other three co-accused were men of good character. From experience, I would say these people (Asians) are no more and no less dangerous that most others when they fancy themselves greatly wronged and are disinhibited by alcohol'.

[Prison report]
Risk assessment – drink, group loyalty, revenge, grudges, unassertive. He said there had always been a feud between the two families and a lot of arguments, but never had he wanted to kill the victim. Though he

132 Murder between men in the family

showed some grief and remorse, he does not accept full responsibility and denies that he has been involved in violent acts
(*Note: he had five previous convictions for assault*). He has been known to carry offensive weapons in the past. He describes himself as a very responsible, caring, confident and affectionate person. It appears that he is quite selfish, has had problems with the police since childhood and is irresponsible in his behaviour.

(*866cf1.2.4)

In many ways, feuds between families are a bit like feuds between nations or neighboring communities. They can go on for a very long time, others may join each of the warring sides, several skirmishes may take place, each side rarely forgets what has been done by the other and usually remembers less about what they have done themselves. In some cases, it is difficult to see how this never-ending spiral can ever come to an end. The historical example of the very long and bloody family feud between the Hatfields and McCoys only ended after nearly 100 years when the modern inheritors of this famous family feud decided to declare an official truce, sign a proclamation of peace and turn the whole thing into a modern 'event' in the form of an annual marathon, remembering the past with a very different theme, 'no feudin,' just runnin.'

Subtype 5. Brothers against others

The previous cases involved murders in which men banded together to kill men from another family with whom they were feuding. These cases differ in that the perpetrators are related to one another, usually brothers or cousins, and act together to kill someone who is neither their kin nor a member of an opposing family group with whom they are feuding. They act as a 'band of brothers' and kill a man who is an outsider. The outsider/s may be someone who has committed an offense against themselves or a member of their family, and the brothers band together to seek revenge. Or, the outsider may have done nothing against either of them or any of their kin, but is attacked and killed in an act of 'brotherly solidarity' against others who belong to a 'category' of persons they hate or despise such as foreigners, gay men, men of color, homeless men, or even supporters of another football team. Similar to the cases of feuding families, these cases also involved perpetrators, brothers/cousins, who were bound together by filial ties and acted together in the killing, but the victims were not from an opposing family with whom they were at war. In these cases, brothers killed in solidarity with one another, or in a joint enterprise performed for the purpose of entertaining themselves, or in an effort to build or maintain a reputation, or in an effort to seek revenge. Whether these murders were initiated or 'justified' as acts of protection or retaliation, or began with their own efforts to harass or intimidate others, one of the important dynamics involved a form of 'solidarity' as brothers acted together in opposition to others.

Murder between men in the family   **133**

Revenge: kills an 'outsider' to avenge an assault against his brother

The group of four young men, the perpetrator (18) and three co-accused were all of a similar age and most belonged to the same family. They were drinking together, some to the state of drunkenness, and decided to revenge an assault that had been perpetrated against one of the *brothers* by a male member (17) of a rival gang/group. They went after him, and once they had found him a fight began, the 17-year-old was killed and the four murderers had their revenge for a previous assault on their brother.

(*165cf1.2.4)

Revenge: perp and his family fight, brother injured, revenge with a bayonet

The perpetrator (21) along with members of his family and a group of young men were involved in a dispute and a fight with another group of youths. The perpetrator's *brother* sustained injuries. The next night, there was a follow up fight, and the victim (20) was speared with a bayonet.

[Context]

On the night prior to the murder an incident occurred involving youths in the area which resulted in the co-accused (*brother of perpetrator*) being injured in the face. The basic trouble appeared to be rival gang warfare. The following evening, a number of people including all four of the accused gather together in the house of the sister of the first two accused. There, they organized themselves into a *'team' with a view to seeking revenge on the rival gang* which was known to be in the vicinity of her house.

(*Note*: He disparaged the term 'gang' saying, 'There was no rival gang, merely a collection of young neds with no moral code').

He armed himself with a bayonet, his brother with a hatchet, another with a knife, and the fourth left the house with the others wielding a bottle. The group ran through the garden of the house and into the street and confronted the rival group. In the ensuing chase, a bottle was thrown by the accused which hit the murder victim on the head temporarily felling him. As he was endeavoring to get up, he was stabbed virtually through the heart by the perpetrator using a bayonet. Death was not instantaneous but occurred in the hospital after all efforts to save his life had failed.

(*284cf1.2.4)

Some brothers acted together in using violence in order to show solidarity with one another, to denigrate someone they deem to be their inferior; to build or maintain a reputation in acts of revenge, and/or simply for entertainment.

134 Murder between men in the family

> *Revenge and the need for a reputation – two brothers and a friend avenge a slight against the perpetrator's brother*

[Note: material from his casefile (★139cf1.2.3) and our interview with him (★736iv.1.2.3).]

[From his casefile]
The perpetrator and his brother came from a violent family with a violent father.

During the afternoon, a fight occurred in a pub between a local 'hard' man (30) and a youth (*the perpetrator's younger brother*). That evening, three men (the perpetrator, his younger brother, and another man) met and decided they should seek *revenge* against the 'hard' man.

[Murder]
All three men armed themselves with knives plus a meat cleaver for the perpetrator's brother. They tracked down the victim (hard man) to another pub where he was drinking with a group of friends. After they sat down, the victim approached them, and the perpetrator and his brother assaulted him with a cosh. The three men then produced their weapons and a pitched battle took place with the three men against the victim and his friends. In the fight, the victim (hard man) was stabbed 29 times in the back by the perpetrator (older brother of the youth who had been assaulted by the hard man earlier that day). He staggered to a nearby police station but died during the ambulance trip to the hospital.

[Charges]
All three men (two brothers and their friend) were charged with the murder of the victim and the attempted murder of another male involved in the fight.

(★139cf1.2.3)

[From our interview with him in prison]
And when you and your co-accused saw him across the road, you went across the road, and was there an argument, or …? Basically, it was about the knife [the day before, the victim (hard man) had threatened his younger brother]. You know, the argument. *And how long did the confrontation last?* From the start, it was about 20 minutes. *Just tell me a bit more detail. You said your co-accused bent down to tie his shoelace? And what happened then?* Me and the guy (victim) were against the wall talking, and he punched me, so I 'went back' and I kicked him in the face as he went down. I kicked him a number of times, and then my co-accused started saying, 'The guys on the floor'. He fell down, and we got stuck in. *How many times did you kick him on the face?* I would say not more than four times, anyway, a couple

of times. *In court, did the pathologist give an estimate of how many times he thought that happened?* It was 29 separate injuries on him. *And you said that your co-accused jumped all over him – what was he doing, kicking and punching?* He was stamping on him. *And where was he stamping on him?* The head. *What were you thinking of then?* The guy's not getting up again. *And when you walked home, what was going through your head and what were you thinking?* I thought the guy was going to be all right. We thought the guy was going to be all right. He got up and he was, 'fucking and cunting', and 'I'm going to do this to you' and all that, and then he fell down. So, we were like [?unclear], you know, and we walked away. I went home. I was shattered [tired], and I went to my work the next day.

(★736iv1.2.3)

While some men act alone in committing a 'hate crime' against a group or an individual who differs from themselves by race, age, religion, sexual preference, social class or some other factor, other men act together in a group. This may give them the 'courage' to use violence or to go the extra step in upping the bar of the amount or type of violence each is willing to commit. The presence of other men may also add an element of 'competition' in who is willing or able to inflict the most pain, do the most damage, or engage in the most extreme, unique, or bizarre actions. In such cases, their actions would appear to be enacted more 'for one another' than 'against the man/men they attack.' In such cases, group solidarity, unity, status, superiority and reputation may figure more highly than the object of their derision who may be despised or deemed inferior. The presence of a spectators may make the violence/murder even more thrilling and bestow even more status on the perpetrator.

Comparisons of Family.Murders and Other.Murders

Qualitative texts from the casefiles and interviews illustrate the diverse nature of Family.Murders between men. These murders were classified into five subtypes of Family.Murder that illustrate their diverse nature. Quantitative data from their casefiles provide a characterization of the 72 Family.Murders and allow us to compare them with 'Other.Murders' that did not involve the family (Table 4.1).

Backgrounds and relationships between perpetrators and victims

The average age of Family.Murderers was 29 years which was slightly older than the men who committed Other.Murders (27 years). The average age of the victims of Family.Murders was 40 years, the same age as the victims of Other.Murders, also 40 years. The perpetrators in both groups were likely to be unemployed at the time of the murder, but the percentage was lower among Family.Murders (60% vs 70%).

136 Murder between men in the family

TABLE 4.1 Murder Event. Family.Murders and Other.Murders

MALE–MALE MURDER	*Family.Murders*	*Other.Murders*
	n = 72	*n* = 352^
	(%)	(%)
BACKGROUND		
– Age:		
– Perpetrators	29 yrs	27 yrs
– Victims	40 yrs	40 yrs
– Unemployed at murder	60%	70%
RELATIONSHIP BETWEEN PERPETRATOR and VICTIM		
– Stranger *(NA.)*	00%	37%
CONFLICTS and DISPUTES		
– On-going Dispute	46%	27%★★★
– Confrontation at Murder	65%	66%
– Prev.viol: Perp.against.vic.	15%	10%
– Prev.viol: Vic.against.perp	21%	08%★★
DRINKING and DRUGS		
– Perp. Drugs	14%	20%
– Perp. Drinking	71%	67%
– if perp. drinking, Drunk	67%	77%
– Drinking 3–6hrs	40%	41%
– Drinking all day	25%	21%
– Vic. Drinking	51%	46%
– if vic. drinking, Drunk	72%	74%
– of those drinking, drink together	36%	29%
MURDER EVENT		
– Home of victim	81%	44%★★★
– One perpetrator	78%	54%★★★
– No Witness	72%	57%★★
– Perpetrator [anger, rage, indignant]	51%	38%
– Injuries = 5 + injuries	63%	72%
CAUSE OF DEATH		
– Strangle	04%	08%
– Stab	54%	46%
– Beat w/object	17%	18%
– Beat w/hands/feet	9%	18%
– Shot	16%	10%

OFFENSE/s		
Murder + 2nd offense (yes)	30%	41%
– if 2nd offense:'property offense':	71%	63%

statistically significant: *p < .05, **p < .01, ***p < .001
^ numbers vary when: (not applicable) and/or (missing data)

Conflicts, disputes and previous violence

Ongoing disputes between perpetrators and victims were common, and were much more likely in Family.Murders than Other.Murders (46% vs 27%*). While confrontations at the time of the murder were common among both groups (65% vs 66%) the content of these confrontations varied greatly across the five subtypes of Family.Murder. Previous violence by the perpetrators against their victims was unusual (15% vs 10%). The data reveal that previous violence by the victims against the perpetrators was more likely in family murders than Other.Murders (21% vs 8%*). That is, one-fifth of the men who were murdered had previously been violent to the family member who murdered them, possibly making these acts of revenge, retaliation or self-defense. Despite this, the majority of these men did not have a previous history of violence by either man against the other.

Drinking, drunkenness and drugs

Drinking and drunkenness were common both among Family.Murders and Other. Murders. Among the perpetrators of Family Murders, 71% of them had been drinking, and 67% of those who had been drinking were defined as drunk. This pattern was fairly similar among the men who committed Other.Murders, as 67% of them who had been drinking, and 77% of those who had been drinking were defined as drunk. Among the victims, about half of them had been drinking at the time they were killed (51% vs 46%), and nearly two-thirds of the victims who had been drinking were defined as drunk (72% vs 74%). About one-third of the perpetrators and victims were drinking together before the murder (36% vs 29%).

Murder event

Family.Murders usually took place in the home of the victim compared to Other. Murders that were much less likely to take place in a home (81% vs 44%*). Further comparisons of Family.Murders and Other.Murders reveal that Family Murders were more likely to involve only one perpetrator (78% vs. 54%*), and no witnesses (72% vs 57%*). Half of the Family.Murderers were defined as angry, in a rage or indignant compared to Other.Murderers (51% vs 38%). Even so the majority of both Family.Murders and Other.Murders inflicted five or more injuries (63% vs 72%).

138 Murder between men in the family

Cause of death

Stabbing was the most common cause of death both in Family.Murders and in Other.Murders (54% vs 47%). Other causes of death included beating with an object (17% vs 18%) and shooting (16% vs 10%). Strangling was rare (4% vs 8%).

Other offenses

A minority of both types of murder involved a second offense (30% vs 41%), and most of these were property offences (71% vs 63%).

Overall, Family.Murders were more likely than Other.Murders to involve an 'ongoing dispute' prior to the murder, more likely to have *no witnesses*, and victims were more likely to be *alone* when they were killed. Compared to Other.Murders, the perpetrators and victims of Family.Murders were slightly more likely to have been drinking, and a majority of those who had been drinking were defined as drunk. Family.Murders were far more likely than Other.Murders to have been committed in the home of the victim, to involve a single perpetrator, and to have had no witness. About half of the Family.Murderers were angry, indignant or in a rage compared to just over one-third of the men who committed Other.Murders.

Summary and conclusions

The family and extended kin group is a complex institution with members of all ages and both sexes who are related through birth and blood or through marriage and cohabitation. These diverse bonds and relationships can be the source of conflicts and disputes. Everything is there: love and affection, conflict and hatred, competition, status, privilege, and more. Although all of the ingredients for conflict are there, the family in its many configurations seems to work fairly well for most people most of the time. But failures can be intense, long lasting, explosive, aggressive, and violent. Murder is rarely the outcome of conflicts within and between families, or any other conflicts, but it does occur, and these cases articulate some of the situations and circumstances in which family relationships and dynamics are involved in events that end in death.

In general, most homicides in the family involve the killing of women and children, but here we have focused only on male–male murders within the broad context of family relations in an effort to examine the nature and diversity of lethal events in which men are both the perpetrators and the victims. We classified family murders between men into five subtypes: 1) Blood relatives (including grandfathers, fathers, sons and brothers); 2) Gay intimate partners; 3) Collateral intimate partner murders – Male victims; 4) Family feuds and feuding families; and 5) Brothers against others. We have focused on the differing relationship between the men who commit these murders and the men they kill. We began with the closest relatives who are related by blood, followed by those related through marriage or cohabitation. The 'collateral murders' of men primarily involved conflicts between men and women in intimate relationships but ended with the killing of another man. This includes men who were trying to protect the perpetrator's woman partner from further abuse, to men who become the 'new male partners' when women separate or divorce husbands/boyfriends who respond by killing her new partner. Feuds between families involve men from one family acting together to murder a man or men from another kin group. Last, we examined when brothers band together to kill a man/men who is neither related to them nor party to a family feud, but an 'outsider' deemed to have caused an 'offense' or a 'category' of person they despise, and brothers band together to attack the transgressor, or act as a unit to kill an outsider for no apparent reason. These murders constitute the breadth of those that occur within the broad context of relations within and between male members of the family with all of its cultural ties, loyalties, conflicts and animosities.

Notes

1. As both grandfathers were over 65, the data from these two cases are analyzed with the murders of Older.Men (Chapter 6), but are used here to illustrate the killing of older men in the family, i.e. data from the two cases have not been double counted.
2. Quote also used in Chapter 8, prison-remorse.

References

Cavanagh, K., Dobash, R. E., and Dobash, R. P., 2005. Men who murder children inside and outside the family. *British Journal of Social Work*, 35, 667–688.

Cavanagh, K., Dobash, R. E., and Dobash, R. P., 2007. The murder of children by fathers in the context of child abuse. *Child Abuse & Neglect*, 31, 731–746.

Dobash, R. E. and Dobash, R.P., 2012. Who died?: Murder of others in the context of intimate partner conflict, *Violence Against Women*, 18, 662–671.

Dobash, R. E. and Dobash, R. P., 2015. *When Men Murder Women*. New York: Oxford University Press. See 'Intimate Partner Collateral Murders, pp. 58–62, and 'Subject Index' p. 332, listing of 'collateral murders/killings.' For Murder.Event: for comparisons: Male–Male Murder and Intimate Partner Murder (of women), 37, 51–66, 283–284.

Dobash, R. P. and Dobash, R. E., 2018. When men murder children. In T. Brown, D. Tyson and P. F. Arias (eds) *When Parents Kill Children: Understanding Filicide*. Cham, Switzerland: Palgrave Macmillan, pp. 81–101.

Ewing, C. P., 1997. *Fatal Families: The Dynamics of Intrafamilial Homicide*. Thousand Oaks and London: Sage, 100–117.

Heide, K. M., 2013. *Understanding Parricide: When Sons and Daughters Kill Parents*. New York: Oxford University Press.

Liem, M. and Koenraadt, F., 2018. *Domestic Homicide: Patterns and Dynamics*. Abingdon: Routledge.

Vance, J. D., 2016. *Hillbilly Elegy: A Memoir of a Family and Culture in Crisis*. New York: Harper Collins. ISBN: 978–0–06–230054.

Websdale, N., 2010. *Familicidal Hearts: The Emotional Styles of 211 Killers*. New York: Oxford University Press.

140 Murder between men in the family

Online and newspapers

Cain and Abel (the first murder), Wikipedia, https://en.wikipedia.org/w/index.php?title=-
Cain_and_Abel&id=897221323 [Accessed May 16, 2019].

Hatfield–McCoy Feud. Available at: https://en.m.wikipedia.org/wiki/Hatfield-McCoy_feud
[Accessed 12 January, 2020].

Romeo and Juliet, (family feud, murder, forbidden love and collateral deaths) Available at:
www.rsc.org.uk/romeo-and-juliet [Accessed May 16, 2019]. https://en.wikipedia.org/w/
index.php?title=Romeo_and_Juliet&oldid=754867238, [Accessed May 16, 2019].

West Side Story, (the fight) (West Side Story Sndtrk – The Rumble/Tonight, YouTube.
com). Available at: www.youtube.com/watch?v=dSeQSSXFSNU

West Side Story, 2020. Steven Spielberg, 20th Century Fox, release December 18, 2020.
Available at: https://en.wikipedia.org/wiki/West-Side-Story Movie (2020)

West Side Story (new Broadway play), opens, February 20, 2020. @Westsidestorybway.com

5
SEXUAL MURDER BETWEEN MEN

Of the 424 male–male murders in the Murder Study, 32 cases (8%) involved a sexual element of some kind. Sexual murders between men are complex and varied. They involve different types of relationships between the perpetrators and their victims, occur in a wide range of contexts and circumstances, and involve various sexual elements in the dynamic and sometimes changing elements of the murder events themselves. In order to capture this diversity, we have used a broad conceptualization of sexual murder that not only includes explicit physical acts of a sexual nature but also includes issues relating to the sexual identity or sexual orientation of the victims and/or perpetrators, as well as accusations about sexual acts that may or may not have occurred but are used to incite violence and/or to 'justify' its use against the victim. The nature of this diversity and complexity is shown in the accounts of sexual murders taken from the casefiles and interviews in the Murder Study, and organized around themes that characterize some of the differing ways in which sex and sexual identity were involved in the situations and circumstances preceding and surrounding these murders. They illustrate the nature of hate crimes involving gay 'bashing' and homophobia; the mixture of motives and dilemmas when sex is exchanged for accommodation or money, cases involving homosexual advances and claims of homosexual advances, murders involving prostitution, sex with children, and serial killing.

There is a vast literature on sexual attacks and sexual murders committed by men against women, but much less on sexual murders committed by men against other men. This reflects several facts: that far more women than men are the victims of sexual violence; that far more sexual murders are committed by men against women than by men against other men; and that women are rarely the perpetrators of sexual murder. These patterns were mirrored in the wider Murder

142 Sexual murder between men

Study that included all types of murder committed by and against men, women and children, with clear gender differences between men and women both as perpetrators and as victims of murder. Across the entire sample of 866 casefiles in the Murder Study, 91% of the *perpetrators* were male ($n = 786$) while only 9% ($n = 80$) were female, which reveals an extreme gender imbalance among perpetrators. The gender imbalance was less extreme among the *victims* of these 786 male perpetrators which included 424 adult, male victims, 271 adult, women victims, 36 boys and 55 girls under age 16 who were murdered by men (see Chapter 1, Murder Study-Casefiles; Dobash and Dobash, 2015, p. 278, 2018). If we focus only on murders committed by men that involved sex, the gender difference among the victims becomes extremely skewed: of the 271 male–female murders, 36% involved sex, while of the 424 male–male murders only (7.5%) involved sex. These gender differences help explain why male–male sexual murders have received much less attention and why the gaze on sexual murder usually turns to male perpetrators and woman victims.

This does not mean, however, that sexual murders between men are unimportant or that they have they been completely ignored. In 'Killing Gay Men, 1976–2001,' Bartlett noted that 'The existing literature relating to sexual crime … pre-supposes a male assailant and a female victim,' but asserted that 'gay sexual homicide 'constitutes a coherent object of study.' Using files from the Crown Prosecution Service and the Home Office Homicide Index, Bartlett focused on 'cases of sexual crime in a context where women are absent' (Bartlett, 2007, p. 573–595), and his study of 77 male–male sexual killings (in Britain) is similar to Stephen Tomsen's (2002) study of 74 convicted men (in Australia) (see other studies of male–male sexual violence and murder).[1]

All those who have examined sexual murders between men, have found them to be complex and difficult to classify.

> Sexually associated killings present a specific category of offences which comprise a huge variety of manifestations. Attempts to find a suitable classification based on aspects such as sexual motivation (sexually motivated murder usually fails to capture the essence of this phenomenon). Situational variables such as intoxication, resistance shown by the victim or the presence of witnesses play a major role in determining whether or not an assault will end fatally and be classified as sexually associated.
>
> *(Birkel and Dern, 2013, p. 323, citing Proulx,*
> *Beauregard, Cusson and Nicole, 2007)*

This reflects our own experience in trying to classify the 32 cases of male–male sexual murder in the Murder Study. Although we encountered some of these complexities in our earlier examination of the sexual murders committed by men against women, we found sexual murders committed by men against other men to be far more varied and complex. While it is important to examine sexual murders where men are both the victims and the perpetrators, this is neither straightforward nor easy. Official figures about male–male sexual murders are often not available, some figures do not specify the gender of the victims (who are usually women) with the result that the minority of male victims of murders involving sex or sexual identity are either unavailable or incorrectly incorporated with findings about women victims. Thus, the need for disaggregation is paramount if we are to focus on male–male murders that occur in a sexual context and obtain further knowledge about such cases.

Main patterns – sexual murders between men

Of the 424 male–male murders in the Murder Study, 32 cases (7.5%) involved a sexual element of some kind. Who are these men? What was their relationship? Had they previously been in conflict? What happened in the murder event? Were there witnesses? Were others involved? What was the nature of the attack and the cause of death? In answering these questions, we begin with the 'main patterns' that characterize all 32 male–male sexual murders, then follow with textual accounts of 'six subtypes' of sexual murder that illustrate the nature and diversity of these murders. Then, we compare 'Sexual murders' with 'Other. Murders' that did not involve sex in order to consider how they are alike and how they differ.

Background and relationship between perpetrators and victims

At the time of the murder, the average age of perpetrators was 25 years, and the average of their victims was 37. The majority of perpetrators were unemployed (67%). Only 7 of the 32 cases of sexual murder (22%) involved men who were *strangers* while in 25 cases (78%) the men were acquainted, and these divided almost equally between relatively short and longer acquaintances of months or years. Most were acquainted through contacts in pubs or clubs, and a few lived together as roommates or as sexual partners.

Conflicts, disputes and previous violence

While 60% involved a confrontation at the time of the murder, only a few of the men had previously been in any form of ongoing dispute (19%).

Drinking, drunkenness and drugs

At the time of the murder, 72% of perpetrators and 47% of the victims had been drinking, and most of them were drunk. By contrast, only 17% of perpetrators were on 'drugs.'

144 Sexual murder between men

Murder event

Most sexual murders were committed by only one man who acted alone (73%). The locations were divided almost equally between private places like homes and residences (47%), and public places like parks, streets or waste ground. The vast majority of sexual murders were not witnessed (80%), and most involved five or more injuries (83%).

Cause of death

The methods used to kill the men varied including: stabbing (60%), followed by strangling (13%), beating with an object (13%), beating with hands and feet (10%), and shooting (3%).

Other offenses (in addition to murder)

Slightly less than half of these murders involved a second offense (43%), and very few of the additional offenses (20%) involved a property offense such as burglary or theft (Table 5.1).

Overall, most sexual murders were committed by one man who was acquainted with the victim, no witnesses were present, and the locations were divided between the home of the victim and public places such as parks, streets, and vacant areas. Three-quarters of the perpetrators and just under half of the victims had been drinking, and most of those who were drinking were drunk. One-third of the perpetrators and victims were drinking together. Stabbing was the most common cause of death, and most murders involved five or more injuries. Nearly half of the sexual murders also involved a second offense, but very few of these involved a property offense.

Sexual murders between men – six subtypes

These murders are variously related to 'sex' and 'sexual identity.' Some involve the sexual act itself, some are about sexual identity, and some are about various sexual practices. In order to deal with this diversity, we have divided these murders into six subtypes that illustrate the different ways in which sex and/or sexual identity were involved in these events. As shown in the narratives, what 'counts' includes varying aspects of the sexual act itself, sexual identity of the perpetrators and/or victims, and various notions that reflect wider social conceptions about the sexual behaviors of men, and between men.

> Sexual murders between men – six subtypes
> 1   Hate crimes against gay men
> 2   Sexual exchanges and mixed messages
> 3   Homosexual advance

Sexual murder between men 145

4 Prostitution
5 Pedophilia – both false claims and previous offences
6 Serial sexual murder.

Subtype 1. Hate crimes against gay men

Some gay men were murdered by men who were not gay or seeking any form of sex from their victim but, instead, baited them, hunted them down and killed them in attacks that were often very vicious and brutal. The men were often strangers, and the victims were killed because of who they were rather than because of anything, sexual or otherwise, they may have done to/with the man or men who killed them. In many of our cases, the killers were fairly young men or adolescents who acted together in a group against a man they 'targeted' for violence, robbery, or both. When acting within the context of a group, they seemed to be emboldened in initiating attacks and seemed to be 'performing' for one another in displays of ever-increasing levels of violence in what might appear to be a competition to introduce differing kinds of attack and elevating the severity. There seemed to be an excitement among the group and a delight in the entire process of stalking and baiting the man selected as prey followed by the drama of inflicting pain, and the competition to introduce different forms of violence with increasing levels of severity and injury. The following cases illustrate how men 'worked' in a group to rob and brutalize gay men who were strangers to them but defined as 'fair game' because they were gay. The first case involved four youths who frequently assaulted and robbed gay men in a public park where gay men went to 'cruise' for sexual partners. The level of violence was brutal, and a sense of fun and pleasure seemed to be gained from the process of luring and attacking the victims before robbing them of money and valuables which the perpetrators believed would be much easier and less risky than robbing others because they thought gay men would be less likely to report the assaults and robberies to the police.

> *Hate crime – strangers – four youths go gay bashing in the park and commit multiple muggings of gay men over many weeks before this vicious attack and murder*
>
> The perpetrator (16) and two or three others of a similar age (co-accused) were drinking in a club and decided to go out 'poof bashing' in a local park. They robbed the victim (25), punched and kicked him, and attempted to throw him over railings onto a railway embankment. One of the perpetrators seems to have been the leading spirit behind the campaign of 'poof-bashing' that resulted in this murder.
>
> [Murder]
> On the evening of the murder, the perpetrator (16) and two others, aged 15 and 16, had been drinking, and at 3am decided to go to the park,

146 Sexual murder between men

a well-known haunt for gay men, to indulge in 'poof-bashing'. They were in the park with two other youths who did not take part in any of the subsequent events, and who were later the principle witnesses for the prosecution. Earlier in the evening, they had been in the park and assaulted a man with the intention of robbing him. When the murder victim entered the park, he was approached by the group who punched him to the ground. He got up and ran off but they chased and caught him and proceeded to punch and kick him into unconsciousness. They then dragged him to some bushes and continued to kick him mainly about the head and neck. During the attack, the victim bled profusely and a large pool of blood was found later.

[Injuries]
The injuries included a fracture of the nasal bone and a hemorrhage which was caused by a severe kick to the neck. He was dragged to the railings which separated the park from an embankment wall which dropped 40 feet to the railway below. The perpetrator pulled down the victim's trousers and kicked and stamped on his private parts. He then tried to lift him over the railings but was unable to do so. During the lengthy attack, the other two youths tried to stop further violence but were unsuccessful. The four youths then left the scene, but the perpetrator returned to administer further kicks to the head of the now moribund body, and also to beat him about the head with a branch which he had broken into several pieces. The body was found the following morning with multiple injuries to the head, face and neck, and bruising to various parts of the body and private parts. The cause of death was inhalation of blood and sub-arachnoid hemorrhage.

[Perpetrator's account]
He said that in order to finance his drinking and cannabis consumption he was regularly stealing and, in the company of others, mugging people in the streets. He said, 'It led us to mugging gays', and for two weeks he and his friends acted together to commit at least ten muggings of gays. He said the normal routine was for two youths to hide and for a third to 'play-bait' the man (pretend they wanted to be to be picked up for sex). He said the 'bait' would lure the man away, and then the others would pounce on him, steal his money and jewelry, and beat him up. He said, 'It was exciting. You felt your adrenalin going. It was a big laugh'. He said four people took part in the crime but two subsequently turned 'Queens evidence' [gave evidence for the prosecution]. He recognized that at the time of the offence that, 'his lifestyle was uncontrollable'.

Sexual murder between men **147**

[Prison governor's report]
He appears to have a rather ambivalent attitude to the offence. He expresses some remorse but admits that 'gay bashing' was regarded by those with whom he mixed as an easy way to earn money as an alternative to stealing. He describes the offense in a rather matter-of-fact manner, and there is nothing to suggest he has genuine feelings of regret. On looking back, he considers he was extremely young and did not know what he was doing.

(★161cf1.4.4)

This group of youths also attacked and robbed gay men both because they were gay and thus easy prey for robbery. That evening, they had already assaulted several gay men in the local park. All the victims were strangers to the perpetrators who worked as a team with a pre-planned approach before attack.

Hate crime – strangers – one night in the park – a group of young males and a 14-year-old girl – three assaults and robberies of gay men, and one murder

[Context and circumstances – trial judge report]
The perpetrator (17) and four others (all teens), and the perpetrator's girlfriend (14) were together in the park late in the evening where they carried out three assaults and robberies between 10.30pm and shortly after midnight. Part of the park was frequented during the late evenings by homosexuals looking for meetings with other homosexuals. Each victim was approached and asked for a cigarette.
–The first victim (27) was threatened with a knife, hit over the head with a bottle, kicked in the body and head, and robbed. The group then went away and the victim left the park. He was not seriously injured and did not consult a doctor.
–The second assault occurred about an hour later against a man (57) who went to the park to meet other homosexuals. He arrived about 11:30pm wearing black boots, a studded black belt and leather bands round his arm, and carrying a knife for his own protection knowing the area to be dangerous. He was assaulted and robbed.
–The third victim (35) was chased, viciously assaulted, robbed, and murdered.

[Injuries]
The injuries were horrific, 83 were noted at the post-mortem including: extensive fractures of the skull, extensive fractures of almost all the bones of the face including the lower jaw bone, and multiple blunt force injuries of the neck, and the front and sides of the chest and limbs. Great force was required to inflict these injuries. The victim was found in the park by a policeman at about 1.30am, and taken to hospital where he died soon afterwards.

148 Sexual murder between men

Earlier, at about 12.30, the same policeman had seen the three males in the park, and they ran off. One of the co-accused, the 14-year-old girlfriend of one of the perpetrators, told the police officer she did not know who the others were. She was taken to the police station and questioned, and her physical participation in the murder was viewed as unlikely.

Meanwhile, the others went to a party taking place nearby where they spoke about what had happened and referred to the victims as 'poofs'. The following afternoon, the perpetrators went to a jeweler and sold a wedding ring they had taken from one of the victims. At the time of the murder, the main perpetrator was employed and had worked for a demolition contractor for about two and a half years before his arrest. He usually consumed about twelve cans of lager on Friday and Saturday nights.

(*282cf1.2.4)

The next man was walking home alone from the pub when he was attacked by two young men who brutalized him and left him near death. Over a few hours, they returned to the scene three times to inflict more injuries, destroy evidence, and raise a false alarm. They gave no motive for their actions against a total stranger, but the nature of the attacks on the sexual parts of his body, the huge number of injuries, and repeat visits to the scene in order to inflict more harm strongly suggest that this was a hate crime directed at a stranger because of his sexual orientation. They later blamed one another and attempted to blame the victim by alleging a homosexual advance.

Hate crime – strangers – two men repeatedly and brutally attack a gay man over several hours

[Context]
The perpetrator (22) and his co-accused (24) killed with severe violence a 23-year-old man who was a stranger to them. The victim had been drinking in a pub and was a bit drunk. While walking home, he encountered the two perpetrators who attacked him. They kicked and punched him unconscious, stripped him naked and dumped him in a hedge. They took his clothes back to the house of one of the perpetrators and burned them. Then, they both changed their own clothes and returned to the scene with a coffee table leg and a screwdriver [the victim was still alive]. The table leg was used to batter the victim and was rammed up his anus. They then stabbed him 68 times with the screwdriver. A boulder weighing 40 lbs was dropped on his head at least twice. He was kicked in the genitals, and there were numerous blows to other parts of his body.

The perpetrators then returned to the same house as before, burned the table leg and tossed the screwdriver. They again returned to the scene, put a coat under the victim's head as a pillow and another coat over his body. About three hours after they encountered the victim, they raised the alarm by rousing the local residents and telling them that they had come across two men attacking the victim. A few hours later, they admitted to the police that they had done it.

No apparent motive was given to the police. At their trial, they alleged for the first time that the victim had been very offensive and *alleged a homosexual advance*. Each blamed the other. One of the perpetrators claimed that the co-accused was responsible for all the violence, and claimed that he had tried to protect the victim. He later retracted this statement, and took his share of the blame.

*(*692cf1.2.8)*

These murders were committed by young men who did not know the men they killed, had no previous contact with them, and were not involved in anything that might be defined as a conflict, a dispute, or a sexual encounter. Instead, they seem to have killed the men simply and solely because of who they were rather than because of anything they may have done to the perpetrator or anything that had taken place between them. 'Gay bashing' is usually a group activity engaged in by several individuals acting together rather than by a single person acting alone. The violence is often fueled by drunkenness, a sense of male comradery, notions of social and/or moral superiority, and the thrill and excitement of doing violence to another with little prospect of being harmed in the process. From the perpetrator's point of view, the social identity of the victim is of paramount importance in viewing him as a 'legitimate' target for violence. At the same time, the perpetrator's sense of his own social identity as someone who is 'not gay 'or does not appear to be so, is also being demonstrated by the perpetrators both to themselves and to others.

In Orlando, Florida on June 12, 2016, a mass shooting in a gay club by a 29-year-old security guard resulted in the wounding of 53 individuals and the deaths of 49 others plus the perpetrator. The mass shooting was followed by a three-hour stand-off involving first responders including the police, firefighters and medical services. It was variously described as a hate crime focused on LGBT people, a terrorist attack motivated by American-led interventions in Iraq and Syria, or an attack on the Hispanic community. Despite these speculations, it was generally described as the 'deadliest incident of violence against LGBT people in U.S. history', and the deadliest terrorist attack in the U.S. since the September 11 attacks in 2001. According to the various accounts, there may have been a mixture of personal, political, and sexual orientations in the behavior and thinking of the perpetrator, and a corresponding mixture of intentions and motives in the events preceding the murder. Was this mass shooting in a gay night club a hate crime against gay people? A political act against foreign nations? A racist attack against Hispanics? Or something more immediate or personal? What was he thinking? Why did he do it?

150 Sexual murder between men

The US Federal Bureau of Investigation (FBI) and the Central Intelligence Agency (CIA) both conducted investigations and found no evidence of communications between the perpetrator and any terrorist organizations, any evidence of the use of gay dating websites or apps, or that he was a patron of the gay nightclub where he shot and killed or wounded nearly 100 people. Some said he may have previously visited the club, and others thought he might have been mixed or confused about his sexual identity. What is clear is that gay and Hispanic people were targeted, and that firearms allowed the perpetrator to greatly increase the number of victims he was able to wound and kill during this event.

In response, the club owner, Barbara Poma, created the onePULSE Foundation in 2017 to fund a memorial site and museum to open in 2020. And in 2019, Madonna released, 'God Control,' a song supporting gun control that depicted a nightclub shooting with explicit images of a shooting in an effort to get viewers to 'wake up' to the effects of such shootings and the need for gun control. Madonna makes a call for gun control in the lyrics and a written statement. The video begins: WARNING: 'This video is disturbing and viewing discretion is advised.' The video ends: 'Every year over 36,000 Americans are killed in acts of gun violence and approximately, (1,000,000) more are shot and injured.'No one is safe. Gun control. Now' (https://youtu.be/zv-sdTOw5cs). (See Beaumont-Thomas, 2019; Pulse Nightclub).

In contrast to the mass shooting in Florida that involved scores of victims killed or wounded by a single perpetrator, most sexual murders between men usually involve only one or a few male perpetrators who kill one victim. Whether the number of perpetrators and victims are many or few, the details of the following cases from the Murder Study provide additional insights into the mixture of messages, intentions, motives, and orientations of perpetrators as they relate to lethal events that somehow involved sex, sexual orientations, or sexual identity.

Subtype 2. Sexual exchanges and mixed messages

Some murders occurred in the context of what appeared to be an 'exchange' of sex for a valued resource such as accommodation, alcohol, drugs, food, clothing, or a job. Unlike hate crimes against gay men that frequently involved strangers, the men in these murders were usually acquainted albeit in various ways and for various lengths of time. Some acquaintances were very brief while others were lengthy. For some men, the exchange of sex for accommodation or the like appeared to have been 'consensual' although the conditions of the arrangement may not have been verbalized or otherwise made explicit. Others said that they did not get involved in any form of 'agreement' to exchange sex for whatever was on offer. Still others claimed that the victim attempted a sexual act that they had not 'signed up to,' such as anal sex, and indicated that they responded violently when subjected to a sexual behavior that was unexpected or undesired.

Sexual murder between men **151**

The circumstances, messages and motives were sometimes mixed, and tables were sometimes turned. Some men had fallen on hard times, been cut adrift from family and or friends, become addicted to alcohol or drugs, were living rough on the streets, or were otherwise in need or vulnerable. Some were gay, some were not, some were unclear about their sexual identity, and some were hiding their identity from their family and friends. Some became involved in 'exchanges' with acquaintances or strangers for things they needed or wanted, and these exchanges sometimes involved sex that may or may not have been wanted or agreed.

Brief acquaintance – met on the street, went to victim's flat to drink, unwanted sexual advance

Can you tell me then what happened – the offense itself? The thing is, I don't really want to [say anything]. My name doesn't go on the sheet? [research questionnaire] *No, no, your name is confidential.* I was attacked. Somebody offered me accommodation. I was drinking with the person and the person attacked me, tried raping me and I hit him. I seen a hammer, and I hit him with the hammer and, unfortunately, he died. *Was this because you were out on the street drinking?* No. I went back to his flat. He met me on the street. He invited me back to his flat. *So, you went back to his flat? You were still drinking?* Then he actually, personally, he tried raping me. *What did he do to you?* He didn't actually do anything, but he attempted to. He dropped his trousers and tried dragging mine down. *And did you think he was dead or …?* No. I believed he wasn't dead at the time. What it was, I actually tied this guy up myself, panicking because he was a big guy and I thought he was going to kill me. I knew how to take the pulse. I told the courts [at his trial]. I took his pulse, and he was alive. I believe the reason he died is because the police weren't quick enough to go and find him.
*(*2011iv1.4.4)*

Brief acquaintance – perpetrator a homeless hitch hiker

The perpetrator (26) was temporarily homeless and between jobs. He was hitch-hiking, was picked up by the victim (34), stayed with the him for a weekend, and engaged in consensual sexual activity. According to the perpetrator, he killed the victim because of shame about the sex activity and in response to a sexual advance. He beat him over the head with a wine bottle, stole possessions from his flat, and left him to die.
*(*674cf1.1.5)*

Situations become even more complex when sex is exchanged for accommodation for a longer period of time. Some type of 'relationship' may be formed, or at least believed to be so in the mind of one of the men and, for him, the relationship becomes something more than a mere exchange. This murder involved an

152 Sexual murder between men

exchange of sex for accommodation but the perpetrator seemed to have been in various stages of denial about his own sexual orientations, lied about his sexual behavior to his friends and family, and in the end claimed that he killed the victim in order to prevent him from revealing their sexual relationship to his family. But at the time of the murder, he told friends his intention was 'to kill a queer,' bragged about having done so, and even took them to see the body.

Three year relationship – sex for accommodation

He (17) admitted to having a sex relationship with the victim (38) and living with him rent-free in return for sex. He said the motivation for the murder was to stop the victim telling his family about the relationship. Before the murder, he told several friends that he planned to kill the victim.
(*567cf1.4.4)

The next case involved sex, murder and a theft on a fairly grand scale that may have been of greatest importance. The perpetrator claimed the murder occurred when the victim attempted to have anal sex with him, but other events, including the robbery of all of the contents of his house, casts some doubt on this motive.

Brief acquaintance, sex exchanged for accommodation. Claimed unwanted sex act but stole the entire contents of his house.

[Context]
He (27) said he'd known the victim (42) for one week after arriving in [city] to look for employment. He booked into the Salvation Army hostel for the homeless, and then went to a pub 'frequented by homosexuals' where the victim offered him a drink. He said he was living rough, and the victim invited him to stay at his flat where they shared a double bed and slept together while naked.

[Murder]
When police questioned him about the murder, he admitted it and said that he struck the victim when he tried to have anal intercourse with him. He said he saw that the victim was seriously hurt (although not yet dead), wondered what to do, and decided to steal his property.

[After the murder – grand theft]
He hired a van, returned to the flat and loaded the entire contents of the flat, which took several trips (the flat was located in a tower block and several residents witnessed him loading furniture). He returned to his home in [another town] and unloaded the goods into his own house. He stole furniture, carpets, pictures, cameras, electrical equipment, and jewelry to value of £3,000 [about $5,000]. He gave some of the goods

Sexual murder between men **153**

to friends, sold others to second hand shops, and put an ad in the local paper advertising other items.

[The body]
The body was found about one week after the murder when a friend returned from holiday and tried to contact the victim. Decomposition and maggot infestation had started.

(★574cf1.4.4)

Murders within the context of an exchange of sex for accommodation were often committed by men who were younger and/or more disadvantaged than the men they killed. While the older men who offered resources in exchange for sex were apparently gay or bisexual, the sexual orientation of the perpetrators was not always clear, and may have varied over time and/or in differing circumstances. While some of the perpetrators were clearly gay and engaged in mutually agreed sexual behavior, others may have been unsure about their sexuality, or were straight men who engaged in behaviors with which they did not agree but did so in order to have a place to live, a job, or the like. Some of the comments of the perpetrators reflect these differing views, or mixed messages, about what they were doing and why.

Mixed messages about sexual orientation

In this case there was a lack of clarity about the sexual orientation of the perpetrator. The victim was a 'well known and well-regarded' member of a particular gay club, but it is unclear whether the perpetrator was 'bating and luring' him with sexual suggestions and innuendo or seeking to engage him in a sexual act. Was the perpetrator gay, prejudiced against gays or mixed about his own sexual orientations? Or was it some combination of these factors? What is clear is that the killing was brutal, and that sex and sexual identity were factors in the events preceding the murder. In the police interview, he began by denying that he knew the victim.

Motive unclear – a sexual flirtation or 'bating' a gay man?

The motive was unclear. There was a sexual context prior to the murder but this could have had different meanings for the victim (43) and the perpetrator (20). The victim was most probably killed because he was a homosexual as evidenced by the very serious violence to his 'private parts.'

[Murder and injuries]
The perpetrator kicked the victim repeatedly all over his body rupturing his kidney and causing multiple fractures to his neck, body, larynx, spine, ribs, and considerable damage to his private parts including his testes and anus. All of the victim's clothing, except one sock and one shoe, were torn

154 Sexual murder between men

from him during the attack. The body was wedged underneath a flight of cast iron steps leading from the emergency exit of an alleyway. He disposed of his own clothes and shoes, and during six hours of police interviews, denied any knowledge of the victim or involvement in the crime.

A sexual flirtation, or 'baiting' a gay man?

[Context]
Earlier in the evening, the perpetrator and victim were seen in conversation inside the nightclub. They were together on the dance floor and the perpetrator had his arm around the victim's shoulder. They were talking and their heads were close together. The perpetrator grabbed the victim by the hips on the dance floor and brought them toward him as they engaged in a simulated sex act. The perpetrator was touching the victim's bottom in a sexual manner. At 2 am, they left the club and were seen in conversation outside. The perpetrator was drunk.

[Motive – unclear]
The perpetrator and victim were seen together outside the club. He may have lured the victim into the alley to have sex and changed his mind and attacked him instead, or he may have lured him in with the promise of sex but actually for the purpose of attacking him because he was a homosexual.

[The body]
The victim was covered in mud and blood, and there was human excreta in his trousers.

[After the murder]
A taxi driver took the perpetrator home, and he later returned to the club at 3.30am wearing different clothing. He appears to have spent the night at his mother's flat who may have helped him dispose of the soiled clothing.

[Police interview]
During the police interview, the perpetrator denied speaking to the victim that night other than saying 'Hello', and denied having any contact with him. He says he can't remember because of drink, yet he remembers other details such as requesting that a particular record be played. The defendant sought to cover his tracks by disposing of his clothing and footwear before his arrest.

[The victim]
The victim was regarded as a homosexual, and was well known and well regarded at the club. Some witnesses say they saw the victim crying about 2 am.

[Trial judge]
The present murder was a particularly savage and brutal attack although no weapon was used. The attack was unprovoked, violent and prolonged, and caused multiple fractures of the larynx, spine and ribs, a ruptured kidney, and considerable damage to the private parts. All the deceased's clothing, except his sock, were torn from him in the course of the attack. The trial judge recommended a tariff of 16 years.

[Lord Chief Justice comment]
'This was a horrifying crime and I do not disagree with the trial judge's tariff.'

(*867cf1.4.4)

The fact that some witnesses saw the victim crying at 2am may suggest that he had taken as genuine the sexualized encounter with the perpetrator on the dance floor earlier in the evening, and that it may have had a romantic meaning for him which was later dispelled when witnesses saw him alive and crying at 2am before he was brutally attacked and killed. Aside from this and other speculations about the possible meanings of the events preceding the murder, the nature and severity of the attack and injuries suggests that the perpetrator was not only intent on killing the man he attacked but the additional and explicit attack upon his genitals clearly focuses attention on the sexual nature of this murder.

Subtype 3. Homosexual advance

Some murderers claimed that a homosexual advance had occurred, and that this was the reason for their lethal response. The 'homosexual advance defense' is neither new nor novel. In some countries, it continues to be used as a legal defense based on the idea that 'the provocation was such that it was capable of causing a "*reasonable man*" to do as the defendant did,' i.e. to kill in response (*Holmes* v *DPP* 1946, cited in Wheatie, 2016, 39, note 5). In cultural terms, this appears to be saying that the 'destruction' of a man's heterosexual status through an unwanted homosexual act upon his body warrants, or justifies, a response up to and including the killing of the man who through such actions 'destroys' or 'alters' his manhood. Although this may no longer serve as a legal defense in many countries, it may still have a certain cultural resonance with members of a jury and may be recounted by perpetrators and their lawyers as part of the context in which the lethal violence occurred. It implies that a 'real man' is a heterosexual man, and that a homosexual act upon his body somehow robs him of that status which, once lost, can never be reinstated. (see Oliver, 1999; Comstock, 1992; Mezey and King, 1992; Mison, 1992; Dressler, 1995; Banks, 1997; New South Wales, 1998; Lunny, 2003; Bartlett, 2007).

In the following cases, perpetrators claimed their lethal actions were in response to a homosexual advance, and these accounts provide insights into the situations and circumstances used in an effort to 'justify' the murder even when such claims are false.

156 Sexual murder between men

Homosexual advance – drinking partners (friends), perpetrator awoke while being sexually abused

The defense claimed that the perpetrator (22) was provoked as he woke to find the victim (59) sexually assaulting him. The perpetrator and victim were drinking partners.

[Murder]
The perpetrator fell asleep and says he woke in great pain to find the victim fellating him to ejaculation and biting his penis (the evidence supports both claims). He killed him by stamping on his face at least six times. The prosecution suggested there was consensual mutual stimulation in which the victim caused him [perpetrator] such pain that he lost his temper and killed him.

[Police interview]
'Well, he was giving me a nosh, a gobble, when I woke up and my bell end [penis] was red raw. I was sick of it, so I jumped up and down on his head a few times. I rang my mam straight away and told her what I did.'

[Defense case]
He claims he reacted because of previous abuse when a boy attempted to rape him in a youth detention center several years before. He had a horror of forced sex, and this constitutes, 'a factor to be taken into account in sentencing.'

[Trial judge]
I wish that one could say that your history is an unusual one but, sadly, so many young men like you abuse drugs and abuse alcohol. Your drugs were prescribed but, in a sense, you abused your drugs by putting alcohol on top, and so you drifted, and one thing led to another.

[Background report in prison]
He claimed two attempted sex attacks on him both in and outside prison, and that he reacted very violently to the alleged attacks. He told a social worker that he was confused about his sexuality and suggested that he was seeing an older man (not the victim), and possibly charging him money for sexual favors.

(*616cf1.4.4)

Homosexual advance against a teenager and a threat against his younger brothers

[Pre-trial psychiatric report]
The perpetrator (17) attacked the victim (47) with three chairs, and broken bits of chairs were found in his flat. The victim had 38 head injuries, and bruising to his chest, arms, and legs. When police asked, 'What

happened?' he said, 'He invited me in for a drink, and we sat down talking and drinking. He tried to touch my balls, so I picked up the chair and smashed it over his head. He reported that the victim said, 'I'm going to fuck you and fuck your brothers.'

(★606cf1.4.4)

While a few of the perpetrators had been sexually assaulted or raped by the man they killed, others knowingly and falsely claimed that they killed in response to a sexual advance or a sexual attack in the hope that this would resonate with members of the jury and result in a finding of 'not guilty' or in a lesser sentence from the judge.

False claim of a homosexual advance
Married man (30) killed practicing homosexual (54) claims homosexual advance – no evidence to support the claim.

(★048cf1.4.4)

False claim of a homosexual advance
Killed for financial gain but claimed a sexual advance – no evidence to support the claim.

(★721cf1.2.8)

Subtype 4. Prostitution

Selling sex for money, whether by women or men, has always been a risky business, but the person at risk often differs when the encounter involves men buying sex from women than when men are buying sex from other men. When men buy sex from women, it is usually the seller (woman) who is at risk from the buyer (man), but the opposite is often the case when men buy sex from other men. The tables may be turned, and it is the male *buyer* of sex rather than the male *seller* of sex who is most at risk of a violent attack, robbery, or both. So, what is happening and what seems to be making the difference? The issue at stake here seems to be at least partially related to the age of the two men. When the buyer of sex is older than the seller, this may render the purchaser more vulnerable to attack. While different issues may be at stake including disagreements about how much is paid or what is actually delivered, the older man seeking to buy sex from a younger man may be the weaker and more vulnerable of the two men not only in terms of his physical strength and prowess, but also in terms of his desirability as a potential sexual partner. This imbalance may, of course, be altered or offset when the older man is more affluent or has a higher social status than the younger man from whom he attempts to buy sex or upon whom he wishes to force his sexual attentions. The following cases illustrate both, and reflect on the contradictory positions of each man in such encounters. They contain mixed messages of disillusionment and anger on the part of the younger men who were selling sex. Disillusionment about themselves, dissatisfaction about their lives as sex

158 Sexual murder between men

workers, and/or anger and resentment directed at the older man who is buying or attempting to buy sex from them. In addition, some men were also trying to rob their customers which brought additional risks to these encounters.

Prostitution – sex worker, alcoholic with five years as a 'rent boy,' kills stranger who refused to pay

This 23-year-old man ('rent boy') had consensual sex with a man, the 53-year-old victim, and when the victim refused to pay, he strangled him and stabbed him at least 22 times.

[Statement to police]
After I had masturbated him and he'd refused to pay, I thought of the five years of me being on the gay scene. It made me sick, and I just lost my temper. Many times, I have helped old ladies across the road and done favors for old people. I have even picked up worms from the road and put them on a patch of grass. If I had been sober, I would never have done something like this.

(*650cf1.4.4)

He saw himself as kind and helpful to people, even to worms, but was resentful about his life as a prostitute, drunk, and angry that he was being cheated out of his fee for sex. By contrast, the psychiatrists viewed him as a drunk who was cold, remorseless, indifferent to others, and someone who refused to learn from his past. Both views were recorded in his casefile. For the next man, a period in prison had kept him away from the public, but this did not last for even one full day after his release. Prostitution, alcohol, and theft were all involved in his immediate return to offending.

Prostitution – first day out of prison, kills stranger who offered money for sex in a public toilet

A 21-year-old man killed a 56-year-old man whom he met in public toilets and who offered him money for sex.

[Police summary]
On the day of the murder, the perpetrator had just been released from prison. He was at home with his parents and drank a bit. He went out in the evening, and when walking home went into the toilets where the victim chatted to him and offered him £10 for sex. He pretended to go along with the idea in order to get the money. When the victim offered the money, he grabbed it, knocked the victim down, kicked him twice, and stole his watch. The victim died within five minutes from asphyxiation due to blood in his lungs.

(*677cf1.4.4)

Subtype 5. Pedophilia – both false claims and previous offenses

The sexual abuse of a child is abhorrent and completely unacceptable, but it is also unacceptable for individuals to take the law into their own hands in response to such behavior. In many respects, those who sexually abuse children are viewed as a 'pariah class' distinct from those who commit all other crimes, including sex crimes committed against adults whether the victims are women or men. There is an intensity about this particular crime that often separates it from all others, places the perpetrators outside the boundaries of comprehension or understanding, and can expose raw and brutal notions about retribution and revenge. Within such a hot cultural context, accusations of the sexual abuse of a child can be dynamite. Once accusations are made, they are almost impossible to retract. Once rumors begin, they are almost impossible to stop. And once in the public domain, some action seems to be 'required.' In the minds of some accusers, almost anything is 'allowed' in response to this offense.[2] The heat that can be generated when claims of child sex abuse are made against an individual, whether true or false, has the power to unleash extreme responses with dire outcomes. Ironically, the strength of feelings against child sexual abuse seem to be contradicted when cases of the sexual abuse of children are known but ignored in schools, churches, families and other institutions (discussed in Chapter 7), but here it is important to stress that while emotions about the sexual abuse of children are intense and the behavior is viewed as abhorrent, this is not a justification for individuals deciding to take the law into their own hands.

Cases from the Murder Study that involved pedophilia went in different directions including: fabrications and false claims of the sexual abuse of a child that were knowingly and falsely made in order to justify an attack on an innocent person; knowledge of a previous incident that occurred in another time and place that were used to rationalize an attack by others at another point in time; claims used by men who wanted to take the law into their own hands and administer their own form of punishment rather than report the offense to the police for processing through the criminal justice system. We begin with false claims and end with vigilantes. In seeking to examine the various ways in which claims about the sexual abuse of children were involved in events that led to a murder, it is essential to reiterate that the response to such offences can never be vigilantes who take it upon themselves to kill in the name of seeking 'vengeance' for those who have been victimized, or do so under the guise of seeking some form of so-called 'justice' for the community at large.

Pedophilia – a false claim and four men kill the man they accuse
Four drunken men began to accuse the victim of abusing children (*a total fabrication according to the Court*). They harassed and assaulted him over a number of days and beat him to death.

160 Sexual murder between men

[Murder and context]

The victim (27) was single and educationally subnormal. The perpetrator (20) and three co-accused, falsely 'claimed he had been 'messing about with the kids' while babysitting his sister's child. A female witness said the police should be notified, but one man replied, 'Why should we?'

Then, they kicked him in the face and head until he fell to the floor and began to bleed from his nose, lips and ears, with blood on his hair and on the carpet. They continued to kick him for several minutes when one man said, 'Why don't we do it properly?' The perpetrator left the room and returned with a razor blade and cut the left side of the victim's face. She (witness) said all four men assaulted the victim from 1 am– 3.15 am. The victim had no chance to defend himself. The witness was sickened by what she saw, recalled seeing one man pull his legs apart and kick him several times in the testicles, and as a final indignity, unzip his trousers, remove his penis, and urinate over the victim's face.

A neighbor reported hearing, 'You fucking bastard', and the victim screaming, 'Don't hit me. Don't hit me', followed by, 'You lying bastard. Tell me the truth. I want the truth'. The witnesses estimated that this continued for the next couple of hours. Another witness said, 'the victim was covered in blood, and [he] was kicking him in the back while the others were standing watching, laughing and shouting insults and obscene phrases at the victim. Finally, an ambulance was called and he was rushed to the hospital.

[Examining doctor]

The injuries included: multiple facial injuries, swelling of his whole face, four deep lacerations to the left side of his face, multiple contusions of his whole body, limbs and genitals, chest and abdomen, and bruising to the back of both hands. His breathing was impaired when he arrived. An x-ray revealed several fractured ribs, major brain swelling and a brain contusion. He showed no signs of recovering consciousness. There were 80 separate marks of violence on his body. He had been tortured for three hours.

*(*1058cf1.2)*

Murder of a supposed pedophile – no evidence

[Trial judge]

It was suggested that rumors had been circulated in the area in which the deceased lived that he had been sexually abusing children, but there was no evidence to that effect. The perpetrator (23) stabbed the victim (20) with broken glass that was embedded in his face, and the injuries to his private parts were bizarre which tends to suggest some sexual connotation but that was not supported in any way by the evidence.

*(*046cf1.4.4)*

Sexual murder between men **161**

A rumor, whether true or false, can quickly lead to what is in effect the forming of a 'posse of vigilantes,' a manhunt and a murder. An accusation of the sexual abuse of a child can become a powerful tool in the hands of one willing to make a false accusation against an innocent person with the sole purpose of destroying them while, at the same time, seeming to become a 'local hero' and an upholder of the moral order.

In the next case, the judge, jury, and evidence agreed that everything began with a false accusation of child abuse before ending with the death of the man falsely accused. At first, the accuser presented himself as behaving in an 'honorable' manner that took on 'heroic' proportions as he led others in the 'just' actions of seeking revenge and ridding the community of the man accused of offending against the child concerned and against the sensibilities of the community at large. Such accusations can be used with effect against those who are weak, vulnerable, and without supporters or defenders, as well as against those who are personal enemies of the perpetrator/s. In the murders of men falsely accused of sexually abusing children, the perpetrators seemed intent on carrying out violence on an individual by creating a rationale for such actions even though they knew the rumor to be false. In the cases presented above, no evidence was presented in court [by police or others] to support the notion that the victim had a history of sexual offences against anyone, children or adults. The rumors had no basis in fact, and this seemed to have been known by the perpetrators who manufactured a story to justify their extreme violence and eventual killing of the man they 'targeted' for attack. These perpetrators were seemingly keen to use violence but, at the same time, sought to justify their violence and attribute their own wrong doing to the person they victimized. They sought to convert their horrific violence into something 'heroic,' 'honorable,' and 'justifiable' by falsely accusing their victim of pedophilia and then, in effect, 'righting the wrong' by torturing and killing him in an act of 'moral outrage.'

Revelations of previous convictions for child sexual abuse

In our interview with this man, he was clearly focused on killing a man he knew had a previous offence for child sex abuse and whom he suspected of making a sexual advance against his five-year-old daughter. He was intent on killing, demonstrated a certain since of pride in the athletic skills used in the process, and killed with no sense of remorse or regret.

Pedophilia – two men claimed sexual abuse of perpetrator's daughter
He (23) said he believed the victim was a sexual abuser who had made advances to his five-year old daughter. He and his co-accused took him

162 Sexual murder between men

to an isolated part of the countryside, beat him unconscious, slit his throat, threw him into a stream, and left him to drown.

[Our interview]

The door went and I answered it, and this guy [victim] is standing there and wanting to speak to my co-accused [*to explain his past offense and that he had not abused the perpetrator's daughter*]. It was automatic, I just clicked. 'Right, I'm going to get him! And we went out, and we took him up into the hills saying we were going to [a remote pub] which is back of the hills, out in the middle of nowhere. I stopped, we got him out of the van, I said to him what he'd done [attempting to sexually abuse my daughter]. He denied it, and I just lashed out at the guy. I literally leathered the guy, and he was unconscious. I knew that because he was lying there and he wasn't moving. And the next thing, he [co-accused] pulled the Stanley knife out and cut his throat. And I'm sort of like 15 feet away by this time, and I'm thinking, 'What's he doing?' And I went back over. I've seen what he's done, blood all over him. I checked his pulse and tried to check his heart and couldn't find anything. I couldn't find anything, and there's a burn [stream] that ran slightly away from us, and we took him in there. Because it's like a defense mechanism kicking in. I don't want to be caught for something. I knew I'd just done something wrong, but the scale of it, you don't realize.

All I know is I went out for the evening, I beat somebody up, and I've been with somebody else who's just come in and killed him. I know enough about it to know that I was as guilty as he is because I was there. And it was, 'Dump the body. We'll act normal'. *And when you said that you leathered him, tell me what you mean, what you did, was it fists?* Physically, I mean I punched him. I punched lumps out of him. I used a couple of moves from karate that I knew. I wouldn't say I actually used karate on him. I used the karate to get him down, because one thing I was taught, don't leave somebody standing in front of you. And I used that, and then I literally just punched lumps out of the guy. *Head or body sort of thing?* I would say the location of the stomach. The two most vulnerable places. Well, that's what you aim for, and I just totally leathered the guy. But to be honest, it wasn't a frenzied attack as such, right. It was very cold and calculated because I knew what I wanted to do, right. And when I had seen that I had went too far, I just stopped, right. He was breathing, you could see he was breathing, but you could see he was out cold, and I thought, 'Enough', that's enough. To me, I had gone to my limit.

And would you have just left him there and drove away? Yes. *You said something earlier that you found out later that he wasn't dead.* No, he wasn't dead. It was superficial. I couldn't find a pulse nor a heartbeat. *So, did he die because he was left?* No, he died because we threw him into the burn/ stream, right. So, yes, I did kill him in that respect. And I thought, this

Sexual murder between men **163**

guy's dead, and it was a case we would need to get rid of him because we couldn't leave him lying in the middle of a stream. The guy drowned. The guy was alive but he actually died of drowning because we threw him in the burn/stream. *And he was unconscious when you threw him in?* Yes.

(*290iv1.2.8)

A previous conviction for child sex abuse is, in effect, a conviction for all time. It never goes away, is difficult if not impossible to explain away, and is often assumed to pose an ever-present threat of being repeated at another time and in another place. This is a past that is, for the most part, difficult if not impossible to escape even for those who have served their time in prison, gone through therapy and changed their orientations and offending behavior. It is often very difficult, if not impossible, to get prisoners to take part in prison programs designed to work with sex offenders, especially offenses against children, precisely because of the stigma attached to such crimes within and outside the prison context, and because of possible recriminations from fellow inmates within the prison itself. These murderers seemed to be seeking some misguided form of 'revenge' and setting themselves up as 'upholders' of a moral order in which they acted as judge, jury and executioner. While the legal process may have already run its course, these perpetrators seemed to think they could 'rerun their own process' as a prelude to assaulting and killing the man. Simply knowing that their victim had a previous conviction for a sexual offense against a child seemed to be enough for them to justify their killing. Such knowledge can become a dangerous tool when revealed within the context of a local community but, as shown in the next case, it can even be used as a rationale for murder within the context of a prison, and even when used by those who have themselves committed a similar offense.

In this case, the murder victim was serving a sentence that involved the sexual abuse of a child when fellow prisoners, who had been convicted for similar offenses, decided to conduct a 'mock trial' in which he was tried, found guilty, and executed in the prison cell shared by all the men.

In prison – a 'mock' trial and execution of a child sex offender by four men serving sentences for similar offenses

[Context]
In prison, the perpetrator (16) and three other prisoners 'executed' a fellow inmate (17) following a 'mock trial' in which the victim was found guilty and *sentenced to hang.*

[Trial judge report]
The victim had been convicted [of a sexual offense against a child] and was waiting to be transferred to complete a four-year sentence. The

164 Sexual murder between men

perpetrator and three co-accused were pretending to other inmates that they were in for GBH, Grievous Bodily Harm, but were, in fact, in prison for sex offences not unlike their victim. They bullied him from his arrival in prison. Then, they tried, sentenced and hanged their fellow inmate.

[Murder]
The victim was subjected to a mock trial for the offence for which he was on remand. At the conclusion of the 'trial', he was sentenced to hang. They planned to execute the hanging at about midnight, and each had their well worked out roles. The four defendants and the victim were all housed in the same cell. About midnight, the victim was gagged, dragged from his bunk, and tied to a chair which was pre-positioned below a noose. The chair was kicked away but it was too short to strangle him and so they had to finish him off by strangling him with two of the men pulling at his legs and the other two tying the noose tighter. The perpetrator acknowledged his part in the killing and admitted that he had put the noose around the victim's neck. The body was left suspended for two hours by which time, and according to their plan, they 'woke up' and pretended to find that the victim had strangled himself.

[Trial judge]
This killing was perhaps the most brutal and callous that it has been my lot to try in some eight years. I am convinced that the defendants were motivated by a pure lust to kill.

(★261cf1.2.8)

A pedophile ring

The sexual abuse of children is usually undertaken by one man who acts alone and may 'groom' the child for a period of time before committing a sexual act against them. Men who groom children in order that they may eventually have sex with them often take their time and entrap the child with 'kindness,' treats, praise, and the like. Most sexual acts against children involve only one man acting against one child, and may occur in families, neighborhoods, and organizations that are respected and viewed as safe places for children. Most do not involve groups of any kind, either of the children who are preyed upon or of the men prey upon them, and most do not end in murder, either of the child victim or of the adult sexual abuser as in the next two cases. It is illegal to have sex with a child and to turn this into a business, but pedophile rings do both. They often prey upon the most disadvantaged and vulnerable children, and sell their sexual 'products' to both heterosexual and homosexual men alike who seek various forms of sexual pleasure with children and young people.

This case reads more like a nineteenth century novel than a true story of sex and murder. As a child, the perpetrator ran away from a foster home and was 'rescued' from the streets only to be ensnared into a ring of child prostitution and exploited for several years before he was able to escape and start a new life. He later discovered that his former 'sex slave master' had retained explicit and compromising photos of him as a child. Fearing that they might somehow be used against him at some time in the future, he and his friends planned to break into the home of his former 'sex slave master' and steal the photographs.

Pedophilia – a Dickensian tale of sex slavery, a 'king,' sex photos, a robbery and murder

[Context]
The murder occurred in the context of several years of sexual abuse when he was a child, and the immediate circumstances of the murder involved a robbery of photos relating to the previous sexual abuse. This 24-year-old gay man and two co-accused set out to rob his previous pedophile master (54), a homosexual employed in a prestigious profession who had corrupted, enslaved and forced him into prostitution when he was a teenager. *The intention was to steal, not to commit murder.*

[Pre-sentence probation officer's interview]
Some years before the murder, when the perpetrator was a teenager, he left his foster home and went to [City] to look for his stepfather. Unable to find him, he wandered the streets unable to sleep for two nights. Eventually, he met up with other boys who lived on the street and introduced him to the 'King', and said he would look after him. He was given a meal, but thinks that he was either drugged or given alcohol because he woke up naked and tied to a bed. He was imprisoned for about six weeks and sexually and physically abused on a regular basis. Once under the control of the 'master', he was allowed out to live as a rent boy (prostitute). The only proviso was that he must present himself to the King between 10 and 2 each day at a well-known cafe. 'He never paid us, we were his, he owned us and enjoyed the power he had over us'. The boys gradually began to rebel which he believes led to the 'disappearance' of some of his friends in unusual circumstances. He eventually broke away from the 'master' and got a job as an electrician, but became aware that his 'master' was looking for him.

He decided to go to the victim's house in order to steal indecent photos previously taken of him, and went with two friends, a male and female. They discovered the house was protected by an alarm system, so decided to gain entry by invitation (since he was known to the householder), and then steal the photos. They gained entry and were asked to spend the night, and it was noted that despite the presence of the perpetrator's friends, the victim still tried to get the perpetrator to go to bed with him.

166 Sexual murder between men

[Murder]
During the night, the perpetrator and his male friend went into the victim's bedroom to look for an alarm key. While the victim was asleep, the perpetrator struck him with a spanner (wrench), and the victim sprang from the bed with a knife and an anti-attack gas canister to defend himself as he was always armed. In the struggle, the perpetrator repeatedly struck the victim with the spanner causing severe head injuries. They overpowered him as he lay on the floor still moving, then placed a silk scarf around his neck and pulled it until he no longer moved and was obviously dead. During the attack, the female friend remained in the room next door. The victim's body was placed head first into a sleeping bag and put under the bed. Then, they left taking some of his possessions with them.

[Arrest and plea]
He was arrested about five weeks later based on information he thinks was supplied by the mother of a friend. When the case came up for trial, he pled guilty rather than face the public disclosure of his previous sexual abuse which only came to light much later in his sentence. Both co-accused pleaded 'not guilty', but both were convicted of murder.

[Trial judge report and sentence]
'He is not a danger to society. There was probably no plan to kill the deceased only to attack and rob him. The deceased's resistance probably led to the killing. In light of the circumstances, I have recommended the lowest possible tariff.'

*(*240cf1.1.5)*

These boys were living on the streets, and their lives were taken over by an older and more powerful man who fed and housed them but also ran a 'business' selling their bodies to other men. Compromising photos were taken and retained for possible sale or distribution, and the retention of the sexualized photos meant they might be used to damage or destroy their lives sometime in the future.

Subtype 6. Serial sexual murder

Although serial murders receive the lion's share of public and media attention, they are actually quite rare. Those that do occur cause a great deal of public alarm, make the front pages of newspapers, and are featured on the daily and nightly news. Some are written into books, made into movies, and receive a disproportionate amount of coverage even among academic researchers and scholars who study criminals and crime. The concern about serial murders exceeds the concern about the much larger number of murders that occur 'one-at-a-time,' and is well beyond the attention given to the huge number of non-lethal attacks that are too

Sexual murder between men **167**

numerous to count. Fear, panic and voyeurism are all involved in the avalanche of publicity given to such cases as the backgrounds and characteristics of perpetrators and victims and the murders are poured over and scrutinized in minute detail. The murder events often read like a gruesome novel that is both real and unreal. The details are riveting because who knows what might happen next, and alarming because it could happen to me. Sex is often involved, and while the victims of serial killers are often women, men may also become targets as shown in this case from the Murder Study that involved the killing of four men within a period of four months. Before finding the last of the four bodies, there was no knowledge among the police, the media or the public that there was a serial killer on the loose. Although the four murders were committed in a short period of time, they took place within the context of two decades of non-lethal attacks against gay men without anyone knowing they were being committed. The perpetrator had no record of offending. For all intents-and-purposes, he was an 'ordinary guy' who lived and worked in the community. For years, he had managed to commit scores of non-lethal sexual attacks against gay men without detection or arrest, without drawing attention to himself, and without any sense in the wider community that these attacks were being committed. Then, he sexually assaulted and killed four men in rapid succession.

Serial killing – four murders in four months following decades of non-lethal sex attacks

The perpetrator (49) was a homosexual man with no known history of offending who had for over 20 years carried out a series of violent and terrifying attacks on solitary men in the [Countryside] near [City]. According to him, *he had perpetrated at least 39 non-lethal attacks on victims that he did not kill.* He stated that the motive was sexual, and he described deriving sexual gratification from the infliction of terror, humiliation and pain. The last of his non-homicidal attacks took place about a month before the beginning of the murders, and he was never arrested for any of these assaults.

[Context]
Following a year of personal misfortune (the death of his mother, deaths of pets, and business problems), his thoughts turned to murder. He was very familiar with the highways and byways of the [Countryside] and regularly travelled widely in the area in hired vans between his home and the locations of his several businesses.

[Murder no. 1]
On the weekend, he killed a 46-year-old man who was an eccentric middle-aged homosexual who lived alone in a ramshackle house fronting onto a major road. Several days before this murder, the perpetrator

168 Sexual murder between men

bought a large combat knife for use as a murder weapon. Two nights later, he pulled up outside the house of the victim in the early hours of the morning. Dressed in black leather and boots that resembled jackboots, he carried out a frenzied attack with the knife, stabbed the victim many times, and inflicted 27 stab wounds to the front and back of his body with the six-inch sheath knife. He also stole a wallet and a swastika flag from the victim's house. [Note: It seems to have been a coincidence that both the victim and the perpetrator shared an interest in Nazism, and the flag was discovered in the perpetrator's house when he was arrested four months after this murder which was the first murder he committed.]

The body was found later face down in the back of his own car. His trousers were around his ankles, his buttocks were exposed, and it was clear that there were wounds visible-on each buttock. The fatal stab wounds to the chest penetrated to the depth of five inches and sliced through the aorta and heart, and also penetrated the lungs, stomach and kidney. In addition, there were three defense wounds to the left hand of the victim.

[Murder no. 2]
On the weekend, two weeks after the first murder, he went to a bar in [City] which is a well-known rendezvous for homosexuals. The victim (28) was a homosexual who attended the bar which was also regularly frequented by the perpetrator. On this occasion, the victim had made a nuisance of himself under the influence of drink or drugs, and at some stage he joined a man dressed in black leather trousers and a black leather jacket, shirt and tie (perpetrator) until they later left the bar together. It is believed that the perpetrator arranged to take the victim back to his home for sex, but instead took the victim, who was drunk, into a nearby forest where he stabbed him to death and left the body in the forest. The victim was last seen at that time, but it was noted that the victim and his friends were all drunks, drug addicts and homosexuals who lived a chaotic lifestyle, and thus no one may have been concerned or raised an alarm when he disappeared from the scene.

His body was not discovered until the perpetrator was arrested [three months later] and only then because of admissions made by the perpetrator himself. Prior to that time, it was not known that the second murder victim was missing or dead. When he was found, his head and right arm were missing, the head clearly removed by a predator such as a fox. His body was naked except for a pair of jeans around his ankles. His head/skull was later found and identified through dental records, keys found nearby, and a fingerprint taken from one hand.

[Post-mortem]
There was severe putrefaction and maggot infestation in the back of the body (he had been dead for 10–12 weeks). However, the front of the body revealed one defined stab wound near the umbilicus, and a T-shirt found near the body had a total of four cuts indicating three stab wounds to the front and one stab wound to the back. Death was caused by stabbing to the abdomen.

[Murder no. 3]
This murder took place two-and-a-half months after the first murder, when he killed a 49-year-old man who lived on a caravan site adjacent to a busy highway where he worked for a company carrying out road works. The victim was awoken by the perpetrator who banged on the caravan door in the early hours of the morning, and when he opened the door he was savagely attacked with the same knife used in the first two murders. He put up a fight, and the perpetrator later told the police that when the victim asked, 'Why?' He answered, 'For fun'. He also told the police that the victim pleaded for his life for the sake of his grandchildren, but to no avail. The perpetrator stole a number of items from the caravan including a video recorder, a mobile phone and a watch. On returning home, he realized that his clip-on-tie must have come off in the fight. He returned to collect it and, at the same time, adjusted the victim's underwear so as to inspect his genitals. The victim was divorced with two daughters, and was not a homosexual. He was described as a shy, self-conscious person who was generally tidy, well-liked and good humored.

[Injuries]
The injuries included 12 stab wounds to the cheek, back, abdomen and body. There were defense wounds and bruises on his left hand. The wounds were caused by a thin bladed, double-edged knife approximately one inch wide and seven inches long. Death was due to multiple stab wounds to the heart and lungs. Because of blood distribution at the scene of the caravan and the site, it was likely that the victim was attacked at the door of the caravan and either came out or was pulled out of the caravan and ended up on the ground where he was found.

[Murder no. 4]
In the early hours of the morning, the perpetrator went to a local beach, a well-known place for nocturnal homosexual trysts. He encountered his fourth victim, a married man (35) with children who appeared to have had a 'secret' life as a homosexual. He was masturbating on the beach when the perpetrator stabbed him to death. He was described by

170 Sexual murder between men

his wife as a happy, caring man who loved his two children and family. She was unaware that her husband had had any other type of relationships, either homosexual or heterosexual.

His body was at the water's edge on the beach, lying on his back with his feet facing up the beach. His trousers were fastened at the waist and his belt was securely fastened, but his fly zip was open. He had a number of stab wounds and there was blood on the beach near where the body was found. His car keys were missing. Death occurred at about 2am. He had been stabbed five times in the chest and abdomen, and once in the back. Three of the wounds were deep and had been caused by a double-edged knife with a blade about 1 inch wide. There were three defense wounds to his right hand. There was no evidence to suggest any recent or past homosexual activity. Blood was found on the sand, and DNA analysis indicated that it belonged to the perpetrator. The car keys were later found in an ornamental fish pond at the back of the perpetrator's house.

The perpetrator was arrested three days later. His black leather jacket bore the blood of victims no. 3 and no. 4. The combat knife (which also bore the blood of the same two victims) was recovered from a bag the perpetrator kept in the front seat of his hired van that contained various tools and property stolen from all the victims except victim no. 2. The police had never heard of the second victim or of his whereabouts, but they were then able to recover his body from [X Forest] with the assistance of a map drawn by the perpetrator when he was later interviewed by the police.

[Trial judge summary]

The jury heard tapes of hours of chilling confessions including references to 'fun' and the repeated description of 'a job well done'. He said the motive was not sexual but 'the relief of pressure', but I question this differentiation in his case. In his 25th interview, weeks after he had been charged, he changed from his previous admission that he had always been alone and claimed that a second man, whom he refused to name, had also been present. He said all four murders had been carried out by a homosexual lover to whom he had given the nickname ['Jet'] after a knife-murderer he saw in a series of horror films. He admitted being present or nearby at three of the murders but not that of victim. no. 2. He provided cynical explanations of how 'Jet' had been in possession of the knife and, for some of the time, the black leather jacket. He admitted he was a predatory homosexual who had enjoyed carrying out 39 non-homicidal attacks, mainly alone. He said his confessions were a combination of knowledge (from his presence at the scene) and hearsay (from 'Jet'), and that they were simply an attempt to protect 'Jet' for reasons of love. He said that none of his other friends or associates knew anything of 'Jet', except that he worked in a hotel as a waiter. This latter suggestion was refuted by evidence in rebuttal. I have no doubt that the jury concluded that 'Jet' was a figment of his imagination.

[Trial judge]
I came to the conclusion that he should never be released because, at the age of 49 and after over 20 years of non-homicidal attacks, he deliberately set in motion a program of savage murders of strangers who had done him no harm whatsoever. He did it 'for fun' and considered it 'a job well done'. He was without mercy for his victims and without the slightest regret or remorse. At one point in cross-examination, he said that he was deriving some enjoyment from the publicity surrounding his trial. He had enjoyed telling the police about the killings. In my view, he enjoyed the trial in a perverse way. In passing sentence, I stated that it would be difficult to find a more dangerous man. He told the police that, but for his arrest, he would have murdered his bank manager the following week. The degree of dangerousness and the likelihood of future re-offending cannot be overstated in this case. Recommendation: 'Never release'.

(★931cf1.4.4)

In January, 2020, a two-year news blackout ended with the conviction and a life sentence of a 36-year-old man described as 'the most prolific rapist in British legal history.' Over two years, he had raped at least 136 young men in Manchester, and probably many more. Acting as a 'good Samaritan,' he lured young men to his flat, drugged them, and filmed himself on his phone as he raped them. He claimed they enjoyed acting out his sexual fantasy of 'playing dead during intercourse,' but this was unanimously rejected by four trial juries who watched hours of explicit footage recorded on his phone. The judge said he showed 'not one jot of remorse,' and considered ordering him to serve a 'whole life term' which would have been the first time this sentence was imposed for a crime other than murder. In this case of male–male rape on a monumental scale, no one was murdered, but it seems reasonable to ask if this might have been the eventual outcome had his ongoing acts of sexual violence not been discovered and stopped (Pidd and Halliday, 2020).

Comparisons of Sexual.Murders and Other.Murders

Narrative texts from the casefiles and interviews illustrate the complexity of Sexual.Murders between men. They were classified into six subtypes in order to illustrate the diverse nature of these murders. Quantitative data from the casefiles provide a characterization of the 32 cases of Sexual.Murders that are compared with 'Other.Murders' that did not involve sex (Table 5.1).

172 Sexual murder between men

TABLE 5.1 Murder Event. Sexual.Murders and Other.Murders

MALE–MALE MURDER	Sexual.Murders	Other Murders
	$n=32$ (%)	$n=392$^ (%)
BACKGROUND		
– Age:		
– Perpetrators	25 yrs	27 yrs
– Victims	37 yrs	40 yrs
– Unemployed at murder	67%	66%
RELATIONSHIP BETWEEN PERPETRATOR and VICTIM		
– Stranger	22%	32%
CONFLICTS, DISPUTES and PREVIOUS VIOLENCE		
– Ongoing Dispute	19%	31%★
– Confrontation at Murder	60%	66%
– Prev.viol: Perp.against.vic.	03%	11%
– Prev.viol:Vic.against.perp	07%	11%
DRINKING and DRUGS		
– Perp. Drugs	17%	20%
– Perp. Drinking	72%	67%
– if perp. drinking, Drunk	73%	71%
– Drinking 3–6hrs	40%	41%
– Drinking all day	14%	21%
–Vic. Drinking	47%	46%
– if vic. drinking, Drunk	72%	64%
– of those drinking, drink together	35%	29%
MURDER EVENT		
– Home of victim	47%	51%
– One perpetrator	73%	56%
– No Witness	80%	58%★★
– Perpetrator [anger, rage, indignant	25%	41%★★
– Injuries = 5 + injuries	83%	70%
CAUSE OF DEATH		
– Strangle	13%	07%
– Stab	60%	47%
– Beat w/object	13%	18%
– Beat w/hands/feet	10%	17%
– Shot	03%	11%

OFFENSE/s		
– Murder + 2nd offense (yes)	43%	39%
– if 2nd offense: 'property offense':	20%	63%★★★

statistically significant: ★$p<.05$, ★★$p<.01$, ★★★$p<.001$
^ numbers vary when: (not applicable) and/or (missing data)

Backgrounds and relationships between perpetrators and victims

The average age of the men who committed a Sexual.Murder was 25 years, which was slightly younger than men who committed Other.Murders (27 years). Male victims of sexual murder were, on average, older than the men who killed them (37 years), but not as old as the victims of Other.Murders (40 years). The perpetrators of Sexual.Murders and Other.Murders were equally likely to be unemployed at the time of the murder (67% vs 66%). Few of the men in either category were strangers (22% vs 32%).

Conflicts, disputes and previous violence

Ongoing disputes between perpetrators and victims were not common, and even less likely in Sexual.Murders than Other.Murders (19% vs 31%★). By contrast, confrontations at the time of the murder were common in both groups (60% vs 66%). The content of these confrontations varied in different subtypes of Sexual. Murders with some more closely associated with issues relating to sexual identity and sexual preferences, and others more about sexual acts and encounters that ranged widely in terms of the specific issues involved. Previous violence by perpetrators against their victims was unusual (3% vs 11%), and previous violence by victims against the perpetrators was a bit less likely in Sexual.Murders (7% vs 11%). While most of the men were not strangers to one another, most did not have a previous history of violence by either man against the other.

Drinking, drunkenness, and drugs

Drinking and drunkenness were common both among Sexual.Murders and Other.Murders. Among the perpetrators of sexual murders, 72% of them had been drinking, and 73% of those who had been drinking were defined as drunk. This was fairly similar among the men who committed Other.Murders, as 67% of them who had been drinking, and 71% of those who had been drinking were defined as drunk. Among all of the victims, nearly half of them had been drinking at the time they were killed (47% vs 46%), and nearly two-thirds of the victims who had been drinking were defined as drunk (72% vs 64%). Many of the men had been drinking for several hours, and about one-third of the perpetrators and victims were drinking together before the murder (35% vs 29%).

Murder event

About half of the victims were murdered in their own home or place of residence (47% vs 51%). Most Sexual.Murders involved only one perpetrator (73% vs 56%), and usually there was no witness to the murder event (80% vs 58%*). Sexual. Murderers were less likely to be defined as 'angry, in a rage or indignant' than Other.Murderers (25% vs 41%*).

Cause of death

Stabbing was more likely to be the cause of death in Sexual.Murders than Other. Murders (60% vs 47%). Shooting was rare in Sexual.Murderers but more likely in Other.Murderers (3% vs 11%). Whether death was caused by stabbing, beating or shooting, the majority of victims in both categories received five or more injuries (83% vs 70%) during the murder event.

Other offenses

Less than half of the sexual murders involved a second offense (43% vs 39%), but very few of the second offenses were property offences (20% vs 63%*). While many of the murders of gay men did involve a robbery or some form of 'property offense,' that ended up on their charge sheet and were a part of the evidence given in their trial, many of the other sub-types of sexual murder, such as those involving accusations of pedophilia, may have involved a second offense but none were related to robbery or 'property.'

In brief, sexual murders were less likely to involve an 'ongoing dispute' prior to the murder. Many gay men were attacked without warning in parks and public places by men who were total strangers and simply focused on attacking a gay man, any gay man. Such events did not begin with an argument or involve any preamble apart from verbal taunting or insulting the gay man before attacking him. The absence of ongoing disputes between perpetrators and their victims not only characterized the killings of men because they were gay, but also men who were pedophiles or accused of pedophilia. In addition, the serial murderer killed strangers with whom he had no prior contact and thus no prior dispute before the killing. Most Sexual.Murders that did involve an 'ongoing dispute,' occurred in the contexts where sex was being traded for accommodation and the like, and those involving claims of an unwanted homosexual advance that may have occurred on more than one occasion and against the objections of the recipient. Sexual.Murders were more likely than 'Other.Murders' to have *no witnesses*. Victims of Sexual.Murders were more likely to be killed when they were *alone*, and the murderers were less likely to have been angry, enraged or indignant at the time of the murder. A minority of Sexual.Murderers were charged with a second offense.

Summary and conclusions

Despite the diverse ways in which sexual identity and various forms of sexual behavior were involved in these murders, they all contained a sexual component that was central to the murder itself and to the dynamic elements leading up to and surrounding these events. It is important to understand the various ways in which sexual behaviors and sexual identities are involved in the social relationships, situations and circumstances as well as the dynamic and unfolding of events that end in outcomes that become lethal. We identify six subtypes of sexual murder between men: 1) Hate crimes against gay men; 2) Sexual exchanges and mixed messages; 3) Homosexual advance; 4) Prostitution; 5) Pedophilia – false claims and offences, and 6) Serial sexual murder. Disaggregation of all of the sexual murders into these six subtypes helps delineate the broad nature of murders committed within a sexual context. Each of the six subtypes of sexual murder identified in the Murder Study may become the subject of still further and deeper examinations in their own right, but it is important that subsequent examinations of sexual murders continue to consider those that are related to the act of sex and to sexual identity, in the ongoing process of gaining a fuller and better understanding of this type of murder.

Notes

1. For other studies of male–male sexual violence and murder, see Comstock (1991, 1992); Hamner (1992); New South Wales (1998); Hearn (1998); Connell (1995, 2000); Meloy (2000); Mouzos and Thompson (2000); Craig (2002); Tomsen (2002); Janoff (2005); Bartlett (2007); Hall (2017); Beauregard and Martineau (2016); Chan (2017, pp. 107–116).
2. For an example, see the *Guardian* (2019, p. 29) involving, 'A group of self-styled "paedophile hunters" who vowed to carry on seeking out child abusers after a case heard in Leeds Crown Court'.

References

Banks, I., 1997. The 'homosexual panic' defence in Canadian criminal law, *Criminal Reports*, 5th series, 371–381.

Bartlett, P., 2007. Killing gay men, 1975–2001. *British Journal of Criminology*, 47 (4), 573–595. http://bjc.oxfordjournals.org/content/47/4/573.full [Accessed November 15, 2019].

Beauregard, E. and Martineau, M., 2016. *The Sexual Murderer: Offender Behaviour and Implications for Practice*. London: Routledge. ISBN: 9781138925410.

Birkel, C. and Dern, H., 2013. Homicide in Germany. In M. C. A Liem and W. A. Pridemore, eds. *Handbook of European Homicide Research*. New York: Springer, 313–328.

Chan, H. C. O., 2017. Sexual homicide: A review of recent empirical evidence (2008 to 2015). In F. Brookman, E. R. Maguire, and M. Maguire, eds. *The Handbook of Homicide*. Chichester: John Wiley & Sons, 105–130.

Comstock, G., 1991. *Violence Against Lesbians and Gay Men*. New York: Columbia University Press.

Comstock, G., 1992. Dismantling the homosexual panic defense. *Law and Sexuality*, 2, 81.

Connell, R., 1995. *Masculinities*. Cambridge: Polity.

Connell, R., 2000. *The Men and the Boys*. Berkeley, CA: University of California Press.

176 Sexual murder between men

Craig, K., 2002. Examining hate-motivated aggression: A review of the social psychological literature on hate crimes as a distinct form of aggression. *Aggression and Violent Behavior*, 7 (1), 85–101. Available at: www.ncjrs.gov/App/publications/abstract.aspx?ID=192583.

Dobash, R. E. and Dobash, R. P., 2015. *When Men Murder Women.* New York: Oxford University Press: *for Murder. Event: Male-Male Murderers* and Sexual Murderers (*of women*), 114–115, 121, 137–151, 291–292.

Dobash, R. P. and Dobash, R. E., 2018. Sexual murder of women intimate partners in Great Britain. In K.Ylllo and M. G.Torres, eds. *Marital Rape: Consent, Marriage, and Social Change in Global Context*. New York, Oxford University Press, 139–162.

Dressler, J., 1995. When 'heterosexual' men kill 'homosexual' men: Reflections on provocation law, sexual advances, and the 'reasonable man' standard. *Journal of Criminal Law and Criminology*, 85, 726–763.

Hall, N., 2017. Hate and homicide: Exploring the extremes of prejudice-motivated violence. In F. Brookman, E. R. Maguire and M. Maguire, eds. *The Handbook of Homicide*. Chichester, West Sussex, UK: John Wiley & Sons, 165–179.

Hamner, K., 1992. Gay-bashing: A social identity analysis of violence against lesbians and gay men. In G. Herek and K. Berrill, eds. *Hate Crimes: Confronting Violence Against Lesbians and Gay Men*. Newbury Park: Sage, 179–190.

Hearn, J., 1998. *The Violences of Men*. London: Sage.

Janoff, D., 2005. *Pink Blood: Homophobic Violence in Canada*. Toronto: University of Toronto Press.

Lunny, A., 2003. Provocation and 'homosexual' advance: Masculinized subjects as threat, masculinized subjects under threat. *Social and Legal Studies*, 12 (3), 311–333.

Meloy, R., 2000. The nature and dynamics of sexual homicide: An integrative review. *Aggression and Violent Behavior*, 5 (1), 1.

Mezey, G. C. and King, M. B. eds., 1992. *Male Victims of Sexual Assault*. Oxford: Oxford University Press.

Mison, R., 1992. Homophobia in manslaughter: The homosexual advance as insufficient provocation. *California Law Review*, 80, 133.

Mouzos, J. and Thompson, S., 2000. Gay-hate related homicides: An overview of major findings in New South Wales. *Trends and Issues in Crime and Criminal Justice*, paper 155. Canberra: Australian Institute of Criminology.

New South Wales, 1998. Attorney General's Department, Criminal Law Review Division, *Homosexual Advance Defence: Final Report of the Working Party*. Sydney: NSW AG.

Oliver, S., 1999. Provocation and non-violent homosexual advances. *Journal of Criminal Law*, 63 (6), 586.

Proulx, J., Beauregard, E., Cusson, M., and Nicole, A., 2007. *Sexual Murderers: A Comparative Analysis and New Perspectives*. Chichester: Wiley.

Tomsen, S., 2002. *Hatred, Murder and Male Honour: Anti-homosexual Homicides in New South Wales, 1980–2000*. Research and Public Policy Series no. 43. Canberra: Australian Institute of Criminology.

Wheatie, S., 2016. The Constitutionality of the 'Homosexual Advance Defence,' Commonwealth Caribbean. *The Equal Rights Review*, 16 (39) note 5. Holmes v DPP [1946], Eastern Caribbean, CA. Dominica, 30 April, 2012, para 21, 'Homosexual Advance Defence' (see Holmes v DPP, [1946]).

Online and newspaper

Beaumont-Thomas, B. 2019. 'Madonna calls for gun control in violent video that depicts nightclub shooting.' *The Guardian*, June 26, 2019 22.02 BST. @ben_bt [accessed

November 16, 2019]. Available at: www.theguardian.com/us-news/orlando-terror-attack [Accessed November 19, 2019].

Guardian, 2019. A group of self-styled 'paedophile hunters' who vowed to carry on seeking out child abusers after a case heard in Leeds Crown Court. the *Guardian*, October 31, 2019, p. 29.

Madonna – 'God control' (Official Music video). https://youtu.be/zv-sdTOw5cs.

Pidd, H. and Halliday, J., 2020. Male rape in Manchester, England – Reynhard Sinaga case. *Guardian*, January 6, 2020. Available at: www.theguardian.com/uk-news/2020/jan/06/reynhard-sinaga-peter-pan-phd-student-who-raped-scores-of-men?CMP=share_btn_link [Accessed January 8, 2020].

Pulse Nightclub, Orlando, Florida, Available at: https://en.wikipedia.org/wiki/Pulse_nightclub [Accessed 16 November, 2019].

6

MURDER OF OLDER MEN

The population of many developed countries is now shifting from a large majority of individuals who are of working age to an increasing proportion of those in or near retirement age and those who are very much older. Without a dramatic increase in the birth rate or a significant increase in the migrant population, some European and Asian countries are increasingly facing a significant in-balance between the working and non-working population. We briefly consider these patterns in Japan, the US, EU, and the UK. Then we ask why this matters, and how it relates to the murders of older men.

- *Japan* provides a clear example of an aging population. In 2014, people aged 65 and older made up 25% of the total population, and with minimal migration and a low birth rate, it is predicted that the elderly will reach over 35% of the population by 2020 (Statistics Bureau of Japan, accessed 17 November, 2019; Ellis and Hamai, 2017).
- In the *United States*, about 14% of the population was over 65 in 2014, and this is expected to rise to 19% by 2025. One US Census Bureau Statistical Brief, 'Sixty-five Plus in the United States' predicted that, 'by the middle of the next century, it might be completely inaccurate to think of ourselves as a Nation of the young: there could be more persons who are elderly (65 or over) than young (14 or younger)!' (US Census Bureau, 1995, U.S. and World Population Clock, 2019).
- In *European countries*, 'in 2018, nearly one-fifth (19%) of the EU population was aged 65 or more,' and 'people aged 80 or more should more than double by the year 2100 to reach 14.6% of the whole population (Eurostat, 2019a; Eurostat, 2019b).

- In the *United Kingdom*, 16% of the population was 65 or older in 2012 and expected to rise. The number of 85-year-olds tripled since the 1970s and is expected to reach two million by 2031. 'In 2018, the life expectancy for men in Britain was 79.4 years, and men are expected to spend 16 years in poor health. By 2050, it is projected that one in four [25%] people in the UK will be aged 65 years and over, an increase from almost one in five in 2018' (UK Office for National Statistics, August, 2019; Eurostat, 2019a; 2019b). Overall, these predictions suggest that nearly 20–25% of the population of these countries will soon be (or are already are) aged 65 or older.

Does this matter? And if so, how does it relate to the murders of older men? The elderly often live alone, experience declining health and a dependency upon others, and experience relative poverty, particularly among the oldest of the old. Many are lonely, dependent, and vulnerable. For some, advanced age and conditions associated with it constitute factors that shape the context and circumstances in which they may be preyed upon by individuals who seek to take advantage of them in differing ways such as stealing from their home or bank account, or make their house a 'hang out' for themselves and their friends, and a few of them are murdered. Using the National Crime Victimization Survey (September 2010), Shannan Catalano, Bureau of Justice Statistics, reported on violence during household burglaries in the US between 2003–2007 (including residents aged 65 or older (see Table 2) and on violence (rape, robbery and assault) during household burglaries (Table 16). None involved homicide, but incidents of violence during household burglaries provides some insight into the small proportion of household burglaries that involved violence, and thus had the potential to end in a homicide (Catalano, 2010, pp. 9–11). Others have examined homicides of the elderly by caregivers (Karch and Nunn, 2011), and documented the 'causes of death' among older homicide victims (Koehler, Shakir and Omalu, 2006).

In a 'Special Issue on Elderly Homicide' in Homicide Studies, Marc Riedel stressed that elderly homicide is important because of the very large increase in the elderly population, and although the number of elderly homicides is small, they have a number of characteristics that differentiate them from other age groups of victims. He refers to 'The 'Senior Tsunami,' as the 'very large increase in the elderly population because those born between 1945–1965 – baby boomers – turned 65 in 2011. Various authors explore different subtypes of the killing of the old including robbery homicide, killing by caretakers, and issues relating to routine activities. They note the general lack of attention to the killing of the elderly compared to other types of homicide, and that there is less research on this category of victim than all others including women, children, and younger men (Riedel, 2013, pp. 123–133).

Concerning 'The Senior Tsunami,' the Official census data from Japan, the US, Europe, and the UK clearly indicate a growing proportion of the elderly in these

180 Murder of older men

populations, and that this is expected to continue. But what does this have to do with homicide and the killing of the elderly? The concept of a 'Senior Tsunami' seems ominous, and when viewed in the context of homicide may seem to imply that countries 'overrun' by old people may experience an increase in the killing of old people. Underlying the specter of being overrun, lies notions of defending against something dangerous or destructive, and the use of a counter attack as a means of defense. All of this sounds both extreme, alarming, and dangerous, so let us step back and consider what all of this might mean with respect to the increasing numbers of the elderly in the population and the possibility of growing numbers of homicides of older men and women.

While the number of homicides among the elderly are likely to increase along with the increasing number of older people in the population, this may not represent an increase in the proportion of the elderly who are murdered which may, in fact, remain at about the same low rate as when there were fewer older people. But is that all we need to know about the killing of the elderly? Does anything else matter? We return to Japan, and note that while they have one of the highest proportions of elderly in the population, they also have one of the lowest rates of homicide in the world. At a cultural level, Japan also bears cultural hallmarks of respect for the elderly, a rejection of violence, and an appreciation of older citizens. While these qualities may not be as strong as they once were, they nonetheless seem to be more in effect than elsewhere. So, our focus on the killing of the elderly cannot simply be a matter of the proportion of the elderly in the population, but must also include issues relating to wider cultural views about old people and their place in society, the general acceptability of the use of violence, and elements of the daily lives of the old including isolation, living alone, and physical and economic dependence that make them more vulnerable to those who might prey upon them.

The killing of older men (and older women) receives far less attention (or none at all), particularly in large studies of homicide that focus on the majority of homicides that involve younger victims and perpetrators, circumstances such as burglary/homicides, and killings involving knives and guns. For example, evidence about the killing of the elderly is absent from two major international reports on homicide compiled by the United Nations Office of Drugs and Crime (UNODC) in 2013 and in 2019). It was also missing from Block and Zimring's (1973) early, foundational study 'Homicide in Chicago, 1965–1970, they focused on the main types of homicide including robbery-killings, killings involving younger victims and offenders, and killings related to guns. While these and other large studies add immeasurably to knowledge about the main types homicide, they are often silent about murders of the elderly and other types of murder that occur less frequently. Although homicides of the elderly are often overlooked in larger studies because of their relatively small numbers, this does not mean that they cannot be examined within large studies. When Carolyn Rebecca Block later returned to the Chicago data and focused on, 'Homicide Against or by the

Elderly in Chicago 1965–2000,' she found that the typical circumstances when the elderly were killed differed from those in which children or young adults were killed, and that there were differences related to the gender and age group of the victim. Dividing the elderly into age groups, she found differences between the killing of women and men, between those who were old and the oldest old, and between those involving robbery, sex, and homicide-suicide (Block, 2013, pp. 154–183). Similarly, there is much to be discovered about the killing of the elderly when these homicides are a central focus of the research (cf., Goetting, 1995; Falzon and Davis, 1998, pp. 371–374; Ahmed and Menzies, 2002; Abrams, et al., 2007).

When the focus turns to the small number of murders that involve the killing of older men, issues apart from burglary can more easily be seen such as those relating to sex, hate crimes, as well as killings by others, such as caretakers or health care providers (Karch and Nunn, 2011). Even when they are not completely ignored, findings about the killing of the elderly may simply report on those over 65 years or 'the oldest old,' and ignore the gender of older victims (Krienert and Walsh, 2010), or their sexual orientation (see Gruenewald and Kelley, 2014 on anti-LGBT homicide). Overall, there is much less research on the murders of older men concerning these and other issues. Concerning sexual homicides, Chan reviewed 47 empirical studies of sexual homicide from 2008–2015, and identified 29 studies containing data about sexual murders of victims who were both male and elderly, including sexual homicides against the elderly in Canada, UK, USA, and Germany (Chan, 2017: 105–130, with studies listed on pp. 126–130). While most studies of sexual murder focus on victims who are female and younger than retirement age, the identification of victims who are both male and elderly makes this a valuable resource in the understudied area of sexual murders of older men.

Even less is known about 'hate crimes' involved in the killing of older men (and women) (Perry, 2001). In 'Hate and Homicide, Exploring the Extremes of Prejudice-Motivated Violence,' Nathan Hall explores the concept of 'hate crimes' which he believes is more accurately defined as 'prejudice,' notes that it is not generally agreed what 'hate crime' means, and that 'it is less nuanced an idea than prejudice, bias, bigotry, hostility, anger, or just a mere aversion to others' (Hall, 2013, 2017, pp. 165–179). Concerning 'hate crimes' and the killing by caretakers or health providers, it is essential to mention the case of Dr. Harold Shipman, a medical doctor in a small town in England who murdered an unknown number of his patients over many years (estimates range up to 250 deaths, with 173 murders recorded in the official statistics for the year 2003). Ultimately, he was convicted of 15 murders of his patients, all were old or very old, and most were women but a few were older men. In his daily practice, he administered overdoses to patients who died shortly after a visit from him but since most of them were old and ill the circumstances did not seem suspicious (White and Ritchie, 2004).

Most killings of older people, whether men or women, occur while they are being robbed, usually in their own home. Some are associated with sex, and a

182 Murder of older men

few appear to be 'hate crimes' possibly reflecting notions of disgust or a disregard of those who are old. Elsewhere, we have examined 'when men murder older women,' and many of the same conditions also apply when men murder older men (see Dobash and Dobash, 2015, 2017), but here, our focus is only on the murders of older men. Using evidence from the Murder Study, we begin with an overview of the 'main patterns' that characterize all 40 murders of older men, followed by narrative accounts of these murders that we classified into three sub-types (hate crimes, theft/murders, and sexual murders). The accounts of these cases illustrate the different situations and circumstances in which older men are murdered by other men, and the dynamic elements involved in these events. Last, we compare the Murders of 'Older.Men' with 'Others.Murders' not of this type in order to consider differences and similarities between them.

Main patterns – murders of older men

Of the 424 cases of male–male murders in the Murder Study, 40 cases (9%) involved men who murdered men aged 65 or older.[1] Using the quantitative evidence from the casefiles, we first describe the 'main patterns' associated with all 40 murders of Older.Men in terms of the relationship between perpetrators and victims, conflicts and disputes, the murder event, and the cause of death (Table 6.1).

Background and relationship between perpetrators and victims

The average age of the perpetrators was 27 years and the average age of their victims was 72 years. Most perpetrators were unemployed (82%). The majority of men were acquainted in various ways, but just over one-third were strangers (38%).

Conflicts, disputes and previous violence

Unlike some of the male–male murders considered in earlier chapters, previous conflicts and disputes between perpetrators and older male victims were rare, and only 8% of the men had been involved in any kind of 'ongoing dispute' prior the murder. Previous violence by the perpetrator against the victim was rare (3%), as was previous violence by the victim against the perpetrator (3%). Almost all of the murders of older men occurred without a history of previous conflicts or disputes between the men. While previous disputes and/or previous violence between perpetrators and their victims were rare, about half of the murder events did involve a confrontation at the time of the murder itself (52%), often involving victims who challenged a man who was trying to steal from him, some were about sex or sexual identity, and a few might best be described as 'hate crimes.'

Murder of older men **183**

Drinking, drunkenness, and drugs

At the time of the murder, over two-thirds of the perpetrators were drinking (69%), and most of those who were drinking were defined as drunk (81%). Very few of the victims were drinking (15%), but the majority of those who were drinking were defined as drunk. Very few of the perpetrators and their victims were drinking together (15%). Only 13% of perpetrators were on drugs.

Murder event

Most older men were murdered in their own home (77%), by one perpetrator (70%). Most murders were not witnessed (88%), and 83% of the older men suffered five or more injuries in the attack.

Cause of death

The methods used to kill older men varied including: strangling (32%), stabbing (24%), beating with an object or instrument (24%), and beating with hands and feet (18%). Death by shooting was rare (3%).

Other offenses (in addition to murder)

Most of the murders of older men also involved a second offense (85%), and the vast majority of the additional offenses (88%) were property offenses such as burglary or theft (Table 6.1).

In brief, the majority of older men were murdered by a single perpetrator (70%) in their own home or place of residence (77%) where they were alone (88%). The majority of perpetrators had been drinking (69%) and were and drunk. While the vast majority of older men were not drinking, if drinking they were more likely to be drunk.

Men murder older men – three subtypes

We categorized the 40 murders of older men into three subtypes in order to examine the diversity within this type of murder, the different contexts in which they occur, and the dynamic elements involved.

> Men murder older men – three subtypes
> 1 Hate crimes against older men
> 2 Murders of older men involving theft or monetary exploitation
> 3 Sex and the murder of older men.

The largest of the three subtypes involved 'theft/murders' that ranged from events that began as relatively 'straightforward' robberies or burglaries to those that

184 Murder of older men

included various forms of ongoing exploitation such as the 'occupation' of the old person's home or personal space and/or ongoing theft of his possessions. Some of the murders of older men involved 'sexual encounters' that took varying forms which will be explored in the narrative accounts. A few can best be described as 'hate crimes' driven by what appears to be a loathing of men who were old, weak and/or vulnerable. Narrative accounts from the casefiles and interviews are used to explore the diversity within each of the three subtypes of the murders of older men. Many of these accounts are lengthy and contain a great deal of detail about the murder event itself as well as the context in which it occurred. Some of the details are particularly disturbing in terms of the level of violence used in the murder and the general treatment of the victim by the men who killed them.

After using the narrative accounts to explore the three subtypes of the murders of older men, we return to the quantitative data and compare 'Murders of older men' with 'Other murders that were not of that type,' and reflect on their similarities and differences. Where there was overlap of the subtypes, such as an older man who was both robbed and sexually assaulted during the murder event, the case was placed in the subtype that seemed to be the most central to the issues involved. Narrative accounts were selected to illustrate both the dynamics involved in the murders of older men and the diversity across these cases. We again warn that the details of some of these accounts are quite horrific, but stress that it is difficult, if not impossible, to understand the nature of these events unless we examine this evidence in some detail. Simply saying that an old man was murdered on X date, and adding another number to the national database of homicides, is not enough if we are to try to understand these events more fully and to use such knowledge in ongoing efforts focused on reducing, and preferably preventing, the killing of those who may be targeted because they are old and vulnerable.

Subtype 1. Hate crimes against older men

We begin and end the narrative accounts with cases we describe as 'hate crimes.' Both are 'outliers' that depart from the Main Patterns discussed above and shown in Table 6.1. Both involved extreme forms of violence in the build-up to the murders that were committed by a group containing perpetrators and witnesses. The first 'hate crime' contained a mixture of factors including a theft, a house 'occupation,' and a group 'performing' for one another and 'competing' to outdo one another in a grueling display of escalating cruelty against a 70-year-old man who became dependent upon the group of local young men and women for company and assistance, but was killed by some members of the group who began by taking money from him and ended by committing a brutal murder. His home was 'occupied' by youths 'hanging out,' watching television, and stealing from him. He was a lonely, feeble old man who was unable to manage his everyday affairs and received support from Social Services. He was killed in his home by

Murder of older men **185**

four young men between 17 and 20 years of age. According to neighbors, they regularly pestered him by banging on the doors and windows of his home until he let them in. They threw wood and mud at him, spat at him and generally made his life a misery. Among his regular visitors was the perpetrator (19) who was usually accompanied by three brothers. Earlier in the day of the murder, they obtained money from the victim, bought 48 cans of lager, and were seen drinking beer and wandering around the housing estate but were not described as drunk. They returned to the old man's house and were unsuccessful in their attempt to rob his gas meter of the coins he fed into it in order to heat his house. Then, the violent torture began.

A 19-year-old and three male friends, aged 17–20, torture a 70-year-old neighbor using a stick, a garden fork, and a stone slab, then burn his body

[Confession to police of 19-year-old perpetrator]
Earlier, one of my pals said, 'Are you going to [victim's name] house?' I said, 'What for?'. He said, 'To do his meter [steal money from his gas meter], cos it's open' [it had already been robbed by another group of males]. So, we went over. He [victim, aged 70] was sitting in the kitchen, and two of my pals were there with another kid I didn't know. I gave him (victim) a can of beer and a cig.

Then, my pal went into the spare bedroom and I followed him in. He found an old sweeping brush and broke off the handles. He gave me it and said, 'Hit him with it'. I took it from him after he had snapped the handle in two again. He told me that it would hurt more with it being shorter. I went into the kitchen, and he was sitting on his own looking at me. I went over to him, and from the back I hit him over the head with the stick. He was sort of turned around and watching me, and he ducked away as I swung out. He wasn't quick enough, and I hit him fairly hard on the head. He said, 'Don't hurt me'. I went into the front room, and one of my pals said, 'You'd better finish him. If you're going to do the job right, do it'.

I got a paving stone from the bottom of the garden and carried it into the kitchen. As I started going towards him, he started to get up out of his chair. I hit him over the head with the paving stone, and he said, 'Don't hit me [perpetrator's name]. Please don't hurt me'. I went back into the front room and said, 'That wasn't good enough'. So, my pal said, 'You'd better go in and finish the job. We can't leave him like that cause if he comes around, he'll start talking'. One of the others went back into the kitchen and started hitting him with the paving slab, and the other pal was telling him to do it harder, and so he did. He must've hit him four or five times with the paving slab.

186 Murder of older men

Then, he sort-of gasped, and I think he stopped breathing. The guy who was hitting him said to take him into the front room. Me and my pal got hold of him and dragged him into the front room. I got a small sort of garden fork, and I stabbed him in his chest with the fork. I did it hard about five or six times to make sure that he was dead. Then, one of my pals, I can't remember which one, said, 'Let's make sure that he's stopped breathing'. Both of them then started stomping on him. They did it a few times each, and then I did it as well. We jumped on his chest and stomach, and I remember that one of them kicked him in his sides as well.

He was dead then, and I threw the fork away, went into the kitchen, turned the light out, and walked out of the kitchen door. Then, we went down to the fish shop and got six pickled onions. We had two each.'

(*858cf1.2.6)

[*Note: In his statement to police, he didn't mention additional events that were later presented in court by police, firemen and neighbors.*]

This ends the perpetrator's statement to the police, but it is not a complete account of the events of that day which also included an attempt to burn the victim's body before the youths went to the fish shop to get their pickled onions, and then continued their rampage by breaking into two other houses and assaulting two women and a man with a broken pool cue. They also attempted to burn the victim's body. Neighbors report a fire that was responded to by firemen and police. The police surgeon and coroner's account reveal the extent of injuries and, last, the trial judge comments about the murder and the social context in which it was committed.

Case continues, additional information

[Police report – witnesses]

On looking out of her window, a neighbor saw smoke and flames coming from the victim's flat. She alerted the other residents in the block who were then evacuated. Others went to the outside of Mr. X's flat, found both doors locked and saw through the window that the fire was coming from the settee and a couple of chairs that seemed to be piled up near the fireplace. Another occupant of the block also went to the outside of his flat, and saw furniture piled up in the middle of the room and 'lit like a bonfire'.

The firemen found his dead body on the floor of the living room with his legs hung over the arm of the settee, and his torso on the floor facing upwards. His legs were badly burned with bone visible. His pet dog was lying on his chest still alive. When they removed the dog, the fireman noticed blood on the body where the dog had been lying. On further examination, they saw puncture wounds to his chest. Police officers

Murder of older men **187**

attended at (midnight) and saw that his head and shoulders were covered by his clothing which had been pulled upwards. Bloodstaining was present across his chest. A police surgeon attended at 1:40am, confirmed his death and noted several stab wounds to the chest and extensive burning of the lower limbs.

[Injuries]
In addition to the fire damage to his body, there were 17 external injuries to his head and face, three injuries to the neck, and about 30 to the chest. The external head and facial injuries consisted mainly of lacerations, abrasions and bruising, although a stab wound was found below the left lower eyelid. A further stab wound had penetrated his mouth. The internal head injuries amounted to fragmentation of all the bones of the lower two-thirds of his face including the cheek bones, lower jaw and nasal bones. The internal bruising was severe, and the external chest injuries included eight stab wounds and a number of irregular abrasions. Internally, there were multiple fractures of the ribs, fragmentation of the breast bone and an almost complete avulsion of the heart from the base. The fatal injuries were mainly to the face and chest, with most of the facial injuries consistent with having been caused by the concrete slab. The chest injuries were consistent with having been caused by the garden fork. The internal injuries of the chest and avulsion of the heart were consistent with being the result of severe compressive force on the chest, perhaps by jumping on the chest. Death was due to multiple injuries.

[Trial judge]
When sentencing, the trial judge called this a 'terrible crime' that began when the defendants failed to get the deceased to leave the kitchen where the gas meter was situated [in order to steal the coins in it].

[Police report presented in evidence to the court]
The police described the area as a housing estate that creates, 'a ready context for the commission of crime', and stated that the standards of discipline and care within the home have not been noticeably lacking, but street life is a powerful influence on young people in the area where high unemployment, criminality, suspicion of authority, and quite intensive policing are facts of life. The risks are that much greater if the buttress of a solid family life is, for whatever reason, weakened.'

(★858cf1.2.6)

The brutality of this murder illustrates an escalation of different kinds of violence with increasing ferocity as the young men egged each other on in an upward spiral of violence. Perhaps the violence became a competition, or a show of masculine

188 Murder of older men

'prowess,' or simply served as a form of entertainment. For the four youths, it was a long day with lots of drinking, lots of violence against several individuals, and a horrific murder of an old man calmly finished with a trip to the fish shop to buy pickled onions. In trying to understand this horrific crime, it was noted that,

> The victim and the offenders lived on a notorious housing estate ... where law-and-order had broken down ... and groups of young males were often seen roaming the streets at night, and the four-co-accused spent much of their time messing about in the streets, drinking, shouting and generally being a nuisance.

The trial judge commented on the breakdown of family ties within this community. In addition, the escalation of violence may also have been associated with the use of a 'violent performance' both as a means of valorization their own masculinity and as a grotesque form of entertainment for the group.

Subtype 2. Murders of Older.Men involving theft or monetary exploitation

Most murders of older men involved some form of monetary gain. Some thefts were committed by strangers, but even more of these murders involved thefts and various forms of exploitation of the older men by acquaintances. Perpetrators included neighbors, those who delivered goods to his home, as well as friends and relatives who spent time in his home and may have provided some form of company or assistance, and felt that such 'assistance' should somehow be 'repaid' by the older man. This may have been done openly and involved 'exchanges' in the form of money, food, alcohol and/or a place to hang-out. Or, indirectly, through stealing items from his home that could be sold for cash, or gaining access to his bank book, credit cards or pension checks that could be taken without his knowledge or consent. Alcohol consumption and drunkenness often played a significant part in these murders. Some perpetrators were drinking and extremely drunk, and decided to rob someone, anyone, to obtain money to continue drinking. Some perpetrators were sufficiently dissipated by the long-term, excessive abuse of alcohol that they selected as their victims those who were old, weak and vulnerable because they were themselves less able to confront younger, more able man.

Theft/murders of Older.Men by strangers

In the Murder Study, 32% of the male–male murders of older men involved 'strangers' who had no previous contact with their victim. As shown in the next three cases, many of these perpetrators were drunk and set out to rob someone in order to get money to continue drinking but, in the process, killed the person they were trying to rob. In one case, the perpetrator was so drunk that he was unaware of whether the target of the robbery was younger or older, a man or a woman, but blindly inflicted a large number of injuries upon them. The fact that numerous injuries were inflicted on men who were older and unlikely to put up much of a fight or to defend themselves in ways that truly threatened the younger man begs the question of why these perpetrators used so much more violence than might have been required to subdue and rob an older man? It should have been easy for this 19-year-old to rob an 81-year-old, and no amount of resistance on the part of the older man was likely to pose a serious threat to him, but he inflicted numerous injuries on the old man, and left him to die.

Drinking, short of money, tries to rob a farmhouse and kills the farmer (age 81)

The male perpetrator (19) with a history of mental health problems was drinking in a pub and decided to rob a farmhouse. When confronted by the farmer (81), he beat him to death by punching and kicking that caused severe injuries, shock and hemorrhaging.

[Context]
The perpetrator had spent the evening drinking, appeared to be short of money and told a friend that he was going out to steal. During the course of the evening in a public house, he had caused trouble through aggressive behavior and brandishing a Stanley knife. The same knife was subsequently found in the farmyard although there is no indication of any weapon being used in the murder.

[Murder event]
In the room in which the victim was assaulted, there was an envelope which was bloodstained and had the fingerprints of the perpetrator. It appears that after the perpetrator left the pub, he went to the farmhouse almost certainly with the intention of breaking in and stealing, and when confronted by the victim he subjected him to a violent attack. The victim's body was discovered the next morning by his nephew.

[Injuries]
The cause of death was due to shock and hemorrhaging caused by multiple injuries including: severe bruising to the facial area resulting in a severe fracture to the facial bones; fractures to the chest bones, both sides of the rib cage, and several injuries on the scalp were consistent with the deceased being struck with a blunt instrument, probably a fist, although kicking was possibly involved.

*(*293cf1.2.2)*

Although some of these men had a history of mental health problems as children or adults, most did not (see Chapter 7, Table 7.1; and Chapter 8, Table

190 Murder of older men

8.1). These findings reveal that the majority of the men who murdered older men had serious problems with alcohol both as children and as adults, and that alcohol abuse was more prevalent among those who murdered older men than among those who committed any of the other types of murder. The majority of those who murdered older men were drunk at the time they committed the murder, and many had previously committed non-lethal acts of violence while trying to steal money to buy more alcohol, like this man who said he didn't intend to kill anyone but just wanted to get more money to continue on a binge.

Perpetrator and two boys murder older man to get money for alcohol

The male perpetrator (23) and two young boys were drinking and sniffing glue, then broke into the home of the male victim (69) and assaulted and murdered him. The perpetrator had a severe drink problem and wanted money for alcohol. He claimed he had no intention to kill and expressed remorse and empathy. In discussing the murder, he had no hesitation in accepting full responsibility for assaulting and killing the victim. He wished to make it clear that he had no intention of killing the man but simply wanted more money for alcohol. He said he felt very sorry for the victim and blamed the offence on his alcohol abuse.

(*140cf1.2.2)

When we interviewed him in prison, this man discussed at length his life, troubles and the killing of the old man. He said he was drunk and broke into the bedroom of a complete stranger in order to rob him so he could continue drinking. During our interview, he provided details about his life before the murder as he traveled to different countries teaching English as a foreign language, about his serious problem with drinking, and of the resulting stress and the toll on his health.

World traveler and alcoholic (30) breaks into bedroom of a sleeping man (83) delivers 50 blows with a hammer, steals money and possessions, tries to escape to Russia but is captured in Poland. Says he 'just wanted to kill someone.'

[Context]
Let's talk about the circumstances surrounding the events that brought you here. What was going on in your life at the time? After a period of trying to stop drinking and to recover, I caught a bus into the city and was drinking on the bus going in. I met someone and she told me there were night clubs up near [area], and to go up there. So, I went up to the area and tried to get into this night club but the bouncer said I was too drunk to go in, so I circled around the back and started climbing to try and find

some sort of entrance to get into this night club. It's all quite vague. I'm not sure what was happening. I reached into a kitchen window of a flat and pulled out a hammer. There was a hammer on the window sill. I got this hammer, and then the next memory I've got is of this open window about two floors up and me climbing up. So, I climbed up and got in this open window.

[Murder]
It was completely dark inside and I was conscious of someone sleeping in the bedroom. I went across to the kitchen and stood there for a moment thinking about what I was going to do. I just went into the bedroom and started swinging the hammer. The person then sat up. It was dark. I couldn't make anything out really but I was conscious of him sitting up and yelling and then I just kept on swinging with the hammer. I can only really go by statements [made in court] of how long I was doing it for, but there were about *50 wounds*. I hit him about 50 times, and then I must have stopped swinging eventually. Then I must have turned the light on. It's not really clear any of this part of it. I must have put a pillow on his head to cover the sight. It was quite horrifying. In the video of the scene I saw later [in court], there was a pullover (sweater) over his head, so I must have put it there. Then I had a bath [in the victim's flat] because I was covered in blood.

Thinking back, had you pictured this before? Had you got a specific intention? Do you think you wanted to steal money? Did you need money at the time? Well, I was poor, yes, so that probably had something to do with it I suppose. *In the [police] reconstruction, had you looked through the flat to look for money and things?* I'd ransacked the bedroom but it was just to take these clothes. I took two [of his] suitcases [and filled them with his] clothes. But the money wasn't well hidden. I noticed from statements [in court] that it was spread all over the bedroom in lots of £3,000, £2,000, in envelopes. There was one under the mattress which would have been the first place a burglar would have looked. There was about £3,000 under the mattress, there was some in his dressing table, some in his cupboard. Just all over the place.

What age was he? He was old, 83. *And, as you've thought back, did you think [stealing money], this is what was up?* Not a material motive, but it's just anger-and-hatred building up over a long time through a lot of things which had happened to me over the years which I started to explain to you [the interviewer] about difficulties in relationships with women, that kind of thing. *And did drinking play its part?* That as well. *Did the police put a motive on it?* No. They didn't class it as burglary. I don't know really....

My life was a mess … I wanted to kill someone. It sounds very brutal but that is it. [Our emphasis, this comment cited in Chapters 6 and 8.]

192 Murder of older men

> [After the murder]
>
> *So, you went on the run?* Yes, the next day I bought a train ticket for Russia but I had to get out [of the train] in Poland to get a visa, so I stayed in Poland. *How did they trace you?* I didn't really cover my tracks at all. I made it easy for them to find me. *And by that time, they knew it was you?* Yes. It was obviously me. There were the fingerprints everywhere. I'd had my fingerprints taken two weeks before that [for another offense]. *So, you came back to England charged with murder?* Yes, I pleaded guilty. *Had you gone on the booze again?* I was drinking a lot then. I was drinking way too much, and I was trying to teach this group of 16-year-olds.
>
> *(*1063iv1.2.6)*

The cases presented above involved theft/murders of older men who were strangers to the men who killed them, and may or may not have been 'selected' for attack on the basis that they were known to be old and thus thought to be an easy target for theft. Some of these victims may simply have been the unlucky ones who, by some fluke or accident, became the target of violence from a man who was blind drunk, unhappy with his life, and lashed out at a stranger who, at least in theory, could have been anyone, young or old, man or woman.

Theft/murders and house occupations of older men by acquaintances

The context of the next case is similar to an earlier case presented in subtype of 'hate crimes' as it is set in the context of a group of young people who used the old man's home as a location for entertainment and 'messing about,' although some of the group, particularly the teenage girls, offered various forms of support and assistance to the old man. Unlike the case cited earlier, the entire group was not involved in this murder. Instead, the older man was murdered by only one of the young people who often visited his house. None of the others were there on the day as he acted alone in an effort to rob the old man in order to continue a drinking session that had gone on for hours. It did not involve the extreme escalation of violence performed as a 'competition' between numerous perpetrators. This robbery and the murder was carried out by a single perpetrator acting on his own and without the group dynamics involved in the earlier case. Nonetheless, it should be understood as occurring in the context of his previous relationship with the victim as a part of a group of young people who occupied his house on many occasions, knew him well, and were accustomed to taking things from him. This murder reflects some of the more usual patterns associated with the killing of older men including: a single perpetrator acting on his own, a robbery in the home of the victim, violence fueled by alcohol, the excessive use of violence, and inflicting many injuries. The false claim of a sexual misdeed by the victim was described in this casefile as a 'cock-and-bull-story,' and rejected by the jury.

Murder of older men **193**

A cuckoo returns to the nest

[Context]

The 22-year-old perpetrator had been drinking heavily and went to rob a 79-year-old man, who actually had no money, and then bludgeoned him to death. The victim was well known in the area and regularly allowed groups of young people to visit and congregate in his house. Some of them used the deceased's home to watch television, drink beer or juice, eat crisps, and generally treat the scene [victim's house] as an 'open house'. There were suggestions that they took advantage of his good nature on some occasions. There is also evidence that he actually encouraged this practice, and it is believed this was merely to provide him with company, there being no evidence to suggest more sinister motives [*see false accusations below*★]. The deceased required assistance to carry on his daily life, and he became the object of attention for several teenage girls who visited regularly, and most showed a genuine concern for his welfare.

[Murder]

The perpetrator had been drinking with friends and needed more money, so he went across the street to the old man's house and attacked him. He did not obtain money but retained his door key presumably in order to return at a later time. He then returned to the pub and continued to drink where he was later confronted by the police and admitted the attack. He made a full and frank admission to the police relating to inflicting injuries upon the deceased and used [as a defense★] a 'cock and bull story' about a sexual attack by the victim upon his sister. His sister categorically denied any such attack. He also claimed self-defense against the 79-year-old victim [claiming the victim] 'produced a knife to attack him, and he struck out, took the knife from him, and stabbed him in the neck'. He denied stamping on him, and further denied any intent to cause him serious injury. When the police arrived [at the pub to arrest him], he taunted them saying, 'I'll tell you who did it if you give us a fiver' [five pounds].

[Post-mortem]

The victim, a 79-year-old widower who lived alone, was found on the living room floor of his home suffering from head and facial injuries. He was alive but was lapsing into unconsciousness and was unable to speak. At the hospital, he was found to be suffering from severe facial bruising, head injuries, stab wounds to the throat, and broken ribs which punctured and collapsed one of his lungs. He suffered a beating with hands or feet resulting in damage to the brain, stab wounds to the throat which

194 Murder of older men

may not have proved fatal, and a severe beating or kicking to the body resulting in 13 broken ribs.

(*1022cf1.2.6)

The next older man was killed by a neighbor who sometimes ran errands for him, but was accused by the older man of stealing. At the beginning of our interview with him, he first implied that he was simply giving a helping hand to the old man, but then said he had broken into his house because he thought something was wrong with him. Next, he revealed that they had argued when the older man accused him of stealing from him, and that he attacked him. He also said that he had his wife call for an ambulance because he thought the older man had had a stroke, and so on, and so forth. Finally, he claimed that he should not have been charged with murder because he said he didn't intend to kill him, and then blamed his wife for his conviction because she acted as a witness against him.

> *He (29) steals from bank book of an older neighbor (65) who reports him to police. He then breaks into the victim's house, argues and strangles him. He denied the murder, but his ex-wife was a witness against him.*

[Context]
On the day of the murder, what happened? I'd called round his flat to see if he was in. *Why were you calling round to his flat?* Because I used to call there and see if he wanted any errands doing. I used to do like bits of shopping for him. When I called round this night, [there was] no answer [so I] knocked on the window. He's sat in the chair watching the TV, and I'm banging. No answer, so I thought there was something wrong. I just broke in, and we had an argument over his bank account being robbed.

He jumped up. Well, he stood up, and I'm just [saying], 'Well, you didn't answer your door. I've been knocking on the window'. So, then we started arguing and he's turned around to me and said, 'Well, I've told your kids [perpetrator's children] that your Dad is going down [to prison] for a long time' [because victim had reported him to the police for withdrawing money from his bank account]. So, I suppose that was the one thing that did wind me up. I grabbed him by the throat, and I was going to punch him but I didn't punch him. I was just holding him by the throat. [I said] 'You've no right doing that', and, 'I'll see you in court'. Then, I pushed him back in the chair, and I left and thought nothing more of it.

I've gone up to my wife's [house] and I've said to her, phone the police or an ambulance. He might have had a stroke. I've just had an argument with him, I'm going to bed, and there was nothing more said about it 'till I was arrested on the Friday morning or the early hours of Saturday morning. I'm charged with suspicion of burglary, and then they charged me with murder'.

And what did they say he'd died of? Asphyxiation, a snapped larynx. *So, when you grabbed him by the throat it actually broke his…?* Larynx or windpipe, whatever you call it. *He died soon after that? And then they charged you with murder?* Unhuh, unhuh. *Did you have any idea that he was dead?* No. *So, all along you were saying that it wasn't a murder?* No. Well, that's why, well, I thought that. I mean when I'd left, I'd run straight up to my wife's house, and I said to her, 'Phone an ambulance'. I says, 'He might have had a stroke' – he had heart problems. Well, at the end of the day, I was charged with murder on the say-so of my ex-wife saying that I'd killed him (she was a witness for the prosecution). She had no idea what it was about.

(*865iv1.2.6)

The next lonely, old man was killed by two perpetrators who were sexual partners, but sex was not involved in the killing. They assisted him with daily chores including cooking and providing advice about his financial affairs while, at the same time, they were stealing money from him. For both the police and forensics, there was some initial confusion about the cause of death which was initially not thought to be suspicious, but with further investigation was found to be a murder.

Two male partners befriend, assist and steal from an intellectually disabled old man living alone. The death was not thought suspicious until the post-mortem.

The perpetrator (29) and his co-defendant (41) were unemployed and 'sponged' off the elderly, lonely, disabled man (69) who was a retired hospital porter. The two men were lovers, but sex was not involved in the murder and the victim was not gay.

[Context]
The victim (69) was a retired hospital porter. He was an only child who was brain damaged at birth, was single all his life, and lived alone in the same house all his life which was described as squalled. He lived in the front room which was the only room in the house that was furnished except for a cooker in the kitchen. He had known the main perpetrator (29) for 18 months, and the co-accused (41) was the victim's own nephew, and all three were quite friendly. The victim went to the perpetrators' home each evening for a meal which they cooked for him. The co-accused (victim's nephew) would often call at his house to check on his welfare and offer advice regarding his benefit entitlements. Both perpetrators were often seen in local bars with the deceased, and were apparently 'sponging' off of him.

[Murder]
About 6pm, a female neighbor saw the two men let themselves into the victim's house. They were only in for a matter of seconds when

196 Murder of older men

they came out and walked away, and between 7–8 pm another female neighbor saw the victim alive. At 10 pm, the neighbor noticed that the front room light was on which was unusual. She thought she heard the door bolt being drawn at 10.30 pm. At 1:00 am, another neighbor saw the nephew of the deceased (co-defendant), who said he could not wake the deceased. On looking through the window, the neighbor saw that the victim was obviously dead, asked the nephew if he wanted to break into the house, and was surprised when he and the other perpetrator did not want to do so.

The woman neighbor ran to a nearby police station, and when the police arrived they found the old man in a collapsed state and noted that no person had attempted to force entry. The nephew/co-accused then kicked the rear door in, led police to his body, became upset, and left the house. The police checked for missing valuables such as his pension book.

[Police surgeon examined the body]
Apart from commenting that the neck tie worn by the victim was tight, there was nothing that was apparently suspicious about the death. The tightness of the necktie had not caused any petechial hemorrhages and therefore caused the doctor no concern.

[Post-mortem]
The examination began with a notion of death from natural causes, but discovered internal injuries to the throat, and that death was caused by a compression injury of the neck. In further interviews with the perpetrator which were tape recorded under caution, he said he had gone to the home of the deceased and had been admitted to the house by him. The two men then went up the stairs to look at a sewing machine and claimed that on the way back down, the victim had fallen down the stairs and the perpetrator had accidentally stood on his throat.

This explanation did not accord with the post-mortem findings, and the questioning continued. Later, he varied his story to say an argument had ensued during which he had taken hold of the victim and shaken him by the shoulders, and that the deceased's head had fallen to one side causing the perpetrator to catch him by the throat. With further questioning, he eventually said that during an argument, he had taken hold of the victim's necktie and swung him round by it, pulled him to his knees, and then delivered a kick to his throat which killed him. He said he then placed the victim on the bed and left him there. When formally cautioned and charged, the perpetrator replied, 'I did it'.

*(*1003cf1.2.2)*

It is difficult to understand why the two men would kill the old man who was for them 'the goose that laid the golden egg.' Why were they arguing? What were they thinking? Overall, the theft/murders of older men involved complete strangers, short-term and long-term acquaintances, and relatives, including the cases of two grandfathers cited in Chapter 4. While most murders of older men were committed by a single perpetrator acting on their own, some involved several men acting together, and a few occurred in the context of a group who 'occupied' his home and stole from him while at the same time providing him with assistance or social contact. Alcohol consumption and drunkenness were common in the theft/murders of older men. For some, the main factor motivating the theft was the desire to obtain more money in order to continue drinking but, instead, ended with a murder.

Subtype 3. Sex and the murder of older men

The murders of older men that contained a sexual element included several different contexts and situations including: claims of a sexual advance, both false and apparently true, that were used to justify the murder; the robbery and murder of gay men who were lured by perpetrators with the prospect of a sexual encounter but whose real intention was to rob and/or to use violence against the victim; and sexual encounters between male prostitutes and their customers that went wrong.

We begin with perpetrators who claimed they killed the older man in response to a 'sexual advance' initiated by the victim. Some claims were supported by the evidence but many were not; and whether true or false, an unwanted sexual advance can never justify a lethal response. As discussed in Chapter 5, such claims were often made in an attempt to deflect responsibility onto the victim and to justify the use of violence in an effort to avoid a conviction for murder. Some murders involved what appeared to be an 'agreement' to engage in a sexual act by the older man who was, in fact, being lured into a situation where he could be robbed. These perpetrators may have had no intention of engaging in a sexual act with the older man, but made a 'proposition' of sex in order to set up the conditions so he could be robbed. In other cases, the men met in a place where it was known that men could have/buy sex and agreed to have sex. Then, for some reason, things changed and the perpetrator, usually the younger man, killed the older man who was his 'customer.' In many ways, the sexual murders of older men are similar to sexual murders involving younger men (see Chapter 5), and the age of the victim made little or no difference, but in others the advanced age of the victim constituted an additional layer of vulnerability as shown in the following cases.

Mixed messages and intentions – sex or robbery, or both?

These cases seem to reflect different understandings between the perpetrators and their victims about what was on offer, what was being discussed, what to expect, what could be extracted from the situation (a job, a place to stay, food or

198 Murder of older men

money, a sexual encounter) and, ultimately, who was 'in charge' of the unfolding events. There were mixed messages about 'who would get what,' and about 'what was meant to happen.' In the first case of mixed messages, the perpetrator, who had a serious problem with alcohol, lured the older man into a secluded location in order to carry out what may have appeared to the older victim as a mutual 'agreement' to have sex while the intention of the perpetrator was to rob him and possibly to have sex with him. The perpetrator brought his younger brother along as a 'look out' for what the younger brother believed was a robbery, but he became a witness both to a sex act and a murder.

> *Drunken perpetrator appeared to offer sex in order to rob an older man, brought his younger brother as a 'lookout,' then engaged in mutual masturbation and killed the older man.*

[Murder]
In the early evening, the perpetrator (21), who was a 'heavy drinker', and his brother went to the pub for a drink and were joined by a young friend. Later, the victim (65), who was known as a homosexual, came into the pub and offered to buy them a drink. The perpetrator thought the older man had a lot of money and so decided to go with him to a secluded location which the victim believed was in order to have sex but the perpetrator thought to rob him.

After closing time at the pub, the two men set off to the park accompanied by his younger brother who was meant to act as look-out while his older brother committed the robbery. After a longer than expected time had elapsed, the younger brother looked over the wall and saw them masturbating each other. Then, he heard a series of cries and thuds, and saw his older brother climbing back over the wall. The younger brother then went to the victim and tried to help him but realized that he was dead. He became very agitated and ran to the nearest bus stop to tell people, then he went to the police station to report what had happened.

[Parole assessment report]
He is the first to acknowledge that alcohol played a considerable part in his life. He was a 'heavy drinker' and his working lifestyle contribute to this. He strongly rejected that he had a problem with alcohol dependency, even though he could identify alcohol-related offending dating back many years. His former Probation Officer indicated that he admitted to drinking to excess, and that this had had a 'devastating effect' on his marriage.

(*186cf1.4.4)

The next murder also involved mixed messages, misinterpretations or misrepresentations about what was on offer, what was to be exchanged, and whether a sexual encounter was part of it. They met in a pub, and the victim offered to help the perpetrator find employment. During our interview, he presented as a personable man who told of a period in his life that involving a great deal of adversity. His partner had rejected him, he had lost his job, moved to a large city, and was finding it difficult to find another job. In recounting the context of the murder, he told of an encounter that was plausible but also a bit naïve about what might have been on offer. Perhaps he was completely unaware of any form of implicit bargain that the victim may have been attempting to negotiate involving the potential of a job in exchange for sex. However, he did say that at a certain point in the encounter he probably should have recognized that this was a possibility. Perhaps he hoped that the 'deal' could be renegotiated or any 'exchange' of sex could simply be ignored. Another account of the events after the murder suggests that robbery may have been a more central factor in these events and not just as an afterthought once the victim was dead. This account is drawn both from our interview with the perpetrator and his casefile.

Strangers meet in a pub. Perpetrator tells of his hard times, victim offers the prospect of a job but later reveals that he wants sex in exchange.

[Interview]
So, how would you have described your life then, round about that time when you were looking for work? Very rough. I think it was one of my lowest points. They always are when a relationship has broken up, and then you're out of the place, and out of work too. I said to my mother I felt as though I was on a slippery slope. Everything I was doing was shit. I just seemed to get into more different bits of bother here and there. I couldn't settle. I found it very strange.

Can you tell me what happened, what led up to the event? I met this guy in the pub, and he said, 'You seem a bit low' and all this, 'What's the matter?' I started [telling my story], and he told me about a building site where he lived, saying he knew the foreman and had got people work. So, I say, I'll come over tomorrow and I'll come and meet the people. He says, 'No, no, I'll take you and show you the place'. So, we got on the bus together on the Saturday and he says, 'There's the building site'. All the [scaffolding and safety] nets were up [but there was no builder on the site], so I knew what was going on [suspecting a sexual approach]. He says, 'Do you want to come in for a cup of coffee?' So, I went into this house which was opposite this building site, sat on the settee, put the telly on, and he left the room.

Fifteen minutes later he come out of the room with a pair of boxer shorts on and said, 'Son, I want you to fuck us and give us some favors for favors.' I jumped up and started to rave. He grabbed me by the nuts and wouldn't let go of me. So, we got into a scuffle, and I turned him

200 Murder of older men

> and we fell on the settee, and I had him by the throat. He had us by the nuts and he wouldn't [let go], and I was yelling at him, 'Get off!', and I'm squeezing him, you know, and there's like a tie on the back of the chair, and I wrapped the tie round him and I was screaming at him, 'Get off us', and he wouldn't let go, and I strangled him.

> [Casefile]
> Shortly afterwards, he phoned his sister-in-law from the victim's flat, and expressed remorse but gave no details about what had happened. Before he left, he stole jewelry from the man's body and money from his pockets, and left his body sitting on the settee. The body was discovered when the perpetrator took friends from the hostel where he was living to the flat, possibly in order to steal more things, and one of them informed the police. Accounts vary, and in one report he says he handed himself into police. He says he took jewelry because he felt the man owed him something since he had provoked him into a terrible criminal act.

> *(*591cf1.4.4)*

His return to the victim's flat accompanied by his friends from the hostel knowing that the man's dead body was there, but also that there might be more property that could be stolen, raises question about the nature of the encounter and his supposed lack of suspicion that a sexual encounter might be initiated by the victim. Was he aware that the invitation was likely to involve an expectation of sex, but thought he could just turn the encounter into a robbery?

Prostitution and robbery

Anonymous sex with a stranger or short-term acquaintance, whether between gay men, gay women, or a man and woman just 'hooking-up,' all involve an element of excitement associated with the unknown, but also contain an element of risk associated with being 'discovered,' and the possible danger of a robbery or assault. The possible risks and dangers vary depending on the particular time, place, and circumstances in which the anonymous sex takes place but, nonetheless, remain an element of such encounters. Whether the sexual encounter is based solely on a social exchange or one that is solely commercial may have little or no bearing on the nature and level of risk to either of the individuals involved, but the awareness and sensitivity to the potential risks is more likely to be known and acted upon by those who engage in sexual encounters with strangers for money. All sex workers, whether men or women, are aware that for various and differing reasons, they could be harmed by the customers who seek sexual services from them. In heterosexual encounters, it is usually the (woman) sex worker/prostitute who is in danger of being harmed by the (male) customer seeking to buy sex from her, but this is not always the direction of the danger when the sexual encounter involves two men. As shown in Chapter 5 on 'Sexual Murder Between Men,' gay men seeking consensual sex from a man may be lured by a straight man who pretends to be offering sex but then turns on him and attacks him either because he is gay or as part of a robbery, or both. Although the circumstances surrounding the sexual murders of older men are not exactly the same as those involving the younger victims, many of the dynamics are sufficiently similar that they need not be recounted again concerning older victims who are killed by younger male sex workers. Thus, only one case is presented here. This narrative is taken both from his casefile and from our interview with him in prison.

Murder of an older man associated with 'cottaging' in a public toilet

[Casefile]
This man (20) was described as very amoral and referred to as a 'psychopath'. He worked as a male prostitute selling himself sexually for money, and killed an older man (65) who was seeking to buy sex in a public toilet. He is possibly a bisexual but described himself as homosexual from an early age.

[Context and circumstances]
He needed money and went to a seaside toilet (known as a 'cottaging' location) and agreed to have sex with the older man. He told alternative stories about what happened including: that there was a dispute about the money; that he decided he didn't want to have sex and became angry when the older man insisted; that he went there to rob a customer and steal his car; and that he just went there to kill someone.

[Murder – several statements to police]
He said he went to a public toilet in order to be picked up. Having agreed to have sexual activity, he went with the victim in his car to an isolated area where he claims the victim went to undo his trouser zip. At this point, he claims he changed his mind and became angry when the victim continued to make sexual advances, lost his temper and punched the older victim. I said, 'Let's talk it over,' so I got him up and we went to the car. We went to this place and he got nasty. He said I'd fucked his chances [of sex that night] and he hit me, so I done him…. He further claims his belt had become undone and that he then wound that belt around the victim's neck. A struggle ensued, but after a short time he overcame the victim who went limp …. 'I hit him. He came at me all aggressive. He went to the ground. I went through his pockets, and then went and got the car ….
Finally, He claimed he was forced to kill the victim in self-defense.

(*816cf1.4.4)

202 Murder of older men

In addition to the information contained in his casefile, we also interviewed this man in prison. His description of what happened before he killed the older man provides more insight into his life and the murder. His description of the murder and the events surrounding it were interspersed with accounts of what was happening in his life at the time, earlier incidents he viewed as important or relevant to understanding him as a person, information about what happened on the night of the murder, and some possible reasons why he did what he did. In this first-person account of the murder and events immediately following it, he reflected on his life in ways that, in his view, provided both rationales and justifications for his actions while, at the same time, also taking responsibility for his actions.

[*Our interview with the same man – in prison*]

[Murder]

'He was on the floor [ground]. I yanked him up and pushed him into the bushes so he's actually being dragged – his head, his hips, bang, bang, I dragged him through the bushes. *You hadn't used the knife? No. Can you think about what was going through your head at the time? What was it? Was it anger because this guy wouldn't back off? Did you want the car? In the end, you stole the car?*

I don't think it was very much to do with him [victim]. It was about me not being able to cope because of my meaningless problems that I had. Because I didn't have the safe surroundings. There are more ways, probably a million ways, I could have dealt with that situation without a doubt, just restrained him. I look back beyond that, at the people I'd stopped from fighting, the situations where I've held somebody at arm's length, women who have got angry with me without me touching them. I can think of a thousand ways that I have done it. I look at that, and I think the responsibility for the murder is mine, and mine alone.

Do you remember when, earlier on [in the interview], I said it was something that was waiting to happen? Well, you could say that was two to three years earlier when the warning signals were there. I was out of that parental guideline then. Yeah, the hold that she [stern and concerned step-mother] had on me was gone. There is no more 'introvert', now I'm the 'extravert'. Imaginary family, and all this sort of thing, but I think, [I lost] a certain amount of self-control, you know, nothing to do with the victim.

I can never say whether I would have tried to move the body or whatever. I can't say that because it didn't get that far. *You left the body, right? And the body was found by the police presumably? No. No? How many days?* I got picked up by the police, I think it was about two or three days later. Yeah, that body was there for two days. They picked me up on the motorway. I pulled the car [stolen from the victim] in [a motorway stop], and the police were already there, and I walked straight into them. I knew they were there, and for whatever reason, I walked straight into them. And then after the next three days – or was it two? I led them to the body, took them to the body, not knowing, not appreciating that the situation was well out of my hands and into theirs.

[The police asked], *How did you do this?* I'd already given them one story, then another, then another, and then another, and then another, It just didn't matter.

Let me ask about your sexuality. You've told me you were living with a woman, and you were having sex with guys as well? So, maybe bi-sexual? Were you concerned yourself about your sexuality? Do you think that was coming out?
I think one of two things: firstly, when I was getting a blow job [from a guy], it would take me at least three to four minutes to get a reaction. I had to work hard. With my [ex-girlfriend], within seconds. She only had to kiss me on the thighs. I saw the gay sex as a release. There was no passion. The thought of kissing another man was appalling.

(*816iv1.4.4)

Statements that the murder had, 'nothing to do with the victim, but was 'about me not being able to cope because of my meaningless problems,' provide some insight into his 'motives' for the murder which he centered solely on his life and the situation in which he found himself. The victim could have been anybody, anywhere, at any time. It seems old man was simply a conduit for the perpetrator's negative emotions and resentments about his life as a prostitute. In that sense, the victim was irrelevant to the perpetrator and could have been anyone. It made no difference who he was. Nonetheless, the fact that the victim was an older man may have made it easier for the perpetrator to act as he did without fear of a 'counter attack' from him.

Hate crime again – fiction and fact – 'Clockwork Orange'

Finally, we return to 'Subtype 1. Hate crimes against older men' with a real-life murder that bears some resemblance to the fictional violence first portrayed in a novel, and then in a film that became infamous and was banned for several decades. The fictional story involved a group of young men who attacked an older man who was homeless, living on the street, feeble, defenseless, and seriously dependent on alcohol. Anthony Burgess's 1962 novel, *A Clockwork Orange*, was made into a film by Stanley Kubrick in 1971. It became the subject of public concern about casual and extreme violence, and was banned by the filmmaker himself in 1973 after public demonstrations following the rape of a Dutch girl by men chanting, 'Singin in the Rain,' which was a copy-cat crime from a violent scene in the movie. The novel and film were produced over a half a century ago, with the story set 'sometime in the near future' which might be 'now.' But does the content of the violence in *A Clockwork Orange* have any relevance today? In

204 Murder of older men

answering this question, we first consider the events in the novel/film using the same format we use to examine cases in the Murder Study. Then, we present a real-life case from the Murder Study that bears some resemblance to this fictional event first presented over half a century ago.

Fiction – the novel and film, 'A Clockwork Orange' – Drunk and engaging in 'a little of the old ultraviolence' against an old man

[Context]
'Clockwork Orange' focuses on a subculture of extreme violence as Alex (main character) and his gang, the 'Droogs' [a contrived word from Russian for friend/buddy], get drunk at the Korova Milk bar on 'quzzle', a drink of milk laced with alcohol, and decide to go out and engage in, 'a little of the old ultraviolence'. Dressed in dramatic and menacing white jumpsuits, 'phantom of the opera' style masks, large cod-pieces over their groins, bowler hats, and carrying long sticks. The gang and their sadistic leader emerge from an underpass intent on wreaking havoc, rape and 'ultra-violence'. They advance singing, 'Singin in the Rain'.

[Violence]
They notice an elderly drunken, scruffy vagrant also mumbling, 'Singin in the Rain'. They stop and 'inspect' the man. A verbal exchange occurs as the older man complains about the lack of law-and-order in society. Then, the gang begin to beat him with their long batons. The violence is extreme, and while the victim is not killed he is left in a heap by his assailants who merrily move on to their next target which presents them with the opportunity to rape a woman in front of her husband, and she ultimately dies from the trauma.

[In prison]
Alex (lead perpetrator) is imprisoned, and aversion therapy is used to turn him away from violence. After his rehabilitation and eventual release from prison, he is recognized and turned upon by some of his former victims. But because of the aversion therapy, he is no longer able to use violence himself and thus becomes the victim of his former victims.

(A Clockwork Orange, *1962 novel, and 1971 film*)

This real-life case from the Murder Study recounts events that while not identical to those in *A Clockwork Orange*, nonetheless, contains many similarities including a senseless and unprovoked attack on an old, homeless man by two very drunk young men who did not know him, had no previous dispute with him, and did not rob or sexually assault him. Instead, they seemed solely intent on embarking on what was referred to as, 'a little of the old ultraviolence.'

Murder of older men **205**

Fact – a real life murder, 'A Clockwork Orange'
– drunk and a little of the old 'ultraviolence' and murder of a homeless old man

[Context]
The perpetrator (27) had no fixed abode and was dossing with an acquaintance. He and his co-accused (27) were both long-term alcoholics and drug addicts. They had been drinking all day and were on their way home or to another drinking venue when they saw an old 'tramp' urinating over a bridge. The victim (72) was an elderly alcoholic who was physically very fragile and weighed under 105lbs.

[Violence and murder]
Words and insults were exchanged, a serious argument developed and they began beating him. The first blow may have been a punch or a slap to the victim's face which knocked him down. While he was lying defenseless, the perpetrator struck him repeatedly with no less than four blows to the left temple delivered with such ferocity that they inflicted multiple skull fractures and brain damage.

[Trial judge]
There is some confusion [and no clarity] about their primary motive. When interviewed and asked why he didn't leave while the victim was disabled, he offered the excuse that he lost his temper and continued to hit the old man with a bottle. His demeanor, and in particular his evidence at trial, suggested that he had absolutely no remorse for what he had done. His description of the attack on the deceased was very cold hearted. His reaction to his conviction and sentence was to utter threats against the witnesses. He was addicted to alcohol and, when possible, also took drugs. He had numerous previous convictions, and led a hopelessly, feckless life. On occasions during drink/drug bouts, he inflicted injuries on himself, but he had no significant mental disorder.
(*1122cf1.2.6)

This murder can best be described as a 'hate crime' committed for no apparent reason, except possibly for fun and entertainment, against an older man who could in no way be viewed as a threat to the younger men who attacked him. As well as being old, the victim was physically very fragile, had nothing that could be stolen, and was not the object of a sexual attack. As stated at the trial, there was 'some confusion [and no clarity] about the primary motive.' Based on all of the accounts in the casefile, it would appear that this murder was committed by two men who were drunk and possibly 'high' and, like the men in *A Clockwork Orange*, were just doing 'a little of the old ultraviolence.'

206 Murder of older men

Comparisons of murders of Older.
Men and Other.Murders

We return to all 40 murders of Older.Men and compare them with Other. Murders that were not of this types in order to consider similarities and differences between them. Who are the perpetrators? Who are their victims? What is their relationship? When, where and how did the murders occur? In asking how these murders are alike and how they differ, we again stress the importance of disaggregating the murders of men into different types in order to examine each more fully. All comparisons are shown in Table 6.1, and here we mention a few differences that were statistically significant (*) and some similarities that should not be overlooked. The comparisons include: background, relationship between perpetrators and victims, conflicts and disputes, drinking and drugs, murder event, cause of death, and charged with another offense in addition to murder.

Backgrounds and relationship between perpetrators and victims

The average age of older victims is an artifact since they were all 65 or older, but it is worth noting the age of older victims compared to the victims of other murders (72 years vs 38 years). Unemployment was common among all male perpetrators, but even more likely among men who murdered Older.Men compared to Other. Murders (82% vs 67%*), a difference that was statistically significant. About one-third of Older.Men and Other.Murders were committed by strangers (38% vs 30%), while the majority were committed by short- and long-term acquaintances and friends.

Conflicts, disputes and previous violence

Ongoing disputes prior to the murder were much less likely when victims were Older.Men compared to Other.Murders (8% vs 32%*). By contrast, 'Confrontations at the time of the murder' occurred in a majority of the murders of Older. Men vs. Other.Murders (52% vs 66%). Many of these 'confrontations' occurred when older men challenged perpetrators in the course of an attempted theft inside their own home. Incidents of 'Previous violence' between the men was unusual across all cases (3% vs 12%). Since most murders of older men did not have a prior history of violence, disputes or conflict between the men, this suggests something apart from a history of personal enmity.

Drinking, drunkenness, and drugs

Many perpetrators had been drinking at the time of the murder (69% vs 68%), and those who were drinking were likely to be drunk (81% vs 72%). By contrast, very few of the older male victims had been drinking at the time they were murdered (15% vs 50%★), but the few victims who had been drinking were likely to be drunk.[2] A few older men were drinking with the man who killed them, but this was less likely among the older male victims than Other.Murders (15% vs 31%★). Perpetrators in both groups were unlikely to be using drugs (13% vs 20%).

Murder event

Older.Men were more likely to be murdered by a single perpetrator (70% vs 56%) while in their 'own home' (77% vs 48%★), and with no witnesses (88% vs 57%★) who might have provided some of form of protection or assistance. At the time, fewer of the killers of older men were angry, indignant or enraged compared to Other.Murders (30% vs 42%★). Even without such emotions, the killers of Older. Men were more likely to inflict five or more injuries on their victims compared to Other.Murders (83% vs 69%). Inflicting a large number of injuries upon a man who is older and thus less likely to be able to resist a robbery, put up a fight, or pose a threat to the perpetrator raises the question of why so much violence was used in the attacks on older men? Orientations to the old including varying levels of disgust, disregard or even a 'hatred' of the old might be involved along with others including drunkenness and east targets for burglary.

Cause of death

While one-third of Older.Men were strangled, this method of killing was very rare among Other.Murders (32% vs 5%★). One-quarter of Older.Men were stabbed to death which was much more common among Other.Murders (24% vs 50%★). One-quarter of the Older.Men were beaten with objects (24% vs 17%) or beaten with hands and feet (18% vs 17%). Very few were shot (3% vs 12%★).

Other offense/s in addition to murder

The killing of Older.Men usually involved a second offense (85% vs 35%★), which was usually a property offense (88% vs 58%★) involving a burglary in his home. These events may have begun with a theft but ended with a murder, or the obverse when a murder then ended with stealing property or personal possessions (see Table 6.1, for all comparisons).

Summary and conclusions

The murders of older men contained three subtypes: hate crimes, theft, and sex. Most murders of older men related to 'burglary' including breaking-and-entering their home by perpetrators who were strangers trying to steal money and personal possessions, and by acquaintances who engaged in various forms of ongoing exploitation of the older men, withdrew money from their bank account, and

208 Murder of older men

TABLE 6.1 Murder Event. Murders of Older.Men and Other.Murders

MALE–MALE MURDER	Older.Men	Other.Murders
	$n = 40$	$n = 384^\wedge$
	(%)	(%)
BACKGROUND		
– Age:		
– Perpetrators	27 yrs	27 yrs
– Victims	72 yrs$^{\wedge\wedge}$	38 yrs
– Unemployed at murder	82%	67%★
RELATIONSHIP BETWEEN PERPETRATOR and VICTIM		
– Stranger	38%	30%
CONFLICTS and DISPUTES		
– Ongoing Dispute	8%	32%★★
– Confrontation at Murder	52%	66%
– Prev.viol: Perp.against.vic.	3%	12%
– Prev.viol:Vic.against.perp	3%	11%
DRINKING and DRUGS		
– Perp. Drugs	13%	20%
– Perp. Drinking	69%	68%
– if perp. drinking, Drunk	81%	72%
– Drinking 3–6 hrs	52%	39%
– Drinking all day	20%	21%
– Vic. Drinking	15%	50%★★★
– if vic. drinking, Drunk	80%$^\wedge$#	71%$^\wedge$
– of those drinking, drink together	15%	31%★
MURDER EVENT		
– Home of victim	77%	48%★★
– One perpetrator	70%	56%
– No Witness	88%	57%★★★
– Perpetrator [anger, rage, indignant]	30%	42%★
– Injuries = 5 + injuries	83%	69%
CAUSE OF DEATH		
– Strangle	32%	05%★★★
– Stab	24%	50%★★★
– Beat w/object/instrument	24%	17%
– Beat w/hands/feet	18%	17%
– Shot	03%	12%★

OFFENSE/s		
* Murder + 2nd offense (yes)	85%	35%***
– if 2nd offense: 'property offense':	88%	58%***

statistically significant: *$p < .05$, **$p < .01$, ***$p < .001$
^ numbers vary when: not applicable and/or missing data
^^ Note: mean age of older men an artifact of sub-sample age of 65+ yrs.
# small numbers

using their home as a crash pad for themselves and their friends where they could hang out, drink and party. Murders that involved some form of 'sexual encounter' included claims of pedophilia, or a sexual attack, and mixed messages about some form of exchange that may or may not have included sex. A few involved male prostitution and disputes about payment, and the like. Some claims of sexual attacks (by the victim against the perpetrator) were known to be false but used in court in an effort to justify the killing and/or to reduce the sentence if they were found guilty. Some sexual encounters were acknowledged but were contested in terms of whether consent had or had not been given. 'Hate crimes' against the old were illustrated in the first and last cases that we define as 'outliers' since they were committed by several perpetrators acting together and contained very extreme levels of violence.

Most older men were murdered by one perpetrator who was trying to rob them in their own home where they were alone without witnesses or anyone who might provide help. While most perpetrators acted alone, when others were present this seemed to alter the dynamics of these events as members of a group seemed to compete with one another in escalating the violence. Two-thirds of the perpetrators and victims were previously acquainted. Most of the men had no 'ongoing disputes' prior to the murder, but half of the murder events did involve a 'confrontation at the time of the murder,' mostly when victims resisted a theft although some involved various issues related to sex. At the time of the murder, over two-thirds of the murderers were drinking, and most of those who were drinking were drunk. While only 15% of the victims were drinking, most of those who were drinking were also drunk. The 'cause of death' varied, including strangling, stabbing, beating with objects or hands and feet. Very few older men were shot.

Notes

1. While only 5 of the 40 older victims (15%) had been drinking at the time of the murder, four of them were defined as drunk.
2. Murder Study: textual accounts of the killing of two grandfathers (612cf.1.2.7 and 641cf1.2.7) were presented in Chapter 4 in order to illustrate the exploitation and murder of older men in the family, but quantitative data for these two cases are included only in this chapter.

210 Murder of older men

References

Abrams, R. C., Leon, A. C., Tardiff, K., Marzuk, P. M., and Sutherland, K., 2007. "Gray murder": Characteristics of elderly compared with nonelderly homicide victims in New York City. *American Journal of Public Health*, 97, 1666–1670.

Ahmed, A. G. and Menzies, R. P., 2002. Homicide in the Canadian prairies: Elderly and nonelderly killings. *Canadian Journal of Psychiatry*, 47, 875–879.

Block, C. R., 2013. Homicide against or by the elderly in Chicago, 1965–2000. *Homicide Studies*, 17 (2) 154–183. https://doi.org/10.1177/1088767913478596.

Block, R. and Zimring, F. E., 1973. Homicide in Chicago, 1965–1970), Jr. of Research in Crime.*Law Criminology*,66 (4),496–510.https://doi.org/10.1177/002242787301000101.

Catalano, S., 2010.Victimization during household burglary. National Crime Victimization Survey. U.S. department of Justice: Office of Justice Programs. Sept. 2010. NCJ227379. Available at: http://bjs.ojp.usdoj.gov/index.cfm?ty=pbdetail&iid=2172 [Accessed November 29, 2019].

Chan, H. C. O., 2017. Sexual Homicide: A Review of Recent Empirical Evidence (2008 to 2015). In F. Brookman, E. R. Maguire and M. Maguire, eds., *The Handbook of Homicide*. Chichester: John Wiley & Sons, 105–130.

Dobash, R. E. and Dobash, R. P., 2015. *When Men Murder Women*. New York: Oxford University Press.*for* Male-Male Murder and Murder of Older Women, 201–220, 260–261, 292, 298, 299.

Dobash, R. E. and Dobash, R. P., 2017. When women are murdered. In: F. Brookman, E. R. Maguire, and M. Maguire, eds., *The Handbook of Homicide*. Chichester: John Wiley & Sons, 131–148 (for murder of older women see 140–142).

Ellis, T. and Hamai, K., 2017. Homicide in Japan. In F. Brookman, E. R. Maguire, and M. Maguire, eds., *The Handbook of Homicide*. Chichester, West Sussex: John Wiley & Sons, 388–411.

Eurostat, 2019a. Eurostat statistics explained, Population structure and ageing, Increase in the share of the population aged 65 years or over between 2008 and 2018 (data extracted in July 2019. Planned article update: July 2020).

Eurostat, 2019b. Eurostat Statistics Explained, Glossary: Life expectancy. EU-28's age pyramid (Data extracted July 2019, planned article updated: July 2020).

Falzon, A. L. and Davis, G. G., 1998. A 15 year retrospective review of homicide in the elderly.*Journal Of Forensic Sciences*, 43 (2) 371–374. https://doi.org/10.1520/JFS16148J.

Goetting, A. 1995. 'Homicide in families and other special populations' (including women, children, and the elderly) (PsycINFO Database Record © 2016 APA).

Gruenewald, J. and Kelley, K., 2014. Exploring anti-LGBT homicide by mode of victim selection. *Criminal Justice and Behavior*, 41 (9), 1130–1152, doi: 10.1177/0093854814541259.

Hall, N. 2013. *Hate Crime* (2nd edition). Abingdon: Routledge.

Hall, N., 2017. Hate and homicide: Exploring the extremes of prejudice-motivated violence. In F. Brookman, E. R. Maguire, and M. Maguire, *The Handbook of Homicide*. Chichester, West Sussex: John Wiley & Sons, 165–179.

Karch, D. and Nunn, K. C., 2011. Characteristics of elderly and other vulnerable adult victims of homicide by a caregiver: National violent death reporting system-17, U.S. States, 2003–2007. *Journal of Interpersonal Violence*, 26, 137–157.

Koehler, S.A., Shakir, A. M., and Omalu, B. I., 2006. Cause of death among elder homicide victims: A 10-year medical examiner review. *Journal of Forensic Nursing*, 2, 199–203.

Krienert, J. L. and Walsh, J. A., 2010. Eldercide: A gendered examination of elderly homicide in the United States, 2000–2005. *Homicide Studies*, 14 (1), 52–71.

Perry, B., 2001. *In the Name of Hate: Understanding Hate Crimes*. New York: Routledge.

Riedel, M., 2013. Special issue on elderly homicides: An introduction. *Homicide Studies*, 17 (2) 123–133.

UK Office for National Statistics. Overview of the UK population, August 2019. (Release date: 23 August 2019) No. 6. The UK's population for over 65's. Available at: www.ons. gov.uk [Accessed November 17, 2019] (population estimates of those aged 16–64; 65 and over; 85 and over; for local areas).

UNODC, United Nations Office of Drugs and Crime, 2013. *Global Study on Homicide 2013: Trends Contexts and Data*. Vienna: UNODC [Accessed April 27, 2013].

UNODC, United Nations Office of Drugs and Crime, 2019 (Vienna), *Global Study on Homicide: Understanding Homicide: Typologies, Demographic Factors, Mechanisms and Contributors* (July) [Accessed December 1, 2019].

US Census Bureau, U.S. and World Population Clock, The United States Population by Age and Sex. Available at: www.census.gov/popclock/world [Accessed November 23, 2019].

US Census Bureau, 1995. Statistical brief: Sixty-five plus in the US. Available at: www. census.gov/population/socdemo/statbriefs/agebrief.html. May, 1995, Economics and Statistics Administration, U.S. Department of Commerce, Statistical Briefs – Robert Bernstein, census.gov [Accessed November 26, 2019].

White, B. and Ritchie, J., 2004. *Prescription for Murder: The True Story of Harold Shipman*. London: Time Warner Books.

Online

A Clockwork Orange, 1971. [Film]. Directed by Kubrick, Stanley. USA: Polaris Productions. Hawk Films, distributed by Warner Bros, released December 19, 1971 (New York), and January 13, 1972 (UK), and February 2, 1972 (US). A Clockwork Orange (film), accessed on November 10, 2019, accessed on November 10, 2019. Available at: https:// en.wikipedia.org/wiki/A_Clockwork_Orange_(film) [Accessed February 27, 2018].

Burgess, A. 1962. [novel] *A Clockwork Orange*. UK: published by William Heinemann. ISBN 0–434–09800–0. OCLC 4205836. https://en.wikipedia.org/wiki/A_Clockwork_ Orange_(novel) [Accessed February 27, 2018].

Statistics Bureau of Japan, 2010 Japan Census. The percentage of the population aged 65 and over increased from 20.2% to 23.0%. p. 3. Available at: www.stat.go.jp/english/data/ kokusei/pdf/20111026.pdf [Accessed 17 November, 2019].

7

LIFECOURSE OF MALE–MALE MURDERERS

Childhood

Who are the men who murdered other men? What were their lives like as children, as adults, and in prison? In the next two chapters, we explore their lives across these three time periods in order to shed light on how they lived, the issues and problems they faced, and their own reflections on their lives and the murders they committed. This is a bit like a 'disjuncture in time travel' through the lives of these men. We have already examined in detail the murders they committed. Here, we will first journey 'back in time' to their lives before they committed murder, then journey 'forward in time' to their lives in prison after they commit murder. When focusing on their lives as children, it is important to remember that none of these men were murderers at this point in time. They were children. They were not murderers. Although it is tempting to interpret everything that happened to them as children, or as adults, as though they were somehow predestined to kill someone at a later point in time, this is a mistake. To see everything in their past life through the lens of our current knowledge of an event that has not yet occurred (the murder), means we are tempted to reinterpret everything based on this knowledge as though no other outcome is possible. In trying to deal with this temptation, we have as much as possible tried to restrict the focus on their lives as children with only a few references to the murder they will later commit. We have tried to strike a balance between observing the patterns that appear to be of relevance from early to later life while, at the same time, trying to avoid over generalizing as we gaze back from our position of certain knowledge that they will, in fact, later kill someone. The journey back in time begins with their lives as children at home, then at school and beyond.

Lifecourse – studying childhood

The research literature on childhood is vast and crosses many fields including education, child development, health care, criminology, and developmental criminology. While much of the research on 'childhood' focuses on the 'normal' progression through intellectual and social learning at varying stages of physical, cognitive and social development, some of it also pays special attention to 'what can go wrong,' and 'when,' and 'why.' For a history of early research on child development, see Collins (2010). Current findings in 'criminology' and 'developmental criminology' that focus on the early onset of offending suggest that individuals who engage in anti-social and/or offending prior to their teens are at greatest risk of becoming persistent offenders who commit the majority of all crimes, and these findings provide insights into the relationship between developmental problems in childhood and subsequent behaviors that are antisocial or criminal. The correlates of childhood offending (which may or may not include offences involving violence) are often associated with constellations of factors including family formation and structure, parental relationships, characteristics of the parents, relationships between parents and children, and characteristics of the children themselves including personality, intellectual capabilities, and behavioral characteristics. This area of study covers a broad scope of disciplines and orientations. The focus may be on the individual biography, on psychological factors, on social factors such as poverty, inequality, discrimination, school, and neighborhoods, on evolutionary psychology, on biology, and others. For an overview of lifecourse criminology, see Carlsson and Sarnecki (2016).

Child development, delinquency, crime and culture

Early research on the relationship between childhood development and crime began in the United States in the 1930s with the work of the husband and wife team, Eleanor and Sheldon Glueck, who conducted a number of studies on child development and crime using a multi-disciplinary approach primarily grounded in bio-psychological thinking. Their most influential study included 500 young 'inmates' at the Massachusetts Reformatory who were compared to a matched sample of 500 'non-delinquents.' On the basis of a ten-year longitudinal study published in the 1950s, they concluded that criminal behavior was age-dependent, beginning in adolescence and tapering off with age, then generally disappearing in adulthood. However, some inmates did not conform to this pattern and became 'chronic offenders' who did not stop committing crime. Their general explanation included human morphology (body types), childhood temperament, and early family childrearing with a strong emphasis on dysfunctional parental factors including lax discipline, erratic punishment and low family control (Glueck and Glueck, 1930, 1950; Laub and Sampson, 1991).

214 Male–male murderers – childhood

In *Patterns in Criminal Homicide* (Wolfgang, 1958), and *The Subculture of Violence* (Wolfgang and Ferracuti, 1967), these pioneers in criminological research conducted extensive studies on the relationship between childhood experiences and crime, and examined anti-social behavior and delinquency among a birth cohort of 10,000 children from ages 10 to 18 (Wolfgang, Figlio, and Selling, 1972; Wolfgang, Thornberry, and Figlio, 1987). Using official data from social services and the police, and highly sophisticated statistical methods, their comparison of delinquent and nondelinquent children set the standard for subsequent research. Focusing on the 'onset of offending,' and the 'continuation or cessation' of criminal behavior, they developed a typology including: 'non-offenders,' 'one-time offenders,' and 'recidivists.' Many of the recidivists were 'non-whites,' and they viewed race and poverty as the main factors associated with a delinquent 'career.' Since then, scholars from different disciplines and with different orientations have continued to examine the lifecourse of offenders and to develop and modify various typologies. Here, we provide a brief overview of a few of these studies, highlight some of the findings, and reflect on some differences between studies of the lifecourse of offenders using 'bio-psychological' and 'socio-cultural' approaches.

Studying the lives of young people – longitudinal studies of large cohorts

David Farrington, a lifecourse criminologist, has been studying the lives of young people in England since the 1970s, and he along with others have published a large body of findings from 'The Cambridge Study in Delinquent Development.' From an early publication on 'public labelling' (Farrington, 1977), to an overview of 'Recent Results from the Cambridge Study in Delinquent Development' in 2013, Farrington and colleagues have championed the use of longitudinal research as the best way to more fully understand behavior (criminal or otherwise) from childhood onwards. They have followed a cohort of young people over many years, tracked changes in their circumstances and offending behavior, and continue to add knowledge about life and crime over the lifespan of this cohort. This large body of work stretches from West and Farrington (1977) to Farrington, Piquero, and Jennings (2013), and beyond. The general focus is on, 'three main issues: the development of offending and antisocial behavior; risk and protective factors at different ages, and the effects of life events on the course of development' (Farrington, 2017, p. 1).

In 1993, Terri E. Moffitt published the findings of her longitudinal study of over 1,000 boys and girls in Dunedin, New Zealand. She was interested in the 'onset' and 'persistence' of anti-social behavior and crime, and her evidence indicated that problematic and anti-social behavior may begin as early as age 10, and advance to more serious crimes, such as robbery and rape by age 22. Her primary focus was on 'individual deficits' such as aggressive temperaments, cognitive abilities, inattention, irritability and impulsiveness that lead to 'weak self-control.'

She reported that the 'early onset offenders' were at greatest risk of becoming lifecourse 'persistent chronic offenders,' and viewed these personal characteristics as *invariant* over the lifecourse, which suggests that if a person suffers from 'temperamental disadvantages' in childhood this will persist throughout their life, and may lead to problematic behavior including crime.

This approach is primarily at the individual level, i.e. bio-psychological, although she does note that negative characteristics and behavior may be exacerbated by the 'social environment' of the home and school. Moffit's two-fold taxonomy: 'Early onset life-long offenders' and 'Late onset offenders who desist' has generally been accepted (Moffitt, 1993, 1997), and others have identified even more types of delinquency and offending (for other typologies, see Carlsson and Sarnecki (2016, pp. 35–41)). Moffitt, and others such Gottfredson and Hirschi (1990) view 'weak self-control' in early childhood as a precursor of offending that begins early and persists throughout life. The notion of 'cumulative continuity' refers to a combination of personality traits (e.g. *individual deficits that lead to weak self-control*) that Moffitt views as *immutable* and thus not subject to any real form of change as the child becomes an adult, e.g. a person who is ill-tempered as a child will tend to be hot tempered as an adult (cited in Carlsson and Sarnecki, 2016, p. 37). Later, Moffit and others did a follow-up on the men at age 26 that appeared to confirm their initial findings (Moffitt et al., 2002).

This may be seen as the route into crime, but is there a route out of crime? From this perspective, the answer is both 'yes' and 'no.' Individuals with the 'immutable' personality characteristics associated with 'weak self-control' begin offending early and do not stop. For them, there appears to be no way out of crime because of personality characteristics that are not subject to change. These are Moffitt's 'Early onset life-long offenders.' But there is a way out of crime for Moffitt's, 'Late onset offenders who desist' as they appear to have what we might think of as a 'fling' with crime mostly during adolescence, but are able to stop behaving badly (desist). Why? Because they do not have the personality traits associated with 'weak self-control' so their 'fling' with crime is over and does not become a life-long pursuit as it does for those with personalities associated with 'weak self-control.' These two types might be viewed as 'basically nice guys' who go through a phase of behaving badly before they grow up and turn into 'nice men.' By contrast, individuals with personalities that are basically flawed in ways that lead to 'weak self-control' begin doing bad things when they are young and are unable to stop. For them, it appears that there is no way out of crime because they can't control themselves. That is who they are, and what they do. In short, they're done, finished for life. Later, we will return to some of these notions including those relating to the possibility of change.

Socio-cultural view of offenders

Using a more socio-cultural perspective, Sampson and Laub (1993, 2003a, 2003b, 2005) locate anti-social and criminal behavior in 'weak informal social controls'

216 Male–male murderers – childhood

in the family, school and among peers. They focus on 'pathways' and potential 'turning points' or 'transition points' associated with significant life events such as graduating from high school, securing employment, and establishing a stable intimate relationship. For them, some individuals are unsuccessful in navigating these transitional stages and drift into persistent offending. They are cut off from informal means of control (i.e. parents, schools) and increasingly come under the control of institutions of the state such as the police, courts and prison. These early life problems and circumstances tend to 'knife off' various informal means of social control (and future life chances) as these boys have more contacts with the formal means of social control embodied in the police, courts and prison. Being exposed to the 'harshness' and negative consequences of contacts with the legal system, especially prison, result in 'stigma' and a 'label' that is difficult if not impossible to shed (see also, Laub and Sampson, 1991, 2001, 2003).

Using concepts from the 'labelling perspective' in the early works of Howard Becker (1963) and Erving Goffman (1963), they note that these processes have the potential to lead to a number of unfortunate consequences such as 'deviance amplification,' an 'altered sense of self,' and the 'shutting off of opportunity' such as employment that, in turn, may lead to an alternative 'master status' and a 'deviant career.' The processes of deviant behavior, formal controls through the justice system, and labelling as a delinquent/offender have an impact on the offender's ability to remain attached to a web of informal social control. Failure to navigate these turning points, along with the stigma of state sanctions, leads to what they term 'cumulative disadvantage.' These failures, along with the rejection of informal means of social control, create a 'pathway' that becomes increasingly narrow as various forms of informal social control become less and less salient as these individuals attempt to navigate an ever-narrowing path through conventional life.

Studying the lifecourse of murderers, and when there are too few to study

Despite the large body of evidence about lifecourse and developmental aspects of those who commit *crime*, there is less evidence about the possible connection between the child and adult lives of those who commit *violence*, and even less about those who commit *murder* (see Scottish Executive, 2001; Smith, 2002; Smith, and McVie, 2003). After decades of research on the lives of young people dating back to the 1970s, Farrington, has observed that 'almost nothing is known about childhood and adolescent predictors of adult violence in large-scale community studies' (Farrington, 2001, p. 66). The main problem for the prospective lifecourse studies is a scarcity of violent offenders, and especially murderers, in studies using longitudinal cohorts. Two examples of this limitation include: the Denver Youth Study, a longitudinal study of 1,530 youngsters residing in 'high-risk neighborhoods, which found only 14 males who had been convicted of homicide (Eisbensen, 2003, p. 4), while two samples of the Pittsburgh Youth Study of 1,517 males yielded only 24 who were charged with homicides (Loeber, 2003, p. 3). Clearly, the very small number of those who commit homicide is not an adequate basis for making generalizations about those who commit murder. In an effort to overcome the problem of the small number of homicides in their studies, Farrington, Loeber, and Beg (2012) used historical data from 1,512 cases collected over a number of years but found only 37 cases (2%) of men convicted of homicide. While noting a lack of evidence about the context and circumstances of the murders, they nonetheless concluded that the best 'predicters' of a homicide were 'environmental and socio-economic variables, and that the best childhood correlates of murder were suspension from school, disruptive behavior, the commission of 'income-generating' crimes, and previous records of violence. They were surprised that no parent–child factors, or those related to psychopathy were able to 'predict' homicide. Despite the problem of small numbers, they nonetheless offered recommendations that, while not unhelpful, could not purport to be based on findings gleaned from only 2% of their sample. The recommendations could have come from anywhere and could have been about most young people. The researchers conclude: 'Interventions should be tailored to alleviate deprivation, curb delinquent peer involvement, improve school performance, and promote effective child-rearing practices' (Farrington, Loeber, and Beg, 2012, p. 120). This is good general advice that has been in the public domain for some time, and we shall return to these issues in the last chapter.

Focusing on the lifecourse of male–male murderers

In order to learn more about the lifecourse of those who commit the relatively rare crime of homicide/murder, it is necessary to use a more *focused and intensive* form of research that has the capacity to gather larger amounts of information across the lifespan of the relatively small number of individuals who commit this particular crime. While it is not possible to obtain data about every factor that might conceivably be associated with those who commit murder, the use of a more intensive approach makes it possible to expand what is currently known about the lifecourse of these particular individuals beyond what can be obtained using other methods. Using a more intensive approach, the findings from the Murder Study expand what is now known about the lives of men who commit murder. As well as adding to existing knowledge about homicide in general and the lifecourse of offenders in particular, these findings may also be of use in the ongoing management and rehabilitation of this type of offender who usually spends much longer in prison and often requires additional or 'enhanced' approaches to rehabilitation within the prison system. Expanding what is known about those who commit this most extreme form of violence may also contribute to efforts focused on interventions earlier in the lives of such men before a serious crime of violence is ever committed.

218 Male–male murderers – childhood

As discussed in Chapter 1, the wider Murder Study contained a total of 866 murderers, including 786 men and 80 woman, who had committed all types of murder against men, women, and children. Elsewhere, we used data from the original sample of all 786 male murderers (who killed men, women, or children) to examine the 'onset of offending' among these men (Dobash et al., 2017). Using straightforward statistical comparisons and multi-variate correspondence analysis, we found that 20% were 'early onset offenders' who committed their first criminal 'act' before age 13 (this did not depend on a 'conviction'); 67% were 'late on-set offenders' who committed an offense after age 13; and 13% had 'no previous criminal record' prior to committing murder. Our analysis of an array of issues across the lifecourse of these male murderers revealed differences in their lives as children and adults. While problems in childhood were common among many of them, 'early onset offenders' were 'more likely' than the other male murderers to have had problems in childhood including problems in their families (parents who separated, fathers who abused alcohol, and fathers who had convictions), and problems in their own behaviour (disruptive at school, taken into care, and/or abused), and they also experienced an array of problems as adults. While those who began offending after age 13, 'late onset offenders,' were not without problems when they were children, they were less likely to have had problems as children than boys who began offending before age 13. As adults, both 'early onset' and 'late onset' offenders experienced a fairly similar array of problems including a lack of educational qualifications, unemployment, alcohol abuse, criminal behavior, and previous convictions including for violent offenses. Once they began offending, whether early or later, many of these men continued to offend, and might best be described as 'persistent offenders'.

Among all 786 male murderers in the wider Murder Study (male perpetrators and both male and female victims), 13% ($n = 99$) had 'no previous convictions' prior to committing murder (Dobash et al., 2007, pp. 255–256). In other publications, we have used data from the wider Murder Study to examine other 'types of murder' and the 'lifecourse' of the men who committed them including: sexual murders against women partners and women acquaintances; the murder of children inside and outside the family; and men who murdered older women. Overall, this forms a fairly large body of findings from the Murder Study about the *lifecourse* of men who murdered women and children (Dobash and Dobash, 2015, 2018a, 2018b). But here, our focus is only on the lifecourse of the 424 men who murdered other men.

Lifecourse of male–male murderers – childhood

All children live their lives in at least three primary domains: the home, the school and their local neighborhood. Each domain plays an important part in early life and provides numerous challenges that were faced by these boys as they progressed

Male–male murderers – childhood **219**

from early childhood to adolescence, and on to adulthood. Here, we examine the childhood of men who later committed murder. This includes early life at home and at school as well as contacts with social, medical and psychological services, and the criminal justice system. We wanted to know about several broad areas of their lives up to age 16: about their parents; about professionals who may have been involved with their parents or other members of their family; who cared for them; if they had ever been taken into care; or physically or sexually abused. How did they get on at school? Did they have issues relating to discipline, sexual problems, mental health problems, or abuse of alcohol or drugs? We wanted to know about offending when they were children including arrests before age 16, convictions, and whether their offences involved theft, serious violence, sexual violence and/or violence against animals. We also wanted to know if they had been in a criminal justice institution for young offenders. In addressing these questions, we use both the *quantitative data* from the casefiles to reflect the overall patterns in the early lives of all of the 424 boys (all male–male murderers), and for each of the Five Types that are compared with other murders not of that type. All findings are shown in Table 7.1.

As we examine their lives as children, we will intersperse evidence showing these patterns along with *narrative accounts* from the casefiles and interviews that illustrate the nature and complexity of these patterns. We begin with 'Problems of their parents/family,' 'professionals involved with their family,' 'disrupted caretaking,' and if they were 'abused as a child.' This is followed by 'problems of the child,' including 'problems at school,' 'discipline problems' along with 'sexual problems, mental health' and alcohol and drug abuse before age 16. Finally, we examine issues relating to early offending and contact with the justice system. The narrative accounts illustrate the nature and diversity of these experiences including both the good and the bad.

Family of origin – parents, family, and other carers

Many of the boys spent their childhood in families that were not unusual among those growing up in mostly working-class areas across the country and, like many other boys of their age, they lived in families that were relatively happy and fairly free of serious problems.

Childhood – parents and family – unproblematic and happy

[Report]
There is no history of family alcohol problems and no history of violence within the household. His father and mother are both in their fifties and both employed, he in construction and she in a care home. He gets on fairly well with his mother although they argue at times. She is nervous and has been on minor tranquilizers. His older sister has

220 Male–male murderers – childhood

been living away for many years. He was fairly close to her and misses her support.

(★102cf1.2.3)

Of the 424 boys, most were born into families with mothers and fathers who were married or cohabiting in a relationship that was recognized by others as a unit, although 41% of the parents had a 'broken relationship.' Although this was higher than the national average at that time, it is nonetheless important to note that the other 59% of the boys spent their childhood in an intact family with both parents as their main caretakers. Of the boys whose parents had a 'broken relationship,' most lived with their single parent usually their mother, some lived with grandparents or other relatives, and others lived with foster caretakers or were in institutional care or some combination of these. While intact families have generally been found to be most beneficial to the development of children, it cannot be assumed that any particular family formation or configuration is always 'good' or 'bad' for children, or that intact families are necessarily free of problems either for the adults or for the children. In a household in which their parents lived together, one or both of their parents may have experienced problems that had a direct or indirect effect upon the lives of their children.

Boys with fathers who abuse alcohol, commit crime and are violent to their mother

Some of the problems experienced by the parents of these boys included fathers who abused alcohol (25%), had a criminal record (16%), were unemployed or economically disadvantaged (18%), and 23% of fathers were violent to their mother. These problems were often entwined, and had ramifications both for the parents themselves as well as for the children who lived with them. When parents have problems, children may feel insecure, afraid and/or angry. They may not know what will happen next, if anyone will be harmed, what might happen to their mother, to themselves, or to their siblings. The following accounts provide some insights into the early lives of the boys who lived in families where their parents, particularly fathers/step-fathers, experienced problems that effected the lives of everyone in the family (Table 7.1).

Father a thief, police frequently visited and searched their home

[Our interview]
You said your Dad did burglaries. Did he get into trouble with the police when you were growing up? Yes. All the time? *Did he ever get lifted?* Loads of times. They used to come and search the house at 3 o'clock in the morning. *Was he in a ring of people doing it, or on his own?* There used to be four or five of them. They grew up together as kids. They used to do shops, safes and things.

(★631iv1.2.3)

Male–male murderers – childhood **221**

Police frequently visited the family – everyone in trouble, never happy

[Our interview]
Anyone in your family in trouble with the police when you were a kid? Yeah, everybody. The local police station could have belonged to us. *And were you happy at home?* I was never happy at home.

*(*2011iv1.4.4)*

Separate examinations of each of the 'Five Types' of male–male murderers reveals that most of these boys spent their childhood in families that were relatively similar with respect to the 'Problems of their parents.' The exception to this was those who lived in a household in which their 'Father (was) violent to (their) mother.' While this was experienced by 23% of 'All' the male–male murderers, it was most likely among those who would later commit a murder in the 'Family' (34%*)[1] and least likely among those who would later commit a 'Sexual' murder (13%) (Table 7.1). Some told us that they directly witnessed their father using violence against their mother, and a few said they saw their mother use violence against their fathers although this was unusual (2%).[2] As children, they could not alter these events and must have felt helpless and fearful for their mother as well as for themselves and their siblings. Perhaps the police would arrest and remove their father, or an ambulance would take their mother to hospital, or they would all have to leave home and try to find a place of safety with relatives, friends, neighbors, or a women's refuge/ shelter. This man told us that his father's violence against his mother wasn't nice for a kid, and that it changed his life.

Father violent to his mother. Not nice. Changes a kid's life.

[Our interview]
Would he [your father] ever say anything to you about it [father's violence to his mother]? Yes. *What would he say?* That he doesn't mean it, and in some ways it's my Mum winding him up and that. Which she did, but it didn't matter what she'd done, she didn't deserve that. I didn't agree with it. And from this day on, when I've seen him, I tell him I'll never forget it. I said, I'll get my own back when I get out [of prison]. *And how does he take it when you say that?* He doesn't like it because I'm straight with him, I tell him straight. I'm not being naïve with him, I'll tell him. And he knows. *So, would you say that's like a principle you've got about hitting, about your Dad hitting your Mum, that it was wrong whatever she might have done to wind him up?* She didn't deserve it. I've seen my friends hitting their girlfriends. You can't tell them. I tried, but they just didn't listen. *What did you try saying?* I just say, listen I've been brought up like that, it's not nice. Like from being a kid. It does put a change into your life.

*(*631iv1.2.3)*

222 Male–male murderers – childhood

In the next case, extreme poverty and his father's drunkenness and violence to various family members formed an ongoing part of his childhood, and continued to be a problem in adulthood as he became a lifelong defender of his mother and siblings. As this boy grew from a child into a man, he left the Army in order to continue trying to protect his mother and siblings from a violent and drunken husband/father who bullied and abused them all.

> ### Childhood – father got drunk, beat his mother, and bullied the family. He tried to protect them, first when he was a boy and later when he was a man.
>
> At age 7, his mother encouraged him to steal purses. She needed money as she had a large family and the children's father didn't provide her with any [support]. When his father got drunk, he would beat up his mother. He would defend her and get hit by his father who also made him and his brothers fight each other. He was in a Special School for the Educationally subnormal for four years. When he left school, he joined the Army but stayed only six months. Two reasons were given: he didn't like discipline, and he wanted to return home as his father was bullying the family while he was away. His father didn't want him home.
>
> *(*641cf1.2.7)*

While any child may initially feel distressed and concerned about their father's use of violence against their mother, they may change their mind over time. If the violence is repeated often enough, it may begin to be viewed as 'normal' in the mind of the child even as they simultaneously view it as 'not normal,' 'not nice,' or 'not significant.' In our interviews with these two men, the first man reflected back on his own dual and contradictory responses to his father's use of violence against his mother, while the second man was less conflicted and defined it as unimportant.

> ### His father violent to his mother – seen as not normal, but you get used to it
>
> [Our interview]
> *So, when he used to be violent to your mum, how serious would her injuries be? Was it black eyes?* Just black eyes, bruises, nothing broken. But it was strange. *Wasn't a normal thing was it? How serious would you say it was, this violence towards your mum?* Well, I think it was a thing that you got used to it.
> *(*591iv1.4.4)*

> ### Father violent to his mother, but he didn't see it as significant
>
> [Our interview]
> *You talked a bit about your mother and father, but just to confirm. There were arguments but no physical violence?* There was the occasional bit of physical violence, my father on my mother, but not severe. I can recall, say,

three occasions. *Pushing and shoving or hitting?* Just a punch to settle an argument, that kind of violence. If my father couldn't win the argument through words, then he'd use violence to win. I wouldn't say the violence was that significant.

*(*1063iv1.2.6)*

Tragedy all around – as a boy, he not only lived in a family in which his father was violent to his mother, but at age six he saw his mother kill his father in self-defense. At school, he had severe learning difficulties and behaved violently, but he had no previous convictions before he committed murder.

Witnessed his mother kill his violent father in self defense

[Report on relevant background]
Prior to this murder, this youthful offender appears to have had considerable difficulties in his life. At age six, he witnessed his mother in self-defense fatally stabbing to death his violently abusive father. She was convicted of manslaughter and sent to prison but the conviction was quashed by the Court of Appeals resulting in her release. At school, he was assessed as having substantial learning difficulties. At the age of 14, his reading ability was judged to be at age 7.5, and he refused to cooperate with remedial teaching. At the time of this offense, he had been referred to the Educational Psychology Department following the last act of violence at school. Although he had no known previous recordable convictions, there is one previous official caution recorded when, at age 12, he was found to be in possession of two large knives at a local fun fair.

*(*1176cf1.2.4)*

Professionals involved with various members of the family

Families that experienced problems may have sought assistance or had contact with social services, medical care, psychologists or psychiatrists. Social work and housing departments may have been involved with issues relating to rehousing whole families for a variety of reasons related to changes in circumstances including new marriages, the birth of a child, violence, divorce, and the like. One or both parents may have been sufficiently unwell that they were unable to adequately care for their children. The nature and content of the 'contacts of various family members' with different professionals during their childhood years provide some insights into the lives they led, including families that had contacts with social services (44%), psychological services (27%), and/or medical care (17%). Contacts with social and health care professionals often involved mothers seeking services for themselves and/or their children involving housing, support from social workers or health care providers. The proportion of families who had contacts with these professionals was

224 Male–male murderers – childhood

fairly similar across all 'Five Types' of murderers, although slightly greater among those who would later commit a murder related to 'Money.'

Various family members may have also had contacts with the police (51%) and/or probation (25%), and these contacts were often related to the actions of the fathers of these boys rather than those of other family members. Contacts with police and probation often involved drunkenness, domestic violence, and/ or other crimes committed by fathers or 'step-fathers.' Of the 'Five Types' of murderers, family contacts with the police during their childhood were most likely among those who would later commit a murder related to 'Money' (61%*) and least likely among those who would later commit a murder in the 'Family' (37%*) (Table 7.1).

The child

Disrupted caretaking

Although some parents/families had problems that involved interventions from various agencies that were primarily directed at these adults, such interventions also have had consequences for the child(ren) in the household. Interventions associated with problems of the parents might, in turn, involve the removal of the child(ren) from the parental home and their placement elsewhere, with another family, a foster home, a children's home, or a residential home. Some parents could no longer care for their children for reasons related to economic disadvantage, unemployment, a broken relationship, domestic violence, substance abuse and/ or poor health. In other circumstances, boys may have been removed from their parental home and spent time in some form of institution for children for reasons more closely associated with the child themselves. A few boys simply left home of their own accord; some were forced to leave by their parents or caretakers; and some were removed by a formal agency, such as social services. The events leading to such outcomes could be painful for all concerned, and long lasting in the memory long after the boy becomes a man.

Before age 16, (23%) of 'All' the boys were 'in care' which may have involved being adopted, living in a foster home, or living in a children's home. For some, this was a successful arrangement, but for others it did not work for a variety of reasons that may have been related to the new 'caretakers,' to the child, or both. But even when these arrangements were successful, there may have been a 'longing' for the 'lost' parent(s), and possibly a search for them that might last for years or even for a whole lifetime. In our interview with this man, he described events of particular importance in his relationship with his adoptive parents including a very happy moment at the seaside with his adoptive father, an explosive event involving a fierce verbal argument with his adoptive mother that was followed by a physical fight between he and his adoptive father, and then he left home forever. He was 15.

Father and son – memory of a happy moment

[Our interview]
Looking back, how would you describe your childhood, in a few words? I'd use one word, 'frantic'. And I would say of my own making, but frantic. *And do you have any happy memories?* One that I can remember, we used to go to the sea-side, and my dad used to be a good swimmer and I used to sit on his shoulders while he swam out, and out, and out, and out, but that was more the feeling of being on my own, with 'My Dad'. That was special.

... same father and son – memory of a sad ending

Were you ever violent towards your [adoptive] mother or father? My dad got it in the end. I was 15 when I left home. That was a fierce fight, verbal, it was verbal between me and my [adoptive] mother. We'd just come back from holiday. It just, the lid just came off, and my [adoptive] father tried to get hold of me to stop me leaving the house. It was this explosion where he found himself being bent over and folded up within seconds. It just totally shook him, and when he got up he looked 20 years older. I was more, ashamed, angry. If I had looked into her eyes, I think she would have been in serious trouble at that time. I had to get out of that house quick. But it was a big explosion. Ohhh, it was shocking.

... another memory – finding his birth mother

[Our interview]
Yeah, all of us were adopted. All adopted … *So, did you ever know your mother and father?* I met my [birth] mother when I was about 15 or 16. I went up to [town where she lived]. Really emotional time that was.

(*816iv1.4.4)

Multiple carers during childhood

The break-up of any parental relationship always involves some form of change in who cares for the child(ren), as well as where and with whom they live. This usually involves a period of readjustment that might result in one or two temporary changes in caretakers as mothers and fathers work out where and with whom their children will live after they separate or divorce. With the ever-increasing rates of separation and divorce, this has become a relatively familiar pattern in the lives of many families that break-up, and then reconstitute in another form that might include new parental figures, new siblings and a new family unit. In many ways, reconstituted families function in a fashion fairly similar to the original family unit, and may be more or less successful. But numerous changes in caretakers

226 Male–male murderers – childhood

are often an indicator that things have failed for a variety of reasons. For some of these boys, one or two moves away from their parents and into a life with other caretakers was a positive move when they were children and also had a lasting effect into adulthood.

Father violent to mother, parents separate, lived happily with his grandmother

[Our interview]

So, in your family, up until the age of 16, who did you grow up with, who was in the house? I stayed with my Gran. Because with her being invalid, I used to go and do all her messages [shopping] and put her in a wheelchair. She used to shuffle places, but she couldn't walk anywhere, she couldn't do steps. She had this, it was more an arthritis, she was only little. I used to, we used to, take her to the seaside, [we have] pictures in her wheelchair. But I stayed with her all the time. I got married from my Gran's.

(*591iv1.4.4)

Being taken into care, and failures when in care

Some family break-ups result in extreme disruptions in caretaking, particularly when these arrangements repeatedly fail and children were moved 'from pillar to post.' Being in care, and having numerous changes of caretakers while in care involves a great deal of changing of where the child lives and with whom they live. Frequent changes of caretakers may also imply 'failures' in arrangements that left these boys even more 'unanchored' and with fewer forms of ongoing and stable support and control from significant adults. Repeated changes in caretakers may be a signal of problems that had not been resolved, or could not be resolved, in each of the different placements. Clearly something was wrong. A large body of research indicates that one important factor in childhood development involves both the quality and the stability of care. While some of those in the Murder Study experienced a least one change in caretaking when they were children, this is not particularly unusual in the current context of family configurations involving parental separations and divorce that result in one or two changes in caretakers as children live with both parents, then a single parent, grandparents or others, and thus experience one or two changes in their primary caretakers. However, research into the relationship between caretaking and various problems in childhood (including educational attainment, criminality and other factors) suggests that there may be a relationship between childhood problems and *many changes* in caretakers (cf., Widom and Maxfield, 2001; Dobash et al., 2007, p. 253).

Nearly one-quarter (23%) of 'All' the boys were 'in care as children,' and 29% of those in care experienced at least 'three or more changes in caretakers' before age 16. This would seem to signal that something is going wrong in these arrangements, and findings from other research suggests that many changes in caretakers is a marker of serious problems. For example, the separate examinations of each of the 'Five Types' of male–male murderers, indicated that those who would later commit a murder related to 'Money' were far more likely than all others to have been 'in care as a child' (33%★), and of those who were in care, *money* murderers were also by far the most likely to have had three or more changes in caretakers (43%★) (Table 7.1).

What might this mean? The fact that men who later commit a murder related to 'Money' were, as children, the most likely to have been 'in care' and also the most likely to have had '3+ changes in caretakers' begs the question of what might be going on. Let us consider what might have been happening in the childhood of these boys, how it might be related to their later lives as adults, and speculate about how this might be related to murders involving money. Numerous changes in 'where' and 'with whom' the boys lived may suggest that they were less likely to be under control or adequately supervised by the changing cast of adults with whom they lived. At the very least, being 'in care' that involved 'numerous changes in caretakers' suggests a lack of stability in who is caring for the child and where they reside. Even if there were no particular problems with the quality of care in each of these placements, each new residence marks a change in their daily routines as well as the 'significant others' upon whom they, as children, depend for their welfare and their sense of security and wellbeing. With fewer anchors and controls, such children may be more likely to fend for themselves or to be taken under the wing of older boys or adults and recruited or coerced into crimes such as shop lifting, drug running, and the like. With time, some boys may become relatively good at illegal activities that make money and thus continue in similar activities which, in effect, constitutes a 'career path' as they increasingly 'specialize' in acquisitive crimes with 'money' at the core of these activities. Although some boys in each of the 'Five Types' of male–male murderers were 'in care' and experienced 'three or more changes in caretakers while in care,' a much larger proportion of those who would later commit murders related to 'money' had these experiences than those who committed 'Other.Murders' not related to money. The difference is statistically significant, and suggests this may be an issue warranting further attention. But what about the others who had been taken into care and experienced 'three or more changes in caretakers' while in care? Each of the other types of male–male murderers contained smaller proportions of boys who had these experiences, but they seem to have been problematic for most boys in this situation.

Childhood – family troubles, running away, petty crime, then put into care

[Our interview]
So why were you in care or why did you go to this [special] school? Well, my dad died when I was ten, and my mother got married again and our step-dad used to beat us up, so I used to run away all the time. And because I was running away, I was shop lifting, this-and-that to feed myself, and I got

228 Male–male murderers – childhood

> caught shop lifting, and they just sent the social worker round so they put me in care.
>
> *(★724iv1.2.5)*

Childhood – in care, changes in caretakers, and crime

[Report]
He was mostly raised by his mother in poverty and with little control but with a lot of love. From age 13–15, he was *in care due to truancy*. [His] siblings were also in care at various points. From age 13, he committed crimes that were mostly car related.

> *(★589cf1.2.3)*

While being taken into care, and living in a foster home or with adoptive parents certainly does not mean that such children are always or necessarily treated badly or that they are physically or sexually abused. Nor does it imply that such abuses never occur to children living with their birth parents within the context of a nuclear family. Nonetheless, children who are taken into care for whatever reason often experience feelings of abandonment and loss of identity. And, some are treated very badly in a context where they are without love, care and support, and this may affect them well into adulthood. Much of this has been captured in two books that provide graphic accounts of the lives of boys in care and incarcerated in homes for boys, one in Florida and the other in England.

In *The Nickel Boys* (2019), Colson Whitehead, the Pulitzer Prize winning author of *The Underground Railroad*, provides an account of the life of an African-American boy who, through a series of mishaps, is taken into care in the Nickel Academy, a segregated reform school in Florida, where he and the other black boys are treated far worse than the white boys, where beating and sexual abuse were common, and punishments could even lead to death in this notorious institution that was finally closed after decades of mistreatment of the boys in their 'care.' It is a story of lost dreams, and ultimately in the death of many boys. This real-life story that reveals extreme forms of injustice, and the author seeks positive changes through the revelation of these wrongs in need of being righted. In *My Name is Why: A Memoir* (2019), Lemn Sissay, an award-winning writer and broadcaster with honorary doctorates from several British universities and Chancellor of the University of Manchester, tells the story of his childhood beginning with being taken at birth from his Ethiopian mother who was required to abandon him and return to her homeland. He was first placed with foster parents who later abandoned him, and then in a series of children's homes. As an adult, he spent years trying to obtain the records and official correspondence about his origins and accounts of his life in various family and institutional settings. The book is filled with photocopies of official correspondence, including baby pictures, letters from social workers, school records, foster parents, and others. Documents in the official file about his childhood, look very similar to the documents in the casefiles of the men in the Murder Study. The outcomes are dramatic: one in tragedy and the other in triumph, as both authors sought to reveal these stories in an effort to seek better lives for children in similar circumstances.

Physical and sexual abuse during childhood

The physical and/or sexual abuse of children may be perpetrated at home by parents, siblings or others, within schools, churches, care homes, or by strangers in public places including institutions streets, alleys and playgrounds. Abuse, whether physical or sexual, may occur when children are very young or in adolescence. Most of it goes unreported, unrecorded, and unattended by those who might come to the aid of the child and make efforts to stop the offending adult from enacting further abuse. It is difficult if not impossible, to know how much physical or sexual abuse of children actually occurs, so official figures are undoubtedly lower than the actual levels of abuse. Whether revealed by themselves or recorded by social workers, general practitioners, or police, the evidence in the casefiles indicate that before age 16, 20% of the boys had been 'physically abused' and 10% had been 'sexually abused'. It should be stressed that some cases of abuse remain untold and thus completely unknown. Some were told but not recorded in official records, and thus were not in the casefiles nor revealed in our interviews with the men in prison. So, this is what we do know.

Of the 'Five Types' of male–male murderers, 'Family' Murderers were the most likely to have been 'physically abused' as children (31%) compared with 18% of 'Other.Murderers,' (31% vs 18%*), see all findings in Table 7.1). Most 'physical abuse' was committed by a male family member including 'step-fathers,' fathers, or other male relatives, and a few said they had been physically abused by their mother, while 'sexual abuse' against the boys included family members as well as neighbors, men in positions of authority within clubs, churches, schools, and strangers who attacked them parks, vacant lots, and the like.

We begin with their reflections about physical chastisement and beatings experienced at the hands of fathers or father-figures, and consider the nature of the abuse, how it was experienced at the time, and reflections about its effects upon them. The first man said that while a certain level of physical chastisement may have occurred, neither he nor his father saw it as 'physical abuse' but viewed it as a normal and usual form of parental discipline.

Parental chastisement, but not viewed as physical abuse

[Our interview in prison]
How about your adopted father, did you get along with him? We got a thrashing off my Dad, but only if it was warranted. He spent a lot of prime time with us.

*(*816iv1.4.4)*

230 Male–male murderers – childhood

The next man did not view it that way. Other cases involving the use of physical violence by fathers against children have already been presented in the earlier section about the fathers who abused alcohol and used violence against their women partners and other members of the family. Here, again we see the overlap of these and other issues.

Physically abused during childhood – describes his childhood as horrible

[Psychology report]
He described his childhood as problematic and characterized by violent beatings from his father …. He claimed that he ran away from home and foster care until he was placed in a secure home. He also talked openly about harming animals and trying to commit suicide at 16 by taking insecticides.

(*237cf1.2.2)

Sexual abuse

The sexual abuse is more likely than physical abuse to go unreported, and the actual figures are likely to be higher than official reports. As stated about Sexual Murders in Chapter 5, the intensity of emotions about the sexual abuse of children is often so great that those convicted of such offences are usually separated from other prisoners for their own safety. Accusations of pedophilia, whether true, false, or suspected, have the power to unleash very extreme responses with dire outcomes including violent attacks and the killing of men accused of violating children. But a contradiction lies at the heart of this matter. At the same time as men who are known or suspected of sexually abusing a child may need to be protected from others, including fellow prisoners, neighbors, or random members of the community, there remains a shameful history of the sexual abuse of children within the family, the community, schools and religious organizations that has sometimes remained untouched even as children revealed their plight and sought assistance from adults they thought might help them.

Strong feelings about the sexual abuse of children and a general rejection of child sexual abuse seem to be contradicted when children report sexual abuse, but are ignored. While not openly and directly endorsing the sexual abuse of children, the focus of some authorities has often seemed to be one of protecting the perpetrators and/or the institutions by refusing to believe the child or accept that the offense occurred in an effort to make the whole thing go away. Seemingly, if the child/accuser is not heard, believed or given validity, their claim of abuse will disappear, things can return to normal, and nothing need be done by those in authority. In some cases, it is only if and when offenses can no longer be ignored, denied or explained away, that circumstances demand that something be done. Since at least as early as the 1980s, scandals have been uncovered in institutions as diverse as the

Catholic Church, national athletic organizations, Hollywood, and many others. The emergence of the #MeToo movement (initially focused on the sexual abuse of women and girls), and expansion to sexual abuses against children and adult men, stands as a testament to the intensity of hitherto unattended claims of such abuse.

Among 'All' the male–male murderers in the Murder Study, a very small minority were known to have been 'sexually abused' (10%) when they were children, and even fewer were identified as having 'sexual problems' (6%) before age 16. While these are two separate issues that include abusive sexual acts committed by others against the child, and sexual problems experienced by the children themselves, they will be discussed together as they sometimes seem to be related. Separate examinations of each of the 'Five Types' of murderers shown in Table 7.1 reveal that the men who committed a 'sexual murder' were most likely to have been 'sexually abused' in childhood (19%) compared with 9% of the men who committed 'Other.Murders' (19% vs 9%*). For some boys, sexual abuse began when they were very young, while others were pre-teens or in their teens when the abuse began. Perpetrates included male family members including fathers, adoptive fathers, uncles, grandfathers, older brothers, and cousins, as well as men outside the family unit. Sexual access to these children was sometimes made relatively easy by virtue of the fact that the sexual aggressor either lived in the same house as the child and/or had easy access to the child as a friend, neighbor, or a trusted member of the school, church or community. Sexual abuse may or may not have involved a phase of 'grooming' in advance. The abuse may have lasted for a short period of time or gone on for many years. While the nature and duration of the sexual abuse varied in each case, it always involved a violation of trust, and may have had adverse effects upon the general development of the child as well as their sexual development.

While only 6% of 'All' the male–male murderers were identified as having 'sexual problems' before age 16, the separate examinations of each of the 'Five Types' of murderers reveal that 26% of the 'Sexual Murderers' had 'sexual problems' when they were children compared with only 4% of 'Other.Murderers' (26% vs 4%*). This stands out as a significant difference between men who later commit a sexual murder compared with men who commit other types of murder. The nature of 'sexual problems' during childhood included such things as the repeated stealing of clothing or underwear off clothes lines, exposing their genitals, excessive masturbation, sexual attacks upon other children including girls or other boys, and engaging in consensual sexual activity with other children at a very early age. In the reports about the 'sexual problems' of these children from various professionals, they were usually careful to stress that the behaviors concerned went well beyond the curiosity of children about sexual parts of the body, 'playing doctor,' and the like. Some raised questions about the possible relationship between the 'sexual abuse' of a child, the development of 'sexual problems' during childhood, and the later perpetration of a 'Sexual Murder.' These findings about sexual issues in childhood, combined with those presented in the next section about 'sexual

232 Male–male murderers – childhood

problems in adulthood,' strongly suggest the need for further explorations of these issues by those with a specific interest in the lifecourse of men who commit serious crimes involving sex.

Abused at care homes – age 3–18

[Psychologist report]
He had a long history in care from ages 3–18. He has been in loads of care units. There is mention of abuse in care, but no details. He referred to periods of his childhood as a 'living hell,' and told me he had been abused in various kids' homes.

*(*156cf1.4.4)*

Sexually abused by boys at school

While at approved school, he was abused on at least two occasions by older boys.

*(*696cf1.4.4)*

Sex with boys – age 10

He says he had homosexual activity with boys when he was ten years old.

*(*1146cf1.1.5)*

Sexual abused by a man – age 11

[Report – psychosexual development]

He told me that he is by inclination a homosexual. He recalled that he was sexually abused by a man when he was 11.

*(*931cf1.4.4)*

Raped by a man – age 13

[Psycho-sexual history]

He told me that he was raped at the age of 13 by a man several years older than him. At the age of 16, he began his first homosexual relationship which lasted for 18 months. During this time, he told me that he was physically assaulted and threatened with knives and a gun on several occasions by his 27-year-old partner.

*(*1004cf1.1.5)*

Problems of the child

We shift from the abuse or mistreatment that others inflicted upon these boys before they were 16 to the actions and problems of the boys themselves. 'Problems of the Child' are separate from the problems of their parents and family discussed earlier. Here, the focus in on the problems of the boys themselves, including:

problems at school, along with problems with discipline, sex, mental health, alcohol, and drug abuse. In addition, we consider their *early offending* including: first arrest, convictions, and time spent in an institution for young offenders. Many of these boys engaged in various forms of mischief that are fairly typical of many children and young people, and while it is possible to look back on such events as early indicators of problems that would later materialize it is essential to be reminded that while many young children engage in various forms of reckless, irresponsible, or even cruel acts, relatively few go on to commit serious crime, violence, or murder. Thus, extreme caution needs to be used in drawing any 'causal' relationships between behaviors in early childhood and later acts of crime and non-lethal as well as lethal violence. This is not to say that there may be no relationship between some of these early and later acts but, rather, to stress that any relationship between them should be drawn with extreme caution and care, and requires much more evidence than can be provided here. Even so, these findings may stimulate further investigations across the lifecourse of those who kill.

Problems at home – a frantic childhood

[Our interview]
I stuck a fork through my oldest brother, through his foot because he got me out of bed on a Saturday morning. My youngest brother told tales on me when I was a kid, so I put a poker (*iron poker for fireplace*) across his head. *What about you? What did you get in trouble for?* Generally, just stealing, ruining people's gardens, smashing windows, greenhouses, digging holes where I shouldn't have been, that sort of thing, you know. Very, very young, cruelty to animals.

(*816iv1.4.4*)

Home was alright, but loved being on the road

[Our interview]
And how would you sort of describe your relationship with your mother and your stepfather? It was alright. I got on, but I don't know why, I just didn't like it at home. I preferred it – being on the road. I loved it. I loved sleeping under the bridges, and just got used to that life. [left home about age 15].

(*2011iv1.4.4*)

Problems at school – learning, discipline, and friends

School is the second primary domain in the lives of all children which, like the family, provides numerous challenges that must be faced as they progress from early childhood into adolescence. Children need to make their way with teachers and other children as well as with the many tasks associated with learning. The learning of specific knowledge as well as various social skills covers a vast array of tasks to perform and master as children develop and mature, and forms much of

234 Male–male murderers – childhood

the foundation upon which each child will continue to develop into adult relationships, the world of work, and life in general. While progress at school forms an important part of the overall process of development, the tasks are not easy, success is not guaranteed, much can go wrong, and things mostly go wrong for children who are already in need.

In 2019, a government report about children excluded (expelled) from schools in England, found that the children who were most likely to be excluded included: pupils with 'Special Educational Needs' (SEN), those eligible for free school meals (economically disadvantaged), those in care and/or in need of social support, and that exclusions were more likely among Black Caribbean pupils, and even more likely among White Irish Travelers and Gypsy/Roma pupils. The findings: SEN children accounted for 78% of those excluded from schools; those from the most disadvantaged families were 45% more likely to be excluded than others; boys with social, emotional and mental health difficulties were 3.8 times more likely to be permanently excluded; Black Caribbean pupils were excluded at three times the rate of White British pupils; and White Irish Travelers and Gypsy/Roma pupils had by far the highest rates of both fixed period and permanent exclusions in state funded schools in England (Weale, 2019). These findings are stark and raise obvious questions about what might be done for these children to keep them in school, and at the same time deal with the problems some of them may cause for teachers and other children in the classroom. Each problem contradicts the other, but both need to be addressed, and both speak about obvious issues about the need for additional funding to support these children and their teachers. These findings also raise other questions that were not asked about what happens later in life to those who are excluded from school or leave for other reasons? What do these children do next week? Or next year? And what might this mean for the rest of their lives? With respect to questions about what might be done while they are still in school, these findings were broadly welcomed by educators who acknowledged the importance of providing early intervention for children in need and those with challenging behavior, but also stressed that government cuts in funding for education in general left them without the additional staff and resources required by children in need, and called upon government to fund the extra resources needed to support these children at school. Left unasked, and thus unanswered, are the questions about what happens next week, next year, and even later, for those who leave school too soon, and thus face adult life with no educational qualifications? We will return to this in the last chapter.

In the Murder Study, our focus on the 'Problems of the Child' begins with problems at school, along with issues related to discipline, sexual problems, mental health, and early abuse of alcohol and/or drugs. Following these issues, we consider early offending and contacts with the justice system. By age 16, the majority of these boys experienced 'problems at school' (63%), and many had 'discipline problems' (43%) (Table 7.1). It is difficult to disentangle one from the other. Some couldn't sit quietly or listen and learn, some couldn't engage with fellow pupils or their teacher. Some may have been hungry, tired, or ill. Many of the boys who began to fail at school, soon began to 'skip' school regularly, and finally stopped attending all together. Over half of the boys (57%) left school before age 16 and 72% left with no educational qualifications,[3] and only 5% obtained a 'A level or higher.' Overall, much was lost from their lives at this early stage in their development. The accounts of life at school are mixed and include stories of academic, social and sporting successes as well as failures along with issues of boredom, bullying, fighting, anti-social behavior, exclusion, and leaving with no qualifications.

School – good at sport and plenty of friends

[Our interview]
Did you ever go to a special education, list D, approved school, residential, anything like that? I finished off school captain in one of the toughest schools in the area. *Why's that then?* Must have just had that personality thing, being able to cope with some of the real characters, you know. It must have taught us like in my shop steward's [union leader at work] thing, you've got to be able to talk with people and understand them. And then get on. But I was always like good at sport so they used to like me to be in the teams. So, cricket, football, basketball, I played for the school. It was all right. *Did you have many friends?* Oh aye, I had plenty. You've always got a lot of friends when you're doing a lot of sports, played for football, cricket teams. I always seemed to get on with people.
(*591iv1.4.4)

School – intelligent, bright but bored, lacked discipline, truanted and left

[Report]
He described his childhood as alright. He was not nervous. There were no major separations during childhood. He has no history of neurotic traits, and started secondary school at age 10 because he was felt to be well above average intelligence. He was bored with the lessons and found it very difficult to accept school discipline. He truanted frequently and was in front of the Children Panel as a result. Despite his academic ability, he was finally sent to an Approved School [residential school for young offenders and/or those beyond parental control] for the last year of his schooling. He actually enjoyed this and felt that it conferred on him a degree of self-discipline. At 16, he left school and completed an apprenticeship as a painter and decorator with a District Council for a period of three years. Since then, he has continued to be fully employed in the painting and decorating trade, and held jobs for reasonable lengths of time with the longest being a period of five years. He has never been dismissed from work but has been made redundant.
(*102cf1.2.3)

236 Male–male murderers – childhood

Problems at school – bullied and fought back

[Our interview]

What about your happiest memory of childhood? Probably when I used to do boxing. I done it when I was about 9 years of age until I was about 16. I liked it, my Ma hated it. She didn't want us to do it, but my father said, 'Let him do it'. My Ma's got loads of trophies in the house. *So, you were pretty good at it?* They [parents] used to come watch in the bars and that, and my father, seemed to change towards me. Most the time he'd be just sitting there saying, 'You're soft, Mammy's boy, sissy, and all that'. And he was trying to make sure I stood up at school. That's why I think I didn't get bullied at school because I wouldn't stand for it. I came home crying one day. My father said, 'Hit him back'. He said, 'If you can't hit him with your hands, pick something up and hit him with it. If you come back here and you haven't done anything, I'm going to take you out and whip you'. So, I went and put him in hospital. I didn't intend to hit him that hard. It wasn't that I hit him hard, it was just that the [iron] bar I hit him with was massive. His family came to the door and all that, but his family knew what he used to do to me when I was younger.

(*631iv.1.2.3)

Enjoyed school, but bullied and left when age 11

He enjoyed his time at primary school but was regularly bullied from the age of 11 because, 'I was effeminate'. He told me that he had no friends at school and did not regularly attend from the age of 11 due to the neurotic condition of 'school refusal'.

(*1004cf1.1.5)

Not attending school, then put into care

[Our interview]

How old were you when you left school? I was put into care when I was 14, but I wasn't going to school for about two years before that. When I got put in care, I was meant to be going to school but the place I was at, they had their own school in the place. But, all they used to do was like – 'shut up everyone' – it wasn't education, it was just watching videos. They just used to put a video on just to keep everyone quiet.

(*724iv1.2.5)

School – No learning and lots of troubles

[Our interview]

Were you happy at school? No. I used to go to school but I never did anything. I used to walk in the snow when it were snowing and still go to school. I never learnt anything. *Did you have friends there or not?* No, but can't remember. *Were you ever in trouble at school?* Always in trouble. Fighting, swearing, general stuff. I mean, they used to lock me up in the classroom and the deputy head's office and stuff like that. I used to jump out of windows to get out of the room. *Is this because you were fighting? Why was this?* Because I was very destructive and I used to just run out of the classes and mess about all the time. *They just couldn't keep you, but how did you get on with your school work?* I didn't. And because they knew I couldn't do it, they used to call me to the back of the class and give me drawing pencils and stuff, and that's why I became an artist really, cos I love drawing. *Did you actually play truant? How often in your last year were you truant?* Every day. *Overall, how would you describe your time at school?* Rubbish. *Why was that?* Cos I didn't like it. Couldn't learn. I wasn't learning. That's what I thought. Personally, I regret it now, cos I should have learnt.

(*2011iv1.4.4)

Sent to a school for maladjusted children, then left when 14

[Background report]
He says his parents often quarreled, his mother was violent to his father and she left when he was six. He developed very anti-social behavior, attended a school for maladjusted children, had psychiatric treatment from ages 10 to 14, used drugs, and had no schooling after age 14.

(*702cf1.2.5)

Mental health problems during childhood

'Mental health problems' during childhood were sometimes identified at a relatively early age. For some, this occurred some time after they entered school when problematic issues may have come to the attention of those outside the immediate family. At this point, various forms of support or intervention may have been sought from professionals such as child psychologists, psychiatrists, doctors, social workers, and others. Before age 16, 13% of 'All' the male–male murderers were defined by various professionals as having 'mental health problems.' Across the 'Five Types' of male–male murderers, mental health problems were most likely among those who murdered 'Older.Men' (22%) and least likely among the 'Confrontational/Fighters' (9%) and those related to 'Money' (12%) (Table 7.1).

Many troubles and seeing a psychologist – age 7

[Our interview]
Were you in any special schools? No, I was seeing a, a psychiatrist. I would say once every three months. *From what age?* I saw my first psychologist when I was about seven, yeah, about seven. *Were you ever in trouble at school?* Yes, continuously. *Continuously, what for?* Stealing, fighting, bunking off school, quite devious. Devious dealing at work as well.

(*816iv1.4.4)

238 Male–male murderers – childhood

Psychological problems – age 8

[Psychologist report]
From the age of eight, he was being seen by a psychiatrist for his behavioral problems. He was in care by age 10, and since his 16th birthday has spent most of his life in custody because of repeated offending, and he is now serving a life sentence for murder. While serving an earlier sentence, he was transferred from prison to a State hospital because of his delusions and hallucinations, and was returned to prison after two years.

(*145cf1.2.2)

Childhood psychological problems relating to truancy, but no contact as an adult

[Psychiatry report pre-trial]
He was seen by child psychological services because of truancy, but has had no contact with psych. services since [he reached] adulthood.

(*102cfl.1.2.3)

Alcohol and drug abuse

'Alcohol abuse' during childhood was a problem for 42% of 'All' of the boys, Of the 'Five Types' of male–male murderers, the abuse of alcohol during childhood was most prevalent among those who murdered 'Older.Men' (52%), but also fairly common among those who committed all the other types of murder. While there was variation in the childhood abuse of alcohol across the 'Five Types' of murderers, these findings suggest that this was often a factor that began in childhood and, as we will see later, continued into adulthood when the use and abuse of alcohol and/or drugs often became entwined with other problems relating to employment, intimate relationships, health, and other issues. Drug abuse during childhood was also a problem for one-third (33%) of these boys.

Drink and drugs – age 13

He started drinking at 13, and later used drugs, especially ecstasy and cannabis.

(*620cf1.2.3)

Alcohol abuse – age 14

[Our interview]
I was drinking at the age of 14. *Drinking a lot?* Yeah. I'd have a drink today if I could. My nerves are bad, very bad. *Are they usually bad?* They have been like this since I have come into prison. I think it is all the years of being on the streets, drinking and stuff, crawling round the country, getting from one end of the country to the other, drunk, you know,

waking up in a doorway of another town and stuff, you know. *And did you start doing this as soon as you were age 15?* Yeah. I left home and just got on the motorway and from that on [I was homeless, drinking and drunk for 15 years].

(*2011iv1.4.4)

Binge drinker – age 15

[Our interview]
And what about the alcohol again, you started at 15? And that was pretty serious stuff? Yes, for a 15-year-old, I'd get drunk three times a week, Thursday, Friday, Saturday night. *So, kind of binge drinking?* Yes, I've always been a binge drinker. *Was that with the sport then?* Yes, because I played senior football when I was 15, so I had access to alcohol. It was all free. So, it played its part, but my mother used to give me what was a lot of money back then, which was enough to get me drunk a few nights. *She was giving you money for that, but did she think…?* She didn't know what I was using it for.

(*1063iv1.2.6)

Some drugs when younger, then just drinking with the lads

[Our interview]
Just a group of lads, we'd all get together and go drinking and that, go for a drink with the others, you know. *Were you doing drugs at all?* Not really. I went off drugs, it was the drink. I had a piece of hash at night or something like that [when I was younger]. When I got older, it was mainly the drink.

(*736iv1.2.3)

Onset of offending, early offending and institutions for young offenders

Contacts with 'Criminal Justice' during childhood included: 'Early Onset, before age 13,' 'First arrest before age 16,' having 'five or more convictions'; if they had 'Convictions for': 'Theft/property,' 'Serious violence,' 'Sexual violence,' 'Violence to animals'; and if they had been in a 'criminal justice institution' for young offenders. Most of the early offenses of these boys involved petty theft, drinking and fighting among groups of boys who were truanting from school, been excluded from school, or had simply left school. Away from school, they had hours to spend hanging around the local park or streets with other boys who were also not at school. Getting drunk or high, pilfering from the local shops, and fighting amongst themselves or with other groups of lads were commonplace and made up much of daily life away from the rigors and routines of life at school. Friends and enemies were made among these peers. Boredom was mixed with 'exciting' activities such as getting drunk or high, fighting and stealing. Some of this would involve encounters with the police and courts, and some of it would

240 Male–male murderers – childhood

foreshadow their future life as they continued into adulthood with orientations and actions begun in childhood. A few began committing crime before their teens or soon thereafter with 21% of 'All' the boys 'Offending before age 13,' (early onset offenders). By age 16, nearly half of these boys (45%) had a record of 'Offending,' and 41% had already had their 'First arrest.' Some were very busy with 'Five or more convictions' (23%), and 27% of the boys had already spent time in a 'criminal justice institution' for young offenders (Table 7.1). For other findings about the onset of offending among these murderers, see Dobash et al. (2007). For many of these boys, a lifetime of problems, delinquency and offending began very young.

From age 7 – starting fires, stealing, fighting, and violence

[Our interview]
So, when was it that you first started getting into trouble for criminal stuff? About when I was 13 or 14. Just thefts. Daft things. Just because of the people I used to knock about with. It's no excuse, but it's just like things happen like that. *And where would you steal from?* Shops, pinch people's bags. *Start fires?* Yes, when I was about seven. *That's pretty young. Tell me about that.* It's just when I was young. I had a thing, they used to call us Magpie, a bird who collects things, because I used to pinch shiny things. I used to take them. I used to put them in this old sewing machine with drawers. Money and all that. I'd keep hold of it. But I used to light fires all the time. I did it in the house once.

(*631iv.1.2.3)

From age 10 – drinking, drugs, and convictions for stealing and wounding

[Post-sentence probation report]
He started fighting at primary school. At secondary school, he truanted to steal cars and shoplift which led to being placed in a home for children with behavioral problems. He started general offending at age ten with lads who were up to age 15. By age 11, he was cautioned for theft and 'wounding-with-intent'. His first conviction was for a head injury to someone caused by him throwing a log. He explains this history of violence by minimizing it, or justifies it by saying that it was a reaction to violence toward his friends or his siblings. He started drinking at 13, and later used drugs, especially ecstasy and cannabis.

(*620cf1.2.3)

'Unexploded bomb' – began offending age 14 including robbery, burglary, assault, criminal damage, drug abuse, risk to women, and in residential care

[Probation report]
The perpetrator's offending began when he was 14, and included all sorts of assault and robbery, indecent assault on a female, threats to kids,

burglary, theft, and criminal damage. He says, his 'offending behavior began when my parents separated'. He described himself as, 'an unexploded bomb'. He was in various residential care establishments, had developed a serious drug problem with 'coke', and was a possible risk to women [mentions three charges for sex offences].

(★191cf1.2.5)

Fun and a sense of pride in winning fights and cruelty to animals

He claimed to have carried out arson attacks notable when trying to burn down an aircraft hangar, as well as the fabricating of a variety of bombs. He talked openly about fighting as a teenager which had involved beating someone senseless and breaking peoples' limbs. He did not express any concerns about his past violence. Indeed, he looked back on them as being fun times for him. There was an element of pride in how he described never having being beaten in a fight, and he seemed amused when discussing cruel acts that he had carried out on animals. When asked whether there was anything worrying about his behavior and the offence which needs to be addressed, he stated clearly that there was not.

(★237cf1.2.2)

For some, the nature and amount of offending reached such a level that they were sent to a care facility for young offenders in an effort to try to prevent them from continuing to commit crime. In some ways, approved schools and various institutions for young offenders may be seen as prisons for those not old enough to go to prison but, in other ways, they may be viewed as schools for children who cannot remain in ordinary schools. In that sense, they stand somewhere between these two institutions.

Doing crime to get a buzz and to be with the lads. By age 13: assault, court, and in detention like a boot camp. Hated police and they hated us.

[Our interview]

So, when was the first time when you were getting into a lot of bother? I think it was when I was 13 or something. A kid tried to pinch my bike off my sister, and I assaulted him. He was 17 or something. I was only 13 or something at the time. I got charged for it and taken to court. *Was it a bad assault then?* Yes, I punched him in the face twice. Section 4, that was the charge I was up for, and they gave me a fright when I was in court. Attendance and that, I didn't like that. *What's attendance?* A Saturday afternoon [detention], for so many hours a week. You get like 24 hours or something, two hours a week and all that. It takes ages to do it. Ex-police and all that. *And what do you have to do for those two hours?* One day you'd do woodwork, the next day they'd have you run 'round a big field with these barrels and all sorts, or sit in a room and ask you why you've been

Male–male murderers – childhood

committing crimes. Basically, it was just like boot camp. And everyone used to hate the police and they used to hate us. It was horrible, I hated it…. *So how would you describe yourself in terms of your previous convictions, your record. How would you describe what you're like?* People used to sit down and talk to us, and that. They'd say, 'Calm down, you're a kid, you can't go round doing things like that'. Because I didn't need to commit crimes, I didn't need it. I never done it for the money, I didn't need money. I used to get plenty of money off my family. It was just to get a buzz really, to get praise and people didn't understand that. Most of my other friends, they used to do it for money, but I never did it for money, and they couldn't understand that. *So, you did it more for?* To be with the lads.

(*631iv.1.2.3)

By age 14 – a dozen offences and in detention

At age 14, he was in court for burglary, criminal damage, etc. He had 12 offenses as a juvenile, was in detention, in an attendance center, and had a supervision order.

(*1058cf1.2)

Summary of childhood – family, school and criminal justice

As children, many of these boys experienced an array of difficulties at home, at school and/or in the community. At home, nearly half of 'All' the 424 boys had parents who had a broken relationship, one-quarter lived in a household where their father was present but abused alcohol and/or was violent to their mother, and one-sixth of their fathers had a criminal record. About half of the families of these boys had contacts with the police and social services, while one-quarter of the families had contacts with probation, and psychologists, and even fewer had contacts with a family doctor. Often, the troubles and difficulties experienced by the parents also resulted in troubles and difficulties for the child. Nearly one-quarter of 'All' the boys were taken into care for reasons relating to one or both parents including their inability to provide adequate care for their children because of poverty or illness, abuse of alcohol or drugs or petty crime, and some were taken into care in order to protect them from physical or sexual abuse at home.

In addition to the problems experienced by the parents/caretakers of these boys, there were also the problems of the boys themselves. These included problems at school (63%), and with discipline (43%). Difficulties in their own lives including: sexual problems (6%), mental health (13%), abuse of alcohol (42%) and drugs (33%), and offending as (21%) of the boys began offending before age 13. By age 16, 45% had begun offending, 41% had their first arrest, 23% already had 5 or more convictions, and 27% had spent time in a criminal justice institution for young offenders (Table 7.1).

TABLE 7.1 Lifecourse-Childhood. Each Type of Male–Male Murderer and Others

Lifecourse-Childhood (pre16)	Confront/ Others	Money/ Others	Family/ Others	Sexual/ Others	O.Men/ Others	#Not typed	All M–M Murderers
MALE–MALE MURDERER	$n=158/$ $/n=266$^	$n=81/$ $/n=343$^	$n=72/$ $/n=352$^	$n=3\,2/$ $/n=392$^	$n=40/$ $/n=384$^	$n=41$	$n=424$
Prob. Parents/Family	% / %	% / %	% / %	% / %	% / %	#	%
Broken rel.^ ^	36 /45^^	45/40	42/41	28/42	30/42	#	41
Alcohol prob. Fa.	26/23	25/24	27/24	12/25	24/24	#	25
Crime record Fa.	17/17	15/17	12/18	15/16	21/16	#	16
Econ. Disadvantage	18/17	25/16	11/19	08/19	25/17	#	18
Fa. viol. to mo.	25/22	17/24	34/20★★	13/24	25/22	#	23 (301)
Prof. w/ Family							
Social services	45/45	47/44	39/45	44/44	41/44	#	44
Medical	13/20	22/15	17/17	17/17	21/16	#	17
Psych.	20/30	30/26	31/26	28/27	32/26	#	27
Police	44/54	61/48★	37/54★	40/54	54/50	#	51
Probation	18/30★★	31/23	22/26	20/25	35/24	#	25
Child Disrupt.Care							
In care as child	19/26	33/21★	18/25	17/24	26/23	#	23
3+change-if in care	20/35★★★	43/26★★★	23/30	28/29	27/29	#	29
Abused as Child							
Physically abused	20/20	19/20	31/18★★	19/20	20/20	#	20
Sexually abused	9/10	06/14	15/09	19/09★	11/09	#	10

Continued

TABLE 7.1 continued

Lifecourse-Childhood (pre16)	Confront/ Others	Money/ Others	Family/ Others	Sexual/ Others	O.Men/ Others	#Not typed	All M–M Murderers
Problems of Child							
Problems at school	57/67★	77/61★★	57/65	65/63	64/56	#	63
Discipline problems	33/48★★	53/40★	34/45	46/43	40/43	#	43
Sexual problems	02/09★	04/06	10/05	26/04★★★	06/06	#	06
Mental health probs.	09/17	12/14	19/13	18/13	22/12	#	13
Alcohol abuse	39/45	37/43	40/42	35/43	52/40	#	42
Drug abuse	36/32	37/32	29/34	38/33	21/33	#	33
Viol. and Crim. Justice							
Early Onset, pre 13	14/25★★	27/19	17/21	25/20	18/10	#	21
Offending, pre16	39/48	57/42★	36/47	43/45	53/44	#	45
First arrest, pre16	35/44	54/37★★★	31/43★	40/41	45/40	#	41
5+ convictions	17/26★★	30/21	20/24	18/23	22/23	#	23
Convictions for:							
Theft/property	29/41	46/36	28/41	21/40	41/38	#	38
Serious violence	14/17	13/16	16/15	19/15	23/14	#	16
Sexual violence	04/03	03/03	01/03	01/03	00/03	#	03
Viol.to animals	02/01	03/01	03/01	00/02	00/02	#	02
Crim.Justice.Instit.	23/27	41/22★★★	15/28★★	24/26	21/26	#	27

^numbers vary when (not applicable) and/or (missing data) ★p < .05, ★★p < .01, ★★★p <.001.
#Not typed, n=41 cases could not be classified due to missing data, etc.
^Each variable contains two percentages for: 'murder type' / 'other.murderers' (%/%)
Example: ^^ [Broken rel. 'Confront./ OtherM' = 36%/45%].
Of 158 parents of Confront. Murderers, 36% had a broken rel./ compared to 45% of the 266 parents of 'Other' murderers.

Male–male murderers – childhood **245**

When each of the 'Five Types' of male–male murderers were examined separately, there were some notable differences in which problems had begun to appear before the boys reached age 13 or before age 16. The childhood backgrounds of those who would later commit a murder related to 'Money' were more likely to have parents with a broken relationship, to be economically disadvantaged/poor, or to be in a family that had contacts with social services, police, and probation. They were the most likely to have been in care, to have had three or more changes in caretakers, to have problems in school, including discipline problems, and to have abused alcohol and drugs. Overall, those who later committed a murder related to 'Money' were the 'most criminogenic' as children: with more than one-quarter of them offended before age 13, over half had their first arrest before age 16, one-third had five or more convictions, and 40% had been in a criminal justice institution for young offenders. By contrast, 'Confrontational/Fighters' were slightly less likely to have had parents with problems, to have experienced 'disrupted caretaking,' problems at school, or other 'problems of the child,' including many of the indicators of 'early offending,' and were less likely although not the least likely of the Five Types of murderers to have been sent to a criminal justice institution for young offenders.

So, what might be going on? It may be that boys who rob, steal or commit other acquisitive acts involving *money*, goods and/or property are more likely to be brought to the attention of police and to be 'processed' within the justice system than the boys who *fight* other boys. If this is so, it should be expected that boys who steal, rather than those who fight, would be more likely to have a police 'record' for their actions and, as such, to be defined as 'early onset offenders.' If this is the case, then the identification of 'early onset of offenders' may be strongly biased against boys who commit crimes involving property rather than those who commit other acts such as fighting which may be overlooked, dismissed, or simply defined as expected behavior among boys provided the physical violence is not too extreme and/or does not result in serious injury or the use of a knife or weapon. The notion that, 'boys will be boys' when they are caught fighting, but not when they are caught stealing, may mean that there may be more/or less reason to call the police about these behaviors which, in turn, has consequences for who becomes an 'offender' and who does not. Indeed, the same issue is raised with respect to the kind of data gathered about youthful offending in the earlier and later versions of The Stockholm Life-Course Project. In their 2016 publication, *An Introduction to Life-course Criminology*, Carlsson and Sarnecki note that changing conceptions about youthful 'fighting' and 'thieving' within the wider society meant that data about 'fighting' was not gathered in the earlier studies because it was not considered to be a problem while thieving was. They explain:

> In Sweden in the beginning of the 1960s, violence was considered a 'natural way' for young boys and men to solve conflicts. Theft, however, was a very serious crime and an indicator of a highly problematic background

and high-risk life circumstances. Thus, among the older samples in The Stockholm Life-Course Project, we have practically no variables that capture use of violence in youth, but a large number of variables that attempt to capture theft. Since the 1960s, of course, there has been a change in how society in general and the criminal justice system in particular, perceives teenage violence. Today, it is a serious social problem and, on the individual level, an indicator of future problem behaviors.

(Carlsson and Sarnecki, 2016, p. 65)

This is not meant to diminish the importance of property crimes committed by those who are young but, rather, to stress the importance of fighting/violence committed by the young. Indeed, other issues may also come into view along with rapidly changing notions about sex and sexuality identity, about domestic violence, and about the elderly and begin to reshape 'what counts,' what 'needs to be counted,' and 'at what stage in life they ought to be counted.' For example, we also found that those who would later commit a murder in the 'Family' were, as children, the most likely of the 'Five Types' to have had a 'father who was violent to their mother' and to have been 'physically abused as a child, but they were least likely to have been 'arrested' before age 16 or to have been in a 'criminal justice institution.' Similarly, those who later commit a 'Sexual' murder were most likely to have been 'sexually abused' as a child and to have been defined as having 'sexual problems' before age 16. For all of the findings, it is prudent to remain sensitive to the possibility of 'retrospective' sensitivities about particular issues and conclusions that are drawn 'after the fact' and aided by the knowledge that an individual has committed a particular type of murder, but it also seems important not to reject any such connections out of hand and/or without more thorough investigations of these issues.

Notes

1. A single asterisk★ indicates statistical significance, with all three levels of significance shown in Table 7.1.
2. Not shown in Table 7.1
3. Reported in Table 8.1.

References

Becker, H. S., 1963. *Outsiders: Studies in the Sociology of Deviance.* New York: Free Press.
Carlsson, C. and Sarnecki, J., 2016. *An Introduction to Life-course Criminology.* Los Angeles, London: Sage.
Collins, W. H., 2010. Historical perspectives on contemporary research in social development. In P. K. Smith and C. H. Hart, eds. *The Wiley Blackwell Handbook of Childhood Social Development,* 2nd edition. Chichester, West Sussex: Wiley-Blackwell, pp. 3–22.
Dobash, R. E. and Dobash, R. P., 2015. *When Men Murder Women.* New York: Oxford University Press.

Dobash, R. P. and Dobash, R. E., 2018a. Sexual murder of women intimate partners in Great Britain. In K.Ylllo and M. G.Torres, eds. *Marital Rape: Consent, Marriage, and Social Change in Global Context*. New York, Oxford University Press, 139–162.

Dobash, R. P. and Dobash, R. E., 2018b. When men murder children. In T. Brown, D. Tyson and P. R. Arias, eds. *When Parents Kill Children: Understanding Filicide*. Cham. Switzerland: Palgrave Macmillan, 81–101.

Dobash, R. P., Dobash, R. E., Cavanagh, K., Smith, D., and Medina-Ariza, J. J., 2007. Onset of offending and life course among men convicted of murder. *Homicide Studies*, 11 (4), 243–271.

Eisbensen, F. A., 2003. Response to Loeber. In M. D. Smith and P. H. Blackman, eds. *The Relationship between Non-lethal and Lethal Violence: Proceedings of the 2002 Meeting of the Homicide Research Working Group*. Chicago: Homicide Research Working Group, 3–7.

Farrington, D. P., 1977. The effects of public labelling. *British Journal of Criminology*, 17 (2), 112–125.

Farrington, D. P., 2001. Predicting adult official and self-reported violence. In G. F. Pinard and L. Pagani, eds. *Clinical Assessment of Dangerousness: Empirical Contributions*. Cambridge, UK: Cambridge University Press, 66–88.

Farrington, D. P., 2017. Introduction. Integrated developmental and life-course theories of offending. In D. P. Farrington, ed., *Advances in Criminological Theory, vol. 14*. Oxford: Routledge, 1–14.

Farrington, D. P., Loeber, R. and Beg, M. T. 2012. Young men who kill: A prospective longitudinal examination from childhood. *Homicide Studies*, 16 (2), 99–128.

Farrington, D. P., Piquero, A. R. and Jennings, W.G., 2013. *Offending from Childhood to Late Middle Age: Recent Results from The Cambridge Study in Delinquent Development*. New York: Springer.

Glueck, S. and Glueck, E., 1930. *500 Criminal Careers*. New York: A. A. Knopf.

Glueck, S. and Glueck, E., 1950. *Unravelling Juvenile Delinquency*. New York. Commonwealth Fund.

Goffman, E., 1963. *Stigma. Notes on the Management of Spoiled Identity*. New York: Simon & Schuster.

Gottfredson, M. and Hirschi, T., 1990. *A General Theory of Crime*. Stanford, CA: Stanford University Press.

Laub, J. H. and Sampson, R. J., 1991. The Sutherland Glueck debate: On the sociology of criminological knowledge. *American Journal of Sociology* 96 (6), 1402–1440. Reprinted in P. Beirne, ed., 1994. *Origins and Growth of Criminology*. Dartmouth Publishing.

Laub, J. H. and Sampson, R. J., 2001. Understanding desistance from crime. In M. Tonry ed., *Crime and Justice: A Review of Research*, Vol. 28, Chicago: Chicago University Press.

Laub, J. H. and Sampson, R. J., 2003. *Shared Beginnings, Divergent Lives: Delinquent Boys to Age 70*. Cambridge, MA: Cambridge University Press.

Loeber, R., 2003. The prospective prediction of homicide in two community samples. Opening address to the Homicide Research Working Group, St. Louis, Missouri, May 2002. In M. D. Smith and P. H. Blackman, eds. *The Relationship Between Non-lethal and Lethal Violence: Proceedings of the 2002 Meeting of the Homicide Research Working Group*. Chicago: Homicide Research Working Group, 3.

Moffitt, T. E., 1993. 'Life course-persistent' and 'adolescence-limited' anti-social behaviour: A developmental taxonomy. *Psychological Review*, 100, 674–701.

Moffitt, T. E., 1997. Adolescence-limited and life-course-persistent offending: A complementary pair of development theories. In T P. Thornberry ed., *Developmental Theories of Crime and Delinquency*. New York: Transaction Publishers, 11–54.

Moffitt, T. E., Caspi, A., Harrington, H., Milne, B., and Pulton, R., 2002. Males on the life-course persistent and adolescence-limited anti-social pathways: Follow-up at age 26. *Development and Psychopathology*, 14, 179–207.

Sampson, R. J. and Laub, J. H., 1993. *Crime in the Making: Pathways and Turning Points through Life*. Cambridge, MA: Harvard University Press.

248 Male–male murderers – childhood

Sampson, R. J. and Laub, J. H., 2003a. Life-course desisters? Trajectories of crime among delinquent boys followed to age 70. *Criminology*, 41, 3555–3592.

Sampson, R. J. and Laub, J. H., 2003b. *Shared Beginnings, Divergent Lives. Delinquent Boys to Age 10*. Boston, MA: Harvard University Press.

Sampson, R. J. and Laub, J. H., 2005. A life-course view of the development of crime. *Annals of the American Academy of Political and Social Sciences*, 602, 12–45.

Scottish Executive, 2001. Homicide in Scotland 2000. *Statistical Bulletin*. Edinburgh: Scottish Executive.

Sissay, L., 2019. *My Name is Why: A Memoir*. Edinburgh, Canongate Books Ltd. ISBN 978-1-78689-234-8.

Smith, D. J., 2002. Crime and the life course. In M. McGuire, R. Morgan, and R. Reiner eds., *The Oxford Handbook of Criminology*. Oxford: Oxford University Press, 702–745.

Smith, D. J. and McVie, S., 2003. Theory and method in the Edinburgh study of youth transitions and crime. *British Journal of Criminology*, 43, 169–195.

West, D. J. and Farrington, D. P., 1977. *The Delinquent Way of Life*. London: Heinemann.

Whitehead, C., 2019. *The Nickel Boys*. London: Fleet, Little, Brown Book Group. ISBN 978-0-7088-9941-0.

Widom, C. S. and Maxfield, M. G., 2001. An update on the cycle of violence. *NIJ Research in Brief*, Washington, DC: U.S. Department of Justice.

Wolfgang, M., 1958. *Patterns in Criminal Homicide*. Philadelphia: University of Pennsylvania Press.

Wolfgang, M. and Ferracuti, F., 1967. *The Subculture of Violence: Towards and Integrated Theory of Violence*. London: Tavistock.

Wolfgang, M., Figlio, R., and Selling, T., 1972. *Delinquency in a Birth Cohort*. Chicago: University of Chicago Press.

Wolfgang, M., Thornberry, T. P., and Figlio, R. M., 1987. *From Boy to Man, from Delinquency to Crime*. Chicago: University of Chicago Press.

Online and newspapers

Weale, S., 2019. Heads urged to expel fewer pupils amid link to vulnerable children, *Guardian*, May 7, 2019, p. 11.

8

LIFECOURSE OF MALE–MALE MURDERERS

Adulthood and in prison

In the last chapter, we examined the childhood lives of the 424 men in the Murder Study. Here, we follow them into adulthood, and then into prison. Like children, adults also live their daily lives in three primary domains: at home, at work rather than at school, and in their local community or neighborhood. Each domain plays an important part in life and presents challenges to be faced and problems to be addressed. Our examination of the adult lives of the 424 men included life at home, at work, and in relation to institutions including social and medical services, police, probation, prison. We wanted to know about their education and employment, intimate relationships, personal problems, criminal behavior, and contacts with professionals. Although what happens in adulthood is not determined by what happens in childhood, the two are nonetheless linked as successes or failures in one phase of life are often carried over into another.

Education during childhood and employment during adulthood constitute one such link as opportunities in the latter are often linked with achievements in the former. Over half of the men in the Murder Study left school before age 16, nearly three-quarters left with 'no educational qualifications' with which to enter the world of work, and three-quarter of the men were 'usually unemployed'. In addition, many of the men either did not established an 'intimate relationship' or had one or more such relationships, but nearly two-thirds of those relationships failed. Men without a job and/or without an intimate partner were often without the social and emotional ties that may have served to 'anchor' them to the daily activities and routines that characterize the lives of most adults.

So, what were the men doing if they were not spending their time at work and/or on the daily routines of domestic life? The evidence provides insights into their 'problems,' their 'criminal behaviors,' and the various 'professionals involved' with them as a consequence of their actions. Their 'problems as adults' included

250 Adulthood and in prison

alcohol abuse, drug abuse, mental health problems, and sexual problems. These and other personal problems affected many men, and certainly more than would be expected among the general population. Their 'criminal behaviors' included persistent criminal behavior, physical and sexual violence, previous convictions, and previous imprisonment. Their lifestyles, personal problems, and criminal behaviors resulted in various professionals being involved in their daily lives, including social services, medical and health care, psychological services, as well as police, probation and prisons. Overall, the adult lives of the majority of these men were characterized by unemployment, broken relationships, alcohol/drug abuse, and crime. Most were 'known' to the local police and courts, often for drunkenness, public disorder, violence, and burglary. The majority were busy committing crime, and it seems the authorities were also very busy catching and prosecuting them. Many of the men lived lives that were sometimes chaotic and punctuated by reckless and dangerous behavior. As shown in the chapter on childhood, many of these problems emerged when they were children and continued into their lives as adults, as many of these men missed, or avoided, the 'webs of conformity' that provide both social control and social support (c.f., Liem, 2016, p. 15). Explaining such behavior is a complicated and difficult task, but as stated by the lifecourse scholars, Sampson and Laub (2004, p. 173), 'adult life course matters,' and focusing only on childhood is not enough. The evidence presented here illustrates why that is so.

The 'anchors' – education, employment and intimate relationships

As in other chapters, the quantitative findings are used to illustrate the 'patterns' shown in the casefiles, and the qualitative text from the casefiles and our interviews are used to illustrate the nature and diversity within these patterns. First, we examine the adult lives of 'All' 424 male–male murderers and for the Five Types of male–male murderers. Then we turn to their lives in prison. Most of the men reached adulthood unprepared to meet the challenges at this stage in their lives. Of 'All' the 424 male–male murderers, 57% left school before age 16, 72% had no educational qualifications, and 72% were usually unemployed. The fact that the majority of all of these men were usually unemployed meant that they were either wholly or partially without this mooring in adult life, but this differed among those who committed different types of murder. When each of the Five Types were examined separately and compared to other men who were not of that type, the men who murdered Older.Men were the most likely to be 'usually unemployed' (84% vs 70%). This is in contrast to the men who committed murders within the Family who were much less likely to be unemployed compared to those who committed Other.Murders (56% vs 75%★).[1] While the majority of the men left school with no qualifications, men who committed murders related to Money were more likely to have failed to achieve qualifications

Adulthood and in prison **251**

(80% vs 63%*). These and other findings about 'All' of the 424 male–male murders, and the separate comparisons of each of the Five Types of male–male murderers are shown in Table 8.1.

The lack of a formal education when they were children made it difficult to obtain employment as adults when some kind of formal qualifications may be required in order to obtain a job. While it is not always necessary to have educational qualifications in order to obtain employment and to be successful in the workplace, those without them are often disadvantaged when seeking employment in competition with others who have finished school and obtained educational qualifications. In addition, the habits of getting out of bed and going to school (no matter how much it may be disliked) are not dissimilar to those of getting out of bed and going to work (no matter how much it may be disliked). Going to work every day, arriving on time, and sticking with a job that may be disliked rather than choosing to be free of such constraints constitute 'lessons for life' that are first learned at home and at school and later translated into the adult world of work even among those who basically dislike both. At worst, this is a grim picture of life as a child and as an adult but, even at its worst, these tasks contain elements that help anchor individuals to the world around them, to the daily routines of life, and to the lives of others who also occupy their world.

We begin the narrative accounts about the adult lives of male–male murderers with the transcript of an unusual case of a man with a serious alcohol problem who neither had nor wanted a job, nor an intimate partner, nor the company of others, and did not care to have a place to call home. We quote him at length, as he repeatedly declares that he did not wish to have such 'anchors' on his life but, instead, just wanted to roam at will and live without social constraints or personal obligations. He saw himself as a 'free spirit' because he was 'on the road,' managed to live rough, was able to drink as much as he liked and when he liked, and did not have to bother with others who only caused trouble and brought bother and grief through arguments and differences of opinion. He was unusual in his almost complete lack of any form of social anchors, or the desire for them.

Life on the road is freedom – life with no anchors, homeless and free to drink

[Our interview]
When I got the touch of the road, that's where I just went. It were like a new road to me, my own boss, go where I want, see what I want. I have covered every bit of this country, seen everywhere. And, I would go back on the road tomorrow, get a sick note and just float off [for 15 years, he travelled, lived on the road, and claimed sickness benefits]. *So, what is it about the road?* I think it is because number one, I like being on my own; and number two, the sense of peace. I mean, if you are in a group, there is always somebody going to end up arguing and stuff like that, but when I was on my own, I could only argue with myself. Couldn't fight myself,

252 Adulthood and in prison

so I preferred it. Now and again I used to go to the Monastery in [city] for a week and get cleaned up and stuff, you know. I can't wait to get back on the road, cos you can have a drink then. Instead, in here [prison], I got the DTs and stuff cos you are not drinking.

Get back on the road again. I love being on the road. *What about being cold and wet and all that?* Well when you are on the road, you have got to learn to survive at the same time. You have got to learn how to make a shelter for yourself. If you have got a sleeping bag with you, you can always find a bit of old polythene sheeting and make a little tent out of it. The sleeping bag will keep you warm and the polythene will keep you dry. Make like a little shack. I have made them on [traffic] islands, little roundabouts, just camped up in the middle. Police come and say you can't stay there. I say, 'No problem, lock me up in the cells for the night'. 'Oh, we can't do that'. I say, 'Well, leave me where I am then'.

Did you spend most of your money on alcohol then? [As an adult living on the road.] Yes. Mainly alcohol, yeah. Not a lot of food. Just mainly alcohol. *So, did you become unhealthy because of that?* Registered alcoholic, and very sick all the time. Ended up in and out of hospitals because of the drink, being sick all the time. *So how much did you drink?* Oh, sometimes, depending on what town I was spending [$$$] a day. *That much? You could drink that much? How could you get that much money?* Well, you just beg. You begged until you got your money, and you are drinking at the same time cos you need a couple of cans down your neck to give you the 'Dutch courage' to start begging. Until the police come, and you get nicked. *Have you ever tried to stop?* I did go to detox and stuff like that, but it didn't do anything. *How many times have you done it, detoxification?* About six times. Stop for a couple of weeks, then end up getting in the mood and going back. *When you say getting in the mood?* Depressed.

*(*2011iv1.4.4)*

This man found it difficult to manage in prison not only because he was no longer 'free' to live a life without connections to others, but also because he got the DTs when he was not able to get enough to drink. Alcohol, and to a lesser extent drugs, were often interwoven into the other problems he experienced. In many cases, it was almost impossible to untangle these factors that cross-cut the lives of these men, and many of the following examples illustrate situations in which several problematic issues were involved at the same time.

In addition to employment, an intimate relationship with a partner, whether with a woman or another man, may also constitute another part of adult life that provides an 'anchor' within the community and membership in a wider group of individuals who might provide various forms of support. It might also have the effect of embedding the individual in many of the routines of daily life and this is especially the case when the couple have children. Intimate relationships

Adulthood and in prison **253**

may be good, stable and endure for a lengthy period of time, or problematic and short-lived. Some may be mixed with good and bad periods, on-and-off periods, and involve various forms of belonging and support mixed with rejection, aggression and violence. In short, intimate relationships can be a very mixed bag of good, bad, and indifference. With the exception of relationships that are thoroughly negative, they may at the very least provide some sense of belonging and identity and include contacts with others that contain an element of responsibility, a sense of belonging, and a source of informal social control. Of 'All' 424 male–male murderers, nearly one-quarter (101 men) had never been in an intimate relationship. Of the 323 men who had ever been in an intimate relationship, 197 of these relationships had failed. At the time of the murder, 300 of the men (70%) were NOT in an intimate relationship. If an intimate relationship, perhaps with children, provides any form of 'anchoring' for the individual, this was missing from the lives of the vast majority of the men when they killed another man. Some never had a relationship that involved living with an intimate partner, but this doesn't mean they didn't have sexual relations or that they never had a child who may or may not have been known to them or been a part of their life.

Single, but has a daughter he didn't know about and has never met

[Prison officer report]
He is single and has never married. He has a daughter who is about eight, but he has never seen her. He found out about her existence a few years ago.
(★156cf1.4.4)

Intimate relationships ended for many reasons including unemployment, alcohol or drug abuse, violence against their partner and/or the children, criminal behavior and imprisonment, and many of these issues were intertwined.

Problems in relationships – affectionate, but drinking, some violence and not sharing domestic work led to a break-up and his depression before the murder

[Report]
A previous relationship with a woman six years older than himself lasted six years. They had two children of their own plus she had three kids from a previous relationship. His second relationship lasted three years, and they had one child. There was a lot of affection between them, but he drank a lot, didn't want a job, and didn't do his share of childcare while his partner was at work.

[Probation report]
He's generally a passive, non-violent man [note: this contradicts the evidence presented at trial], but he was violent to his partner on one

254 Adulthood and in prison

occasion ['only once' common claim]. They broke up several times for a couple of days, and finally she left him three months prior to the murder. After the break–up, he spent most of his time in the pub, hanging round, and drinking. Witnesses in the pub on the day of the offence say all he talked about was, 'his distress at the end of the relationship'. Nine days before the murder, he sought doctor's advice for depression and sleeplessness.

(*589cf1.2.3)

For this man, the loss of his intimate relationship seemed to have been related to his general state of being at the time he committed the murder. Both he and other men who frequented the same pub recounted his state of distress after his wife left him three months prior to the murder. His nearly 'non–stop' drinking in the pub, may have contributed to his general state of being, his wife's departure and the murder [he was drunk at the time]. By contrast, the next man was not sorry for anything, couldn't understand why his wife applied for a divorce, was pleased that she was not able to get a protection order against him, and made contradictory claims that he thought his marriage was happy and that he was never happy.

Denies abusing his wife, even though she sought legal protection from him

[Psychologist report]
He reported to another psychologist that, 'he was extremely surprised when his wife applied for a divorce', and stated that, 'she was the most uncaring, the biggest bully, unsympathetic, and that there had not been a happy day in the five years [of their marriage].' He also said that he thought the marriage was happy, and denied any abuse against his wife although he admitted they had their rows. He said he was pleased that she had been unable to get an injunction against him [because of his violence against her].

(*253cf1.2.2)

The next man said he had been violent to his woman partner [only once, a common claim], and that he was sorry for his violence but attributed 'blame' to the type of alcohol he was drinking when he was violent and on occasions when he had been arrested.

Violence to intimate partner – but claims it was 'only once,' and after drinking

[Our interview]
How did you two [perpetrator and common-law wife] get on? I mean, did you have a lot of arguments or? We had our moments, but I suppose that's expected in most relationships. *Did you ever hit her?* I did once yeah, only

once. We sat down afterwards, a few days afterwards because I felt like shit, you know, I felt like absolute fucking shit. And, she said that she'd been thinking about it and what would have caused it. Basically, I'd been drinking vodka and I'm not a vodka drinker. And I sat there and I thought. Well, actually that's funny that she should say that because each time I've had vodka I've been arrested.

(*876iv1.2.3)

Problems as an adult

Alcohol and drug abuse

Among 'All' of the murderers, 57% habitually abused alcohol and 35% frequently abused drugs. For men who abused alcohol and/or drugs, the impact on their lives was often quite extreme, and usually entwined with other issues including unemployment, poor health, broken relationships, violence, crime and arrest. For many, alcohol and substance abuse took over their lives. For some, consumption to excess occurred nearly every day while others 'binged' a few days in every week when they spent all the money they had and stayed as drunk or high as long as possible. Many began consuming to excess when they were children or teenagers, and this shaped their lives as adults. For some, it formed a primary or central part in the murder itself which took place when they were drunk and/or high, because they were drunk and/or high, and/or as they tried to steal in order to get money to stay drunk and/or high. Of the Five Types of murderers, alcohol abuse was much more apparent in the lives of men who murdered an Older Man (75%) when compared with Other. Murderers (55%). This is shown as (75% vs 55%*) in the table, and the asterisk indicates that the difference was statistically significant. By contrast alcohol abuse was least likely among men who committed murder for Money (48%). Although, alcohol abuse was a problem for many men who committed other types of murder: Family (63%), Confrontational/Fighters (55%), and 'Sexual' murderers (54%) (Table 8.1).

Drinking and drugs – all day, every day

[our interview]
I started drinking badly. *So how much?* I used to get up in the morning at 11 or 12 o'clock. Drink, take Valium and cannabis, and just drink all day and all night, every day. Most days there would be some kind of drug and alcohol. It would be the same every day basically. *How much would you drink each day?* If I went to the bar, I would drink ten cans of red stripe [lager], and then I would start drinking vodka and Bacardi rum. I could drink a bottle of Bacardi. *A full bottle?* Yes, like between me and my friend, between the two of us, and that was just for about an hour or so, two hours. *A full bottle?* Yes.

(*631iv.1.2.3)

256 Adulthood and in prison

Jobs lost through drinking, and three previous convictions related to drinking

[Report]
At age 19, he married a local girl of the same age. Because of employment difficulties caused by heavy drinking, they and their 2-year-old son moved to live with his parents. While living with his parents, his wife and son died tragically in a house fire. On leaving school, he commenced employment in a local supermarket for a few weeks before being employed as a crane driver in a steel works for four years, but he was sacked for drinking. He then obtained a labouring job with the district council, but after two months he was again sacked for drinking. There then followed a long period of unemployment until he obtained another laboring job, but once again he was paid off very quickly because of his drinking habits. At the time of the offence, he had been unemployed for six months.

[Previous convictions]
He had three previous convictions for housebreaking with intent to steal, breach of the peace, and drunk and incapable, all resulted in fines.
(*140cf1.2.2)

Another report about this man commented on his lifelong problem with alcohol that began in childhood and continued into adulthood until he was unable to begin the day without a drink. He killed during a robbery to get money to continue drinking, said he had no intention to kill anyone, and expressed both empathy and remorse for his actions, but said that he just wanted money to buy more alcohol.

Alcohol abuse from childhood to adulthood, then killed to get money for drink

[Report]
He started drinking regularly at the age of about 14 with a group of friends. Later, following the death of his wife and son, his drinking increased dramatically until the time of his offence when he had to take his first drink early in the morning in order to allay withdrawal symptoms.
(*140cf1.2.2)

This man told us a familiar story of his years of drinking to excess, difficulties with his jobs, failed ambitions, problems with women, poor health, and constantly running away from all his problems. His stories of travel, writing and lecturing paint a bleak picture of his daily life. In his description of constant drinking and drunkenness, he notes the negative effects upon his health, and failed attempts to 'get healthy.' Then, he told us, 'I wanted to kill someone,' which in the end he did. While very drunk, by inflicting 50 hammer blows on an elderly man while robbing him in his own bedroom.

Years of drinking, working, failing – stressed, worn out and just wanted to kill someone

[Our interview – context and circumstances]
If we can talk about your life at the time and then talk about the event itself. What was going on in your life at the time, months before, weeks before? I'd been travelling a lot, for ten years or so. If you'd been travelling the way I'd travelled which was moving around a lot and finding a job here and there and never having that much money. It tends to wear you out after a while. I'd had quite a few difficult relationships with women as well, so I was emotionally worn out and drinking a lot. I'd been drinking heavily for 15 years [began age 15] and so, physically, I was worn out as well. I'd just come back from [another country].

I'd been drinking very heavily, and I'd been trying to be a writer for a long time. For about ten years, I'd had some success but not much. So, I'd failed as a writer. I came back to [*my country*], and I'd split up with a woman and I'd run away from that and I came back and stayed with some friends, and I was trying to get healthy [stop drinking]. I just couldn't get healthy. In the past, I'd been down lots of times through similar things, and I'd always managed to pick myself up by resting for a while, and then I'd bounce back. And I was just completely worn out, physically and emotionally. I was getting older as well. I was 30 then, and I just couldn't keep living that kind of life any more. This constantly moving and the stress involved and being drunk and hung over most of the time, and trying to teach....

My life was a mess ... I wanted to kill someone. It sounds very brutal but that is it.
*(*1063iv1.2.6). [Our emphasis, this comment is cited in Chapters 6 and 8.]*

Although 'alcohol abuse' was a problem for a majority of the murderers, the fact that it was most prevalent among men who murdered Older.Men (75%) lends support to the notion that those dissipated by alcohol appeared to 'select' the easiest and most vulnerable of targets, such as older people. Other 'easy' targets include the disabled, homeless people living on the streets, gay men who might be reluctant to report a robbery, and the like. Details of cases involving the abuse of alcohol and the murder and such victims have been presented in earlier chapters that focused on each of the Five Types of male–male murder. For some men, alcohol became THE all-consuming activity that dominated their daily life and shaped their actions at the time of the murder and the days, weeks and months preceding it. Drug abuse was also a problem for one-third (35%) of 'All' male–male murderers, and was most prevalent among those related to Money (42%), and least among those in the Family (29%). Drug abuse might also involve thefts to get money to buy drugs, others related to the business of drug dealing including the payment of debts and retaliation for deals that went wrong. By contrast, those within the Family were usually committed by men who were addicted to drugs or 'high' on drugs (and sometimes also on alcohol) at the time (Table 8.1).

Little money, but spent most of it on alcohol and drugs

He was on benefits [social welfare], but most of the money was spent on drink and drugs. He had been consuming large quantities of alcohol daily, mainly sherry, cider and canned beer. He also used cannabis, amphetamines and Temazepam.

*(*1122cf1.2.6)*

Long-term abuse of drugs and alcohol

He admitted to previous barbiturate and intravenous heroin abuse by the age of 17, and several years of abuse resulted in six admissions to hospital for detoxification. During the peak of his alcohol abuse, he was drinking at least a bottle of gin throughout the day and admitted to withdrawal shakes and excessive vomiting. In more recent years, he admitted to drinking in binges.

*(*1004cf1.1.5)*

Long-term abuse of alcohol and/or drugs usually dated back to childhood or early teens, and made it difficult to earn a living and/or stay in a relationship. For some, the consumption of alcohol and/or drugs seemed to be the most important element in their life. They spent most of their time and money on alcohol and/or drugs, and often got into difficulties when they were drunk or high.

Mental health problems as an adult

In adulthood, one-quarter (25%) of 'All' the murderers were defined as having a 'mental health problem,' and this was highest among those who murdered in the Family (34%) followed by Confrontational/Fighters (29%*), and lowest among those who committed murders related to 'Money' (21%). The nature of mental health problems ranged from relatively brief bouts of depression involving visits to their doctor and prescriptions for 'anti-depressants,' to prolonged periods of deep anxiety or depression, self-harm and/or attempted suicide. Some conditions were identified in early childhood by psychiatrists or psychologists, while others only came to attention later in adulthood, at the time of the murder, or at the trial (Table 8.1).

This case involved a man who spoke about alcohol, drug abuse, and his mental health, a combination of problems he experienced from childhood to adulthood, and at the time of the murder. Together, they underscore several issues/problems related to alcohol and drug use including family problems and mental health, and in his case an attempted suicide. He, and other men like him, spoke of a combination of problems with their family, women, intimate relationships,

Adulthood and in prison **259**

employment, alcohol and/or drug abuse, along with a sense of 'uselessness,' a lack of hope, a sense of 'no way out' of their problems, and an ongoing sense of anxiety and unease. The list of distress is long and complex.

History of mental health problems from childhood onwards

[Psychiatric report, pre-trial]
[As a child], he was seen by child psychological services because of truancy. And three years ago [before the murder], he took an overdose of prescribed tablets during a period of separation from his girlfriend when he was extremely distressed because he had no access to his daughter for one year. The suicide attempt was half-hearted as he contacted the Samaritans immediately after taking the tablets.

(*102cfl.1.2.3)

Although a quarter of 'All' of the male–male murderers were defined as having 'mental health' problems, very few involved mental health problems that were so extreme that the individual was judged by professionals to be 'insane,' completely unstable, and/or an ongoing threat to everyone around them as shown in the next case which was both extreme and unusual in the level of severity of the condition and the ongoing and high level of threat to others. In short, there were very few cases that took on the characteristics of those depicted in films such as 'Silence of the Lambs' in which Anthony Hopkins plays 'Hannibal Lector,' an intelligent but insane man who engaged in cannibalism, and other films such as 'Henry: Portrait of a Serial Killer' that depict extreme mental health conditions and compulsions among those who kill. While such extreme cases do sometimes exist in real life, they are far from the norm and are very rare.

Judged mentally insane after committing more murders in prison

[Hospital doctor]
It was obvious from his disturbance that he was insane. He could not be regarded as responsible for his actions in any measure. The man has a compulsion to kill.

[Trial judge]
Wherever he may be placed he will constitute a continuing threat to the safety of any person in whose presence he may come [after the first murder sent to mental health institution where he murdered two other patients, resulting in a prison sentence].

(*1146cf1.1.5)

Sexual problems and sexual violence as an adult

In adulthood, of 'All' the murderers (18%) were defined as having 'sexual problems.' These problems ranged widely from men who were confused about their sexual

260 Adulthood and in prison

identity or sexual preferences, to various forms of aggressive or 'inappropriate' sexual behaviors, and holding antagonistic and/or extremely aggressive views about the sexual behaviors or orientations of others. As might be expected, men who committed a 'sexual' murder were by far the most likely to have been defined as having a 'sexual problem' compared with all 'Other.Murderers' (54% vs 15%*). By contrast, 'Confrontational/Fighters' were least likely to have been defined as having a 'sexual problem' (12%*). Of equal importance were the reports regarding previous incidents and criminal convictions for 'sexual violence.' Again, it is men who commit a sexual murder who are most likely to have a history and a conviction for sexual violence (19% vs 8%*). As the following accounts indicate some of these men began an early career of sexual violence, sexual abuse and with violent behavior continuing into their adult lives. Background reports from various professionals indicate that the men who eventually commit a sexual murder were far more likely to have previously been defined as having sexual problems and perpetrating sexual violence both as a child and an adult. While the following examples are mostly associated with sexual violence against children there were also examples of sexual violence against adults.

Sexual problems in adulthood – confused and conflicted

[Prison report]
He lived a chronic lifestyle at the time of the offense with alcohol and drugs a problem, as well as an inability to manage anger and a stated past of sexual abuse when age 14 he was fellated and felt both pleasure and confusion. When the victim [of the murder] tried to become intimate with kisses and cuddles, he says he became angry because that was not what he wanted. He blocked out the fact that he initiated the encounter and vented his anger and shame onto the victim. He claims his thoughts went back to his first sexual encounter when he was abused by a man. In his mind, he blamed the victim for that earlier offense [*that was committed years earlier by someone else*].
(*867cf1.4)

Sexual problems and violence in childhood and adulthood

[Background report]
He had sexual relations with his sisters from age 8 years – initially 'exploration', then, age 10/11, intercourse.

[Later, as an adult]
He was known to give boys money and favours in return for acts of gross indecency. He had a prison sentence for buggery of a 15-year-old male. When released from prison, he was homeless with his mental state deteriorating. The police summary describes him as loquacious and with no remorse.

(*584cf1.4.4)

Years of serious sexual assaults on children and adults

Many previous offences back to age 14, and when aged 19 he received 4 years custody for buggery (5 charges) and gross indecency. When age 21, he was released from custody and underwent 1-month assessment at a clinic specializing in treatment of men who sexually abuse children. There, he revealed that he first began offending against young children when he was about 12 years old. Since then, he admits that he has continually been offending against a whole range of children. When asked specifically how many offences he committed, he replied 'thousands'.

[Another report]
In our opinion, his pattern of offending over the years has been underpinned by an increasing desire to have power and control over other individuals in an attempt to make himself feel superior and omnipotent. His probation records indicate his offending behavior prior to the current offence had become increasingly manipulative, coercive and sophisticated involving fantasies about targeting younger, more vulnerable boys, 'the abuse of which would result in their death'. He has a history of buggery over a five year period of young and vulnerable victims. He does not act on impulse. On the contrary, from previous assessments and from our own observations, he appears to be an extremely dangerous calculating individual with the intelligence and social skills to befriend potential victims and secure their trust and confidence prior to abusing them.

(★1079cf1.4.4)

Contacts with social, psychological, and health care professionals

Serious involvement with professionals was relatively absent from the lives of these men. Fewer than one-quarter of 'All' 424 men had contacts beyond the infrequent and common levels of the social services (21%), medical services (22%) or psychological/psychiatric services (25%). This was despite the fact that over half had problems with alcohol, over one-third had problems with drugs, nearly one-fifth had sexual problems, and this is without considering other medical, social and/or psychological problems they may have experienced such as chronic health conditions, physical injuries and illnesses that are not uncommon in the population at large and particularly among blue-collar workers. Despite the nature and level of their problems, these men did not generally seek nor receive assistance from these professionals. It may be that they did not want to have contact with them, that they felt unable to seek assistance from them, or that they viewed all such contacts negatively. For whatever reason, the majority of these men were not in receipt of assistance from various professionals (Table 8.1).

262 Adulthood and in prison

Criminal behavior as an adult – persistent crime and previous convictions

As explored in the chapter on childhood, many of these men could be considered 'persistent chronic' offenders. In the main, this pattern persisted into their adult lives. The vast majority were consistently involved in criminal activity and this is reflected in the levels of convictions. Many of the men encountered a considerable amount of contact with the police, courts, probation and prison. Persistent criminal behavior was common and this hardly varied across all Five Types (81%) and a similar proportion (85%) had a least one previous conviction and this was also consistent for all types. However, it is worth noting that almost all of the men who killed an elderly man had at least one previous conviction (94%).

Just over two-thirds (67%) had five or more previous convictions and this was most likely for men who murdered for Money (74%) and least likely for men who murdered within a Family (56%★). Around half had served at least one with prison sentence. In short, the majority of these men were busy committing crimes, being arrested, being convicted and spending time in prison. This does not reflect the crimes that went undetected or were not processed through the legal system. Offenses involved public drunkenness, thefts on the street and from shops, auto thefts, burglary from houses, violence on the street, and domestic violence. Some involved a mixture of property offenses and violence (Table 8.1).

Five convictions for theft and assault

[Police report]
Five previous convictions, one for theft of a car and four for assault (worked as a bouncer). For one of the assaults, he served three months in prison, but no other offences since then. He joined the Army at 16, and served [abroad] and on security missions.

(★287cf1.2.3)

Twelve convictions mostly for burglary, and five prison sentences

[Previous convictions]
12 convictions, 5 custodial sentences mostly for burglary but also 1 conviction for violence – 3 months for causing bodily harm by kicking.

(★867cf1.4.4)

Thirty-three convictions and several sentences in prison

[Police report]
Numerous convictions for: drunkenness, theft, burglary, property damage, wife assault, and two for 'non-serious' assault' on police while being arrested.

(★1122cf1.2.6)

Many burglaries

[Psychology report]
At the time of the offence, he was committing burglaries on a regular basis, and smuggled drink and cigs onto the ships [where he worked].

(*237cf1.2.2)

Previous convictions for assault

Convictions for 'minor assaults' were fairly common among 'All' of the men (41%), but somewhat less likely for those who murdered Older.Men (28%) and those who killed in the context of a Family murder (31%). For some men, minor assaults involved the normal activities associated with jobs such as 'bouncing.' For others, this was just the usual way of dealing with negative encounters with other men that frequently ended in a fight with fists and feet, or one that escalated with the use of instruments such as clubs, bricks, stones, and household furniture, or went still further with the use of weapons, such as knives. As noted earlier it is possible that fights among men were often not treated seriously, not seen as crimes, whereas, the evidence in male–male murders demonstrates that 'fights' can be very dangerous (Table 8.1).

Fighting in a motorcycle gang
This man had a much-deserved reputation for being a violent and aggressive character who had belonged to various motorcycle gangs.

(*876cf1.2.4)

Previous convictions for violence, but never in prison

[Prison report]
He has never served a custodial sentence. He has previous charges for 'wife assault' and for 'police assault' and for 'Breach of the Peace'. All were dealt with by fines. He admits he is liable to lose his temper easily although he feels that he has mellowed in the last years. In his younger days, he was frequently involved in gang warfare and, as a result, has numerous facial scars. In general, he has been able to form stable relationships with the opposite sex, and he denies that he was unfaithful to either girlfriend. He was violent to his first girlfriend on one occasion after she had separated from him and he found her with another man. He deeply regrets the situation which he finds himself in at present.

(*102cf1.2.3)

Previous violent attack on neighbor and road rage attack
He was violent to neighbors with whom he had a dispute, and put his fist through their front door. In a 'road rage' incident, he was enraged about something the other driver did, chased him, grabbed him and punched him about the head.

(*619cf1.2.5)

264 Adulthood and in prison

Among 'All' the men, 17%, had a previous conviction for a Serious assault. These assaults involved inflicting serious injury and/or the use of instruments, clubs and weapons. The use of knives included those that were more obviously seen as weapons such as combat knives, but also included kitchen knives, pin knives and others that might be found in every household or in the pockets of many men, and might be used for everyday purposes as well as in fights and lethal attacks. In the UK, guns may be legitimately owned and licensed by farmers, hunters, and members of shooting clubs, but there can be little doubt about the seriousness of an attack that involved the potential or actual use of a firearm against another individual.

Attacks using knives

His previous offences have all included the use of a knife. While in the Army, he was charged with stabbing a cook in an argument and sentenced to nine months detention. As a civilian, he argued with a man he believed had stolen his sister's video, held a knife to the man's face and headbutted him before leaving. He served six months in prison.

(★852cf1.4.4)

Guns and firearms – given a gun and keeping it

[Our interview]
Had you used a gun before, had you handled a gun before [the murder]? I had used air pistols, air rifles, but never used a proper gun. *You said it was a shot gun?* Yes. *Where did you get the gun?* I'd been to my friend's house (co-accused), and somebody was there who had it on them and they gave it to me. *Did you ask for it?* No. but because I was going on about my sister [who committed suicide], he said, "Here, go and sort it [shoot sister's partner who he thought caused her suicide] knowing that I would go and do it. I ended up keeping this gun.

(★631iv.1.2.3)

Note: he did not kill the man he blamed for his sister's suicide, but killed someone else.

'Out of Sight' before the murder – no offending, no previous convictions, no prison

Although most of the men were not strangers to the justice system, a few had never had contact with the police, been arrested, gone to court and/or been convicted of anything prior to committing murder. These men may have committed some kind of 'offense' that came to the attention of the police, but it was dealt with informally, and thus they had no official record of arrest or conviction. The following man appeared to be living 'a crime-free life' until he was older, although he actually began offending years earlier and was only caught and convicted much later. In such cases, the term, 'late onset offender,' may portray an inaccurate picture of someone who appears to have started offending at a later stage in life but, in reality, was not 'caught' offending until he was older. Cases such as these may require a refinement of the concept of the 'late onset offender' in order to differentiate between those who actually begin offending at an older age and those who simply get caught at a later stage in life.

Onset of offending in late 30s – fraud and drunk-and-disorderly, but no prison

[Our interview]
What about yourself then, you said that you were never into bother with the police until you were 47? No, I would have been about 40, early 40s, 41. *What was that for?* Fraud. *What sort of fraud?* Cheque cards and stuff. *So how many times have you been arrested?* Just the once. I got a two-year suspended sentence. *Just for the fraud?* Aye. *Any other than the offence that you're in here for?* Drunk and disorderly once. *How old were you then?* Late 30s I would say. *That's it?* Aye.

(*591iv1.4.4)

Previous charges but no convictions. Threats with a gun, very dangerous.

[Report]
He had no previous convictions, but several charges leading to court appearances. Ten months before the murders, he entered a car dealership, demanded money and threatened the owner with a pistol. He was also charged with conspiring with three others including his brother, to obtain £30,000 from an insurance company by reporting a bogus burglary.

[Probation report]
He was a member of a shooting club and owned five firearms legally under license.

(*615cf1.2.5)

Summary – adulthood and at the time of the murder

While the offences of a few of the men remained hidden from view for some time, the vast majority of the men had previous convictions, and nearly half had served at least one prison sentence before they committed murder. The reasons for their previous prison sentences varied, but many involved offences that were fairly similar to the one in which they killed another man, although a few were markedly different. As adults, nearly three-quarters of the 424 male–male murderers were chronically unemployed, and slightly fewer had either never been in an intimate relationship or had been in one that failed. Many of these men were without the 'anchors' of work and/or an intimate relationship. Over half of them had serious problems with alcohol abuse, one-third had problems with drug abuse,

266 Adulthood and in prison

both of which often began in childhood and continued into adulthood. Persistent criminal behavior was a way of life for over three-quarters of the men, nearly all had at least one previous conviction and two-thirds had five or more convictions. The police were an ever-present part of the lives of nearly three-quarters of the men, and nearly half had previously been to prison. While unemployment, alcohol abuse, failed relationships and persistent crime were common in the adult lives of the majority of 'All' of the 424 men who murdered another man, there was considerable variation in some of the attributes across the Five Types murderers: 'Confrontational/Fighters,' 'Money,' 'Family,' 'Sexual murder,' and murders of 'Older.Men.' In relation to the research literature on the lifecourse of offenders, these men would best be defined as 'lifecourse persistent, serious offenders.'

After the murder – life in prison

In our examination of the childhood lives of these men, we went 'back in time' to their lives as children *before* they committed a murder. Now, we journey 'forward in time,' past their adult lives and *past* the murder, and examined life in prison. We will focus on behavior and discipline in the daily routines of prison life, and their orientations to personal change and reform as they look back at themselves, the murder they committed, and the person they killed as part of the process of working toward personal change and reform. For those convicted of murder, it is not sufficient to just serve the allotted number of years and the prison doors will automatically open and they will be released. In addition to serving their allotted time in prison, they must maintain discipline in their own behavior and their relations with prison staff and other prisoners. In addition, they must successfully complete various programs designed to focus on their offense and their offending behavior before they can be considered for parole. For those convicted of 'Murder,' this is essential, not optional. Simply serving the specified time in prison is not enough to warrant release. Given the seriousness of their crime and the potential danger such offenders might pose to the public should they be released into the community, they must address what they have done, accept responsibility for their actions, and confront the various attitudes and behaviors associated with the murder they committed as part of the process of rehabilitation they must undertake while they are in prison. Parole cannot be considered without the successful completion of these programs which, along with their discipline record, will form part of any future judgements made by the parole board.

Numerous reports about their behavior and progress, are made by prison governors, prison officers, psychologists, medical staff, probation officers, clergy and others. Some reports focus on daily life at work, on the landing, during meals and recreation, while others focus on their participation and progress on programs designed to assist them in addressing issues such as alcohol and drug abuse, violence, and gambling. All of this, and much more, is contained in each man's casefile, and we have organized this information along with the transcripts of our tape-recorded interviews with the men into three main areas about life in prison: 1) 'behavior in prison' described as a 'model prisoner' or 'uncooperative,' or with many discipline reports; 2) 'judgements of professionals' about their 'mental health,' 'risk to public safety,' and 'dangerousness' inside prison and potential danger should the parole board consider their release; 3) 'orientations to the victim and the murder' including expressions of 'remorse' for the murder, and 'empathy' with the victim (Table 8.2). The main patterns include evidence from the case-files and our interviews with these men in several prisons that housed different categories of prisoners from those defined as 'high risk' to those nearing release. All of the men had been in prison for at least four years, and some had been in for much longer.

Behavior – 'model' prisoners and discipline reports

What happens in prison? How do convicted lifers behave, relate to prison officers, prison staff, and other prisoners? Do they cooperate, cause trouble, or both? How do they live their lives in prison? Discipline reports provide a record of problems they may experience, or problems they may cause on the landings, at work, in the gym, the dining hall, the showers, and in their own cell. The daily regime of the prison presents numerous opportunities for behavior that is cooperative or problematic for themselves as well as for other prisoners, prison officers, and other staff. All of this constitutes their daily life in prison, and the record of the way they live that life forms a part of their personal casefile, which provides insights into many facets of their life and conduct. These records and the information in them will form a part of the overall view of the man and his progress that will be presented to the parole board if/when they consider his possible release back into the community.

Model prisoner

We begin with what might be the goal of men serving a life sentence – a positive report from the prison governor sent to the parole board as they considered his parole and possible release on a life license. This man had 41 previous convictions, mostly for property offenses, before receiving a life sentence for stabbing to death a shopkeeper during a robbery. In his report, the prison governor notes that while he was obviously a very busy burglar, he was not a violent or cruel man in his conduct within the prison either with fellow prisoners or prison staff, nor in terms of what was known about his treatment of members of his own family. In addition to serving his time in prison, his good behavior inside the prison and what appeared to be a positive orientation to his family members outside prison, both figured as indicators that reflected positively on his personal conduct, but also suggested that he had a meaningful 'anchor' on the outside in the form of a supportive family. This is the profile of a 'model prisoner.'

268 Adulthood and in prison

Model prisoner – positive report from the governor (41 previous convictions)

[Prison governor to parole board]
The positive factors to be considered are that he is quite clearly a family oriented and caring man. He is quite happy to interact with staff and shows compassion for other individuals when appropriate. In short, I have never seen any evidence of him being a cruel or callous individual, quite the reverse.

(*090cf1.2.2)

Of the 424 men, only 18% could be described as a model prisoner. They had good records of behavior, none or few discipline reports, and caused little or no trouble for staff or other prisoners at work, in the gym, the dining hall, exercise yard, or in their cell. Accounts of behavior in prison ranged from those with few discipline reports, sometimes over many years, to those who were 'uncooperative,' had numerous discipline reports and showed little progress over time.

Uncooperative and many discipline reports

Most men (83%) (including some model prisoners) had received at least one 'discipline report,' sometimes over many years, which might have involved minor infractions of rules, but 42% of the men had received 10 or more discipline reports, and some might have involved very serious infractions including violence, drugs/alcohol, hostage taking, and escape attempts. The men who killed Older Men were most likely to have ten or more discipline reports (60% vs 40%*) and Family murderers were least likely (26% vs 44%*). In addition, 31% of all the men were defined as 'uncooperative' with prison staff, refused to work, or caused problems at work, on the landings, recreation areas and elsewhere. Men who murdered for money were most likely to be 'uncooperative' (41% vs 29%*). A few caused problems that were so serious they received an increase in the length of their sentence and/or a conviction for an additional offense, such as assault. Here are some examples of issues relating to discipline and cooperation within the prison (Table 8.2).

Bully, violence, deals drugs and demands sex in return

[Prison report]
A high risk of escape. Some violence to male prison staff. Other reports indicate satisfactory behavior, and all say he is polite to staff. He has no contact with psychology or probation [no offender programs]. Makes no attempt to address his offending behavior. He has links with sophisticated criminals. Survives well in custody, although he is relatively manipulative. He deals drugs and gets sexual favors in return. Several references in prison reports about his 'sexual importunate behavior', describe him as a bully.

(*665cf1.2.5)

Adulthood and in prison **269**

Previous time in prison with additional time added for a stabbing while in prison

[Senior prison officer for parole board]
This is an extremely worrying and serious case. He has a serious criminal record with a previous 9-year sentence for rape during which he incurred a further 18 months for a stabbing. He is a large man which adds to the danger. He has a poor custody record and is negative about his prospects.

(★056cf1.2.2)

Prison discipline – 10 reports including fighting and assault on a prison officer

[Prison report]
He has had 10 adjudications including an offence against discipline, abusive conduct, assault on a prison officer, and fighting.

(★237cf1.2.2)

A danger to women prison officers

[In prison]
Note on his prison record: 'female officers and females in general should be aware of this man as he appears to dislike all female members of staff'.

(★6161cf1.4.4)

Prison discipline – five positive drug tests but continues to use drugs and alcohol

[Prison report]
He continues to use drugs and alcohol in prison. He has had five positive drugs tests in prison but denies he has a drug problem. He has been on a 'drugs course' but it has had no effect.

(★869cf1.4.4)

For some of the men, problematic behavior, infractions against the rules, discipline reports and uncooperative behavior remained a constant over many years. Others had a bad start when they entered prison but began to change over time. Later, we consider the issue of making personal changes in their attitudes about the murder and the person they killed as well as changes in their own behavior. But here, a bit of background about the previous behavior of this man illustrates the difficulty of achieving such changes, and that this process can be very long, and the outcome uncertain.

... previous offending:

Previous prison for robbery and rape. After release, he murdered his male partner in theft over his share of the money they had stolen.

270 Adulthood and in prison

[Report]
At age 18, he was sentenced to five years on three counts (conspiracy to abduct women, robbery, and rape). With three or four others, they abducted three women, two of whom were prostitutes with the intention of making them work for them as prostitutes. During this sentence, he was disruptive and violent to staff. He committed murder soon after his release from prison.

(★702cf1.2.5)

... same man after years in prison:

Disruptive – moved prisons 20 times, segregated, dirty protest, some change after eight years

[Prison reports]
Articulate and intelligent, but grossly immature, denies guilt, demanding, self-opinionated, uncooperative, physically threatening, disruptive and violent to staff.
Into drugs, bullying, intimidation of other inmates – moved frequently – 20+ prisons.
On segregated, dirty protest.

[Eight years into sentence]
Behavior improving, more friendly and able to communicate with staff, but deteriorated again, although there is some lasting improvement.

(★702cf1.2.5)

It can take years of input from numerous professionals before a man begins to see himself as an offender in need of any form of intervention. He may have had contact over many years with various professionals who have tried to persuade him to address his offending behavior and make changes in himself, particularly in relation to his offending behavior.

Changing pattern of discipline reports over many years during a 16-year sentence

[Medical officer – early in his sentence]
He now accepts that he targets vulnerable individuals who have put him down, and then uses all means possible to discover their weaknesses and then to degrade them. He is extremely dangerous in all forms of group therapy. Risk factors: aggression, cold and detached behavior, criminal lifestyle and unstable lifestyle, deviousness and lack of empathy, subversive and disruptive.

... a later report – after nine years in prison ....

[Prison behavior – later in his sentence]
Good, mature, positive to staff and inmates, but with 27 discipline reports (over 9 years), although none in the last year. The reports were mostly for disobedience, plus 3 for drugs/alcohol, and 2 for violence. He has regular contact with his family and plans to live with his parents on release.

... still later ...

[Prison report – still later in his sentence]
He feels remorse, and takes responsibility for the offence. Three risk factors: drug and alcohol abuse, unstable lifestyle, and anger.

(*867cf1.4.4)

Judgements of professionals in prison

Mental health

Among 'All' of the male–male murderers, 20% were defined by various professionals as having 'mental health problems.' Some of these evaluations were long-standing going back as far as early childhood, while others were not identified until later when the men were adults or after they had committed murder and entered prison. The nature of these mental health problems varied, including depression, self-harm, possibility of suicide, and mental states involving delusions and paranoia. Since the term 'mental health' covers such a broad spectrum of conditions, it is necessary to consider more closely the nature of any particular condition in relation to if/how it might be related to violence and murder. Across the Five Types of murderers, those who murdered Older.Men were most likely to have been defined as having some kind of 'mental health problem' (28%), compared to Confrontational/Fighters (14%*) who were least likely to have been identified as having issues relating to 'mental health' (Table 8.2).

Risks to public safety and dangerousness inside and outside prison

As noted, regular reports about the men commented on their personal behavior, interactions with others, risks to themselves and others inside the prison, and possible risks outside the prison should they ever be released. While most of the men were not viewed as an extreme threat inside the prison, some were, and the possibility that a man might take hostages or attempt to escape were taken very seriously. Just under two-fifths (39%) of all the murderers were judged to be dangerous, and 45% were considered a 'risk to public safety.' Confrontational/Fighters were least likely to be judged to be dangerous (24%*) and a risk to public safety (32%). The men who murdered Older.Men were the most likely to be assessed as dangerous (53% vs 38%*) (Table 8.2). In our analysis of the casefiles and in interviews it was

272 Adulthood and in prison

apparent that these judgements were often subject to change either way – more positive or more negative. Basically, what we report here is the assessments at the time we carried out the research. A personal note regarding our own safety while conducting interviews within the various prisons: although we arranged with prison officials to be alone with the men when we interviewed them in order to ensure that the interviews were confidential and that this was obvious to the men concerned, our own safety was always taken very seriously by the prison staff who issued us with a personal alarms should this be needed, and the men were aware that we could seek assistance should it be required. The need never arose.

Demanding, intimidating, aggressive to other prisoners, and might take hostages

[Lifer Liaison Officer report]
He has a rigid, intolerant thought process. Impossible standards of behavior, work practices, cleanliness, politeness, etc., and expects same from others. If they fail to meet his [impossible] standards, he sees it as a serious moral lapse and responds very sternly. This shows in his prison work record. He has had a series of jobs in various workshops, each lasts only a short time before he finds faults, refuses to compromise, and resigns. *There are concerns that he might take hostages [their emphasis]*. (*619cf1.2.5)

Risk to public safety and dangerousness

[Previous probation report]
He was a member of a shooting club and owned five firearms legally under license.

[In prison – high risk, several escape attempts]
Report from prison regarding the planning of an escape with three others involving the timing of dog patrols, seeking access to the chapel, enquiring about martial arts protective clothing. Grey paint and papier-mâché were found in the cell of one of his accomplices. Transferred to another higher security prison where he was involved in a *possible escape attempt* and inciting unrest. Transferred to Special Secure Unit and his category was changed to *Exceptional Risk*. Six years after the start of sentence, on Cat A (High Escape Risk) *[their emphasis]*.

*(*615cf1.2.5)*

In addition to judgements about the risks the men might pose within the prison, concerns about the possible 'risk to public safety' and 'dangerousness' were ever present in considerations about how safe it might be to release a man into the community in considerations about parole. At this point, judgements about the potential risk to public safety and dangerousness were of vital importance, and involved assessments about their behavior inside the prison as well as views about the potential danger to those outside the prison should they be released on parole. These judgements were influenced by their record of behavior and discipline reports in the daily life of the prison. They also considered their willingness to participate on programs that focused on their offending behaviors, such as alcohol and drug abuse, violence, and the like, and their willingness to focus on their orientation to 'their murder' and 'their victim.' Issues of 'remorse' and 'empathy' were of particular importance in these programs.

Orientations to 'their victim' and 'their murder' – remorse and empathy

Among 'All' the male–male murderers, 34% expressed 'No remorse' for their murder, and 43% expressed 'No empathy' with their victim. The flip side of asking who was 'not sorry' and who 'didn't care,' is asking who, upon later reflection, 'is sorry' about the murder, and who 'does care' about the victim. Of the Confrontational/Fighters' only 22% had 'no remorse' (meaning that 78% did have a sense of remorse about the murder), so Fighters were the most likely of the male–male murderers to be 'sorry' about the murder they committed. This was bore out in our interviews with Confrontational Fighters many of whom expressed deep regret about the murder and the person they killed. More of them expressed regret and sorrow about the murder than those who committed other types of murder. Why might that be so? For them, the murder may have been 'more personal' because it involved people they knew who were fairly similar in age. While these individuals may have been 'enemies in a fight' the enmity between them may not have been so extreme that they had a strong desire to kill the man with whom they had a fight. By contrast, a greater proportion of those who murdered Older.Men were assessed as having 'no remorse' for the murder (43% vs 33%) and 'No empathy' for the man they killed (58% vs 42%*). Mostly, they killed older men while they were trying to steal from them in their home, often in an effort to obtain money for alcohol and/or drugs, and killed the older man when he challenged them. Although they may have had nothing against the older man in advance of the lethal encounter, the fact that he challenged him may have 'inflamed' them, and this may help explain the large number of injuries often inflicted upon older victims who, by virtue of their age and infirmity, were less likely to represent a challenge to a younger man. Among the men who committed murders related to Money, 34% expressed 'no remorse' about the murder, and 43% had 'no empathy' for their victim. Many of these men, like those who murdered Older.Men, killed while in the act of committing a burglary or in the context of dealing drugs, and may have been relatively indifferent or antagonistic to the person they killed (Table 8.1).

> *No remorse for the murder and no empathy with the victim*
> *No empathy for the victim, did the world a favor*

274 Adulthood and in prison

[Prison report]
When asked about victim empathy, he said, 'There was no victim. I did the world a favour by killing the victim'.

(*6161cf1.4.4)

No remorse for the murder

[Prison – principal officers report]
Despite his outwardly friendly and co-operative nature, he is clearly a calculating and somewhat manipulative man who has demonstrated little remorse for his actions.

(*724cf1.2.5)

No remorse for the murder, egotistical, lacks remorse, blames others

[Report at prison induction]
[Egotistical and *lack of remorse*] He is a man almost incapable of showing genuine remorse, totally selfish and somewhat of a bully as well. As long as life is going along in his favor he can be quite pleasant and coopera-tive. Say 'no', and his stance changes dramatically. He then displays im-mature almost childish behavior and becomes very difficult to manage.

[Later report]
There is *no remorse* towards the victim nor towards his family. He is a selfish individual whose only concern in life is himself. Outwardly happy, cheerful, extrovert, all the clichés, trying desperately to appear to adhere, but he is a man who requires his gratification instantly. He shows a total lack of thought about people other than himself. He has little tolerance for other people. Throughout my interview, he spoke mainly of himself and did not show much concern for his co-accused other than to blame them.

(*1058cf1.2)

Four murders – no remorse, no regrets and would have killed more

[Prison report]
He told me that although four killings occurred there could have been many more. If an opportunity to kill presented itself and he didn't do it he felt as if 'it was an opportunity lost'. He enjoyed the publicity fol-lowing a crime, although this was not 'an overriding passion' and he was quite explicit that he had absolutely no regrets about the injuries and the killings. He felt no remorse.

(*931cf1.4.4)

While some expressions of remorse contained elements of self-pity and a pri-mary focus on the effects upon themselves (such as loss of their freedom and the conditions of imprisonment), others expressed feelings of sorrow about the murder they committed while, at the same time, attempting to partially excuse themselves because of their young age, dependence on alcohol, extreme drunkenness, and other factors associated with deflection and/or minimization of responsibility.

No remorse for the murder, then some remorse but excuses himself because of age

[Prison governor's report]
He recognized that at the time of the offence his lifestyle was uncontrollable. He appears to have a rather ambivalent attitude to the offense. He expresses some remorse but admits that 'gay bashing' was regarded by those with whom he mixed as an easy way to earn money as an alternative to stealing. He describes the offense in a rather 'matter-of-fact' manner, and there is nothing to suggest he has genuine feelings of regret. Later in his sentence, he did appear to express remorse, but he considers that his behavior did not deserve a life sentence. On looking back, he considers he was extremely young and did not know what he was doing.

*(*161cf1.4.4)*

No intention to kill, just wanted money for alcohol, good intentions and change, but alcohol could still pose a problem after release

[Report]
When discussing his offense, the perpetrator fully appreciates the gravity of it and has stated, 'It was sheer stupidity. There was no need for it'. He has no hesitation in accepting full responsibility for assaulting and killing the victim. He wishes to make it clear that he had no intention of killing the man but simply wanted more money for alcohol. He feels very sorry for the victim and blames the offence on his alcohol abuse.

[But]....
The prison officers in his hall agreed that alcohol has not been a problem for several months. He recognizes the serious nature of his alcohol abuse and has good insight into the change it has on his personality. He derived good support from AA (Alcoholics Anonymous) and intends to renew his membership of the organization on his release. However, it must be acknowledged that if he remains unemployed and without nearby family support there is a considerable risk of him again abusing alcohol. His alcohol abuse has certainly been associated with a number of violent episodes in the past which predate the present offence.

*(*140cf1.2.2)*

276 Adulthood and in prison

With feelings of remorse and empathy come feelings of pain and regret

Expressions of 'remorse' and 'regret' are generally thought to be foundational in the process of rehabilitation, and serve as stepping stones in individual efforts to change personal orientations and behaviors that relate to the murder. There may be various reasons for expressing remorse for the murder. At one extreme, the feelings of remorse for the murder may include feeling sorry for oneself because 'it' somehow 'just happened' and as a consequence 'I am in prison.' At the other extreme, feelings of remorse for the murder may include deep feelings of sorrow both because a man is dead and because they are the one who killed him. Below, we hear from men who expressed both feelings of empathy and remorse, some seem to have been deeply felt both in the immediate aftermath of the murder and later in prison, some remain mixed.

'I will be sorry even after I have done my time'

[Statement to police]
I just wanted to say that at the time it happened, the killing, I was drunk, very drunk. If I had been sober, I would never have done something like this. I just lost my temper and I went too far. I wish the guy was alive. *I'm sorry for what I done, and even when I done my time, I shall still be sorry.*

[Psychiatric pre-trial report – a different view]
He was cold and remorseless, refused to discuss events in detail. His personality [*excessive drinker who didn't learn from experience and had little regard for others*] were not amenable to medical treatment.

(*650cf1.4.4)

Deep remorse for the murder of an alcoholic man who was, 'the love of my life'

[Trial judge]
At all times, he was obsessed with the deceased. They lived together [as intimate partners] in various places for about ten years, and he was financed by the deceased's income. The deceased was a talented man with a flawed personality manifesting itself in alcoholism. When the victim lost his job because of alcoholism, the defendant became extremely anxious because he feared he might lose his relationship and his home. He was prescribed Diazepam and Temazepam but his doctor did not perceive any serious psychiatric disturbance. The defendant is aged 37, and has no history of violence. *The deceased was the love of his life.* I do not consider that he is a continuing danger, except for himself. His *remorse seems very genuine.* The recommendation [length of sentence] is the lowest I have yet made, and deliberately so.

(*1004cf1.1.5)

In prison – thinking about his actions, taking responsibility and facing remorse

[Probation report]
He has never tried to justify himself, to claim either provocation or self-defense, or to minimize the serious nature of what occurred. He has 'a high degree of remorse and an awareness of how this offense has impacted on the victims' families. He appears to struggle with the knowledge that he has participated in bringing someone's life to an end and the impulsive, thoughtless nature of an action which he never intended would have the consequences it had.

(*1174cf1.2.3)

Prison programs – working to change attitudes and behaviors

When in prison, men convicted of murder must participate in various programs regarding their ways of thinking and future relationships with others if and when they return to the community. They must think about and learn to manage themselves in different settings including the family and intimate relationships, the workplace, the pub and other contexts. The primarily cognitive behavioral programs are designed to assist them in learning skills that should be useful in their thinking about themselves and in their relationships with others. For an evaluation of prison-based cogitative behavioral programs (see Friendship et al., 2002). These programs are not just aimed at thinking and behavior associated with experiences after release, they are also oriented to learning social and thinking skills that may assist them in coping with prison. Prison presents inmates with all sorts of challenges that might turn into aggression and violence and learning to negotiate these encounters, and even to 'walk away' can be very important. Because of the seriousness of their offense, it is essential that relevant issues are addressed before they can be considered for parole. Even then, it is not sufficient to simply have taken the courses but that they have learned from them, have taken the messages on board, and have made sufficient progress at changing their problem behaviors and attitudes to make themselves less risky to others.

Looking back with/without regret, looking forward with/without resolve

Progress toward personal change is difficult, and some men continually refuse to make any effort to change themselves or their behavior while others undertook the challenge. Some of the men behaved badly and caused problems within the prison, some simply refused to communicate, some refused to participate in any of the prison programs related to their offending behavior or to accept responsibility for their crime, and for these and other reasons they were considered to be a potential danger should they be released.

278 Adulthood and in prison

Prison programs – refuses to communicate or participate for many years

He seems to be mostly uncommunicative, but gives different responses to different professionals. He refuses to engage in any offence-related work, is uncommunicative, reclusive, has no remorse, and is emotionally flat.

(★714cf1.2.7)

Prison programs – refused to participate for five years

[Prison review board summary]
For the first four–five years of his sentence, he saw his crime as manslaughter, refused to attend Alcohol, Anger Management, and Skills courses. He conceded that he had used excessive violence but [claims to] have no recollection of how or when he inflicted the fatal wounds.

[Probation report – nine years into his sentence]
He's always had difficulty accepting he perpetrated such a violent and frenzied attack.

(★716cf1.4,4)

Prison programs – refuses to participate for 15 years

He has been in prison for almost 15 years during which time he has made no effort to address any of the risk factors and displays no insight into his offending behavior. In view of the above it can only be concluded that this man's level of risk has not decreased and therefore would continue to present a risk to the community should he be released. I therefore recommend that he remain with the high security status until such time as he begins to accept more responsibility for his offence and starts to address his offense behavior.

(★237cf1.2.2)

Prison programs – working class lifestyle and crime

[Our interview]
It hasn't been good for us but since this sentence really, I've learnt how to control my temper. When I was out there, I couldn't. That's because of my childhood, the way I was brought up. But some people never understand that. Like Psychology [Department] in here, I was trying to explain to her [Psychologist] and she didn't understand it. *Why didn't she understand it?* Because she was like from a middle-class area, she hadn't seen nothing like this before. She was a bit shocked, basically. She thought like because I'm in for murder and that, that was an excuse I was using. But being brought up in a rough area, it's just violence all through your family, obviously you're going to turn to that. If you're pushed in a cupboard, you're going to turn to fight. It's just second nature. She said "No, it's not." I said "Oh, all right."

(★631iv1.2.3)

Adulthood and in prison **279**

Same man continues....

Prison programs – refuses to talk, then convinced to talk and things become easier

[Our interview]
How often do you talk to people, either inside or out of prison [e.g. family], about your offence? Never. Outside, I don't talk to nobody about it outside. This is only the second time I've spoken about it. *Is that right, in all these years?* Aye. because I didn't want to at first, and when I did this report for psychology, she said you've got to talk. I said I'm not, and she said, 'You've got to'. I said, 'Listen, I was naïve. It's not something someone wants to be impressed by'. I said I don't want to talk about what I've done. She said, 'You won't get released from prison if you won't talk about it'. She said this for about three days, trying to get me to speak about it. And I did eventually because the Prison Officer said, 'You've got to talk about it. This is your chance now to open up', and I nearly didn't. Even though I didn't agree with it, talking about it, because it is sad, know what I mean. I didn't agree with talking about it.

Well, what made you agree to talk to us then, for the research? Because I've got to talk about it anyway. I've got to start learning to talk about it. Because if I don't, it's an excuse for them to keep me in prison. *You said before something about bottling up is the worst thing that you can do.* That's one of the things the doctor told us, 'Try and talk about the offence, it'll make it easier'. Which it did.

(*631iv1.2.3)

These cases illustrate that resistance to change can be intense and long lasting. Men can go for years without addressing either the offense itself or their own attitudes and behaviors associated with it. In the first case of long-term resistance, prison staff continued to encourage this man to participate on the programs, and this was eventually effective when he entered a program. In the next two accounts, the men's orientations to the crime and to themselves changed from when they were on trial to early in their sentence, and after several years in prison. The first man began with no remorse and an unwillingness to engage with staff and spent his first few years causing problems for staff and himself, but after five years in prison he began to engage positively with staff and to make efforts to 'turn himself around,' but even then there was a concern about his future prospects if he returned to abusing alcohol.

In prison, engages with programs, and changes in thinking and actions

[Our interview]
Have you done any offender programs? Aye, aye. I've done alcohol awareness. I done a Quaker course over two days for an alternative to violence project.

280 Adulthood and in prison

That was a volunteer course. Cognitive skills, ETS (Enhanced Thinking Skills). Twelve sessions of a 16-session drug rehabilitation course. After 12 sessions, I jacked it in because all they were talking about was heroin and I knew everything about heroin then, so I wasn't sitting around with junkies. *In terms of the courses that you've been on what's been the most useful, or the most interesting?* The ETS (Enhanced Thinking Skills) – it opened my mind up. *To what?* To think, think before you act – that's the best course I've ever done. *What kinds of things did you enjoy?* The whole thing about the ETS is – if you get into an argument, step back a wee bit, think about the consequences short term, long term, midterm – whatever. Think about it – and then decide. *And do you think you've used that?* Oh, aye. That's how I'm doing education. I never done any education before.

Nothing like that before. *So, what motivated you then?* The ETS opened my mind up to what I could do and what I canny do, right.

(*818iv1.2.3)

From no remorse and no empathy to personal change over time

[Pre-trial report]
No remorse or emotion. At the time of examination, he did not show any evidence of emotion when talking about the assault on the victim. There was no evidence of grief or remorse at all. There was 'evidence of a personality disorder, as evident from his chaotic lifestyle'.

[Prison report – early in prison sentence]
Few interests, unable to tolerate frustration, will not persist with difficulties, depression, attempts to obtain hooch or drugs, gambles or gets in debt, appears tense unable to relax. Plays a key role in the wing drugs/hooch-scene. Has suicidal tendencies and suffered depression. On occasion, admitted to hospital for depression. He was housed in the prison segregation unit for his own protection.

[After five years in prison]
In interview he presented as someone who has a positive attitude to his current situation and who is motivated to make progress. He tells me that he has good external support. Staff speak well of him and have no complaints about his work or attitude. [But] expressed reservations about success outside prison vis. alcohol.

(*1122cf1.2.6)

In the next example a prolific sexual offender against vulnerable boys and young men persistently refused to participate in any programs. The following narrative demonstrates that potential progress may be possible when he agrees to participate in a specialist sex offender program.

After years in prison agrees to participate in sex offender program

[Probation officer's report]
In conclusion, we concur with the numerous other assessments high-lighted in this report, that his callous unconcern for others over the years, combined with his highly manipulative nature and apparent incapacity to experience remorse regarding feelings of guilt, make him *particularly high risk of re-offending in the future and dangerous to the public*. To his credit, he has recently acknowledged that without specialist help, he remains high-risk of re-offending, and has now agreed to take part in prison 'Sex Offender Treatment Programme'. He was in receipt of psychological input while in 'X' Prison and expressed a desire for long-term psychiatric intervention including psychotherapy.

*(*1079cf1.4.4)*

This man discussed his own process of learning while in prison and offered advice to younger prisoners.

Personal change over time – programs help you see things clearly, stay calm, and walk away from trouble

[Prison report – early in his sentence]
Risk factors initially identified: 'aggression, cold and detached behavior, criminal lifestyle, unstable lifestyle, deviousness, lack of empathy, subversive, and disruptive'.

[Our interview – later in his sentence]
Programmes. What sort of things have you done? I've done the ETS (Enhanced Thinking Skills), that's the new one, the head banging one. I've done that and got a good mark. 'Anger management', 'Alcohol awareness', 'Relationships'. That's all the ones they've asked us to do.

But are you saying then that you don't think that anything that these courses have taught you will help you when you're out? Oh, it helps, it helps you look at situations, you can see them a bit clearer, a bit quicker and gives you that little bit of an edge more. But the main point of the whole thing is you've got to stop getting into the situation.

What about since you've been in, something you said earlier was there's a lot of violence in prison. Have you found anything you've learnt on the courses helpful for keeping out of bother since you've been in? Aye, it's best, doing this ETS thing where you're going through 20 sessions, where you've got a camera on you, camera in the room, a probation, a psychologist, a screw, you're going through these play roles and they explain things to you. You look at films and you look to see what you first see, and then you can see something clearly, and its' different. You might think something's happening and then when you sit back to look at it it's something totally different. They're good. You learn. You learn.

You're probably interviewing a few different lifers now. There's other ones, lads, very hot tempered. Then suddenly they're talking to you later and saying, 'fucking hell, I shouldn't have done that'. I hope I'm not swearing too much. Me, I'm more calm. I can control. I'll say, 'Listen man, don't lose your temper. Think of the courses. Walk away from the thing, or you could be fighting every other day in jail'. Cos when you're surrounded by a load of young ones, which is unbelievable, all they're interested in is drugs, drugs and more drugs.

(*591iv1.4.4)

Summary – adulthood and life in prison

The adult lives of the men who committed murder were generally problematic. Most entered adulthood with weak anchors to a conventional life. The majority left school early with no qualifications, were unemployed and had a broken intimate relationship or none at all. Many had serious problems with alcohol and/or drug abuse, and a few had mental health problems. Persistent criminal behavior along with previous and numerous convictions were a common feature of life, with nearly half of the men having a previous conviction for violence, and nearly half of them had previously been in prison. For some, the murder was the end of a personal history of violence against others. This was the background they brought to prison. For some, prison was nothing new. Although nearly half the men had been in prison before, serving a sentence for 'murder' presents new and different challenges. In Britain, anyone convicted of 'murder' is required to serve a minimum term (tariff) before they can be considered for parole and released into the community where they will remain under supervision for the rest of their life and always remain subject to a recall to prison.

Being granted parole is dependent on accepting responsibility for *their* murder and undertaking the arduous task of confronting the behaviors and modes of thinking associated with the murder. Many men found it difficult to accept responsibility for *their* murder. In its strongest form, this involved complete denial of the murder (someone else did it), claims that the victim deserved it, or a total loss of memory, as well as minimization of the violence and the like. An important aspect of such 'cognitive scripts' is a distancing from their own orientations and actions along with the objectification of the victim that somehow 'just died.' A few men steadfastly held to such views, others were shameful and repentant from the beginning of their sentence, while most progressed, albeit sometimes very slowly, to participate in prison programs oriented to confronting their problematic thinking and behavior. It is difficult to 'embrace' notions of remorse about the murder, empathy for the victim, and to admit *their* culpability for the murder. The evidence presented here reveals that some men maintained their original modes of thinking, were unable to take the 'role of the other' (the victim), and were unwilling to consider such notions even from the professional staff who were trying to help them through the difficult process of changing their thinking and behavior.

So, what's next? – The world outside

In our interviews with men in prison, the last question we asked was 'How do you see your future?' Although it was not our intention, this was in fact a very cruel question. Some of the men were silenced by it, others seemed not to know what to say, and some seemed to withdraw into themselves in what seemed like a silent form of contemplation about what might actually be outside the prison walls, what they might do out there, and how they might manage. So, what next? 'What next?' is in fact a very big question about hopes, dreams, and fears about the life he might lead outside the prison walls. The answers may have been realistic, or unrealistic. They may have simply been dreams of the life they would like to lead but, in reality, thought it unlikely that they would ever be able to lead. Their thoughts may have also been laced with notions about their own personal frailties and what they might do about them, about the certainties that had previously been embodied in their daily routines that characterized the life they led before they killed someone and went to prison. So, 'what next?' is not only a very big question for the men we interviewed about the life they might hope to lead outside the prison walls, it is also a very big question for everyone else who lives in that world outside the prison walls.

Life after prison

The question, 'So, what next?' for the men who have committed a murder includes a myriad of issues that relate to the 'reform' and 'reintegration' of these particular men both inside and outside of prison. What immediately comes to mind are the various programs offered to men while they are inside prison that focus on their offence and offending behavior with a view to dealing with the particular issues that relate to the murder they committed and brought them into prison. A necessary addition to what happens while they are in prison are various efforts related to employment, resettlement, housing, and other aspects of daily life that must be addressed once they return to the community. The evidence regarding 'what happens next' when men leave prison is not encouraging. Some may make it on the outside and some may not and may, instead, continue the lifestyle associated with crime and violence.

Will these men succeed in creating a more conventional lifestyle, desist from crime and avoid returning to prison? The answer is not encouraging. In the US, research exploring the nature of desistance from crime after imprisonment, basically considers why a man might 'go straight,' and explores the 'turning

284 Adulthood and in prison

points' in their adult lives and 'anchors' in conventionality that are often very weak. What chance is there for 'lifers' with considerable 'baggage' that began in early life, continued into adulthood, have spent after many years in prison, and then leave prison with few opportunities and with modes of thinking and behavior that are not conducive to a positive 're-start' in life? Will they desist? The evidence indicates that men convicted of homicide are extremely unlikely to commit another homicide, but a reasonable proportion of them will commit further crime such as burglary and robbery, as well as infractions of parole such as drunkenness, drug taking, and the like, that will send them back to prison (Liem, 2013).

Is it possible for 'lifers' to turn themselves around and become a 'new' person? Some lifecourse criminologists have reached quite pessimistic conclusions about the prospect of desistance from crime. While stressing the importance of social control and social roles in adult life, they have generally paid little attention to the processes and mechanisms associated with these 'anchors' of social control. According to Liem (2016) there is another way of conceptualizing the route to desistance that focuses on understanding the *transition process*. While lifecourse researchers stress the significance of milestones and the importance of social control, not much attention has been paid to how these connections operated to create modes of thinking and behavior associated with desisting from crime, i.e. the *process* of moving away from crime. Some lifecourse researchers have certainly advanced thinking about the 'pillars of desistance,' finding that they do not simply rest on marriage and employment, but also include 'cohesive stable relationships,' a wider network of family relations, and steady employment that make a difference (Liem, 2016). Even so, they have not investigated the *process* of moving away from crime, which Liem labels a 'Transforming into a better self.'

One of the early efforts to study the process of desisting from crime stressed the importance of 'cognitive shifts' that are necessary for desistance (Giordano, Cernkovich and Rudolph, 2002, p. 1000). Mostly using qualitative data, they and other researchers investigated the 'subjective changes' that effect 'individual identity and the processes of self-reform and transformation of identity (Maruna, 2001; LeBel et al., 2008.). Having collected 'redemption' stories from ex-offenders they identified 'hooks for change' that appear to involve cognitive shifts leading to rejection of the old self and the creation of replacement behavior. Consequently, the new 'self' replaces external control with internal controls. For Liem, this means that one of the answers to the desistance puzzle 'appears to be in a mind-set' of the offender and a 'belief in self-efficacy' (Liem, 2016, pp. 11–19). These conclusions are important and have implications for lifers, but most of the findings are about men who committed less serious crimes than murder and have been imprisoned for relatively short periods of time, and not about those who committed very serious crimes and have spent many years in prison.

In, *Changing Violent Men* (2000), we tried to contribute to the study of desistance and examine the process of personal change in a research evaluation that compared two different criminal justice responses to men convicted of using violence against their woman partner. Men convicted of violence against their intimate partner were sentenced by the court either to one of the usual sanctions (such as a fine, a short sentence, admonishment or probation) or required to attend CHANGE, a feminist-oriented cognitive behavioral program that worked on modes of thinking and changes in behavior. The aim of the research was to assess whether men who completed the program were more likely to stop using violence against their woman partner than men who were sentenced to the traditional sanctions such as fines. In the Violent Men Study, we assess the cessation of violence using follow-up interviews with 122 male abusers and their women partners, we also learned a great deal about *why* men might change (Dobash et al., 2000; particularly Chapter 8, 'Why Men Change' pp. 147–174; see also, Morran, 2013).

Our interviews with these violent men and their women partners led us to conclude that any intervention aimed at desistence had to include a combination of 'respectful retribution' such as a criminal justice sanction, along with a positive program that required men to accept responsibility for *their* violence and to learn new ways of thinking and behaving. One task that the men found painful, was looking back on *their* violent behavior with honesty and candor, and talking explicitly about its consequences for others as well as for themselves. We found 'Three Stories of Change': 1) men who cannot or will not change despite the nature of the intervention; 2) men who engage in limited and temporary change maintained under the watchful eye of the enforcers of law and the threat of sanctions; and 3) men who changed their violent behavior and associated attitudes and began to regulate their own behavior (Dobash et al., 2000, p. 151). Follow-up interviews and questionnaires after one year suggested that the successful men began to recognize and acknowledge the impact their behavior had on others, particularly their partners and children. One important change involved the realization that they were not merely an 'object' that was acted upon by outside events and by others but a 'subject' who made decisions including whether to use violence. As a part of building the new non-violent self they needed to shed their exculpatory language about justifications, minimization, denial and the blaming of others. Finally, changes in behavior needed to be lasting and sustained for life not abandoned at the first hurdle (Dobash et al., 2000).

There is little evidence about desistance from crime and personal change among men released from prison after serving very long sentences for murder, but there are a few studies that venture into this domain. Marieke Liem, Chair of the Violence Research Initiative at Leiden University, has produced the first substantial study focused on this topic, *After Life Imprisonment* (Liem, 2016). She conducted intensive interviews with 68 men who had committed homicide and spent decades in prison before being released on parole. Many of the men she interviewed had been sent back to prison because of a parole violation or a new offense, and these findings provide important insights into the problems faced by

TABLE 8.1 Lifecourse-Adulthood. Each Type of Male–Male Murderer and Others

Lifecourse – Adulthood	Confront. / Others	Money/ Others	Family/ Others	Sexual/ Others	O.Men/ Others	#Not typed	All M–M Murderers
MALE–MALE MURDERER	$n=158$/ /$n=266$^	$n=81$/ /$n=343$^	$n=72$/ /$n=352$^	$n=32$/ /$n=392$^	$n=40$/ /$n=384$^	$n=41$	N = 424
Ed. and Employment	% / %	% / %	% / %	% / %	% / %		%
Left sch.before 16^^	55/59^^	55/56	51/58	57/57	60/56	#	57
No Education Qual.	69/74	80/63★★	68/73	70/72	73/72	#	72
A level or higher	07/04	05/05	12/04★	07/05	05/05	#	05
Usually unemployed	63/77★★	66/70	56/75★★★	64/72	84/70	#	72
Intimate Relationships							
Family dysfunction	26/26	31/25	30/25	19/27	23/27	#	26
Bkdown relationship	61/62	66/60	68/59	67/60	70/60	#	61^^^
Problems as Adult							
Econ. Disadv.(poverty)	22/17	18/17	09/20★	17/18	22/17	#	18
Alcohol abuse	55/57	48/59	63/55	54/57	75/55★★	#	57
Drug abuse	37/33	42/35	29/37	36/36	33/36	#	35
Mental health Probs.	29/18★	21/26	34/23	25/25	26/24	#	25
Sexual Problems	12/21★	16/18	25/16	54/15★★★	20/17	#	18
Sexual Viol, not DV.	09/07	13/08	08/09	19/08	09/09	#	09
Criminal Behavior							
Persistent crim. beh.	84/79	81/80	81/80	73/81	87/80	#	81

Physical viol in gen.	51/43	49/45	32/49★★	57/45	28/47★★	#	46
At least 1 prev. conv.	85/85	86/85	80/86	77/86	94/84	#	85
5+convictions	68/67	74/65	56/69★	57/68	70/66	#	67+
At least 1 convict. for:							
Minor assault	42/41	44/40	31/43★	34/42	28/42	#	41
Serious assault	16/20	14/18	17/20	27/17	15/17	#	17
Serious sex assault	09/09	13/08	08/09	19/08★	09/09	#	09
Previous Prison	46/46	57/43	31/43★	33/46	53/45	#	46
Professional Involved							
Social services	21/21	20/21	17/22	23/21	30/19	#	21
Medical	18/24	22/20	23/22	18/22	24/21	#	22
Psych/ Psychiatric	27/22	26/25	28/25	33/25	35/24	#	25
Police	78/78	84/77	66/80★	75/78	85/74	#	78
Probation	28/38★★	33/34	37/34	36/34	57/31★★★	#	34

^numbers vary when (not applicable) and/or (missing data) ★*p* < .05, ★★*p* < .01, ★★★*p* < .001

#Not typed, *n* = 41 cases could not be classified due to missing data, etc.

^Each variable contains two percentages for: 'murder type' / 'other.murderers', (% / %)

^^['Left school before 16,' contains: % in that Type / and % of 'Others' not in that type.

^^^n=323 includes only men who had ever been in a long-term intimate relationship

Example: ^^[Left School before age 16] 'Confront./ Others' = 55/59]. *Of the 158 Confront. murderers, 55% left school before age 16 compared to 59% of the 266 'Other' murderers.*
Tip: to focus on <u>one</u> column, fold paper lengthwise and place over all other columns.

TABLE 8.2 Lifecourse-In.Prison. Each Type of Male–Male Murderer and Others

Lifecourse - In Prison	Confront/ Others	Money/ Others	Family/ Others	Sexual/ Others	O.Men Others	#Not typed	All M–M Murderers
MALE–MALE MURDERER	$n = 158/$ /$n = 266$^	$n = 81/$ /$n = 343$^	$n = 72/$ /$n = 352$^	$n = 32/$ /$n = 392$^	$n = 40/$ /$n = 384$^	$n = 41$	N-424
	%/%	% / %	% / %	% / %	% / %		%
Behavior in prison							
Model prisoner^^	**21/16**^^	19/18	21/17	21/18	08/19	#	18
Uncooperative	26/35	41/29★	26/33	33/31	28/32	#	31
Discipline.report 1+	84/83	86/82	78/84	78/83	85/83	#	83
Disc. report, 10+	41/42	46/40	26/44★	44/40	60/40★	#	42
Judgements of professionals in prison							
Mental health-prison	14/22★	19/19	23/19	21/20	28/19	#	20
Risk public safety	32/52★★★	47/44	44/44	50/44	43/58	#	45
Dangerousness	24/47★★★	44/38	44/38	47/38	53/38★	#	39
Orientations to – victim and murder							
No Remorse	22/40★★★	42/32	31/34	37/33	43/33	#	34
No empathy	31/49★★★	46/42	39/44	53/42	58/42★	#	43

^numbers vary when (not applicable) and/or (missing data) ★$p < .05$, ★★$p < .01$, ★★★$p < .001$.
#Not typed, $n = 41$ cases could not be classified due to missing data, etc.
^Each variable contains two percentages for: 'murder type' / 'other.murderers', (% / %)
^^['Model prisoner', contains: % in that Type / and % of 'Others' not in that type.
★$p < .05$, ★★$p < .01$, ★★★$p < .001$.
Example: ^^ [Model prisoner] 'Confront./ Others' = 21/16]. *Of the 158 Confront. murderers, 21% were 'model prisoners' compared to 16% of the 266 'Other' murderers.*
Tip: to focus on <u>one</u> column, fold paper lengthwise and place over all other columns.

these 68 men. Liem was interested in assessing two possible explanations of desistance. Do men change and desist because they established new social and personal anchors such as employment and a relationship? Or, is desistance more about shedding an older crime-based *persona* and creating a new more conventional identity? She concluded that neither explanation was adequate. One major problem for the men was overcoming the 'serious disruption of a lengthy imprisonment' that made reentry very problematic. While some of the men appeared to achieve a turning point, such as establishing an intimate relationship or finding a job, these 'hooks' often did not work. The relationships some men established were sometimes chaotic and some of the women also had serious problems such as substance abuse and mental illness. While these might be seen as 'bad choices,' it must be acknowledged that choices are limited for an ex-con who committed a homicide and then spent decades in prison. In addition, jobs were scarce for men with such a background who would, quite rightly, be subject to security checks that would exclude them from many jobs. A history of a serious offense, and a lack of skills and connections don't generally lead to employment.

Liem suggests that men do not find a job and then change themselves. It is the other way around. Changing the 'mind-set' must come first, although this does not necessarily lead to employment. Pre-existing ties had mostly evaporated and the wider network of family and kin were 'not receptive.' These men were not able to establish the 'hooks' needed for reentry and for desistance. Some men did change their thinking and 'persona' and adopt a more positive outlook, but even those who created a 'better version' of self were unlikely to succeed. Her evidence suggests that those who projected a new image had 'been schooled in redemption stories' often learned in prison (for a similar process in the United States, see, Dashka (2020)). This was apparent both for men who succeeded and for those who failed. Does this mean their narratives were 'inauthentic?' Maybe? Importantly, these men continued to face the problems of their past: substance abuse, mental health problems and a 'crime-ridden lifestyle,' and were also coupled with solving legal issues and obtaining housing. Those who succeed were most likely to have a sense of 'self-efficacy' including responsibility and control over their lives. Based on Liem's evidence about desistence and personal change among 'lifers,' she concluded that 'thinking' comes first, then 'hooks and turning points' may follow. The findings from our own research on changes among men who abuse their intimate partners leads us to the same conclusion, and also our own belief that while the road to personal change is very difficult and the outcome is not certain, the journey is not without hope and is worth the effort.

Note

1. A single asterisk* indicates statistically significant differences, with the specific levels of significance shown in Table 8.1 Lifecourse-Adulthood.

290 Adulthood and in prison

References

Dobash, R. E. Dobash, R. P, Cavanagh, K., and Lewis, R., 2000. *Changing Violent Men*. Thousand Oaks and London. Sage.

Friendship, C., Blud, L., Erikson, M., and Travers. R., 2002, 'An evaluation of cognitive behavioural treatment for prisoners. Findings 161.' The Research, Statistics Directorate. London: Home Office.

Giordano, P. G., Cernkovich, S. A., and Rudolph J. L., 2002. Gender, crime, and desistance: Toward a theory of cognitive transformation. *American Journal of Sociology*, 107 (4), 990–1064.

LeBel, T, Burnett, R., Maruna, S., and Bushway, S., 2008. The 'chicken and egg' of subjective and social factors in desistance from crime. *European Journal of Criminology*, 5 (2), 131–159.

Liem, M. C. A., 2013. Homicide offender recidivism: A review of the literature. *Aggression & Violent Behavior*, 18, 19–25.

Liem, M. C. A., 2016. *After Life Imprisonment: Reentry in the Era of Mass Incarceration*. New York: New York University Press.

Maruna, S., 2001. *Making Good: How Ex-convicts Reform and Rebuild Their Lives*. Washington, DC: American Psychological Association Books.

Morran, D., 2013. Desisting from domestic abuse: Influences, patterns and processes in the lives of formerly abusive men. *The Howard Journal of Criminal Justice*, 52 (3), 306–320.

Sampson, R. J. and Laub, J. H., 2004. A general age-graded theory of crime among delinquent boys: Lessons learned and the future of life-course criminology. In D. Farrington, ed., *Advances in Theoretical Criminology: Testing Integrated Developmental and Life Course Theories of Offending*. New Brunswick, NJ: Transaction, pp. 165–181.

Online and newspapers

Dashka, S., 2020. How to get out of prison. *New York Times Magazine*, 5 January, 2020.

9

MALE–MALE MURDER

Evidence from the Murder Study

A close examination of 'murder events' and the 'situations and circumstances' in which they occur are central to our efforts to provide a fuller understanding of when men murder other men. Evidence was taken from our wider Murder Study that included a sample of 866 casefiles of 786 men and 80 women convicted of all types of murder and 200 interviews with 180 men and 20 women serving a sentence for murder. Details of the Murder Study are presented in Chapter 1.

In *Male–Male Murder*, our focus is only on men who murdered other men. Evidence from the casefiles of 424 male–male murderers, reveal some main patterns across these cases. The age of the perpetrators ranged from 27–29 years. The age of their victims ranged from 33–37 years. The average age of older victims was 72 years, which is an artifact as victims in this group were all aged 65 or over. The majority of the men were unemployed, most were drinking at the time of the murder, and those who were drinking were usually drunk. Some of the men perpetrators and victims were drinking together. A minority of the men used drugs. Most of the murders involved only one perpetrator and were not witnessed, although some involved a group of perpetrators and numerous witnesses, and these were often particularly brutal. The majority of the murders involved some kind of 'confrontation' during the murder event itself often as victims challenged a man who was burgling their home or during some kind of exchange in the street, park or pub. Most deaths involved five or more injuries, usually stabbing and/or beating with hands and feet, or instruments such as clubs, bricks, and other blunt objects. Although some perpetrators were angry or indignant at the time, many were devoid of such emotions. Some murders involved a 'prior dispute' between the men or some form of 'previous violence' between them. In order to examine these and other issues, we developed a typology of male–male murder that allowed us to consider these cases in greater detail and to have a

292 Evidence from the Murder Study

better understanding of what might be happening, and why. Developing a typology of male–male murder was extremely difficult as discussed in Chapter 1. The Five Types of male–male include: Confrontational Murders/Fighters; Murder for Money/Financial Gain; Family Murders between men; Sexual Murders between men; and Murder of Older.Men.

Confrontational Murders/Fighters

Confrontational Murders/Fighters were the largest group of murderers, $n = 158$ (37%). Among them, we identified six subtypes: 1) groups, conflicts and confrontations; 2) confrontations involving disputes and 'slights to self"; 3) confrontations involving disputes and 'slights against others'; 4) the 'fair fight' – men agree to fight'; 5) 'collateral victims: bystanders and displacement of violence'; and 6) confrontations involving 'identification with a wider group/organization.' While these six subtypes represent variation in this overall type, they all involve a similar context: conflicts, disputes and fighting over reputations where the perpetrator felt he or his group had been insulted or humiliated and used violence to regain and/or to enhance his reputation. In interviews with men and in their casefiles, it was clear that their behavior was very much like fighters in England who went out for a 'laff' and those in Australia who engaged in fighting as a form of entertainment. Focusing on the murder event, the evidence reveals that nearly half of the men murdered in a group context, that many were drinking and three-quarters of those who were drinking were drunk. Victims were less likely to have been drinking, but those who had been drinking were equally likely to be drunk. Many confrontational murders took place in public locations such as pubs, parks and vacant lots. Very few of these cases included a second offense, such as burglary, which reinforces the notion that issues such as 'reputations' were of importance rather than any form of monetary gain. The main 'cause of death' was stabbing. Confrontations, often involved long-running conflicts and previous aggressive encounters. Some studies emphasize the 'trivial' nature of disputes, the importance of gangs, spontaneous responses of perpetrators, and the existence of rules of 'engagement' associated with a 'fair fight.' By contrast, we did not find evidence of widespread gang activity, nor that the circumstances were 'trivial.' Instead, these perpetrators viewed the 'slights' as serious and consequential to their reputation and self-image which they felt must be defended. The majority of Confrontational murders were not spontaneous. Many involved ongoing disputes that led to confrontations that were usually one-sided with victims that were more vulnerable than the perpetrator(s) or were made disproportionally more vulnerable as perpetrators 'introduced' knives, clubs or other 'weapons' used to overwhelm and kill the victim. We have long been critics of the notion of the 'fair fight,' and discussed this in various chapters. The question to address here is why would a generally aggressive and violent man (most perpetrators) engage in a 'fair fight' when he knows that his best chance of 'winning' is to do as much as possible to take advantage of the situation including producing a knife, a club, a brick, or even a gun. Overall, Confrontational/Fighters were exactly that. They killed in the context of a fight, often alone but sometimes as part of a group, and often linked to an ongoing dispute that led to the confrontation in which they committed murder.

Murder for Money/Financial Gain

The 81 cases (19%) of the male–male murders involved money or some form of financial gain. Among them, we identified seven main subtypes: 1) thefts, burglary and robbery; 2) drug-dealing disputes; 3) criminal activity and 'share-outs'; 4) informal personal debt; 5) gangs, conflicts over territory and resources; 6) unlawful activity and disputes with officials, and 7) contracts to kill. They were more likely than Confrontational murders to involve strangers, although many victims were known to the perpetrators including neighbors. Only a few of these murders involved an 'ongoing dispute,' but nearly half of them did involve a 'confrontation' during the murder event. Nearly one-third of them took place in the home of the victim, and most involved only one perpetrator. The contexts and circumstances included a burglary where the primary intention was to steal money or property, and the murder occurred when a perpetrator was interrupted by the victim and he responded with lethal violence. Most of these murders did not seem to involve a prior intent to kill. One distinct aspect of most murders for money was the commission of another offense, usually a property offense. Ongoing disputes were less likely than in other murders, and perpetrators were less likely to have been drinking, although those who had been drinking were likely to be drunk. Similarly, the victims were unlikely to have been drinking, but if drinking they were also likely to be drunk. Some of these murders involved perpetrators and victims who were friends and neighbors. Most were not planned, although those involving drug dealing or disputes between neighbors or officials were usually planned, deliberate and vengeful. Very few involved elaborate schemes to deal with the body, but those related to drug-dealing cases were different, and sometimes involved strenuous efforts to obliterate the body, either as an expression of extreme hatred and/ or in order to eliminate evidence of the murder.

Murder between men in the family

Using a broad definition of family, we classified 72 (17%) cases as family murders. While families are considered locations of strong emotional, affectionate and filial ties, they are also locations of exceptionally strong animosities as adult offspring fall out with parents and parents disown their adult children. More broadly, feuds within and between families are legendary and the subject of cautionary tales such as Romeo and Juliet. While identifying and classifying family-based murders may seem straight forward, this was not the case. We identified five subtypes involving male–male murder: 1) blood relatives, 2) gay intimate partners; 3) collateral intimate partner murders – male victims; 4) family feuds and feuding families; and 5) brothers against others. Ongoing disputes were more likely in Family Murders than Other Murders, and one-fifth of them involved previous violence by the victim against the perpetrator which suggests the possibility that some of these murders involved revenge. Nearly three-quarters of the perpetrators had been drinking at the time of the murder and, once again, those who were drinking were drunk. Victims were much less likely to be drinking, about one-half, but they too were drunk. The use of drugs was unusual. Three-quarters of these murders were committed by a single perpetrator, and slightly more took place in the victim's home. Over half of the victims were stabbed to death, and one-third involved a second offense, usually a theft.

Murders of grandfathers and fathers mostly involved disputes about authority and control, and about money. Murders of gay intimate partners often occurred in a context of intense conflicts between the partners and previous violence between them. Intimate partner collateral murders of men included men trying to protect their daughter from an abusive male partner who responded by killing her protector. We also identified 'male assistors' such as police and lawyers who were providing help to the perpetrator's woman partner, and also 'new male partners.' Collateral victims included fathers and mothers trying to protect their daughter from her male partner/abuser, as well as divorce lawyers; and new male partners. Family feuds and feuding families are not unusual. Some become infamous cases in the media, advice columns, and in legends, and some involve 'brawls' in the streets between members of families at war. Murders involving brothers sometimes involve the killing of one another, and may also involve brothers 'ganging' together against others.

Sexual murder between men

In 32 cases (8%) sex and sexual identity were related to the murder. These cases involved the greatest amount of diversity both in the context and circumstances of the murders, and among those who were murdered. We used a broad definition of sexual murder including various sexual elements involved in these murders, and identified six subtypes of sexual murders between men: 1) hate crimes against gay men; 2) sexual exchanges and mixed messages; 3) homosexual advance; 4) prostitution; 5) pedophilia – false claims and offenses; and 6) serial sexual murder. Hate crimes committed against gay men often occurred late at night in public locations where gay men were vulnerable to attacks. Some attacks were carried out by groups of young men, often involving a robbery coupled with serious antagonisms against gay men. Most did not involve strangers, and few involved ongoing disputes, although confrontations during the murder itself were fairly common. Some sexual murders involved mixed 'messages' between the perpetrator and victim about what was being exchanged, and some involved confusion about the sexual identity of victims and/or the perpetrators. The context of some of these murders involved attempts to lure victims into dangerous situations by pretending to offer sex when the intention was to rob them. False accusations of pedophilia involved vigilantes attacking vulnerable individuals while claiming to be 'principled enforcers' acting in moral outrage to 'protect the community.' The chapter also includes a complicated murder involving modern sex slavery of children and the eventual murder of the 'king.' Again, the majority of these perpetrators had been drinking and were drunk. With the exception of the hate murders, most sex murders involved only one perpetrator and one victim, and no witnesses. Most of the men were stabbed to death. Some of the subtypes included only a few cases, and there was only one serial murder.

Murder of older men

There were 40 cases (9%) of men who murdered older men, aged 65 and older. These included three subtypes: 1) hate crimes against older men; 2) murders of older men involving theft or monetary exploitation; and 3) sex and the murder of older men. An important characteristic of these murders was the significant difference in the average ages of the victims (72) and perpetrators (27), a difference of 45 years while the age difference in the other types of male–male murder was no more than 15 years. The age difference was an important factor in these murders as the perpetrators seemed to choose victims who lived alone, and were vulnerable through disability, ill health and age. Almost all of these perpetrators had serious problems with alcohol, the majority had been drinking and were drunk at the time of the murder. Some left the pub in order to rob the 'old man' in the house nearby so that they could get money to continue drinking. Older men were mostly murdered in their own home, often as part of a burglary. Very few of the victims had been drinking but the few who were drinking were also drunk. Hatred of the elderly was demonstrated in cases that involved extreme violence and torture. The victims were objectified as despicable, and easy targets for theft and casual violence. Most killers were known to the victims and this added to their vulnerability. Ongoing disputes were extremely rare, although confrontations during the murder itself were not, especially when the victim caught the perpetrator in the act of burglary, remonstrated with him and was then attacked and killed. Murders of Older.Men where rarely witnessed and most older men were killed in their own home. One-third of older men were strangled to death, while others were stabbed, beaten with objects or beaten with hands and feet. Very few were shot. Most of these murders involve a second offense, almost always a property offense.

Lifecourse of male–male murderers

Lifecourse – childhood

After examining each of the Five Types of Male–Male Murder, we turned to the men themselves and examined their lives from childhood, to adulthood, and

296 Evidence from the Murder Study

then on to their lives in prison. We conducted interviews with the men in prison, beginning with a discussion of their childhood, followed by life as an adult including the murder and, finally, their life and progress in prison. This allowed the men to talk openly about their past before we asked the more difficult and demanding questions about the murder they committed, their life in prison, efforts to reform, and reflections about what might be ahead at the end of their sentence. This structure took the form of a natural history that progressed chronologically and seemed to aid in gathering information that was meaningful and that progressed to the most difficult of topics both for the person answering the questions and for the person asking them. The same structure was used in gathering data from their casefiles, albeit without the interpersonal elements involved in the interviews. Ironically, we began the research with the notion that it would be far more demanding to conduct personal interviews with the men than to gather data from the casefiles, but found the opposite. It was, in fact, easier to interview the men in person, albeit in a prison cell, than it was to read their casefiles. It is not clear why that should be so, and it may be that this would not always be the case in other areas of research that are equally challenging.

Most of the men were born into families where their parents were in an established marital or long-term cohabiting relationship, but these families were not always ideal. Two-fifths of the parents had a broken relationship, a quarter of the boys had a father who had a problem with alcohol and/or used violence against their mother, and one-fifth of the boys lived in neighborhoods that were disadvantaged. Social Services and the police were involved with about half of the families, and one-quarter of the boys' families had contact with probation, almost exclusively associated with criminal behavior of their father or father figure. Either because of problems in their family or because of issues associated with their own behavior, nearly one-quarter of the boys experienced alternative forms of caregiving during childhood. Some spent time with their grandparents, some were in foster care, and one-quarter of the boys spent time in an institution for young offenders. For many of those in care, the arrangements did not work, and nearly a third of those in care experienced three or more changes in caretakers which is generally viewed as a marker of important problems and concern about the future.

Life at school marked an important 'turning point' for many of the boys who did not fare well in the school environment. For various reasons, around two-thirds had problems at school and about two-fifths experienced discipline problems both at school and at home. Some boys could not learn, others found the 'regime' impossible to navigate and had conflicts with teachers and other students, while some were seriously disruptive. By the age of 13, and certainly before age 16, problems began to emerge, particularly with the abuse of alcohol that was experienced by two-fifths of the boys, while one-third of them abused drugs, and 13% of them had mental health problems that involved social and psychological services. Some of these boys engaged in shoplifting, vandalism and fighting, but for some, these acts were more frequent and serious. By age 13, one-fifth of the boys had committed an indictable offense. By age 16, nearly half of them had been arrested at least once and one-quarter of them had been convicted five or more times. These convictions usually involved property crime; some involved violence. One-quarter of the boys had spent time in a juvenile criminal justice institution and could be defined as 'early-onset' offenders.

In our interviews, some men told us about 'drifting' into crime often with their friends. They were expelled from school or just stopped going, and what mattered was the street, the park, and their pals who were in a similar position. It is important to stress that our data regarding problematic behavior reflects habitual patterns, and not casual experiences such as a few incidents of shoplifting or drunkenness. For some of these boys, persistent and serious problems began at an early age. As shown in Chapter 7 on childhood, and some problems were more apparent in the early lives of those who would later commit different types of murder. For example, men who murdered for money were more likely than those who committed Other. Murders to have been 'in care as a child,' and to have had 'three or more changes' in caretakers while in care. They were also the most likely to have 'problems at school,' 'discipline problems,' to have 'offended before age 13,' and 'offended before age 16,' to have had their 'first arrest before age 16,' to have had 'five or more convictions' (usually for theft), and were also most likely to have been in a 'criminal justice institution' before age 16. In short, the childhood lives of those who would later commit a murder related to 'Money' were as children the most likely to have been in care, to have experienced three or more changes in caretakers, to have problems at school, to begin offending before the age of 16, and to have been incarcerated in a criminal justice institution for juveniles. In short, they were most likely to have the profile of an early onset offender. Conversely, among the Five Types of Male–Male Murderers, the Confrontational/ Fighters were least likely to have had 'problems at school,' 'mental health problems,' 'early onset of offending before age 13,' and to have had 'five or more convictions' before age 16. Overall, there were mixed experiences in the childhood experiences and problems among those who would later commit each of the Five Types of Male–Male Murder. While these were not necessarily harbingers of their lives as adults, nonetheless, many of them did not benefit from the 'anchors' of family, school, and community associated both with social control and with opportunities that affect their future lives as adults.

Lifecourse – adulthood

Over half of the 424 male–male murderers left school before age 16, had no educational qualifications, and were unemployed. Most were poorly equipped to enter the world of work, and lacked both the qualifications and work habits needed for employment. Many were unable to hold-down a job and the majority went in and out of work. Some established intimate relationships, but many of

298 Evidence from the Murder Study

these relationships were fraught, and the majority did not last. The main problem for many was a lifestyle that was not conducive to adult life. Some continued to spend much of their time at the pub or on the 'street.' Removed from the world of family and work, many of the men drifted in-and-out of crime particularly thieving, drunkenness, and violence. Alcohol, and to a less extent drug abuse, featured in the lives of many of these men, with a daily routine of drinking to excess. 'Persistent criminal behavior' was common to most of the men, with property and violent offenses being familiar aspects of daily life. This resulted in numerous encounters with the police, convictions, and nearly half of the men had previously served time in prison. While these problems affected many of the men, some were more likely than others to experience these problems.

Of the Five Types of Male–Male Murderers, those who murdered 'Older. Men' were more likely than the others to have 'left school before age 16,' to be 'unemployed,' to have a 'broken intimate relationship' or none at all, to 'abuse alcohol,' to engage in 'persistent criminal behavior,' to have 'at least one previous conviction,' to have 'five or more previous convictions,' to have been on 'probation,' and to have 'previously been to prison.' In addition, the men who murder Older.Men were also the most likely to have had professionals involved in their life including social services, medical, psychological or psychiatric services, police, and probation. Conversely, among the Five Types of Male–Male Murderers, those who committed a murder in the 'Family' were less likely than the others to have 'left school before age 16,' to have 'no educational qualifications,' to be 'unemployed,' to 'abuse drugs, to have 'five or more previous convictions,' and to have 'previously been to prison.' In addition, the men who committed a Family.Murder were also least likely to have had involvement with social services and police. Overall, those who murdered Older.Men often stood out as the most criminogenic and the most problematic compared with those who committed other murders. However, the lives of many of the others were also characterized by such issues and problems.

Lifecourse – in prison

All of the men in the Murder Study had received a life sentence for murder. Those convicted of murder (not manslaughter) receive a 'life sentence' with a 'tariff' (a recommendation of the number of years they should serve before being considered for parole). However, the final decision is based on their behavior in prison and on successful completion of various programs oriented to issues relating to their offending behavior, e.g. alcohol, drugs, gambling and the like, and their orientation to *their* murder and *their* victim including a focus on genuine regret, remorse and empathy. Even parole and release from prison do not mean they are completely 'free,' forgotten, or beyond the reach of the justice system. Even after release, those convicted of murder remain on a 'life license' for the rest of their life, and can be returned to prison for violations of parole.

Nearly half of 'All' the men had previously been to prison, and were familiar with routines, regulations about behavior, punishment for violations, and the like. They were also familiar with methods used to obtain alcohol and drugs, about problematic relations with fellow inmates and prison staff, and other challenges of life in prison. Evidence in the casefiles included discipline reports and progress reports written by prison staff including prison officers, psychologists, doctors, and prison governors. These reports, along with first-person accounts in our interviews with men in prison, provide insights into how they lived their lives in prison and how they progressed toward possible release and the world outside.

A few of the 424 men were described as a 'model prisoner' (18%). Most (83%) had at least 'one discipline report,' which was not generally a cause for concern among prison staff nor a serious detriment to their future prospects of parole. However, 42% of the men had 'ten or more discipline reports' which was a cause of concern and a detriment to future prospects of parole. Nearly one-third of 'All' the men were judged to be 'uncooperative,' which is a marker of problems, nearly half (45%) were described as a 'risk to public safety,' and 39% were described as 'dangerous.' Of the Five Types of Male–Male Murderers, those who murdered 'Older Men' were least likely to be defined as a 'Model prisoner,' and most likely to have 'ten or more discipline reports,' to be defined as 'dangerous,' to have 'no remorse,' and 'no empathy.' At the same time, men who committed a murder related to 'Money' were most likely to be defined as 'uncooperative.' However, it is notable that 'Confrontational/Fighters' were less likely to be defined as having 'mental health' problems or a 'risk to public safety,' and they were more likely to express 'remorse' and 'empathy.'

After years of researching violence and murder, we conclude that these issues are complex and deeply embedded in the social contexts in which they occur. We have attempted to add to existing knowledge about the Murder Event in all of its diversity by conceptualizing Five Types of Male–Male Murder. In addition, we have examined the lives of male murderers. In an effort to expand what is known about the lives of men who commit murder, we have drilled down into their worlds as children, adults, and in prison. Another lesson we have learned in our studies of violence and of men who use violence, is that change is possible.

NAME INDEX

Abrams, R.C. 181
Ahmed, A. G 181
Alcohol Change UK 17
Alcohol Focus 17
Anderson, E. 7
Archer, J. 3, 16

Bandura, A. 21
Banks, I. 155
Bartlett, P. 142, 155
Barton, A.H. 24
Beaumont-Thomas, B. 150
Beauregard, E. 142, 175
Becker, H.S. 216
Beeghley, L. 2, 4, 5, 6, 19
Beg, M.T. 217
Bennett, T. 105
Benson, D. 16
Birkel, C. 142
Block, C.R. 26, 74, 181
Block, R. 26, 74, 180
Blud, L. 290
Bourgois, P. 7, 8
Brookman, F. 15, 18, 19, 24, 26, 28, 40, 41, 44, 77, 78, 79
Burgess, A. Clockwork [the Novel] 203
Burgess, A. Clockwork [the film] 203, 204
Burnett, R. 290
Bushway, S. 290
Bye, E.K. 17, 18

Carrington, K. 10
Cartwright, D.T. 10

Caspi, A. 248
Catalano, S. 78, 179
Cavanagh, K. 24, 57, 110, 119
CDC 19
Cernkovich, S.A. 284
Chan, H, C.O. 175, 181
Cloward, R.A. 5
Cohen, A.K. 5
Cohen, D. 8
Collier, D. 24
Collins, W.H. 213
Comstock, G. 155
Connell, R. 175
Copes, H. 10, 11, 40, 79
Craig, K. 175
Cusson, M. 142

Daly, M. 5, 26, 39, 40, 41
Dashka, S. 289
Davis, G.G. 181
D'Cruze, S. 2, 26, 29
Dern, H. 142
Dobash, R.E. 15, 21, 22, 23, 24, 26, 29, 33, 57, 110, 119, 142, 182, 218, 227, 240, 285
Dobash, R.P. 15, 21, 22, 23, 24, 26, 29, 33, 57, 110, 119, 142, 182, 218, 227, 240, 285
Dodd, V. 18
Drass, K.A. 74
Dressler, J. 155
Durrkheim, E. 4, 25

Eisbensen, F.A. 216
Eisner, M. 2, 4, 5, 22
Elias, N. 3, 4
Elkin, M. 77, 78
Ellis, A. 40
Ellis, W. 177
Elwert, G. 2
Erikson, M. 290
European Monitoring Centre 86
Eurostat 178, 179
Ewing, C.P. 113

Falzon, A.L. 181
Farrington, D.P. 214, 216, 217
Felson, R.B. 75
Ferracuti, F. 7, 214
Figlio, R. 214
Fischer, D.H. 8
Flewelling, R.E. 25
Forest 17
Forsythe, C.J. 10, 11
Francis, B. 2
Fraser, A. 44, 55
Freeman, J.B. 9
Friendship, C. 277

Ganpat, S.M. 27
Gilbert, P. 3
Giordano, R.G. 284
Glueck, E. 213, 216
Goetting, A. 181
Goffman, E. 216
Gorski, P. 5
Gottfredson, M. 215
Graycar, A. 9
Gruenewald, J. 181

Hadfield, P. 106
Hall, N. 181
Halliday, J. 171
Hamai, K. 177
Hamner, K. 175
Harrington, H. 248
Hasang, O.S.M. 17
Hearn, J. 175
Heide, K.M. 113
Hempel, C.G. 24
Herzfeld, M. 8
Hirschi, T. 215
Hobbs, D. 95
Hochstetler, A. 10, 11, 40
Home Office 2
Homicide Index 40

Horowitz, R. 15, 16
Hough, R.M. 26

James, M. 6
Janoff, D. 175
Jennings, W.B. 214
Jones, H. 26

Kaplan, A. 24
Karch, D. 179, 181
Karstedt, S. 22
Kawachi, I. 5
Kelley, J. 181
Kennedy, B. 5
Kennedy, L.W. 25
Killias, M. 10
King, M.B. 156
Koehler, J.L. 179
Koenraadt, E. 110
Krienert, J.L. 181
Kubrick, S., Clockwork 203, 204
Kuhn, T. 24

Lamnek, S. 20
LaPorte, J. 24
Laub, R.J. 25, 215, 216, 250
Lazarsfeld, A.H. 24
LeBel, T. 284
Leistra, G. 8
Lemos, G. 19
Leon, A.C. 210
Levoy, J. 4
Liem, M.C.A. 27, 110, 250, 284, 285
Lister, S. 106
Loeber, R. 217
Luckenbill, D.S. 13, 14, 15, 25
Lunny, A. 155
Lyman, S.M. 20

Maguire, M. 75
Manthey, J. 17
Martineau, M. 175
Maruna, S. 284, 290
Marzuk, P.M. 210
Maxfield, M.G. 226
McCorkle, K.D. 26
McIntosh, A. 10
McVie, S. 19, 20, 216
Medina-Ariza, J.J. 34
Meloy, R. 175
Menzies, G.C. 155
Menzies, R.P. 181
Merton, R.K. 25

302 Name index

Miethe, T.D. 23, 74
Miles, C. 18
Millon, D.H. 24
Milne, B. 248
Mison, R. 155
Moffitt,T.E. 214, 215
Morran, D. 285
Morris, P.K. 9
Mouzos, J. 175
Mullins, C. 105

National Crime Survey 179
New South Wales 155
Nicole, A. 142
Nieuwbeerta, P. 27
Nisbett, R.E. 8
Nunn, K.C. 179, 181

Oakes, J. 9
Ohlin, L.E. 5
Oliver, S. 155
Omalu, B.I. 179

Pegg, S. 2, 26, 29
Peristiany, J.G. 8, 40
Perry, B. 181
Pidd, H. 171
Pike, S. 26
Piquero, A.R. 214
Pitt-Rivers, J.D. 8
Polk, K. 15, 25, 26, 27, 40, 41
Powdermaker, H. 9
Pridemore, W.A. 5, 17
Probst, C. 17
Proulx, J. 142
Pulton, R. 247

Ranson, D. 27
Regoeczi, W.C. 23, 74
Rehm, J. 17
Riedel, M. 179
Ritchie, J. 181
Rudolph, J.L. 284
Ryle, M. 17
Rylett, M. 17

Sampson, R.J. 25, 215, 216, 250
Schwartz, G. 15, 16
Scott, J. 10
Scott, M.B. 20
Scottish Executive 216
Scottish Government 2
Seawright, J. 24

Shakir, A.M. 179
Shield, K.D. 17
Short, J.F. 7
Silverman, R.A. 25
Sissay, L. 228
Smith, D. 34
Smith, D.J. 216
Soothill, K. 2
Spierenburg, P. 2, 3
Spiers, G. 4
Statistics Bureau of Japan 176, 210
Strodtbeck, F.I. 7
Sutherland, E. 7
Sutherland, K. 210

Tardiff, K. 210
Tavuchis, N. 21
Taylor, R. 64
Tedeschi, J.T. 75
Thompson, S. 175
Thrasher, F. 7
Tomsen, S. 155
Topalli, V. 87
Travers, R. 290

UK Office of National Statistics 179
UNODC 3, 180
US Census Bureau 178
US Department of Justice 106

Vance, J.D. 129

Walklate, S. 2, 26, 29
Walmsley, R. 40
Walsh, J.A. 181
Weber, M. 4, 5, 25
Websdale, N. 129
West, D.J. 214
Wheatie, S. 155
White, B. 181
Whitehead, C. 228
Widom C. S 226
Wikipedia, Cain and Abel 107, 140
Wikipedia, Chicago School 7
Wikipedia, Hatfield–McCoy 128,
    129, 140
Wikipedia, Pulse nightclub 150
Wikipedia, Romeo and Juliet 126, 140
Wikipedia, West Side Story Film 2020
    127, 140
Wilkinson, R.W. 5
Williams, J. 64
Williams, K.R. 25

Wilson, A.V. 26
Wilson, M. 5, 26, 40, 41
Winlow, S. 106
Wolfgang, M.E. 7, 25, 214
Wright, R. 75, 87, 105
Wyatt-Brown, B. 8, 9

YouTube, Madonna – 'God control' 150
YouTube, West Side Story Sndtrk 127, 140

Zahn, M. 26

SUBJECT INDEX

Page numbers in **bold** denote tables.

A Clockwork Orange 203–5
abused during childhood *see* Lifecourse-
  Childhood, abused physically, abused
  sexually
Adam and Eve *see* Cain and Abel
adulthood (perpetrators) *see*
  Lifecourse-Adulthood
Africa 2, 4
age (perpetrators) 41, 75, 108, 143,
  182, 291, 299
alcohol 16–18, 20, **71**, **104**, **136**, **172**, **208**,
  282, **286**, 298–9; *see also* Lifecourse-
  Adulthood, alcohol abuse; Lifecourse-
  Childhood, alcohol use/abuse
American West (early) 10
Australia 9, 10, 15, 142, 292

background, of perpetrator 41, 68, **71**, 75,
  102, **104**, 108, 135, **136**, 143, **172**, 173,
  182, 206, **208**, 291
behavior in prison 266–73, **288**
body 22
bouncers 58, 95
bragging 53–4
Britain 18, 142; *see also* England/Wales;
  UK/Britain
brothers 113, 132–5
Bureau of Justice Statistics 179
burglary, burglary homicides 77–86,
  179, 200
bystanders 61–4

Cain and Abel 107
Cambridge Study in Delinquent
  Development 214
Canada 181
Caribbean countries 2, 6, 86
cause of death 43, 70, **71**, 76, **104**, 109,
  136, 144, **172**, 183, **208**, 291
Central America 2, 4, 6, 86
Central Intelligence Agency (CIA) 150
childhood, of perpetrators **243–4**; *see also*
  Lifecourse-Childhood
childhood, research (child development,
  delinquency, education, lifecourse
  criminology) 213–17
child murders 15
child physical abuse, of perpetrators **243**;
  see also Lifecourse-Childhood, abused
  physically
child sexual abuse, of perpetrators 161–6,
  243; *see also* Lifecourse-Childhood,
  abused sexually
Chicago 15, 180–1
Chicago School 7
'Clockwork Orange' 203–5
code (the code) 7, 11, 40
cognitive scripts 20–2, 282, 284, 289
cognitive shifts 282–4
collateral murders 61–4, 110, 118–26, 138–9
conflicts, disputes and previous violence
  42, 68, **71**, 75, 102, **104**, 108, **136**, 137,
  143, **172**, 173, 182, 206, **208**, 291

Subject index

context specific approach 22
contract killing 99–100
convictions/offending, as adult 262–5,
    286–7; *see also* Lifecourse-Adulthood
convictions/offending, as child 239–45,
    244, **286**, 297–8; *see also* Lifecourse-
    Childhood
criminal careers 6
criminal gangs 93–5
criminology 7, 214
Crown Prosecution Service 142
Cuidad Juarez, Mexica 87
culture/subculture of violence and
    crime 6–7, 11–12

dangerousness **288**
'dare' 48
data collection (casefiles and interviews),
    analysis, disaggregation *see*
    Murder Study
data (homicide data) 2–3, 5, 15–16,
    18–19, 24, 27–8, 291–9; *see also*
    Murder Study
debts 92, 221
Denver Youth Study 216
deprivation, disadvantage 12, 217, 216, 282
desistance, from crime 284–5
Developmental Criminology 213–14
disadvantage 12, 216, 296
disaggregation 24–32, 142; *see also* Murder
    Study
discipline **244**, 299; *see also* Lifecourse-
    Childhood
displacement of violence 61–3
disputes *see* conflicts, disputes and
    previous violence
dog 57
drinking, drunkenness and drugs 42–3,
    69, 70, **71**, 75, 76, 103, **104**, 109, **136**,
    137, 143, **172**, 173, 183, 206, **208**
drug cartels 87
drug dealing 6, 8–10, 12, 86; films,
    books, TV 87
drugs, use/abuse, as adult **286**, 298–9; *see
    also* Lifecourse-Adulthood, drug abuse
drugs, use/abuse, as child **244**; *see also*
    Lifecourse-Childhood, drug abuse
drinking/drunkenness, as adult **286**; *see
    also* Lifecourse-Adulthood, alcohol
    use/abuse
drinking/drunkenness, as child **244**;
    see also Lifecourse-Childhood,
    alcohol abuse
Dutch Homicide Monitor system 27

education/school 218–19, 233–7,
    249–51, **286**
elderly homicide 178–82
empathy 273–7, **288**
employment **286**
England/Wales 1, 2, 19, 23, 28, 44, 292
England/Wales, Home Office Homicide
    Index 142
Europe, European countries EU 178, 179
Eurostat 178–9
'expressive' homicides 70

fair fight 16, 39, 57–60, 292
family (carers, parents) *see* Lifecourse-
    Childhood
family, kin/kinship, feuds 4, 107,
    126–32, 216
family murders *see* Murder Type (and
    subtypes): family murders between men
father violent to mother **243**; *see also*
    Lifecourse-Childhood, father violent
    to mother
FBI Supplementary Homicide Reports,
    SHRs 79
female murderers 1
fight 39–41, 60–1
fighters *see* Murder Type (and subtypes):
    confrontational Murder (fighters)
fighting 10–11, 41, 53–4
Finland 17
firearms, gun 15, 19, 61, 264–5; *see also*
    cause of death
Five Types of Male-Male Murder 1,
    22, 29–32, 292, 295, 298–9; *see also*
    Murder Types (separate entries for each
    type of murder)
football club 65

gangs 4, 5–6, 41, 44, 86
'gay bashing' 149
gender 2–3, 10, 142, 181
gender imbalance, of murder perpetrators
    and murder victims 142
Germany 181
government officials 96–9
grandsons kill grandfathers 111–13
group allegiance 64–8
groups 4, 43–9, 64–7, 145
gun control 150

hate crimes 145–50, 175, 181, 184–8, 205
Hatfield and McCoy family feud 128–9
homicide, historical trends 3–5, 10–12
homicide rates 2, 8, 9

306 Subject index

homicide (murder) research 6–11, 13–29;
  see also Murder Study
homicide-suicide 181
homosexual advance 155–7
'hooks and turning points' 289

identity 4, 7
inequality 5–6, 12
injuries *see* cause of death
'instrumental' homicides 70
insult 55–7
intimate relationships 284–5, 289

Jamaica 6, 9–10
Japan 178, 179, 180

kinship 4
knives 18–20, 43, 46, 264; *see also*
  cause of death

label, labelling 216
LGBT homicide 181
LGBT people in US 149–501
life after prison 283–5, 289
life in prison 266–7; *see also*
  Lifecourse-In.Prison
life license, life sentence, tariff *see* murder,
  sentence for
lifecourse-Adulthood 249–66, **286–7**,
  297–8; abused wife 254; alcohol abuse
  255–8, 282, **286**, 298; convictions
  264–5, **286–7**; convictions for assault
  263–4, **286–7**; criminal behavior
  262–5, 282, **286–7**, 298; drug abuse
  255–8, **286**, 298; education 249, 282,
  286; intimate relationships 250–5,
  286, 297–8; mental health 258–9,
  286; sexual problems, sexual violence
  259–61, **286**; professionals involved
  261, **287**; unemployed 282,
  286–7, 291, 298
Lifecourse-Childhood 212–46, **243–4**,
  295–7; abused physically 229–32, **243**;
  abused sexually 229–32, **243**, 246;
  alcohol use/abuse 238–9, **244**, 296;
  convictions **244**; discipline/disruptive
  at home 233, **244**; disrupted caretaking
  (in care) 224–9, **243**, 297; drug abuse
  238–9, **244**, 296; education *see* school;
  family 218–24, **243**, 296; father violent
  to mother 220–3, **243**, 246, 296; in
  care 224, **243**, 297; mental health
  problems 237–8, **244**, 297; offending
  239–41, 297; onset of offending

214–15, 239, **244**, 245, 297; parents/
  carers 218–24, **243**, 296; problems of
  the child 233–46, **244**; professionals
  involved with family 223–4, **244**;
  school 216, 233–7, **244**, 296–7; young
  offenders institution 241–2, **244**
lifecourse criminology 214–18
Lifecourse-In.Prison 266–89, 298–9;
  behavior 267–8; dangerousness 271–3;
  discipline reports 268–71; empathy
  273–7; mental health-prison 271;
  model prisoner 267–8; prison programs
  (attitudes and behaviors) 277–83;
  remorse 273–7; risk to public safety
  271–3; uncooperative 268–71, **288**
lifecourse of murderers, research 216–27
lifecourse, research 213–18

Madonna 150
male honor/masculine honor 3, 8, 9,
  39–40
mass murderers 1
mental health 237–8, **243–4**, 258–9, 271,
  286–7, **288**, 297
mixed messages about sexual orientation
  153–5, 197–8
model prisoner 267–8, **288**, 299
modern state and violence 4
murder event 12–13, 22, 23, 42, 69, **71**,
  76, 103, **104**, 109, **136**, 137, 144, **172**,
  174, 183, 207, **208**, 291, 299; *see also*
  Type of Murder (and subtypes) for each
  type of murder
murder, history 2–5
murder, modern societies and cultures 5–6
murder, sentence for 23, 291, 298
Murder Study 1–2, 20, 22–4, 28–33,
  217–8; casefiles 23–4; context specific
  approach 22; data collection 23–4;
  disaggregation 22, 22; interviews 24;
  Nud*ist/QSR 24; qualitative and
  qualitative data 23–4; strategic sites
  (prisons interviews) 24; typologies
  28–9, 29–32
Murder Type (and subtypes):
  confrontational murders (fighters)
  10–11, 30, 39–69, **71–2**, 245, **243–4**,
  245, **286–7**, **288–9**, 292–3, 299; six
  subtypes (*list*) 43, 292; Subtype 1.
  Groups, conflicts and confrontations
  43–50; Subtype 2. Confrontations
  involving disputes and 'Slights to
  Self' 50–5; Subtype 3. Confrontations
  involving disputes and 'sights against

others' 55–7; Subtype 4. The 'fair' fight - men agree to fight 57–61; Subtype 5. Collateral victims, bystanders and displacement of violence 61–4; Subtype 6. Confrontations involving 'Identification with a wider group/organization' 64–8; *see also* murder event

Murder Type (and subtypes): family murders between men 31, 107–39, **136–7**, **243–4**, **245**, **286–7**, **288–9**, 293–4, 298; five subtypes (*list*) 110, 138, 294; Subtype 1. Blood relatives 110–14; Subtype 2. Gay intimate partners 114–18; Subtype 3. Collateral intimate partner murders - male victims 118–26; Subtype 4. Family feuds and feuding families 126–32; Subtype 5. Brothers against others 132–5; *see also* murder event

Murder Type (and subtypes): murders for money/financial gain 30–1, 70–103, **104–5**, **243–4**, **245**, **286–7**, **288–9**, 293, 299; seven subtypes (*list*) 76–7, 293; Subtype 1. Thefts, burglary and robbery 79–86; Subtype 2. Drug dealing, disputes and murder 86–91; Subtype 3. Criminal activity, 'share-outs' and murder 91–2; Subtype 4. Personal debts, disputes and murder 92–3; Subtype 5. Gangs, conflict over control of territory and resources 93–6; Subtype 6. Unlawful activity, disputes with officials and murder 96–9; Subtype 7. Contract to kill 99–101; *see also* murder event

Murder Type (and subtypes): murders of older men 32, 178–209, **208–9**, **243–4**, **245**, **286–7**, **288–9**, 295; three subtypes (*list*) 183, 295: Subtype 1. Hate crimes against older men 145–50, 183, 184–8; Subtype 2. Murders of older men involving theft or monetary exploitation 183, 188–97; Subtype 3. Sex and the murder of older men 183, 197–205; *see also* murder event

Murder Type (and subtypes): sexual murders between men 31–2, 141–75, **172–3**, **243–4**, **245**, **286–7**, **288–9**, 294–5, 298–9; six subtypes (*list*) 144–5, 175, 294; Subtype 1. Hate crimes against gay men 145–50; Subtype 2. Sexual *exchanges* and mixed messages 150–5; Subtype 3. Homosexual advance 155–7; Subtype 4. Prostitution 157–8; Subtype 5. Pedophilia - both false claims and previous offences 159–66; Subtype 6. Serial sexual murder 166–71; *see also* murder event

murder, of women 14–15, 142

National Crime Victimization Survey 78, 179
National Homicide Index 18
Netherlands 27
New Zealand 214
night time economy 95
no previous convictions 264–5
Northern Ireland 4
norm enforcers 22
Norway 17
Nud*ist/QSR 24

onePULSE Foundation 150
onset of offending (early) 214–18, 239–43, **244**, 245, 297; *see also* Lifecourse-Childhood, convictions, offending, onset of offending
onset of offending (late) 245; *see also* Lifecourse-Adulthood, offending
older people 178–82
Orlando, Florida 149–50
other offense/s in addition to murder 43, 70, **72**, 76, 103, **105**, 109, **137**, 138, 144, **173**, 174, 183, 207, **209**

parole 282
pathways 216
patricide 108
paedophile, pedophilia 159–66; *see also* child sexual abuse
paedophile ring 164–6
poverty and homicide, violence 8, 9
program for offenders, inside prison 277–82
perpetrators, women 3
prostitution 157–8
psychopaths 1
prostitutes, prostitution, men 200–3
pub 52–3, **286**; *see also* Lifecourse-Adulthood, alcohol abuse

qualitative data 24
quantitative data 23

rationalizations (justifications): for murder 40–1; for violence 22
rehabilitation, reform 217, 277–82, 283–5
reintegration 283–4

308 Subject index

relationship between perpetrator and
victim (for each type of murder) 15, 41,
68, **71**, 75, 102, **104**, 108, 135, **136**,
143, **172**, 173, 182, 206, **208**
relative deprivation 5
remorse 273–7, **288**
reputation 87
research about homicide/murder 15–28
'risk to public safety' **288**
robbery (England/Wales) 77–9; *see also*
burglary, burglary homicides
Romeo and Juliet 126–7
routine activities 22

school *see* Lifecourse-Childhood
Scotland 1, 2, 19, 23
Scottish/Irish background 8
sectarian murder 645–7
self-defense 14
serial sexual murder 166–71
serial killers 1
serial killing, of older people 181
sexual advance 155–7
sexual exchanges 150–3
sexual messages 153–5
sexual murder *see* Murder Type (and
subtypes): sexual murders between men
sexual orientation 153–5
'share-outs' 91
shot *see* cause of death
'slights against others' 55–7
'slights against self' 50–3
stab *see* cause of death
'stare' 50–1
strangle *see* cause of death
stigma 216
slavery 9
social controls 215
social science, Sociology 5
sons kill fathers 113
SPSS, quantitative data and analysis 23; *see
also* Murder Study
Statistics Bureau of Japan 178
Stockholm Life-Course Project 245–6
subcultures of violence and crime 6–12, 214
Sweden 17

tariff *see* murder, sentence for
territory 93–4
theft (and murder of old men) 188–92
theory (perspectives, explanations) of
crime, violence and/or homicide:
bio-psychological 215; criminological
213–17; cultural 6–7; ethnographic 7–8;

evolutionary psychology 5, 26; historical
4–5; labelling 216; lifecourse 213–15;
psychological 22; sociocultural 5–6,
215–6; sociological 5; sub-cultural 6–7,
9–12; symbolic interactionism 13–14,
20–1
'thinking', what thinking? (cognitive
scripts) 20–3, 26, 282–4, 289; *see also*
rationalizations (justifications)
transition points, transition process
(personal change) 216, 277–85, 289
types of murder *see* Murder Types
(subtypes)
typologies of homicide 24–6, 28–9;
developing 28–9; importance of 24–5;
Murder Study-five types of male-male
murder 28–32

UK/Britain, burglary and robbery 79
UK/Britain, murder (homicide) 79
UK, elderly homicide 179, 181
UK Office for National Statistics 179
United Nations Office of Drugs and
Crime UNODC 3
United Nations Office of Drugs and
Crime (UNODC) 3, 180
US Bureau of Justice Statistics 78
US Census Bureau Statistical Brief, 'Sixty-
five Plus in the United States' 178
US Centers for Disease Control and
Prevention (CDC) 19
US Department of Justice 77
US Department of Justice (Uniform Crime
Reporting program of the FBI) 37
US elderly homicide 181
US Federal Bureau of Investigation
(FBI) 25, 79, 150
US Southern/Northern background
8–9, 10

victim precipitation 13–15
victims of murder *see* Murder Type
(subtypes)
violence against male intimate partners
114–18
violence against woman partners 14–15,
253–5
violence and crime, historical trends 3–11
violent cultures and subcultures 5–12
violent events 12–13, 22

West Side Story 127
Women's Aid 22
World Population Clock 178